enVision® Florida MATHEMATICS

Volume 1 Topics 1–6

Authors

Robert Q. Berry, III
Professor of Mathematics
Education, Department of
Curriculum, Instruction and
Special Education, University
of Virginia, Charlottesville,
Virginia

Zachary Champagne
Assistant in Research
Florida Center for Research
in Science, Technology,
Engineering, and
Mathematics (FCR-STEM)
Jacksonville, Florida

Eric Milou
Professor of Mathematics
Rowan University,
Glassboro, New Jersey

Jane F. Schielack
Professor Emerita
Department of Mathematics
Texas A&M University,
College Station, Texas

Jonathan A. Wray
Mathematics Supervisor,
Howard County Public
Schools, Ellicott City,
Maryland

Randall I. Charles
Professor Emeritus
Department of Mathematics
San Jose State University
San Jose, California

Francis (Skip) Fennell
Professor Emeritus of
Education and Graduate
and Professional Studies,
McDaniel College
Westminster, Maryland

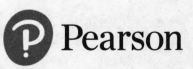
Pearson

Boston, Massachusetts   Chandler, Arizona
Glenview, Illinois   New York, New York

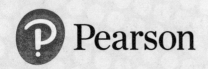

ISBN-13:   978-0-13-491273-8
ISBN-10:   0-13-491273-X

5   20

 CONTENTS

TOPICS

🌴 DIGITAL RESOURCES

📶 Go Online | PearsonRealize.com

INTERACTIVE STUDENT EDITION
Access online or offline

VISUAL LEARNING
Interact with visual learning animations

ACTIVITY
Use with *Solve & Discuss It, Explore It,*
and *Explain It* activities and Examples

VIDEOS
Watch clips to support *3-Act
Mathematical Modeling* Lessons
and *enVision® STEM Projects*

PRACTICE
Practice what you've learned and
get immediate feedback

TUTORIALS
Get help from *Virtual Nerd*
any time you need it

MATH TOOLS
Explore math with digital tools

GAMES
Play math games to help you learn

KEY CONCEPT
Review important lesson content

GLOSSARY
Read and listen to English and
Spanish definitions

ASSESSMENT
Show what you've learned

PEARSON
realize
Everything you need for
math anytime, anywhere.

Use Positive Rational Numbers

TOPIC 2
Integers and Rational Numbers

TOPIC 3

Numeric and Algebraic Expressions

TOPIC 4 Rational Number Operations

TOPIC 5

Represent and Solve Equations and Inequalities

TOPIC 6
Understand and Use Ratio and Rate

Mathematics Florida Standards (🌐MAFS)

GRADE 6 ADVANCED

RATIOS AND PROPORTIONAL RELATIONSHIPS

MAFS.6.RP.1 Understand ratio concepts and use ratio reasoning to solve problems. (Major Cluster)

MAFS.6.RP.1.1 Understand the concept of a ratio and use ratio language to describe a ratio relationship between two quantities.

MAFS.6.RP.1.2 Understand the concept of a unit rate a/b associated with a ratio $a:b$ with $b \neq 0$, and use rate language in the context of a ratio relationship.

MAFS.6.RP.1.3 Use ratio and rate reasoning to solve real-world and mathematical problems, e.g., by reasoning about tables of equivalent ratios, tape diagrams, double number line diagrams, or equations.

MAFS.6.RP.1.3a Make tables of equivalent ratios relating quantities with whole-number measurements, find missing values in the tables, and plot the pairs of values on the coordinate plane. Use tables to compare ratios.

MAFS.6.RP.1.3b Solve unit rate problems including those involving unit pricing and constant speed.

MAFS.6.RP.1.3c Find a percent of a quantity as a rate per 100 (e.g., 30% of a quantity means 30/100 times the quantity); solve problems involving finding the whole, given a part and the percent.

MAFS.6.RP.1.3d Use ratio reasoning to convert measurement units; manipulate and transform units appropriately when multiplying or dividing quantities.

MAFS.6.RP.1.3e Understand the concept of Pi as the ratio of the circumference of a circle to its diameter.

MAFS.7.RP.1 Analyze proportional relationships and use them to solve real-world and mathematical problems. (Major Cluster)

MAFS.7.RP.1.1 Compute unit rates associated with ratios of fractions, including ratios of lengths, areas and other quantities measured in like or different units.

MAFS.7.RP.1.2 Recognize and represent proportional relationships between quantities.

MAFS.7.RP.1.2a Decide whether two quantities are in a proportional relationship, e.g., by testing for equivalent ratios in a table or graphing on a coordinate plane and observing whether the graph is a straight line through the origin.

MAFS.7.RP.1.2b Identify the constant of proportionality (unit rate) in tables, graphs, equations, diagrams, and verbal descriptions of proportional relationships.

MAFS.7.RP.1.2c Represent proportional relationships by equations.

MAFS.7.RP.1.2d Explain what a point (x, y) on the graph of a proportional relationship means in terms of the situation, with special attention to the points $(0, 0)$ and $(1, r)$ where r is the unit rate.

MAFS.7.RP.1.3 Use proportional relationships to solve multistep ratio and percent problems.

THE NUMBER SYSTEM

MAFS.6.NS.1 Apply and extend previous understandings of multiplication and division to divide fractions by fractions. (Major Cluster)

MAFS.6.NS.1.1 Interpret and compute quotients of fractions, and solve word problems involving division of fractions by fractions, e.g., by using visual fraction models and equations to represent the problem.

MAFS.6.NS.2 Compute fluently with multi-digit numbers and find common factors and multiples. (Additional Cluster)

MAFS.6.NS.2.2 Fluently divide multi-digit numbers using the standard algorithm.

MAFS.6.NS.2.3 Fluently add, subtract, multiply, and divide multi-digit decimals using the standard algorithm for each operation.

MAFS.6.NS.2.4 Find the greatest common factor of two whole numbers less than or equal to 100 and the least common multiple of two whole numbers less than or equal to 12. Use the distributive property to express a sum of two whole numbers 1–100 with a common factor as a multiple of a sum of two whole numbers with no common factor.

MAFS.6.NS.3 Apply and extend previous understandings of numbers to the system of rational numbers. (Major Cluster)

MAFS.6.NS.3.5 Understand that positive and negative numbers are used together to describe quantities having opposite directions or values (e.g., temperature above/below zero, elevation above/below sea level, credits/debits, positive/negative electric charge); use positive and negative numbers to represent quantities in real-world contexts, explaining the meaning of 0 in each situation.

MAFS.6.NS.3.6 Understand a rational number as a point on the number line. Extend number line diagrams and coordinate axes familiar from previous grades to represent points on the line and in the plane with negative number coordinates.

MAFS.6.NS.3.6a Recognize opposite signs of numbers as indicating locations on opposite sides of 0 on the number line; recognize that the opposite of the opposite of a number is the number itself, e.g., $-(-3) = 3$, and that 0 is its own opposite.

MAFS.6.NS.3.6b Understand signs of numbers in ordered pairs as indicating locations in quadrants of the coordinate plane; recognize that when two ordered pairs differ only by signs, the locations of the points are related by reflections across one or both axes.

MAFS.6.NS.3.6c Find and position integers and other rational numbers on a horizontal or vertical number line diagram; find and position pairs of integers and other rational numbers on a coordinate plane.

MAFS.6.NS.3.7 Understand ordering and absolute value of rational numbers.

MAFS.6.NS.3.7a Interpret statements of inequality as statements about the relative position of two numbers on a number line diagram.

MAFS.6.NS.3.7b Write, interpret, and explain statements of order for rational numbers in real-world contexts.

MAFS.6.NS.3.7c Understand the absolute value of a rational number as its distance from 0 on the number line; interpret absolute value as magnitude for a positive or negative quantity in a real-world situation.

MAFS.6.NS.3.7d Distinguish comparisons of absolute value from statements about order.

MAFS.6.NS.3.8 Solve real-world and mathematical problems by graphing points in all four quadrants of the coordinate plane. Include use of coordinates and absolute value to find distances between points with the same first coordinate or the same second coordinate.

MAFS.7.NS.1 Apply and extend previous understandings of operations with fractions to add, subtract, multiply, and divide rational numbers. (Major Cluster)

MAFS.7.NS.1.1 Apply and extend previous understandings of addition and subtraction to add and subtract rational numbers; represent addition and subtraction on a horizontal or vertical number line diagram.

MAFS.7.NS.1.1a Describe situations in which opposite quantities combine to make 0.

MAFS.7.NS.1.1b Understand $p + q$ as the number located a distance $|q|$ from p, in the positive or negative direction depending on whether q is positive or negative. Show that a number and its opposite have a sum of 0 (are additive inverses). Interpret sums of rational numbers by describing real-world contexts.

MAFS.7.NS.1.1c Understand subtraction of rational numbers as adding the additive inverse, $p - q = p + (-q)$. Show that the distance between two rational numbers on the number line is the absolute value of their difference, and apply this principle in real-world contexts.

MAFS.7.NS.1.1d Apply properties of operations as strategies to add and subtract rational numbers.

MAFS.7.NS.1.2 Apply and extend previous understandings of multiplication and division and of fractions to multiply and divide rational numbers.

MAFS.7.NS.1.2a Understand that multiplication is extended from fractions to rational numbers by requiring that operations continue to satisfy the properties of operations, particularly the distributive property, leading to products such as $(-1)(-1) = 1$ and the rules for multiplying signed numbers. Interpret products of rational numbers by describing real-world contexts.

MAFS.7.NS.1.2b Understand that integers can be divided, provided that the divisor is not zero, and every quotient of integers (with non-zero divisor) is a rational number. If p and q are integers, then $-\left(\frac{p}{q}\right) = \frac{(-p)}{q} = \frac{p}{(-q)}$. Interpret quotients of rational numbers by describing real-world contexts.

MAFS.7.NS.1.2c Apply properties of operations as strategies to multiply and divide rational numbers.

MAFS.7.NS.1.2d Convert a rational number to a decimal using long division; know that the decimal form of a rational number terminates in 0s or eventually repeats.

MAFS.7.NS.1.3 Solve real-world and mathematical problems involving the four operations with rational numbers.

EXPRESSIONS AND EQUATIONS

MAFS.6.EE.1 Apply and extend previous understandings of arithmetic to algebraic expressions. (Major Cluster)

MAFS.6.EE.1.1 Write and evaluate numerical expressions involving whole-number exponents.

MAFS.6.EE.1.2 Write, read, and evaluate expressions in which letters stand for numbers.

MAFS.6.EE.1.2a Write expressions that record operations with numbers and with letters standing for numbers.

MAFS.6.EE.1.2b Identify parts of an expression using mathematical terms (sum, term, product, factor, quotient, coefficient); view one or more parts of an expression as a single entity.

MAFS.6.EE.1.2c Evaluate expressions at specific values of their variables. Include expressions that arise from formulas used in real-world problems. Perform arithmetic operations, including those involving whole-number exponents, in the conventional order when there are no parentheses to specify a particular order (Order of Operations).

MAFS.6.EE.1.3 Apply the properties of operations to generate equivalent expressions.

MAFS.6.EE.1.4 Identify when two expressions are equivalent (i.e., when the two expressions name the same number regardless of which value is substituted into them).

MAFS.6.EE.2 Reason about and solve one-variable equations and inequalities. (Major Cluster)

MAFS.6.EE.2.5 Understand solving an equation or inequality as a process of answering a question: which values from a specified set, if any, make the equation or inequality true? Use substitution to determine whether a given number in a specified set makes an equation or inequality true.

MAFS.6.EE.2.6 Use variables to represent numbers and write expressions when solving a real-world or mathematical problem; understand that a variable can represent an unknown number, or, depending on the purpose at hand, any number in a specified set.

MAFS.6.EE.2.7 Solve real-world and mathematical problems by writing and solving equations of the form $x + p = q$ and $px = q$ for cases in which p, q and x are all nonnegative rational numbers.

MAFS.6.EE.2.8 Write an inequality of the form $x > c$ or $x < c$ to represent a constraint or condition in a real-world or mathematical problem. Recognize that inequalities of the form $x > c$ or $x < c$ have infinitely many solutions; represent solutions of such inequalities on number line diagrams.

MAFS.6.EE.3 **Represent and analyze quantitative relationships between dependent and independent variables.** (Major Cluster)

MAFS.6.EE.3.9 Use variables to represent two quantities in a real-world problem that change in relationship to one another; write an equation to express one quantity, thought of as the dependent variable, in terms of the other quantity, thought of as the independent variable. Analyze the relationship between the dependent and independent variables using graphs and tables, and relate these to the equation.

MAFS.7.EE.1 **Use properties of operations to generate equivalent expressions.** (Major Cluster)

MAFS.7.EE.1.1 Apply properties of operations as strategies to add, subtract, factor, and expand linear expressions with rational coefficients.

MAFS.7.EE.1.2 Understand that rewriting an expression in different forms in a problem context can shed light on the problem and how the quantities in it are related.

MAFS.7.EE.2 **Solve real-life and mathematical problems using numerical and algebraic expressions and equations.** (Major Cluster)

MAFS.7.EE.2.3 Solve multi-step real-life and mathematical problems posed with positive and negative rational numbers in any form (whole numbers, fractions, and decimals), using tools strategically. Apply properties of operations to calculate with numbers in any form; convert between forms as appropriate; and assess the reasonableness of answers using mental computation and estimation strategies.

MAFS.7.EE.2.4 Use variables to represent quantities in a real-world or mathematical problem, and construct simple equations and inequalities to solve problems by reasoning about the quantities.

MAFS.7.EE.2.4a Solve word problems leading to equations of the form $px + q = r$ and $p(x + q) = r$, where p, q, and r are specific rational numbers. Solve equations of these forms fluently. Compare an algebraic solution to an arithmetic solution, identifying the sequence of the operations used in each approach.

MAFS.7.EE.2.4b Solve word problems leading to inequalities of the form $px + q > r$ or $px + q < r$, where p, q, and r are specific rational numbers. Graph the solution set of the inequality and interpret it in the context of the problem.

GEOMETRY

MAFS.6.G.1 **Solve real-world and mathematical problems involving area, surface area, and volume.** (Supporting Cluster)

MAFS.6.G.1.1 Find the area of right triangles, other triangles, special quadrilaterals, and polygons by composing into rectangles or decomposing into triangles and other shapes; apply these techniques in the context of solving real-world and mathematical problems.

MAFS.6.G.1.2 Find the volume of a right rectangular prism with fractional edge lengths by packing it with unit cubes of the appropriate unit fraction edge lengths, and show that the volume is the same as would be found by multiplying the edge lengths of the prism. Apply the formulas $V = \ell wh$ and $V = bh$ to find volumes of right rectangular prisms with fractional edge lengths in the context of solving real-world and mathematical problems.

MAFS.6.G.1.3 Draw polygons in the coordinate plane given coordinates for the vertices; use coordinates to find the length of a side joining points with the same first coordinate or the same second coordinate. Apply these techniques in the context of solving real-world and mathematical problems.

MAFS.6.G.1.4 Represent three-dimensional figures using nets made up of rectangles and triangles, and use the nets to find the surface area of these figures. Apply these techniques in the context of solving real-world and mathematical problems.

STATISTICS AND PROBABILITY

MAFS.6.SP.1 Develop understanding of statistical variability. (Additional Cluster)

MAFS.6.SP.1.1 Recognize a statistical question as one that anticipates variability in the data related to the question and accounts for it in the answers.

MAFS.6.SP.1.2 Understand that a set of data collected to answer a statistical question has a distribution which can be described by its center, spread, and overall shape.

MAFS.6.SP.1.3 Recognize that a measure of center for a numerical data set summarizes all of its values with a single number, while a measure of variation describes how its values vary with a single number.

MAFS.6.SP.2 Summarize and describe distributions. (Additional Cluster)

MAFS.6.SP.2.4 Display numerical data in plots on a number line, including dot plots, histograms, and box plots.

MAFS.6.SP.2.5 Summarize numerical data sets in relation to their context, such as by:

MAFS.6.SP.2.5a Reporting the number of observations.

MAFS.6.SP.2.5b Describing the nature of the attribute under investigation, including how it was measured and its units of measurement.

MAFS.6.SP.2.5c Giving quantitative measures of center (median and/or mean) and variability (interquartile range and/or mean absolute deviation), as well as describing any overall pattern and any striking deviations from the overall pattern with reference to the context in which the data were gathered.

MAFS.6.SP.2.5d Relating the choice of measures of center and variability to the shape of the data distribution and the context in which the data were gathered.

MATHEMATICAL PRACTICE

MAFS.K12.MP.1.1 Make sense of problems and persevere in solving them.

MAFS.K12.MP.2.1 Reason abstractly and quantitatively.

MAFS.K12.MP.3.1 Construct viable arguments and critique the reasoning of others.

MAFS.K12.MP.4.1 Model with mathematics.

MAFS.K12.MP.5.1 Use appropriate tools strategically.

MAFS.K12.MP.6.1 Attend to precision.

MAFS.K12.MP.7.1 Look for and make use of structure.

MAFS.K12.MP.8.1 Look for and express regularity in repeated reasoning.

CORRELATION TO LANGUAGE ARTS FLORIDA STANDARDS (LAFS)

LAFS.6.SL.1.1 Engage effectively in a range of collaborative discussions (one-on-one, in groups, and teacher-led) with diverse partners on grade 6 topics, texts, and issues, building on others' ideas and expressing their own clearly.

   a. Come to discussions prepared, having read or studied required material; explicitly draw on that preparation by referring to evidence on the topic, text, or issue to probe and reflect on ideas under discussion.

   b. Follow rules for collegial discussions, set specific goals and deadlines, and define individual roles as needed.

   c. Pose and respond to specific questions with elaboration and detail by making comments that contribute to the topic, text, or issue under discussion.

   d. Review the key ideas expressed and demonstrate understanding of multiple perspectives through reflection and paraphrasing.

LAFS.6.SL.1.2 Interpret information presented in diverse media and formats (e.g., visually, quantitatively, orally) and explain how it contributes to a topic, text, or issue under study.

LAFS.6.SL.1.3 Delineate a speaker's argument and specific claims, distinguishing claims that are supported by reasons and evidence from claims that are not.

LAFS.6.SL.2.4 Present claims and findings, sequencing ideas logically and using pertinent descriptions, facts, and details to accentuate main ideas or themes; use appropriate eye contact, adequate volume, and clear pronunciation.

LAFS.68.RST.1.3 Follow precisely a multistep procedure when carrying out experiments, taking measurements, or performing technical tasks.

LAFS.68.RST.2.4 Determine the meaning of symbols, key terms, and other domain-specific words and phrases as they are used in a specific scientific or technical context relevant to grades 6–8 texts and topics.

LAFS.68.RST.3.7 Integrate quantitative or technical information expressed in words in a text with a version of that information expressed visually (e.g., in a flowchart, diagram, model, graph, or table).

LAFS.68.WHST.1.1 Write arguments focused on discipline-specific content.

   a. Introduce claim(s) about a topic or issue, acknowledge and distinguish the claim(s) from alternate or opposing claims, and organize the reasons and evidence logically.

   b. Support claim(s) with logical reasoning and relevant, accurate data and evidence that demonstrate an understanding of the topic or text, using credible sources.

   c. Use words, phrases, and clauses to create cohesion and clarify the relationships among claim(s), counterclaims, reasons, and evidence.

   d. Establish and maintain a formal style.

   e. Provide a concluding statement or section that follows from and supports the argument presented.

LAFS.68.WHST.2.4 Produce clear and coherent writing in which the development, organization, and style are appropriate to task, purpose, and audience.

CORRELATION TO ENGLISH LANGUAGE DEVELOPMENT STANDARDS (ELDS)

ELD.K12.ELL.MA.1 English language learners communicate information, ideas and concepts necessary for academic success in the content area of Mathematics.

ELD.K12.ELL.SI.1 English language learners communicate for social and instructional purposes within the school setting.

Math Practices and Problem Solving Handbook

 The **Math Practices and Problem Solving Handbook** is available at **PearsonRealize.com**.

MAFS.K12.MP.1.1 **Make sense of problems and persevere in solving them.**

MAFS.K12.MP.2.1 **Reason abstractly and quantitatively.**

MAFS.K12.MP.3.1 **Construct viable arguments and critique the reasoning of others.**

MAFS.K12.MP.4.1 **Model with mathematics.**

MAFS.K12.MP.5.1 **Use appropriate tools strategically.**

MAFS.K12.MP.6.1 **Attend to precision.**

MAFS.K12.MP.7.1 **Look for and make use of structure.**

MAFS.K12.MP.8.1 **Look for and express regularity in repeated reasoning.**

A rancher is building a fence on a 200-foot stretch of field. He has 30 posts and 225 feet of fencing. He plans to place one post every 6 feet. Will he have enough posts to build the fence as planned?

6 ft

200 feet stretch of field

Total 30 posts

Can I see a pattern or structure in the problem or solution strategy? I can see that one post is needed for every 6 feet.

How can I use the pattern or structure I see to help me solve the problem? I can write an equation that finds the number of posts needed for 200 feet.

Do I notice any repeated calculations or steps? Each post covers a 6-foot distance.

Are there general methods that I can use to solve the problem? I can divide the total distance to be fenced by the distance between posts.

Other questions to consider:
• Are there attributes in common that help me?
• Can I see the expression or equation as a single object or as a composition of several objects?

Other questions to consider:
• What can I generalize from one problem to another?
• Can I derive an equation from a series of data points?
• How reasonable are the results that I am getting?

Math Practices and Problem Solving Handbook

Standards for Mathematical Practice

Make sense of problems and persevere in solving them.

Mathematically proficient students:

- can explain the meaning of a problem
- look for entry points to begin solving a problem
- analyze givens, constraints, relationships, and goals
- make conjectures about the solution
- plan a solution pathway
- think of similar problems, and try simpler forms of the problem
- evaluate their progress toward a solution and change pathways if necessary
- can explain similarities and differences between different representations
- check their solutions to problems.

Reason abstractly and quantitatively.

Mathematically proficient students:

- make sense of quantities and their relationships in problem situations:
  - They *decontextualize*—create a coherent representation of a problem situation using numbers, variables, and symbols; and
  - They *contextualize* – attend to the meaning of numbers, variables, and symbols in the problem situation
- know and use different properties of operations to solve problems.

Construct viable arguments and critique the reasoning of others.

Mathematically proficient students:

- use definitions and problem solutions when constructing arguments
- make conjectures about the solutions to problems
- build a logical progression of statements to support their conjectures and justify their conclusions
- analyze situations and recognize and use counterexamples
- reason inductively about data, making plausible arguments that take into account the context from which the data arose
- listen or read the arguments of others, and decide whether they make sense
- respond to the arguments of others
- compare the effectiveness of two plausible arguments
- distinguish correct logic or reasoning from flawed, and—if there is a flaw in an argument—explain what it is
- ask useful questions to clarify or improve arguments of others.

  Go Online | PearsonRealize.com

Model with mathematics.

MAFS.K12.MP.4.1

Mathematically proficient students:
- can develop a representation—drawing, diagram, table, graph, expression, equation–to model a problem situation
- make assumptions and approximations to simplify a complicated situation
- identify important quantities in a practical situation and map their relationships using a range of tools
- analyze relationships mathematically to draw conclusions
- interpret mathematical results in the context of the situation and propose improvements to the model as needed.

Use appropriate tools strategically.

MAFS.K12.MP.5.1

Mathematically proficient students:
- consider appropriate tools when solving a mathematical problem
- make sound decisions about when each of these tools might be helpful
- identify relevant mathematical resources, and use them to pose or solve problems
- use tools and technology to explore and deepen their understanding of concepts.

Attend to precision.

MAFS.K12.MP.6.1

Mathematically proficient students:
- communicate precisely to others
- use clear definitions in discussions with others and in their own reasoning
- state the meaning of the symbols they use
- specify units of measure, and label axes to clarify their correspondence with quantities in a problem
- calculate accurately and efficiently
- express numerical answers with a degree of precision appropriate for the problem context.

Look for and make use of structure.

MAFS.K12.MP.7.1

Mathematically proficient students:
- look closely at a problem situation to identify a pattern or structure
- can step back from a solution pathway and shift perspective
- can see complex representations, such as some algebraic expressions, as single objects or as being composed of several objects.

Look for and express regularity in repeated reasoning.

MAFS.K12.MP.8.1

Mathematically proficient students:
- notice if calculations are repeated, and look both for general methods and for shortcuts
- maintain oversight of the process as they work to solve a problem, while also attending to the details
- continually evaluate the reasonableness of their intermediate results.

TOPIC 1

USE POSITIVE RATIONAL NUMBERS

? Topic Essential Question

How can you fluently add, subtract, multiply, and divide decimals? How can you multiply and divide fractions?

Topic Overview

Topic Vocabulary

- reciprocal

Lesson Digital Resources

INTERACTIVE STUDENT EDITION
Access online or offline.

VISUAL LEARNING ANIMATION
Interact with visual learning animations.

ACTIVITY Use with *Solve & Discuss It, Explore* and *Explain It* activities, and to explore Exampl

VIDEOS Watch clips to support *3-Act Mathematical Modeling Lessons* and *STEM Pr*

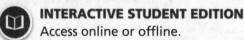

Go online | PearsonRealize.com

Stocking UP

▶ Stocking Up

When shopping for groceries, it is useful to set a budget and stick to it. Otherwise, you may buy items you do not need and spend more money than you should. Some people avoid overspending by bringing cash to pay for their groceries. If you bring $50 in cash, you cannot spend $54. Think about this during the 3-Act Mathematical Modeling lesson.

PRACTICE Practice what you've learned.

TUTORIALS Get help from *Virtual Nerd*, right when you need it.

MATH TOOLS Explore math with digital tools.

GAMES Play Math Games to help you learn.

KEY CONCEPT Review important lesson content.

GLOSSARY Read and listen to English/Spanish definitions.

ASSESSMENT Show what you've learned.

enVision® STEM Project

Did You Know?

Engineering is the **application of math and science** to solve problems.

Engineers solve problems by designing and building products, materials, machinery, structures, transportation vehicles, and so many other things.

Engineers work in nearly every area from chemical and electrical engineering to biomedical and oceanographic engineering.

Engineers design equipment to make you safer.

Engineers find ways to **improve and enhance performance** of all kinds of products.

Engineers help keep you healthy.

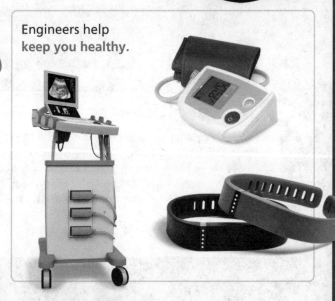

Your Task: Improve Your School

Think like an engineer! Take a walk around the inside and the outside of your school building. Make a list of specific things or areas that need improvement. Then choose one idea and do some background research to gain an understanding of factors that might impact improvement efforts. In the next topic, you and your classmates will learn about and implement the engineering design process to propose possible ways to make the improvements.

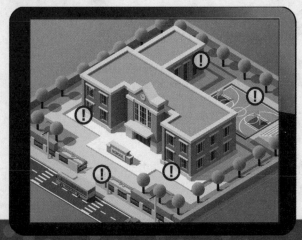

Vocabulary
Choose the best term from the box to complete each definition.

compatible numbers
decimal
divisor
estimate
quotient

1. Numbers that are easy to compute mentally are _____.

2. The number used to divide is the _____.

3. A(n) _____ is an approximate answer.

4. The result of a division problem is a(n) _____.

Whole Number Operations
Calculate each value.

5. $4\overline{)348}$

6. $9{,}007 - 3{,}128$

7. 35×17

8. $7{,}964 + 3{,}872$

9. $22\overline{)4{,}638}$

10. 181×42

Mixed Numbers and Fractions
Write each mixed number as a fraction. Write each fraction as a mixed number.

11. $8\frac{1}{3}$

12. $5\frac{3}{5}$

13. $2\frac{5}{8}$

14. $3\frac{4}{9}$

15. $\frac{24}{7}$

16. $\frac{43}{9}$

17. $\frac{59}{8}$

18. $\frac{32}{5}$

Verbal Expressions
19. How are the expressions "$\frac{1}{4}$ of 12" and "12 divided by 4" related?

Decimals
20. What decimal does this model represent? Explain.

Prepare for Reading Success

Write what you already know about the lesson content. Then write a question that you want answered about the lesson content.

Lesson Title	What I Know	Questions I Would Like Answered
Fluently Add, Subtract, and Multiply Decimals		
Fluently Divide Whole Numbers and Decimals		
Multiply Fractions		
Understand Division with Fractions		
Divide Fractions by Fractions		
Divide Mixed Numbers		
Solve Problems with Rational Numbers		

Go Online | PearsonRealize.com

Solve & Discuss It!

 ACTIVITY

Maxine is making a model windmill for a science fair. She is connecting 4 cardboard tubes together vertically. Each tube is 0.28 meter in length. What is the combined measure of the connected tubes?

Use Appropriate Tools
You can use decimal grids to calculate with decimals.

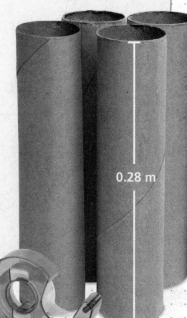

0.28 m

I can...
add, subtract, and multiply decimals.

MAFS.6.NS.2.3 Fluently add, subtract, multiply, ... decimals using the standard algorithm for each operation.
MAFS.K12.MP.5.1, MP.6.1, MP.7.1

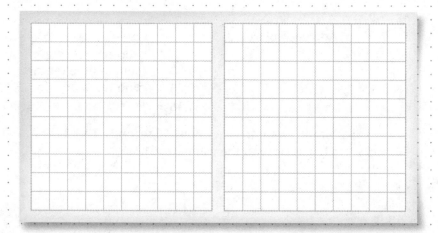

Focus on math practices

Look for Relationships Suppose that Maxine made another windmill model by connecting 4 cardboard tubes that are each 2.8 meters long. What is the combined measure of this model? What relationships do you see in the factors you used here and above? Explain how this helps you solve the problem.

 VISUAL LEARNING

EXAMPLE 1 **Add Decimals**

Scan for Multimedia
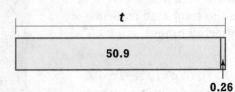

Kim and Martin swam 50 meters. Martin took 0.26 second longer than Kim. What was Martin's time in the race?

Be Precise Why is precision important when working with decimals?

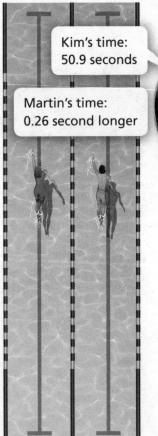

Kim's time: 50.9 seconds

Martin's time: 0.26 second longer

Find 50.9 + 0.26.

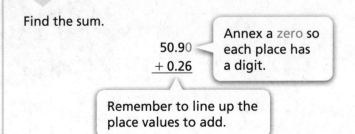

Estimate first by rounding each addend.

50.9 rounds to 51.   0.26 rounds to 0.3.

51 + 0.3 = 51.3

Find the sum.

```
  50.90
+  0.26
```
Annex a zero so each place has a digit.

Remember to line up the place values to add.

Add each place.

```
  1
 50.90
+ 0.26
 51.16
```
You can regroup the sum of nine tenths and two tenths.

Martin swam the race in 51.16 seconds. The sum 51.16 is close to the estimate, 51.3.

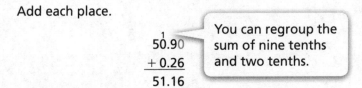 **Try It!**

Suppose that Martin finished the race 0.47 second after Kim. What was Martin's time in the race? Use an estimate to check that your answer is reasonable.

Convince Me! If Martin finished the race 0.267 second after Kim, you would need to add 0.267 to 50.9 to solve the problem. How is adding 0.267 to 50.9 different from adding 0.26 to 50.9?

EXAMPLE **2** **Subtract Decimals**

  ACTIVITY ASSESS

Amy ran a race in 20.7 seconds. Katie finished the race 0.258 second before Amy. How long did it take Katie to run the race?

Find 20.7 − 0.258.

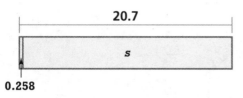

Estimate the difference by rounding.

$$20.7 - 0.3 = 20.4$$

0.258 rounds to 0.3.

To find the difference, line up the place values.

20.700 ·········· Annex zeros as placeholders.
− 0.258

Subtract each place. Regroup as needed.

$$\begin{array}{r} \overset{\scriptscriptstyle 6\,\overset{9}{\cancel{10}}\,10}{20.7\cancel{0}\cancel{0}} \\ -\ 0.258 \\ \hline 20.442 \end{array}$$

Katie ran the race in 20.442 seconds. 20.442 is close to the estimate, 20.4, so the answer is reasonable.

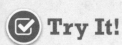 **Try It!**

Suppose that Katie finished the race 0.13 second before Amy. What was Katie's time in the race? Use an estimate to check that your answer is reasonable.

EXAMPLE **3** **Multiply Decimals**

What is the area of this antique map? Use the formula $A = \ell w$ to find the area of the map.

Multiply as you would with whole numbers. Then place the decimal point in the product. Annex zeros if needed. The number of decimal places in the product is the sum of the number of decimal places in the factors.

$$\begin{array}{r} 3.25 \\ \times\ 2.5 \\ \hline 1625 \\ +\ 6500 \\ \hline 8.125 \end{array}$$

3.25 ·········· 2 decimal places (hundredths)
× 2.5 ·········· 1 decimal place (tenths)

8.125 ·········· 3 decimal places (tenths times hundredths equals thousandths)

The area of the antique map is 8.125 ft².

2.5 ft

3.25 ft

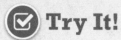 **Try It!**

How do you determine where to place the decimal point in the product?

0.43 ·········· ☐ decimal place(s)

× 0.2 ·········· ☐ decimal place(s)

0.086 ·········· ☐ decimal place(s)

Annex zeros if needed.

| To add decimals, line up place values and add. Regroup as needed. | $\begin{array}{r} \overset{1}{5}0.90 \\ +\ 0.26 \\ \hline 51.16 \end{array}$ | To subtract decimals, line up place values and subtract. Regroup as needed. | $\begin{array}{r} \overset{6}{2}\overset{9}{0}.\overset{10}{7}\overset{10}{0}\overset{}{0} \\ -\ 0.258 \\ \hline 20.442 \end{array}$ |

To multiply decimals, multiply as you would with whole numbers. Then use the number of decimal places in the factors to place the decimal point in the product.

$$\begin{array}{r} 1.35 \\ \times\ 4.6 \\ \hline 810 \\ +\ 5400 \\ \hline 6.210 \end{array}$$

Do You Understand?

1. **?Essential Question** How can you add, subtract, and multiply with decimals?

2. **Generalize** How is adding and subtracting decimals similar to and different from adding and subtracting whole numbers?

3. What can you do if a decimal product has final zeros to the right of the decimal point?

4. **Critique Reasoning** Diego says that the product of 0.51×2.427 will have five decimal places. Is Diego correct? Explain.

Do You Know How?

In 5–10, find each sum or difference.

5. $5.9 + 2.7$

6. $4.01 - 2.95$

7. $6.8 - 1.45$

8. $9.62 - 0.3$

9. $2.57 + 7.706$

10. $15 - 6.108$

In 11–16, place the decimal point in the correct location in the product.

11. $4 \times 0.94 = 376$

12. $5 \times 0.487 = 2435$

13. $3.4 \times 6.8 = 2312$

14. $3.9 \times 0.08 = 312$

15. $0.9 \times 0.22 = 198$

16. $9 \times 1.2 = 108$

In 17 and 18, find each product.

17. 5.3×2.7

18. 8×4.09

Practice & Problem Solving

In 19–27, find each sum or difference.

19. $2.17 - 0.8$

20. $4.3 + 4.16$

21. $46.91 - 28.7$

22. $4.815 + 2.17$

23. $5.1 - 0.48$

24. $27 + 0.185$

25. $9.501 - 9.45$

26. $14 + 9.8$

27. $12.65 + 14.24$

In 28–33, find each product.

28. 7×0.5

29. 12×0.08

30. 24×0.17

31. 0.4×0.17

32. 1.9×0.46

33. 3.42×5.15

34. Write an equation that illustrates the following: A number with two decimal places multiplied by a number with one decimal place. The product has only two nonzero digits.

35. The Bright-O Shampoo Factory includes 1.078 ounces of vanilla oil in a 6.35-ounce bottle of shampoo. How much of the bottle of shampoo is **NOT** vanilla oil?

In 36–38, use the graph to solve.

36. The fastest speed a table tennis ball has been hit is about 13.07 times as fast as the speed for the fastest swimming. What is the speed for the table tennis ball?

37. **Look for Relationships** How fast would 1.5 times the fastest rowing speed be? Before you solve, tell the number of decimal places in your answer.

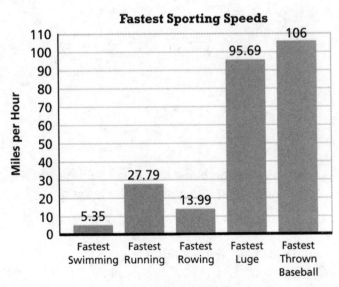

38. Which activity has a recorded speed about 7 times as fast as the fastest rowing speed?

39. Matthew bought a jersey, a pennant, and a hat. He paid with a $50 bill and some money he borrowed from his friend. If Matthew got $6.01 in change from the cashier, how much did he borrow from his friend to pay for all the items?

```
Sports Shop
New York, NY 10014

11:01AM 001 JAN01 2017

Jersey       39.99
Pennant      10.25
Hat          13.75

Total:
Cash:

Change:       6.01

THANK YOU FOR SHOPPING
AT THE SPORTS SHOP
```

40. Anna's running time for a race was 23.1 seconds. Another runner's time was 5.86 seconds faster. Find the other runner's time.

41. **Higher Order Thinking** Explain why 0.25×0.4 has only one decimal place in the product.

42. The wings of some hummingbirds beat 52 times per second when hovering. If a hummingbird hovers for 35.5 seconds, how many times do its wings beat?

43. The students at Walden Middle School are selling tins of popcorn to raise money for new uniforms. They sold 42 tins in the first week. How much money did they make in the first week?

POPCORN $9.25 each

Assessment Practice

44. Use the information in the table to solve each problem.

    🌐 6.NS.2.3

Trails in Everglades National Park

Trail	Length (kilometers)
Bayshore Loop	3.2
Coastal Prairie	12.1
Rowdy Bend	4.2
Snake Bight	2.6

PART A

What is the combined length in kilometers of the Bayshore Loop trail and the Rowdy Bend trail?

PART B

How many kilometers longer is the Coastal Prairie trail than the Snake Bight trail?

🔊 Go Online | PearsonRealize.com

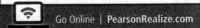
Solve & Discuss It!  ACTIVITY

Some friends went to lunch and split the bill equally. If each person paid $6.75, how many people went to lunch? Use a diagram or equation to explain your thinking.

Guest Check

CHECK NUMBER 984796

Food $$

Drinks $$

Total $27

TAX

Thank You TOTAL

> **Reasoning** How can you use reasoning to create a representation of the problem?

I can...
divide whole numbers and decimals.

MAFS.6.NS.2.2 Fluently divide multi-digit numbers using the standard algorithm. **Also 6.NS.2.3**
MAFS.K12.MP.2.1, MP.3.1, MP.6.1, MP.7.1

Focus on math practices
Reasoning Suppose $7.00 was added to the bill for a dessert that everyone shared. How much more does each person have to pay?

EXAMPLE 1 **Divide Whole Numbers by Whole Numbers**

Scan for Multimedia

A tortilla bakery makes 863 packages of tortillas to sell to restaurants. Each restaurant receives the same number of packages as a complete order. How many restaurants can receive a complete order?

There are 18 packages in a complete order.

Use Structure How can you use structure to divide 863 by 18?

Find $863 \div 18 = n$.

A bar diagram can be used to represent the problem.

packages of tortillas | 863 |

packages per box | 18 → n → n, completely filled boxes

Use compatible numbers to estimate $863 \div 18$.

$$900 \div 20 = 45$$

The quotient of $863 \div 18$ is about 45, so the first digit of the quotient will be in the tens place.

Start by dividing the tens.

$$\begin{array}{r} 4 \\ 18\overline{)863} \\ -72 \\ \hline 14 \end{array}$$

Step 1 Divide
Step 2 Multiply
Step 3 Subtract
Step 4 Compare

Next, bring down the ones. Repeat the steps as needed to complete the division.

$$\begin{array}{r} 47\,R17 \\ 18\overline{)863} \\ -72\downarrow \\ \hline 143 \\ -126 \\ \hline 17 \end{array}$$

The answer is reasonable since 47 is close to the estimate, 45.

The bakery can sell complete orders to 47 restaurants.

✓ Try It!

Workers at an electronics company pack 2,610 smart phones in boxes. Each box holds 9 smart phones. How many boxes do they fill?

$$\begin{array}{r} 9\overline{)\,2,\ 6\ 1\ 0} \\ -\ 1\ \ 8 \\ \hline \\ \qquad 8\ \ 1 \\ - \\ \hline 0 \\ \qquad 0 \\ - \\ \hline 0 \end{array}$$

Convince Me! Why is the first digit of the quotient in the Try It! not in the same place as the first digit of the quotient in Example 1?

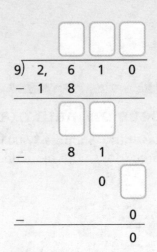

How can you write a decimal quotient when dividing whole numbers?

Find $180 \div 8$.

Estimate. Because $180 \div 10 = 18$, start dividing in the tens place.

Divide the tens and ones.

```
   22
8)180
  -16↓
    20
  -16
     4
```

Write the remainder as a decimal. Place the decimal point and annex a 0 in the tenths place.

Then complete the division.

```
    22.5
8)180.0
  -16↓
    20
  -16↓
    40
   -40
     0
```

EXAMPLE **3** **Divide Decimals**

Use the division algorithm to divide with decimals.

A. Find $809.40 \div 12$.

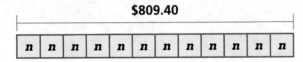

$809.40

| n | n | n | n | n | n | n | n | n | n | n | n |

Use compatible numbers to estimate, and then divide to solve.

809.40 is close to 840, and $840 \div 12 = 70$.

Place the decimal point in the quotient above the decimal point in the dividend.

```
   67.45
12)809.40
  -72↓
    89
   -84↓
     54
    -48↓
      60
     -60
       0
```

The quotient 67.45 is close to the estimate of 70, so the answer is reasonable.

$809.40 \div 12 = 67.45

B. Find $4.20 \div $1.40.

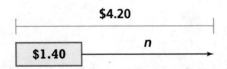

$4.20

$1.40   n

Multiply both the divisor and the dividend by the same power of 10 that will make the divisor a whole number.

Multiply 1.40 and 4.20 by 10^2 or 100.

```
       3              3
1.40)4.20    140)420
                -420
                   0
```

Divide. Place a decimal point in the quotient if needed.

$4.20 \div $1.40 = 3$

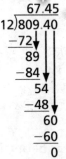 **Try It!**

Divide.

a. $65 \div 8$ **b.** $14.4 \div 8$ **c.** $128.8 \div 1.4$

To divide by a decimal, rewrite the decimal so that you are dividing by a whole number. Multiply both the divisor and the dividend by the same power of 10. Then divide as you would with whole numbers.

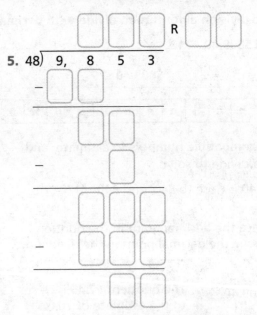

$$35.2 \div 0.16$$

$$
\begin{array}{r}
100 \\
\times\ 35.2 \\
\hline
200 \\
5000 \\
+\ 30000 \\
\hline
3{,}520.0
\end{array}
$$

$$
\begin{array}{r}
100 \\
\times\ 0.16 \\
\hline
600 \\
+\ 1000 \\
\hline
16.00
\end{array}
$$

$$
\begin{array}{r}
220 \\
16\overline{)3{,}520} \\
-\ 32 \\
\hline
32 \\
-\ 32 \\
\hline
0
\end{array}
$$

Do You Understand?

1. **? Essential Question** How can you divide whole numbers and decimals?

2. When dividing with decimals, why is it necessary to multiply both the divisor and the dividend by the same power of 10?

3. **Use Structure** Explain how you can decide where to place the first digit of the quotient for 6,139 ÷ 153.

4. **Use Structure** How do you know where to place the decimal point in the quotient when dividing a decimal by a whole number?

Do You Know How?

5. 48)9, 8 5 3   R

In **6** and **7**, divide. Record remainders.

6. 2,789 ÷ 36

7. 18)153

In **8** and **9**, divide. Write remainders as decimals.

8. 4)139

9. 215 ÷ 2

In **10** and **11**, divide.

10. 5)34.75

11. 215.25 ÷ 5

In **12** and **13**, divide. Annex zeros if needed to write remainders as decimals.

12. 5.3 ÷ 0.2

13. 0.4)8.9

Go Online | PearsonRealize.com

Practice & Problem Solving

Scan for
Multimedia

Leveled Practice In **14** and **15**, divide.

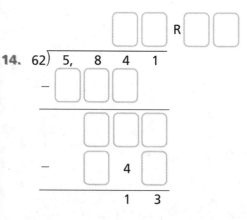

14. 62) 5, 8 4 1

15. 4) 3 5 0 .

In 16–19, divide. Record remainders.

16. 2,593 ÷ 21

17. 19)6,927

18. 9)2,483

19. 968 ÷ 38

In 20–23, divide. Write remainders as decimals.

20. 5)56

21. 232 ÷ 40

22. 44 ÷ 10

23. 4)2,626

In 24–27, divide.

24. 6)$54.18

25. 187.2 ÷ 8

26. 7)6.3

27. 137.5 ÷ 5

In 28–31, divide. Annex zeros if needed to write remainders as decimals.

28. 6.4 ÷ 0.8

29. 0.6)0.2430

30. 52.056 ÷ 7.23

31. 0.745)9.089

---

32. Ants are one of the Thorny Devil lizard's favorite foods. It can eat 45 ants per minute. How long would it take this lizard to eat 1,080 ants? Express your answer in minutes.

33. Critique Reasoning Henrieta divided 0.80 by 20 as shown. Is her work correct? If not, explain why and give a correct response.

$$
\begin{array}{r}
0.40 \\
20\overline{)0.80} \\
-80 \\
\hline
0
\end{array}
$$

34. Which brand of fruit snacks costs less per pound? How much less?

Fruit Snacks
Brand A   Brand B
15 lb   25 lb
$16.20 $22.25

35. Be Precise How many times as much does each item cost in 2010 as in 1960?

Item	1960 Cost	2010 Cost
Movie Ticket	$0.75	$9.75
Regular Popcorn	$0.25	$4.10
Regular Drink	$0.35	$3.08

Movie Ticket _____

Regular Popcorn _____

Regular Drink _____

36. Higher Order Thinking Kendra has 5.5 pounds of popcorn and wants to package it equally in 50 bags. How can she use place-value reasoning to find the amount of popcorn to put in each bag?

37. You and a friend are paid $38.25 for doing yard work. You worked 2.5 hours and your friend worked 2 hours. You split the money according to the amount of time each of you worked. How much is your share of the money? Explain.

Assessment Practice

38. What is the value of the expression $1,248 \div 25$?
 6.NS.2.2

Ⓐ 49

Ⓑ 49 R 9

Ⓒ 49.9

Ⓓ 49 R 23

39. Which expression has the same solution as $3,157 \div 41$? 6.NS.2.2

Ⓐ $1,852 \div 24$

Ⓑ $1,928 \div 25$

Ⓒ $2,079 \div 27$

Ⓓ $2,184 \div 28$

Solve & Discuss It! ACTIVITY

The art teacher gave each student half of a sheet of paper. Then she asked the students to color one fourth of their pieces of paper. What part of the original sheet did the students color?

Model with Math How can you use a picture to represent the problem?

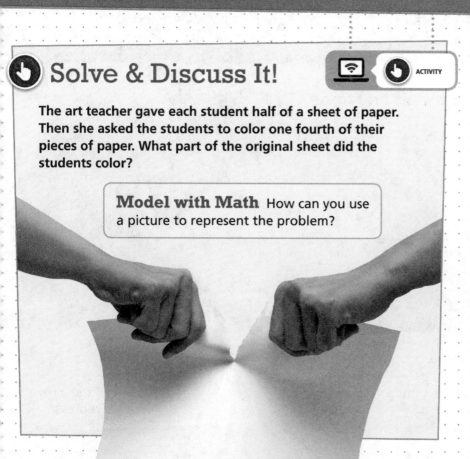

I can...
use models and equations to multiply fractions and mixed numbers.

Prepares for MAFS.6.NS.1.1 Apply and extend previous understanding of multiplication and division to divide fractions by fractions. ... e.g. by using visual fraction models and equations to represent the problem. ...
MAFS.K12.MP.2.1, MP.3.1, MP.4.1, MP.6.1

Focus on math practices
Reasoning Should your answer be less than or greater than 1? Explain.

? **Essential Question** How can you multiply fractions and mixed numbers?

  VISUAL LEARNING

EXAMPLE **1** **Multiply Unit Fractions**

Scan for Multimedia

There was $\frac{1}{4}$ of a pan of lasagna left. Tom ate $\frac{1}{3}$ of this amount. What fraction of a whole pan of lasagna did Tom eat?

To find a part of a whole, multiply to solve the problem.

Find $\frac{1}{3} \times \frac{1}{4}$.

ONE WAY Divide one whole into fourths.

> Divide $\frac{1}{4}$ into 3 equal parts.

> Divide each of the other $\frac{1}{4}$s into 3 equal parts.

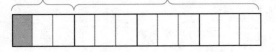

12 parts make one whole, so one part is $\frac{1}{12}$.

$$\frac{1}{3} \times \frac{1}{4} = \frac{1 \times 1}{3 \times 4} = \frac{1}{12}$$

Tom ate $\frac{1}{12}$ of a whole pan of lasagna.

ANOTHER WAY

> Shade 1 of the 3 rows yellow to represent $\frac{1}{3}$.

> Shade 1 of the 4 columns red to represent $\frac{1}{4}$.

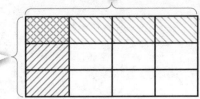

The orange overlap shows the product $\frac{1}{3} \times \frac{1}{4}$.

1 out of 12 parts are shaded orange.

$$\frac{1}{3} \times \frac{1}{4} = \frac{1 \times 1}{3 \times 4} = \frac{1}{12}$$

Tom ate $\frac{1}{12}$ of a whole pan of lasagna.

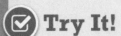 **Try It!**

Find $\frac{1}{4} \times \frac{1}{5}$ using the area model. Explain.

$\frac{1}{4}$ ⋯⋯⋯⋯⋯ 1 of ☐ rows

$\frac{1}{5}$ ⋯⋯⋯⋯⋯ 1 of ☐ columns

Convince Me! Why is the product of $\frac{1}{4} \times \frac{1}{5}$ less than each factor?

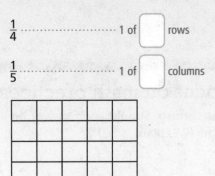

EXAMPLE **2** 👆 **Multiply Fractions**

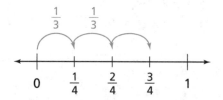

Find $\frac{2}{3} \times \frac{3}{4}$ using a number line.

$\frac{1}{3}$ means 1 of 3 equal parts, so $\frac{1}{3}$ of $\frac{3}{4}$ is $\frac{1}{4}$.

$\frac{2}{3}$ means 2 of 3 equal parts, so $\frac{2}{3}$ of $\frac{3}{4}$ is 2 times $\frac{1}{4}$.

$\frac{2}{3} \times \frac{3}{4} = \frac{6}{12}$ or $\frac{1}{2}$

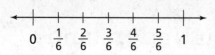

✅ Try It!

Find $\frac{3}{4} \times \frac{4}{6}$ using the number line. Explain.

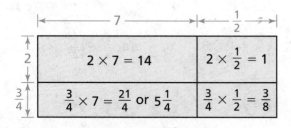

EXAMPLE **3** 👆 **Multiply Mixed Numbers**

Find $7\frac{1}{2} \times 2\frac{3}{4}$.

Estimate first. $7\frac{1}{2}$ times $2\frac{3}{4}$ is about 8 times 3.
So, the answer should be about 24.

ONE WAY You can use an area model to find the partial products. Then add to find the final product.

← 7 →	← $\frac{1}{2}$ →
2 $2 \times 7 = 14$	$2 \times \frac{1}{2} = 1$
$\frac{3}{4}$ $\frac{3}{4} \times 7 = \frac{21}{4}$ or $5\frac{1}{4}$	$\frac{3}{4} \times \frac{1}{2} = \frac{3}{8}$

$14 + 1 + 5\frac{1}{4} + \frac{3}{8} =$

$14 + 1 + 5\frac{2}{8} + \frac{3}{8} = 20\frac{5}{8}$

> $5\frac{1}{4}$ is renamed $5\frac{2}{8}$.

ANOTHER WAY You can use an equation to find the product. Rename the mixed numbers and then multiply.

$$7\frac{1}{2} \times 2\frac{3}{4} = \frac{15}{2} \times \frac{11}{4}$$
$$= \frac{165}{8}$$
$$= 20\frac{5}{8}$$

Because $20\frac{5}{8}$ is close to the estimate of 24, the answer is reasonable.

✅ Try It!

A clothing factory makes T-shirts. If each machine makes $3\frac{1}{3}$ T-shirts per hour, how many T-shirts does one machine make in $4\frac{1}{2}$ hours? Write and solve an equation.

You can find the product of fractions or mixed numbers.

Multiply the numerators.

Multiply the denominators.

$$\frac{2}{5} \times \frac{3}{4} = \frac{2 \times 3}{5 \times 4} = \frac{6}{20} \text{ or } \frac{3}{10}$$

$$3\frac{1}{3} \times 1\frac{1}{2} = \frac{10}{3} \times \frac{3}{2} = \frac{10 \times 3}{3 \times 2} = \frac{30}{6} \text{ or } 5$$

Rename mixed numbers as fractions.

Do You Understand?

1. **Essential Question** How can you multiply fractions and mixed numbers?

2. **Reasoning** Is the product of $\frac{3}{6} \times \frac{5}{4}$ equal to the product of $\frac{3}{4} \times \frac{5}{6}$? Explain.

3. **Construct Arguments** Why is adding $\frac{3}{9}$ and $\frac{6}{9}$ different from multiplying the two fractions?

4. Tina has $\frac{1}{2}$ of a pan of cornbread left from a dinner party. She eats $\frac{1}{2}$ of the leftover part the next night. How much of the whole pan does Tina eat? Write and solve an equation.

5. **Construct Arguments** Explain how you would multiply $5 \times 2\frac{1}{2}$.

6. In Example 1, find the fraction of a whole pan of lasagna that Tom ate if he started with $\frac{7}{8}$ of a pan.

Do You Know How?

7. Find $\frac{5}{6} \times \frac{1}{2}$. Use the model to help solve.

8. Find $\frac{3}{4} \times \frac{4}{9}$.

In 9–16, find each product.

9. $\frac{2}{3} \times \frac{1}{2}$

10. $\frac{5}{9} \times \frac{1}{9}$

11. $\frac{7}{10} \times \frac{3}{4}$

12. $\frac{1}{3} \times \frac{1}{4}$

13. $\frac{5}{6} \times \frac{3}{7}$

14. $\frac{3}{5} \times \frac{11}{12}$

15. $\frac{4}{10} \times \frac{2}{5}$

16. $\frac{3}{4} \times \frac{2}{9}$

In 17 and 18, estimate the product. Then complete the multiplication.

17. $2\frac{3}{4} \times 8 = \frac{\boxed{}}{4} \times \frac{8}{1} = \boxed{}$

18. $4\frac{1}{2} \times 1\frac{1}{4} = \frac{\boxed{}}{2} \times \frac{\boxed{}}{4} = \boxed{}$

Practice & Problem Solving

In 19 and 20, find each product. Shade the model to help solve.

19. $\frac{1}{3} \times \frac{5}{6}$

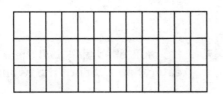

20. $\frac{2}{3} \times \frac{1}{12}$

In 21–28, find each product.

21. $\frac{7}{8} \times \frac{1}{2}$

22. $\frac{2}{5} \times \frac{1}{12}$

23. $\frac{5}{7} \times \frac{7}{9}$

24. $\frac{1}{2} \times \frac{3}{4}$

25. $\frac{1}{4} \times \frac{7}{8}$

26. $\frac{5}{6} \times \frac{9}{10}$

27. $\frac{1}{4} \times \frac{1}{8}$

28. $\frac{1}{3} \times \frac{3}{7}$

In 29–36, estimate the product. Then find each product.

29. $2\frac{1}{6} \times 4\frac{1}{2}$

30. $\frac{3}{4} \times 8\frac{1}{2}$

31. $1\frac{1}{8} \times 3\frac{1}{3}$

32. $3\frac{1}{5} \times \frac{2}{3}$

33. $3\frac{1}{4} \times 6$

34. $5\frac{1}{3} \times 3$

35. $2\frac{3}{8} \times 4$

36. $4\frac{1}{8} \times 5\frac{1}{2}$

In 37 and 38, use the diagram at the right.

37. Linda walked $\frac{3}{4}$ of the length of the Tremont Trail before
stopping for a rest. How far had Linda walked on the trail?

38. The city plans to extend the Wildflower Trail to make it
$2\frac{1}{2}$ times its current length in the next 5 years. How
long will the Wildflower Trail be at the end of 5 years?

Tremont Trail
$3\frac{1}{2}$ miles

Seton Trail
$1\frac{1}{4}$ miles

Wildflower Trail
$2\frac{3}{8}$ miles

39. The world's smallest gecko is $\frac{3}{4}$ inch long. An adult male Western Banded Gecko is $7\frac{1}{3}$ times as long. How long is an adult male Western Banded Gecko?

40. **Higher Order Thinking** In Ms. Barclay's classroom, $\frac{2}{5}$ of the students play chess. Of the students who play chess, $\frac{5}{6}$ also play sudoku. If there are 30 students in Ms. Barclay's class, how many play chess and sudoku?

41. The Boca Grande Causeway in Florida is about $1\frac{4}{9}$ times as long as the Golden Gate Bridge in San Francisco. The Golden Gate Bridge is about 9,000 feet long. About how long is the Boca Grande Causeway?

42. If $\frac{7}{8}$ is multiplied by $\frac{4}{5}$, will the product be greater than either of the two factors? Explain.

43. **Be Precise** To amend the U.S. Constitution, $\frac{3}{4}$ of the 50 states must approve the amendment. If 35 states approve an amendment, will the Constitution be amended?

44. A scientist had $\frac{3}{4}$ of a bottle of a solution. She used $\frac{1}{6}$ of the solution in an experiment. How much of the bottle did she use?

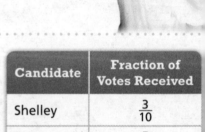

45. In the voting for City Council Precinct 5, only $\frac{1}{2}$ of all eligible voters cast votes. What fraction of all eligible voters voted for Shelley? Morgan? Who received the most votes?

Candidate	Fraction of Votes Received
Shelley	$\frac{3}{10}$
Morgan	$\frac{5}{8}$

Assessment Practice

46. Which of these equations is equivalent to $1\frac{1}{2} \times 3\frac{1}{5} = 4\frac{1}{2}$? 🔊 6.NS.1.1

ⓐ $4\frac{1}{2} \div 3\frac{1}{5} = 1\frac{1}{2}$

ⓑ $1\frac{1}{2} \div 4\frac{1}{2} = 3\frac{1}{5}$

ⓒ $1\frac{1}{2} \div 3\frac{1}{5} = 4\frac{1}{2}$

ⓓ $3\frac{1}{5} \div 4\frac{1}{2} = 1\frac{1}{2}$

47. Which of these equations is equivalent to $\frac{3}{4} \times 8\frac{1}{5} = 6\frac{3}{20}$? Select all that apply. 🔊 6.NS.1.1

☐ $\frac{3}{4} \div 8\frac{1}{5} = 6\frac{3}{20}$

☐ $6\frac{3}{20} \div \frac{3}{4} = 8\frac{1}{5}$

☐ $6\frac{3}{20} \div 8\frac{1}{5} = \frac{3}{4}$

☐ $\frac{3}{4} \div 6\frac{3}{20} = 8\frac{1}{5}$

☐ $8\frac{1}{5} \div 6\frac{3}{20} = \frac{3}{4}$

1. Vocabulary How can you use a *compatible number* to estimate a quotient when dividing a decimal by a whole number? *Lesson 1-2*
🌐 6.NS.2.3

2. Keaton is building a rectangular tabletop and wants to put a metal border around the edge. The length of the tabletop is 1.83 meters and the width is 0.74 meter. Use the formula $P = 2\ell + 2w$ to find the perimeter of the tabletop. *Lesson 1-1* 🌐 6.NS.2.3

Norbert's Nursery

Flower	Price per Flat
Petunia	$5.25
Daisy	$7.65
Begonia	$8.40

3. Norbert's Nursery is having a sale. Flats of flowers are priced as marked, including tax. Jake buys 2 flats of petunias, 3 flats of daisies, and 1 flat of begonias. If he pays with a $50 bill, how much change should Jake receive? *Lesson 1-1* 🌐 6.NS.2.3

4. Marguerite is selling space in an advertisement book for a community fund-raising event. Each $\frac{1}{4}$ page in the book costs $15.50. What is the cost for $\frac{3}{4}$ page? *Lesson 1-1* 🌐 6.NS.2.3

Ⓐ $62.00   Ⓑ $46.50

Ⓒ $20.67   Ⓓ $11.63

5. What is the value of $170 \div (4 \times 5)$? *Lesson 1-2* 🌐 6.NS.2.2, 6.NS.2.3

6. Lucia walks $2\frac{3}{4}$ miles on Monday. On Monday, she walks $1\frac{1}{2}$ times farther than on Tuesday. Which equation can be used to find how far Lucia walks on Tuesday? *Lesson 1-3* 🌐 6.NS.1.1

Ⓐ $2\frac{3}{4} \times 1\frac{1}{2} = 4\frac{1}{8}$ Ⓑ $2\frac{3}{4} + 1\frac{1}{2} = 4\frac{1}{4}$

Ⓒ $2\frac{3}{4} \div 1\frac{1}{2} = 1\frac{5}{6}$ Ⓓ $1\frac{1}{2} \div 2\frac{3}{4} = \frac{6}{11}$

How well did you do on the mid-topic checkpoint? Fill in the stars.

MID-TOPIC PERFORMANCE TASK

Nyan Robotics Team received their challenge for the year and has to buy parts to build their robot for competitions.

Parts List

Part	Cost per Part
Beam	$5.95
Channel	$8.50
Motor controller	$99.75
Motor mount	$17.55
Gear	$12.15
Sprocket	$3.00
Wheel	$18.90
Axle	$4.35

PART A

Team members Eric and Natalia secure a grant for $75.00 to buy beams and channels. If the team needs 3 beams and 6 channels, will the grant cover the cost? If so, how much of the grant will remain? 🐱 6.NS.2.3

PART B

Team members Corinne, Kevin, and Tomas decide to share the cost of 2 motor controllers and 4 wheels equally. How much does each member need to contribute? 🐱 6.NS.2.3

PART C

Nyan Robotics has a budget of $99 to buy sprockets, axles, and gears. If they spend $\frac{2}{3}$ of the budget on sprockets, how much money from the budget remains to buy axles and gears? 🐱 6.NS.1.1

Stocking **UP**

MAFS.K12.MP.4.1 Model with mathematics. Also MP.1.1, MP.2.1, MP.3.1, MP.5.1, MP.7.1, MP.8.1

MAFS.6.NS.2.3 Fluently add, subtract, multiply, and divide multi-digit decimals using the standard algorithm for each operation.

ACT 1

1. After watching the video, what is the first question that comes to mind?

2. Write the Main Question you will answer.

3. Construct Arguments Predict an answer to this Main Question. Explain your prediction.

4. On the number line below, write a number that is too small to be the answer. Write a number that is too large.

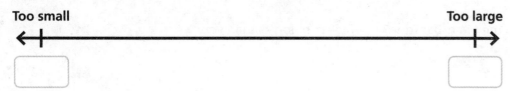

Too small   Too large

5. Plot your prediction on the same number line.

6. What information in this situation would be helpful to know? How would you use that information?

7. Use Appropriate Tools What tools can you use to get the information you need? Record the information as you find it.

8. Model with Math Represent the situation using the mathematical content, concepts, and skills from this topic. Use your representation to answer the Main Question.

9. What is your answer to the Main Question? Is it higher or lower than your prediction? Explain why.

Go Online | **PearsonRealize.com**

10. Write the answer you saw in the video.

11. Reasoning Does your answer match the answer in the video? If not, what are some reasons that would explain the difference?

12. Make Sense and Persevere Would you change your model now that you know the answer? Explain.

Reflect

13. Model with Math Explain how you used a mathematical model to represent the situation. How did the model help you answer the Main Question?

14. Reasoning How did you represent the situation using symbols? How did you use those symbols to solve the problem?

SEQUEL

15. Model with Math The store purchases boxes of pasta for $0.82 and cans of sauce for $1.62. How much profit does the store make from this purchase?

Go Online | **PearsonRealize.com**

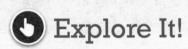 Explore It!

Students are competing in a 4-kilometer
relay race. There are 10 runners.

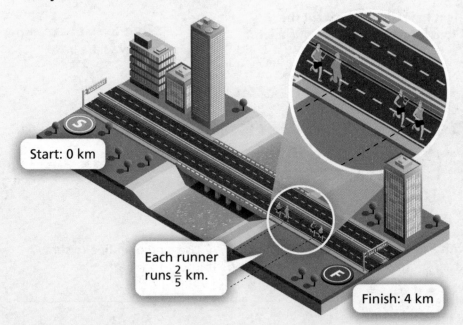

Start: 0 km

Each runner
runs $\frac{2}{5}$ km.

Finish: 4 km

I can...
use models and equations to
represent fraction division.

MAFS.6.NS.1.1 Interpret and compute quotients
of fractions, and solve word problems involving
division of fractions by fractions, e.g., by using visual
fractional models and equations to represent the
problem. ...

MAFS.K12.MP.2.1, MP.4.1, MP.7.1

A. Use the number line to represent the data for the race.

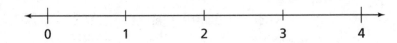

0   1   2   3   4

B. Use multiplication or division to describe your work on the number line.

Focus on math practices

Model with Math Describe what a number line would look like if there
were 10 runners each running $\frac{1}{2}$ kilometer in a 5-kilometer race.

EXAMPLE 1 **Divide Whole Numbers by Fractions**

Scan for
Multimedia

Mr. Roberts has a board that is 3 feet long. He plans to cut the board into pieces that are each $\frac{3}{4}$ foot long to build a set of shelves. How many shelves can he make?

Use Structure How many $\frac{3}{4}$s are in 3?

| 0 ft | 1 ft | 2 ft | 3 ft |

ONE WAY Write 3 as a fraction with a denominator of 4, $\frac{12}{4}$. Think of division as repeated subtraction.

Board $\underset{\underline{\hspace{4cm}}}{\overset{\frac{12}{4} \text{ ft}}{}}$

Each shelf $\boxed{\frac{3}{4} \text{ ft}} \xrightarrow{s \text{ shelves}}$

$$\begin{array}{cccc} \frac{12}{4} & \frac{9}{4} & \frac{6}{4} & \frac{3}{4} \\ -\frac{3}{4} & -\frac{3}{4} & -\frac{3}{4} & -\frac{3}{4} \\ \hline \frac{9}{4} & \frac{6}{4} & \frac{3}{4} & 0 \end{array}$$

Mr. Roberts can make 4 shelves.

ANOTHER WAY Use a number line to show 3 feet. Divide it into $\frac{3}{4}$-foot parts.

So, $3 \div \frac{3}{4} = 4$.

When the divisor is less than 1, the quotient is greater than the dividend.

Mr. Roberts can make 4 shelves.

☑ Try It!

A board is 6 feet long. How many $\frac{2}{3}$-foot-long pieces can be cut from the board? Use the number line to show your work.

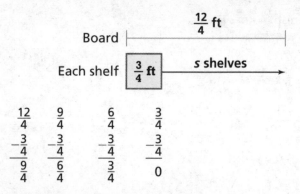

Convince Me! Why is the number of pieces that can be cut from the board greater than the number of feet in the length of the board?

EXAMPLE **2** Divide Fractions by Whole Numbers

  ACTIVITY ASSESS

How much cake will each person get if 3 friends decide to share half a cake equally? Find $\frac{1}{2} \div 3$.

Draw a picture to show $\frac{1}{2}$.

$\frac{1}{2}$

Divide $\frac{1}{2}$ into 3 equal parts.

$\frac{1}{2} \div 3$

Each part is $\frac{1}{6}$ of the whole.

$\frac{1}{2} \div 3 = \frac{1}{6}$

Each person will get $\frac{1}{6}$ of the cake.

 **Try It!**

Make a diagram to find $\frac{2}{3} \div 4$.

EXAMPLE **3** **Use Relationships to Divide Whole Numbers by Fractions**

You can use what you know about dividing fractions to find and use a pattern. Look at the division and multiplication sentences at the right. Find and use a pattern to solve $4 \div \frac{2}{3}$.

The pattern shows that when you divide by a fraction, you get the same result as when you multiply by its reciprocal.

$8 \div \frac{4}{1} = 2$	$8 \times \frac{1}{4} = 2$
$5 \div \frac{1}{2} = 10$	$5 \times \frac{2}{1} = 10$
$3 \div \frac{3}{4} = 4$	$3 \times \frac{4}{3} = 4$

$4 \div \frac{2}{3} = 4 \times \frac{3}{2}$

Rewrite the problem as a multiplication problem using the reciprocal of the divisor.

$= \frac{4}{1} \times \frac{3}{2}$

$= \frac{12}{2}$ or 6

Two numbers whose product is 1 are called **reciprocals** of each other. If a nonzero number is named as a fraction $\frac{a}{b}$, then its reciprocal is $\frac{b}{a}$.

 **Try It!**

Use the pattern in the table above to find $8 \div \frac{3}{4}$.

$8 \div \frac{3}{4} = 8 \times \boxed{} = \boxed{}$

To divide a whole number by a fraction:

> Write the whole number as a fraction.

$$14 \div \frac{4}{7} = \frac{14}{1} \div \frac{4}{7}$$

$$\frac{14}{1} \times \frac{7}{4} = \frac{98}{4} \text{ or } 24\frac{1}{2}$$

> Multiply the whole number by the reciprocal of the divisor.

To divide a fraction by a whole number:

> Write the whole number as a fraction.

$$\frac{4}{7} \div 14 = \frac{4}{7} \div \frac{14}{1}$$

$$\frac{4}{7} \times \frac{1}{14} = \frac{4}{98} \text{ or } \frac{2}{49}$$

> Multiply the fraction by the reciprocal of the whole number.

Do You Understand?

1. **? Essential Question** How can you represent division of fractions?

2. **Reasoning** Draw a diagram to represent $8 \div \frac{2}{3}$. Then write an equation to show the solution.

3. **Reasoning** Is $4 \div \frac{3}{2}$ the same as $4 \div \frac{2}{3}$? Explain.

4. How can you write any nonzero whole number as a fraction?

5. **Look for Relationships** How does the quotient compare to the dividend when the divisor is a fraction less than 1?

6. What division equation is represented by the diagram?

Do You Know How?

In **7–14**, find each reciprocal.

7. $\frac{3}{5}$

8. $\frac{1}{6}$

9. 9

10. $\frac{7}{4}$

11. $\frac{5}{8}$

12. 16

13. $\frac{7}{12}$

14. $\frac{11}{5}$

In **15–22**, find each quotient.

15. $6 \div \frac{2}{3}$

16. $12 \div \frac{3}{8}$

17. $\frac{1}{4} \div 3$

18. $\frac{2}{5} \div 2$

19. $2 \div \frac{1}{2}$

20. $3 \div \frac{1}{4}$

21. $9 \div \frac{3}{5}$

22. $5 \div \frac{2}{7}$

Go Online | PearsonRealize.com

Name: _____

Practice & Problem Solving

Leveled Practice In **23** and **24**, complete each division sentence.

23. $6 \div \boxed{} = 12$

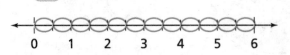

0   1   2   3   4   5   6

The number line shows 6 wholes.

24. $\frac{2}{3} \div \boxed{} = \frac{2}{9}$

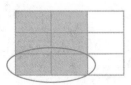

···

In **25** and **26**, find each quotient. Draw a diagram to help.

25. $\frac{3}{5} \div 3$

26. $2 \div \frac{2}{5}$

···

In **27–30**, find each reciprocal.

27. $\frac{3}{10}$

28. 6

29. $\frac{1}{15}$

30. 3

···

In **31–38**, find each quotient.

31. $36 \div \frac{3}{4}$

32. $2 \div \frac{3}{8}$

33. $18 \div \frac{2}{3}$

34. $9 \div \frac{4}{5}$

35. $\frac{1}{6} \div 2$

36. $\frac{2}{3} \div 3$

37. $\frac{3}{5} \div 2$

38. $\frac{1}{4} \div 4$

···

39. A worker is pouring 3 quarts of liquid into $\frac{3}{8}$-quart containers.
How many of the containers can she fill? Write and solve
a division equation.

3 quarts $\frac{3}{8}$ quart

In 40–43, use the given information.

A tortoise can move 600 ft in $\frac{2}{3}$ h.

A snail can move 120 ft in $\frac{3}{4}$ h.

A sloth can move 250 ft in $\frac{5}{8}$ h.

40. **Higher Order Thinking** Without doing any calculations, how can you use the information given to tell which animal moves the fastest?

41. **Reasoning** The quotient $250 \div \frac{5}{8}$ tells about how far a sloth may move in one hour. How far can a sloth go in 90 minutes? Justify your reasoning.

42. The quotient $600 \div \frac{2}{3}$ tells about how far a tortoise may move in one hour. Find that distance.

43. Write and solve an equation to find how far a snail can go in one hour.

44. A waitress pours $\frac{3}{4}$ gallon of orange juice equally into 5 pitchers. What fraction of a gallon of orange juice is in each pitcher? Use the rectangle to represent the problem. Then write an equation to show the solution.

The rectangle represents 1 whole gallon. Draw lines to represent $\frac{3}{4}$ gallon first. Then divide that into 5 equal parts.

Assessment Practice

45. Select all the math statements that have the same solution. 🕐 6.NS.1.1

☐ $12 \div \frac{2}{3} = \frac{12}{1} \times \frac{3}{2}$

☐ $\frac{2}{3} \div \frac{1}{27} = \frac{2}{3} \times \frac{27}{1}$

☐ $16 \div \frac{4}{5} = 16 \times \frac{5}{4}$

☐ $12 \div \frac{3}{2} = 12 \times \frac{2}{3}$

☐ $24 \div \frac{4}{3} = 24 \times \frac{3}{4}$

46. Select all the math statements that are true. 🕐 6.NS.1.1

☐ $\frac{1}{3} \div 3$ is $\frac{1}{3} \div \frac{3}{1} = \frac{1}{3} \times \frac{1}{3}$

☐ $\frac{4}{5} \div 5$ is $\frac{4}{5} \div \frac{5}{1} = \frac{4}{5} \times \frac{1}{5}$

☐ $\frac{7}{8} \div 8$ is $\frac{7}{8} \div \frac{1}{8} = \frac{7}{8} \times \frac{8}{1}$

☐ $\frac{2}{3} \div 6$ is $\frac{2}{3} \div \frac{6}{1} = \frac{2}{3} \times \frac{1}{6}$

☐ $\frac{4}{9} \div 4$ is $\frac{4}{9} \div \frac{1}{4} = \frac{4}{9} \times \frac{4}{1}$

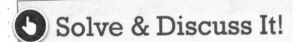 
Lesson 1-5
Divide Fractions by Fractions

Go Online | PearsonRealize.com

A granola bar was cut into 6 equal pieces. Someone ate part of the granola bar so that $\frac{2}{3}$ of the original bar remains. How many $\frac{1}{6}$ parts are left? Use the picture to draw a model to represent and find $\frac{2}{3} \div \frac{1}{6}$.

$\frac{2}{3}$

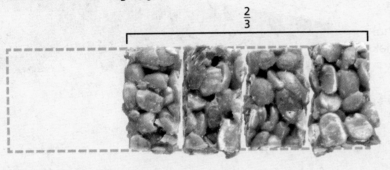

Model with Math You can model with math by dividing a whole into equal parts.

I can...
divide a fraction by another fraction.

MAFS.6.NS.1.1 Interpret and compute quotients of fractions, and solve word problems involving division of fractions by fractions, e.g., by using visual fractional models and equations to represent the problem. ...

MAFS.K12.MP.4.1, MP.7.1

Focus on math practices
Use Structure How can you use multiplication to check your answer?

37

VISUAL LEARNING

 EXAMPLE 1 👁 **Use an Area Model to Divide Fractions**

Scan for Multimedia

Simon buys $\frac{1}{2}$ yard of material to make footbags. How many footbags can Simon make? Find $\frac{1}{2} \div \frac{1}{6}$.

Simon uses $\frac{1}{6}$ yard of material for each footbag that he makes.

Model with Math How can you use an area model to represent the division?

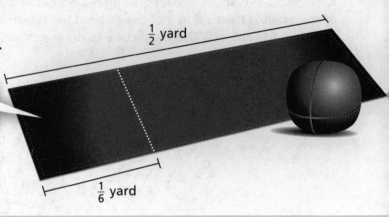

$\frac{1}{2}$ yard

$\frac{1}{6}$ yard

STEP 1 Draw an area model to show the dividend, $\frac{1}{2}$.

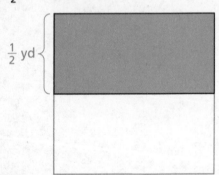

$\frac{1}{2}$ yd

Then find how many $\frac{1}{6}$s are in $\frac{1}{2}$.

STEP 2 Divide the same area model into $\frac{1}{6}$s to show the divisor.

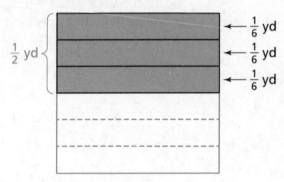

$\frac{1}{2}$ yd

← $\frac{1}{6}$ yd
← $\frac{1}{6}$ yd
← $\frac{1}{6}$ yd

There are three $\frac{1}{6}$s in $\frac{1}{2}$.

So, $\frac{1}{2} \div \frac{1}{6} = 3$.

Simon can make 3 footbags.

☑ **Try It!**

Use the number line below to represent $\frac{1}{6} \times 3 = \frac{1}{2}$. Then write an equivalent division sentence.

0   1

Convince Me! How are the dividend, divisor, and quotient represented on the number line?

EXAMPLE **2** Use Another Area Model to Divide Fractions

 ACTIVITY   ASSESS

How much of a $\frac{3}{4}$-cup serving is in $\frac{2}{3}$ cup of yogurt?

STEP 1 Find $\frac{2}{3} \div \frac{3}{4}$. Show $\frac{2}{3}$ and $\frac{3}{4}$.

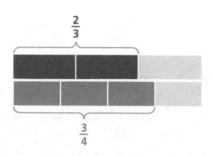

STEP 2 Multiply the denominators to find the common unit of twelfths to compare $\frac{2}{3}$ and $\frac{3}{4}$.

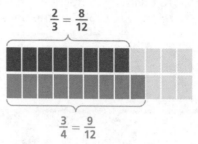

$$\frac{2}{3} = \frac{8}{12}$$

$$\frac{3}{4} = \frac{9}{12}$$

$\frac{2}{3}$ is divided into 8 equal parts, while $\frac{3}{4}$ is divided into 9 equal parts.

So, $\frac{2}{3}$ cup is $\frac{8}{9}$ of a $\frac{3}{4}$-cup serving.

 Try It!

Find $\frac{1}{4} \div \frac{3}{8}$. Draw an area model.

 EXAMPLE **3**  Divide Fractions

Andrew has $\frac{3}{4}$ gallon of orange juice. He wants to pour it into $\frac{1}{6}$-gallon containers. How many containers can Andrew fill?

Find $\frac{3}{4} \div \frac{1}{6}$. To divide by a fraction, rewrite the problem as a multiplication problem using the reciprocal of the divisor.

$\frac{3}{4} \div \frac{1}{6} = \frac{3}{4} \times \frac{6}{1}$ — $\frac{6}{1}$ is the reciprocal of $\frac{1}{6}$.

$\quad\quad = \frac{18}{4}$ or $4\frac{1}{2}$

Andrew can fill $4\frac{1}{2}$ containers.

$\frac{3}{4}$ gallon

$\frac{1}{6}$ gallon

Try It!

How wide is a rectangular strip of land with a length of $\frac{3}{4}$ mile and an area of $\frac{1}{2}$ square mile? Use the area formula: $A = \ell \times w$.

$\frac{1}{2} = \frac{3}{4}w \rightarrow \frac{1}{2} \div \boxed{} = w \rightarrow \frac{1}{2} \times \boxed{} = w \rightarrow w = \boxed{}$

The strip of land is $\boxed{}$ mile wide.

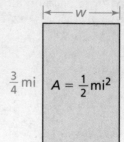

$\frac{3}{4}$ mi $A = \frac{1}{2}$mi²

To divide a fraction by a fraction, rewrite the division equation as a multiplication equation.

> To divide by a fraction, multiply by the reciprocal of the divisor.

$$\frac{4}{5} \div \frac{3}{10} = \frac{4}{5} \times \frac{10}{3} = \frac{40}{15} \text{ or } 2\frac{2}{3}$$

Do You Understand?

1. **? Essential Question** How can you divide a fraction by a fraction?

2. **Critique Reasoning** To find the quotient of $\frac{2}{5} \div \frac{8}{5}$, Corey rewrites the problem as $\frac{5}{2} \times \frac{8}{5}$. Explain Corey's mistake and how to correct it.

3. **Reasoning** Is the quotient of $\frac{3}{5} \div \frac{6}{7}$ greater than or less than $\frac{3}{5}$? Explain.

4. How is dividing a whole number by a fraction different from dividing a fraction by a fraction?

Do You Know How?

In 5–7, write a division sentence to represent each model.

5.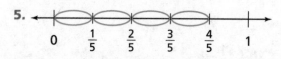

6.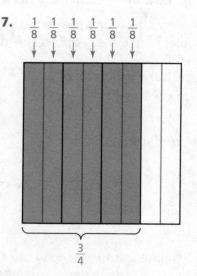

7.

In 8–11, find each quotient.

8. $\frac{3}{4} \div \frac{2}{3}$

9. $\frac{3}{12} \div \frac{1}{8}$

10. $\frac{1}{2} \div \frac{4}{5}$

11. $\frac{7}{10} \div \frac{2}{5}$

Go Online | PearsonRealize.com

Name: _____

Practice & Problem Solving

Scan for
Multimedia

In 12 and 13, complete each division sentence using the models provided.

12. $\frac{1}{3} \div \frac{1}{12} = \boxed{}$

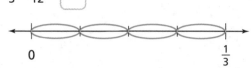

0                    $\frac{1}{3}$

13. $\frac{2}{5} \div \frac{1}{10} = \boxed{}$

$\frac{1}{10}$ $\frac{1}{10}$ $\frac{1}{10}$ $\frac{1}{10}$

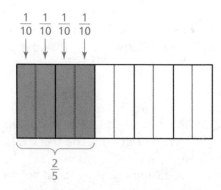

$\frac{2}{5}$

In 14–25, find each quotient.

14. $\frac{2}{3} \div \frac{1}{3}$

15. $\frac{1}{2} \div \frac{1}{16}$

16. $\frac{1}{4} \div \frac{1}{12}$

17. $\frac{6}{7} \div \frac{3}{7}$

18. $\frac{5}{14} \div \frac{4}{7}$

19. $\frac{5}{8} \div \frac{1}{2}$

20. $\frac{7}{12} \div \frac{3}{4}$

21. $\frac{2}{7} \div \frac{1}{2}$

22. $\frac{4}{9} \div \frac{2}{3}$

23. $\frac{7}{12} \div \frac{1}{8}$

24. $\frac{3}{10} \div \frac{3}{5}$

25. $\frac{2}{5} \div \frac{1}{8}$

26. Be Precise A large bag contains $\frac{12}{15}$ pound of granola. How many $\frac{1}{3}$-pound bags can be filled with this amount of granola? How much granola is left over?

27. Higher Order Thinking Find $\frac{3}{4} \div \frac{2}{3}$. Then draw a picture and write an explanation describing how to get the answer.

28. The area of a rectangular painting is $\frac{1}{6}$ square yard. The width is $\frac{2}{3}$ yard. What is the length of the painting? Use the formula $A = \ell \times w$.

29. Solve for n in the equation $\frac{13}{16} \div \frac{1}{6} = n$.

30. Model with Math A cafeteria uses $\frac{1}{6}$ pound of coffee to fill a large coffee dispenser. The cafeteria has $\frac{2}{3}$ pound of coffee to use.

a. Complete the model at the right to find how many coffee dispensers the cafeteria can fill.

b. Write a division sentence that describes the model and tells how many dispensers can be filled.

$\frac{2}{3}$ {

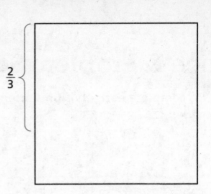

31. Model with Math A full load for a small truck to haul is $\frac{2}{3}$ ton of gravel. The truck is hauling $\frac{1}{2}$ ton of gravel.

a. Complete the model below to find how much of a full load the truck is hauling.

b. Write a division sentence that describes the model and tells how much of a full load the truck is hauling.

$\frac{1}{2}$ ton gravel

$\frac{2}{3}$ TON CAPACITY

$\frac{1}{2}$

$\frac{2}{3}$

32. Use Structure How many $\frac{1}{4}$-inch pieces can be cut from a piece of metal $\frac{5}{8}$ inch long?

33. Write a problem that could be solved by finding $\frac{5}{8} \div \frac{2}{5}$.

34. Which division sentence is shown by the model at the right?

6.NS.1.1

$\frac{1}{9}$ $\frac{1}{9}$ $\frac{1}{9}$ $\frac{1}{9}$ $\frac{1}{9}$ $\frac{1}{9}$

Ⓐ $\frac{2}{3} \div \frac{1}{9} = 6$

Ⓑ $\frac{1}{9} \div \frac{2}{3} = \frac{1}{6}$

Ⓒ $6 \div \frac{1}{9} = 54$

Ⓓ $6 \div \frac{2}{3} = 9$

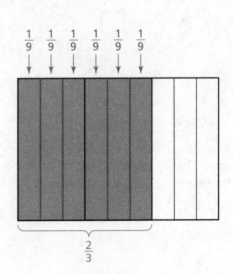

$\frac{2}{3}$

Solve & Discuss It!

  ACTIVITY

A jeweler has a $5\frac{1}{2}$-inch strip of silver wire that she is cutting into $1\frac{3}{8}$-inch pieces. How many pieces can she make?

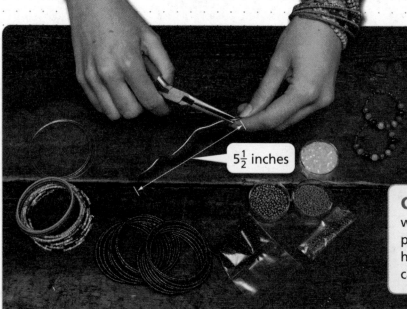

$5\frac{1}{2}$ inches

Lesson 1-6
Divide Mixed Numbers

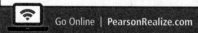 Go Online | PearsonRealize.com

I can...
divide with mixed numbers.

MAFS.6.NS.1.1 Interpret and compute quotients of fractions, and solve word problems involving division of fractions by fractions, e.g., by using visual fractional models and equations to represent the problem. ...

MAFS.K12.MP.1.1, MP.2.1, MP.7.1, MP.8.1

Generalize How can you use what you know about solving problems with fractions to find how many pieces the jeweler can make?

Focus on math practices

Generalize Explain how to use estimation to check whether your answer is reasonable.

43

EXAMPLE 1 Divide a Mixed Number by a Mixed Number

Scan for Multimedia

Damon has $37\frac{1}{2}$ inches of space on his car bumper that he wants to use for bumper stickers. How many short bumper stickers can Damon fit side by side on his car bumper?

$37\frac{1}{2}$ inches

GO GREEN GO Long = 15 inches

I ♥ ROBOTS Medium = $10\frac{3}{4}$ inches

 Short = $6\frac{1}{4}$ inches

STEP 1 Estimate $37\frac{1}{2} \div 6\frac{1}{4}$.

Bumper space |———— $37\frac{1}{2}$ in. ————|

Short sticker | $6\frac{1}{4}$ in. | —— *n* stickers ——→

$37\frac{1}{2} \div 6\frac{1}{4}$
↓   ↓
$36 \div 6 = 6$ ← Use compatible numbers to estimate the quotient.

So, $37\frac{1}{2} \div 6\frac{1}{4} \approx 6$.

STEP 2 Find $37\frac{1}{2} \div 6\frac{1}{4}$. Write each mixed number as a fraction.

$37\frac{1}{2} \div 6\frac{1}{4} = \frac{75}{2} \div \frac{25}{4}$

$= \frac{75}{2} \times \frac{4}{25}$ ← Use the reciprocal of $\frac{25}{4}$ to write a multiplication problem.

$= \frac{300}{50}$ or 6

Because 6 is the estimate, the quotient is reasonable. Damo can fit 6 short bumper stickers on his car bumper.

☑ Try It!

How many medium bumper stickers can Damon fit side by side on his car bumper? Find $37\frac{1}{2} \div 10\frac{3}{4}$.

Convince Me! Why do you multiply $\frac{75}{2}$ by $\frac{4}{43}$ to divide $37\frac{1}{2}$ by $10\frac{3}{4}$?

$37\frac{1}{2} \div 10\frac{3}{4} = \frac{75}{2} \div \boxed{}$

$= \frac{75}{2} \times \boxed{}$

$= \boxed{}$

Damon can fit $\boxed{}$ medium bumper stickers on his car bumper.

EXAMPLE **2**   ACTIVITY   ASSESS

EXAMPLE 2 — Divide a Whole Number by a Mixed Number

Kayla drives her new car to work every day. It uses $1\frac{3}{5}$ gallons of gas for each round trip. How many round trips to work can Kayla drive on a full tank of gas?

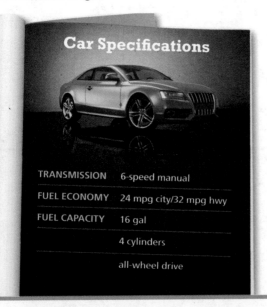

Car Specifications

TRANSMISSION	6-speed manual
FUEL ECONOMY	24 mpg city/32 mpg hwy
FUEL CAPACITY	16 gal
	4 cylinders
	all-wheel drive

STEP 1

Estimate using compatible numbers.

$$16 \div 1\frac{3}{5} \rightarrow 16 \div 2 = 8$$

So, $16 \div 1\frac{3}{5} \approx 8$.

STEP 2

$$16 \div 1\frac{3}{5} = \frac{16}{1} \div \frac{8}{5}$$

> Write the whole number and mixed number as fractions.

$$= \frac{16}{1} \times \frac{5}{8}$$

> Multiply by the reciprocal of the divisor.

$$= \frac{80}{8} \text{ or } 10$$

The estimate, 8, is close to the quotient, 10. The answer is reasonable. Kayla can drive 10 round trips to work on a full tank of gas.

EXAMPLE 3 — Divide a Mixed Number by a Whole Number

Lillian hikes the trail in 4 hours. She hikes the same number of miles per hour. How many miles did Lillian hike each hour?

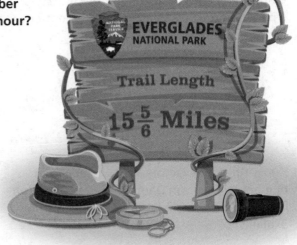

EVERGLADES NATIONAL PARK

Trail Length

$15\frac{5}{6}$ Miles

STEP 1

Estimate using compatible numbers.

$$15\frac{5}{6} \div 4 \rightarrow 16 \div 4 = 4$$

So, $15\frac{5}{6} \div 4 \approx 4$.

STEP 2

$$15\frac{5}{6} \div 4 = \frac{95}{6} \div \frac{4}{1}$$

> Write the mixed number and whole number as fractions.

$$= \frac{95}{6} \times \frac{1}{4}$$

> Multiply by the reciprocal of the divisor.

$$= \frac{95}{24} \text{ or } 3\frac{23}{24}$$

The estimate, 4, is close to the quotient, $3\frac{23}{24}$. The answer is reasonable. Lillian hikes $3\frac{23}{24}$ miles each hour.

 Try It!

Divide.

a. $20 \div 2\frac{2}{3}$

b. $12\frac{1}{2} \div 6$

To divide with mixed numbers, write mixed numbers and any whole numbers as fractions.

Use the reciprocal of the divisor to rewrite the problem as a multiplication problem.

$$5\frac{1}{3} \div 1\frac{1}{3} = \frac{16}{3} \div \frac{4}{3} = \frac{16}{3} \times \frac{3}{4} = \frac{48}{12} \text{ or } 4$$

Finally, multiply and use the estimate to check whether the answer is reasonable.

Use compatible numbers to estimate.

$$5 \div 1 = 5$$

Do You Understand?

1. **Essential Question** How can you divide with mixed numbers?

2. **Generalize** When dividing mixed numbers, why is it important to estimate the quotient first?

3. **Reasoning** In Example 1, how many long bumper stickers can Damon fit side by side on his car bumper? Will there be uncovered space? Explain.

4. What is the difference between dividing fractions less than 1 and dividing mixed numbers?

Do You Know How?

In 5–13, find each quotient.

5. $2\frac{5}{8} \div 2\frac{1}{4} = \frac{21}{8} \div \boxed{}$

$$= \frac{21}{8} \times \boxed{}$$

$$= \boxed{}$$

6. $3 \div 4\frac{1}{2}$

7. $18 \div 3\frac{2}{3}$

8. $1\frac{2}{5} \div 7$

9. $5 \div 6\frac{2}{5}$

10. $8\frac{1}{5} \div 3\frac{3}{4}$

11. $2\frac{1}{2} \div 4\frac{1}{10}$

12. $2\frac{2}{3} \div 6$

13. $6\frac{5}{9} \div 1\frac{7}{9}$

Practice & Problem Solving

Leveled Practice In **14–25**, find each quotient.

14. $10 \div 2\frac{1}{4} = \frac{10}{1} \div \boxed{}$

$= \frac{10}{1} \times \boxed{}$

$= \boxed{}$

15. $9\frac{1}{3} \div 6 = \frac{28}{3} \div \boxed{}$

$= \frac{28}{3} \times \boxed{}$

$= \boxed{}$

16. $1\frac{3}{8} \div 4\frac{1}{8} = \frac{11}{8} \div \boxed{}$

$= \frac{11}{8} \times \boxed{}$

$= \boxed{}$

17. $2\frac{2}{3} \div 8 = \frac{8}{3} \div \boxed{}$

$= \boxed{} \times \boxed{}$

$= \boxed{}$

18. $4\frac{1}{3} \div 3\frac{1}{4} = \frac{13}{3} \div \boxed{}$

$= \boxed{} \times \boxed{}$

$= \boxed{}$

19. $1 \div 8\frac{5}{9} = \frac{1}{1} \div \boxed{}$

$= \boxed{} \times \boxed{}$

$= \boxed{}$

20. $3\frac{5}{6} \div 9\frac{5}{6}$

21. $16 \div 2\frac{2}{3}$

22. $2\frac{5}{8} \div 13$

23. $3\frac{6}{7} \div 6\frac{3}{4}$

24. $2\frac{1}{3} \div 1\frac{1}{3}$

25. $3\frac{3}{4} \div 1\frac{1}{2}$

26. Beth is making a rope ladder. Each step of the ladder is $2\frac{1}{3}$ feet wide. Beth has a rope that is 21 feet long. How many steps can she make from the rope?

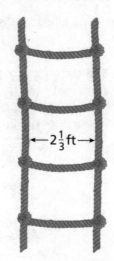

←$2\frac{1}{3}$ ft→

27. The area of this rectangle is $257\frac{1}{4}$ in.². Find side length w.

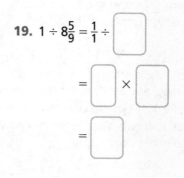

$257\frac{1}{4}$ in.²

$10\frac{1}{2}$ in.

w

In 28 and 29, use the picture.

28. The larger room is twice as long as the smaller room. How long is the larger room?

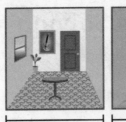 

29. If the length of the smaller room is divided into 4 equal parts, how long is each part?

$20\frac{4}{5}$ feet   ?

30. **Make Sense and Persevere** Luis has 3 pounds of ground turkey to make turkey burgers. He uses $\frac{3}{8}$ pound per burger to make 6 burgers. How many $\frac{1}{4}$-pound burgers can Luis make with the remaining turkey?

31. **Higher Order Thinking** If $9 \times \frac{n}{5} = 9 \div \frac{n}{5}$, then what does n equal? Explain.

32. Margaret uses $1\frac{3}{4}$ teaspoons of key lime zest to make 12 key lime cupcakes. She wants to make 30 cupcakes. How much key lime zest will Margaret use?

33. **Use Structure** A gem store in Fort Lauderdale received a shipment of $1\frac{1}{2}$ pounds of moonstone crystals. If these moonstone crystals were separated into 6 equal bags, how much would each bag weigh?

34. The owner of an aquatic store used $17\frac{1}{2}$ gallons of water to fill aquariums. He put $5\frac{5}{6}$ gallons of water in each aquarium. How many aquariums did he fill?

35. Write an explanation to a friend about how you would estimate $17\frac{1}{5} \div 3\frac{4}{5}$.

Assessment Practice

36. A restaurant has $15\frac{1}{5}$ pounds of alligator meat to make tasty alligator dishes. 🏴 6.NS.1.1

PART A

Each pot of alligator stew requires $2\frac{3}{8}$ pounds of alligator meat. Which solution shows how many pots of alligator stew can be made?

Ⓐ 36 pots; $15\frac{1}{5} \times 2\frac{3}{8}$

Ⓑ $\frac{5}{32}$ pot; $2\frac{3}{8} \div 15\frac{1}{5}$

Ⓒ 7 pots; $15\frac{1}{5} \div 2\frac{3}{8}$

Ⓓ 6 pots; $15\frac{1}{5} \div 2\frac{3}{8}$

PART B

The restaurant could make a smaller pot of alligator stew that uses $1\frac{3}{5}$ pounds of alligator meat. How many more smaller pots of alligator stew can be made than the larger pots?

Go Online | PearsonRealize.co

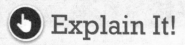 Explain It!

 ACTIVITY

Lesson 1-7
Solve Problems with Rational Numbers

Go Online | PearsonRealize.com

Jenna feeds her cat twice a day. She gives her cat $\frac{3}{4}$ can of cat food each time. Jenna is having a friend take care of her cat for 5 days. To prepare, she bought 8 cans of cat food. Did Jenna buy enough cat food?

I can...
solve multistep problems with fractions and decimals.

MAFS.6.NS.1.1 Interpret and compute quotients of fractions, and solve word problems involving division of fractions by fractions, e.g., by using ... equations to represent the problem. ...

MAFS.K12.MP.2.1, MP.3.1, MP.6.1

A. What do you need to know before you can answer the question?

B. How can you determine which operations to use to solve the problem?

Focus on math practices

Reasoning To find out whether she has enough cat food, Jenna multiplies, divides, and compares. Explain how Jenna may have solved the problem.

VISUAL LEARNING

EXAMPLE 1   **Solve Multistep Problems with Fractions**

Scan for Multimedia

A farmer is building a small horse-riding arena. The fencing around the arena is built using three rows of wood planks. The farmer decided to use wood planks that are $8\frac{1}{2}$ feet long, so he ordered 130 of these wood planks from a local lumberyard. Did he order enough wood planks to build the arena?

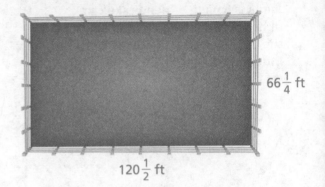

$66\frac{1}{4}$ ft

$120\frac{1}{2}$ ft

Find the perimeter of the arena.

$$P = 2 \times 120\frac{1}{2} + 2 \times 66\frac{1}{4}$$

$$= 241 + 132\frac{1}{2}$$

$$= 373\frac{1}{2} \text{ ft}$$

The farmer needs enough wood planks for 3 times the perimeter.

$$3 \times 373\frac{1}{2} = 1{,}120\frac{1}{2} \text{ ft}$$

Divide to find how many $8\frac{1}{2}$-foot-long planks are needed.

$$1{,}120\frac{1}{2} \div 8\frac{1}{2} = \frac{2{,}241}{2} \div \frac{17}{2}$$

$$= \frac{2{,}241}{2} \times \frac{2}{17}$$

$$= \frac{4{,}482}{34} \text{ or } 131\frac{14}{17}$$

The farmer needs at least 132 wood planks to build the fencing. He did not order enough wood planks.

☑ **Try It!**

The farmer decided that he ordered enough planks for an arena that measured $115\frac{1}{4}$ ft by $63\frac{1}{2}$ ft. Is he correct? Explain.

Convince Me! What questions do you need to answer to solve the Try It!?

EXAMPLE **2**

Solve Multistep Problems with Decimals

A 26.2-mile marathon is being planned. Water stations and medic tents must be placed along the route.

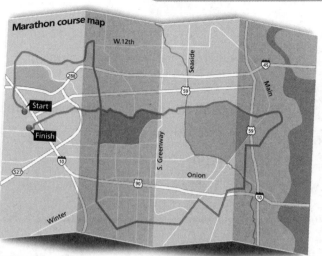

Marathon course map

A. Water stations are being set every 2.62 miles along the marathon route and at the start line. How many water stations are needed?

> Divide 26.2 by 2.62 to find the number of water stations along the route.

$$26.2 \div 2.62 = 10$$

$$10 + 1 = 11$$

> Add 1 to include the water station at the start line.

A total of 11 water stations are needed for the marathon.

B. There are 5 medic tents equally spaced along the marathon route, including one at the starting line and one at the finish line. Where should the other 3 medic tents be placed?

Be Precise You can be precise by calculating accurately when you solve problems.

> Divide 26.2 by 4 to find the location for the first medic tent after the one at the starting line.

$$26.2 \div 4 = 6.55$$

$$6.55 \times 2 = 13.1 \qquad 6.55 \times 3 = 19.65$$

> Double the distance to find the location of the third tent.

> Triple the distance to find the location of the fourth tent.

The fifth tent is at the finish line.

The medic tents are placed at the starting line, at 6.55 miles, at 13.1 miles, at 19.65 miles, and at the finish line.

Try It!

The number of runners who finish the marathon is 320. Runners donate $2.50 for each mile they run. How much money is donated? Explain.

$$26.2 \times \boxed{} = \boxed{} \text{ miles}$$

$$\boxed{} \times \$2.50 = \boxed{}$$

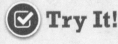

When solving multistep problems with fractions or decimals:

- decide the steps to use to solve the problem.
- choose the correct operations.
- identify the information you need from the problem.
- correctly use the information.
- calculate accurately.
- interpret solutions and check that the answer is reasonable.

Do You Understand?

1. **? Essential Question** How can you solve problems with rational numbers?

2. **Be Precise** Meghan has $5\frac{1}{4}$ yards of fabric. She plans to use $\frac{2}{3}$ of the fabric to make 4 identical backpacks. To find how much fabric she will use to make the backpacks, Meghan multiplies $5\frac{1}{4}$ by $\frac{2}{3}$. What else does Meghan need to do to find how much fabric she needs for each backpack?

3. **Critique Reasoning** Each side of a square patio is 10.5 feet. The patio is made up of 1.5-foot by 1.5-foot square stones. What is the number of stones in the patio? Look at the solution below. Does it include all the steps needed to solve the problem? Explain.

   $10.5 \times 10.5 = 110.25$

   $110.25 \div 1.5 = 73.5$

Do You Know How?

4. Devon records 4 hours of reality shows on her DVR. She records comedy shows for $\frac{3}{8}$ of that amount of time. Devon watches all the reality and comedy shows in half-hour sittings.

   a. Find the number of hours of comedy shows that Devon records.

   b. Find the total number of hours of reality and comedy shows that Devon records.

   c. Find the number of half-hour sittings needed to watch all the shows.

5. An auto mechanic earns $498.75 in 35 hours during the week. His pay is $2.50 more per hour on weekends. If he works 6 hours on the weekend in addition to 35 hours during the week, how much does he earn?

   a. What questions do you need to answer to solve the problem?

   b. How much does the auto mechanic earn? Explain.

Practice & Problem Solving

In 6–8, use the picture at the right.

6. You buy 3.17 pounds of apples, 1.25 pounds of pears, and 2.56 pounds of oranges. What is your total bill rounded to the nearest cent?

Oranges
$1.09 lb

Apples
$0.99 lb

Pears
$1.19 lb

7. A student pays for 8.9 pounds of apples with a $10 bill. How much change does the student receive?

   a. What do you do first to solve the problem?

   b. What do you do next?

8. A customer pays $3.27 for oranges and $4.76 for pears. How many pounds of fruit does the customer buy?

   a. What do you do first to solve the problem?

   b. What do you do next?

9. **Critique Reasoning** Students put $2\frac{1}{4}$ pounds of trail mix into bags that each weigh $\frac{3}{8}$ pound. They bring $\frac{2}{3}$ of the bags of trail mix on a hiking trip. Can you determine how many bags of trail mix are left by completing just one step? Explain.

10. Three fifths of the T-shirts in a T-shirt shop are blue. Five eighths of those T-shirts are on sale. One third of the blue T-shirts that are on sale are size medium. What fraction of the shop's T-shirts are blue T-shirts that are on sale and are size medium? Explain.

In 11 and 12, use the diagram.

A community garden is made up of three gardens: a vegetable garden, an herb garden, and a flower garden.

Community Garden

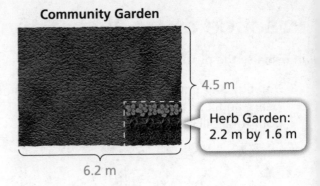

4.5 m

Herb Garden: 2.2 m by 1.6 m

6.2 m

11. The area of the vegetable garden is 0.4 of the area of the community garden. What is the area of the vegetable garden?

12. The area of the flower garden is 9.7 square meters greater than the herb garden. What is the area of the flower garden?

13. **Reasoning** At the end of a party, $\frac{3}{4}$ cup of smoked fish dip is left. Jim divides $\frac{4}{5}$ of the leftover smoked fish dip equally between 2 friends. How much dip does each friend get?

14. Students are planning a 3-day hiking trip in the Everglades. The hike covers a distance of 18.5 kilometers. The students hike 0.28 of the total distance the first day. If they split the remaining distance equally between the second and third days, how far will they hike on day 3?

15. **Higher Order Thinking** Kelly buys three containers of potato salad at the deli. She brings $\frac{4}{5}$ of the potato salad to a picnic. How many pounds of potato salad does Kelly bring to the picnic? Describe two different ways to solve the problem.

POTATO SALAD WEIGHT 1.03 lb

POTATO SALAD WEIGHT 1.12 lb

POTATO SALAD WEIGHT 1.6 lb

Assessment Practice

16. Students make $84\frac{1}{2}$ ounces of liquid soap for a craft fair. They put the soap in $6\frac{1}{2}$-ounce bottles and sell each bottle for $5.50. Which expression shows how much students earn if they sell all the bottles of liquid soap? 🌐 6.NS.1.1

   Ⓐ $71.50; $\left(84\frac{1}{2} \div 6\frac{1}{2}\right) \times 5.50$

   Ⓑ $92.18; $\left(84\frac{1}{2} \div 5.50\right) \times 6$

   Ⓒ $18.50; $\left(84\frac{1}{2} \div 6\frac{1}{2}\right) + 5.50$

   Ⓓ $99.86; $\left(84\frac{1}{2} \times 6\frac{1}{2}\right) \div 5.50$

17. Claire mowed 5 lawns last week. She mowed each lawn in $\frac{7}{12}$ hour. She mowed the same lawns this week in $\frac{5}{12}$ hour each using her new lawn mower. How many times longer was Claire's time to mow all the lawns last week than this week? 🌐 6.NS.1.1

How can you fluently add, subtract, multiply, and divide decimals?
How can you multiply and divide fractions?

Vocabulary Review

Complete each definition and then provide an example of each vocabulary word.

Vocabulary   reciprocal   dividend   fraction   product

Definition	Example
1. The answer to a multiplication problem is called a _____.	
2. The _____ is the quantity to be divided.	
3. To write a division expression as multiplication, you multiply by the _____ of the divisor.	

Use Vocabulary in Writing

Explain how to use multiplication to find the value of $\frac{1}{3} \div \frac{9}{5}$. Use the words *multiplication*, *divisor*, *quotient*, and *reciprocal* in your explanation.

Concepts and Skills Review

LESSON **1-1** **Fluently Add, Subtract, and Multiply Decimals**

Quick Review

To add or subtract decimals, line up the decimal points so that place-value positions correspond. Add or subtract as you would with whole numbers, and place the decimal point in the answer. To multiply decimals, multiply as you would with whole numbers, then place the decimal point in the product by starting at the right and counting the number of places equal to the sum of the number of decimal places in each factor.

Example

Add, subtract, or multiply.

```
  22.6        22.6          22.6    1 decimal place
+ 12.4      - 12.4        × 12.4    1 decimal place
  35.0        10.2          904
                           4520
                        + 22600
                         280.24    2 decimal places
```

Practice

Add, subtract, or multiply.

1. $91.2 + 89.9$　　　　**2.** $902.3 - 8.8$

3. 5×98.2　　　　**4.** 4×0.21

5. $62.99 - 10.83$　　　**6.** $423.22 + 98.30$

7. 4.4×6　　　　　**8.** 7×21.6

9. $24.52 - 9.6$　　　　**10.** $369.45 + 32.42$

11. 12.5×163.2　　　**12.** 16×52.3

13. $121.3 + 435.7$　　　**14.** $201.7 - 104.6$

LESSON **1-2** **Fluently Divide Whole Numbers and Decimals**

Quick Review

To divide decimals, multiply the divisor and the dividend by the same power of 10 so that the divisor is a whole number. Then use an algorithm for whole-number division.

Example

Find $2.75 \div 0.05$.

```
    55.
5)275.
  -25
   25
  -25
    0
```

Multiply the divisor and the dividend by the same power of 10 to divide with whole numbers.

Place the decimal point in the quotient and divide.

Practice

Divide.

1. $9.6 \div 1.6$　　　　**2.** $48.4 \div 0.4$

3. $13.2 \div 0.006$　　　**4.** $10.8 \div 0.09$

5. $45 \div 4.5$　　　　**6.** $1,008 \div 1.8$

7. $1.26 \div 0.2$　　　　**8.** $2.24 \div 3.2$

9. $35.75 \div 55$　　　　**10.** $120.4 \div 602$

11. $330 \div 5.5$　　　　**12.** $1.08 \div 0.027$

Quick Review

Multiply the numerators to find the numerator of the product. Multiply the denominators to find the denominator of the product.

Example

Find $\frac{2}{3} \times \frac{5}{6}$.

For $\frac{5}{6}$, shade 5 columns.

For $\frac{2}{3}$, shade 2 rows.

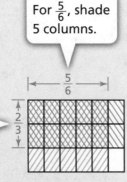

10 of the 18 rectangles are in the overlap area. So, $\frac{2}{3} \times \frac{5}{6} = \frac{10}{18}$ or $\frac{5}{9}$.

Practice

Find each product.

1. $\frac{2}{3} \times \frac{3}{8}$

2. $\frac{1}{4} \times \frac{3}{5}$

3. $\frac{1}{6} \times \frac{1}{8}$

4. $\frac{4}{7} \times \frac{4}{7}$

5. $\frac{6}{7} \times \frac{1}{2}$

6. $\frac{3}{8} \times \frac{8}{3}$

7. $\frac{2}{3} \times \frac{1}{3}$

8. $\frac{7}{8} \times \frac{3}{2}$

9. $2\frac{1}{3} \times 4\frac{1}{5}$

10. $4\frac{1}{2} \times 6\frac{2}{3}$

11. $3\frac{3}{5} \times 2\frac{5}{7}$

12. $14\frac{2}{7} \times 4\frac{3}{10}$

Quick Review

To divide by a fraction, use the reciprocal of the divisor to rewrite the problem as a multiplication problem.

Example

Find $4 \div \frac{4}{5}$.

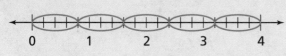

$4 \div \frac{4}{5} = 4 \times \frac{5}{4}$

Use the reciprocal of the divisor.

$\frac{4}{1} \times \frac{5}{4} = \frac{20}{4}$ or 5

Find $\frac{3}{4} \div \frac{1}{8}$.

$\frac{3}{4} \div \frac{1}{8} = \frac{3}{4} \times \frac{8}{1}$

Rewrite the problem as a multiplication problem.

$\frac{3}{4} \times \frac{8}{1} = \frac{24}{4}$ or 6

Practice

Find each quotient.

1. $7 \div \frac{1}{2}$

2. $6 \div \frac{2}{5}$

3. $2 \div \frac{1}{8}$

4. $8 \div \frac{4}{9}$

5. $\frac{1}{2} \div \frac{1}{4}$

6. $\frac{8}{10} \div \frac{1}{5}$

7. $\frac{5}{6} \div \frac{3}{8}$

8. $\frac{1}{3} \div \frac{1}{2}$

9. $5 \div \frac{5}{16}$

10. $\frac{7}{12} \div \frac{3}{4}$

11. $20 \div \frac{5}{6}$

12. $16 \div \frac{1}{4}$

13. $\frac{4}{5} \div \frac{1}{8}$

14. $5 \div \frac{1}{10}$

15. $\frac{7}{11} \div \frac{1}{11}$

16. $4 \div \frac{2}{8}$

Quick Review

To divide by a mixed number, rename each mixed number as a fraction. Then use the reciprocal of the divisor to rewrite the problem as a multiplication problem.

Example

$6\frac{1}{2} \div 1\frac{1}{6} = \frac{13}{2} \div \frac{7}{6}$

> Rename the mixed numbers as fractions.

$\frac{13}{2} \div \frac{7}{6} = \frac{13}{2} \times \frac{6}{7}$

> Write the problem as a multiplication problem using the reciprocal of the divisor.

$\frac{13}{2} \times \frac{6}{7} = \frac{78}{14}$ or $5\frac{4}{7}$

> Multiply. Rename the fraction quotient as a mixed number.

Practice

Find each quotient.

1. $6\frac{3}{8} \div 4\frac{1}{4}$ **2.** $9 \div 2\frac{2}{7}$

3. $3\frac{3}{5} \div 1\frac{1}{5}$ **4.** $5\frac{1}{2} \div 3\frac{3}{8}$

5. $3\frac{2}{5} \div 1\frac{1}{5}$ **6.** $12\frac{1}{6} \div 3$

7. $12 \div 1\frac{1}{2}$ **8.** $3\frac{1}{2} \div 2\frac{1}{4}$

9. $8 \div 1\frac{1}{4}$ **10.** $10\frac{1}{2} \div 1\frac{3}{4}$

11. $3\frac{3}{4} \div 2\frac{1}{2}$ **12.** $60 \div 3\frac{1}{3}$

Quick Review

When solving multistep problems:

- decide the steps to solve the problem.
- choose the correct operations.
- identify the information you need from the problem.
- correctly use the information.
- calculate accurately.
- check if the answer is reasonable.

Example

Jane's garden is 3.4 meters by 6.5 meters. If fencing costs $2.25 per meter, how much will it cost to enclose Jane's garden?

Step 1: Find how much fence is needed.
3.4 + 3.4 + 6.5 + 6.5 = 19.8 meters

Step 2: Multiply to find the cost.
19.8 × 2.25 = $44.55

Step 3: Estimate to check.
3 + 3 + 7 + 7 = 20 meters
20 × 2.00 = $40.00

$40 is close to $44.55, so the answer is reasonable.

Practice

Daisy has one cucumber that is 3 inches long and another cucumber that is 5 inches long. She cuts the cucumbers into $\frac{3}{8}$-inch-thick slices and adds them to a salad. How many $\frac{3}{8}$-inch-thick slices does Daisy have?

1. Write division expressions to represent the first steps in the problem.

2. Solve. Then explain your answer.

Go Online | PearsonRealize.com

Pathfinder

Shade a path from START to FINISH. Follow the solutions in which the digit in the hundredths place is greater than the digit in the tenths place. You can only move up, down, right, or left.

I can...
multiply and divide decimals. 🌐 6.NS.2.3

START
↓

$\begin{array}{r} 22.04 \\ \times\quad 9 \\ \hline \end{array}$	$7.2\overline{)42.12}$	$\begin{array}{r} 53.08 \\ \times\quad 2.4 \\ \hline \end{array}$	$\begin{array}{r} 0.18 \\ \times\quad 1.5 \\ \hline \end{array}$	$7\overline{)0.28}$
$25\overline{)28}$	$\begin{array}{r} 3.71 \\ \times\quad 0.6 \\ \hline \end{array}$	$2.5\overline{)23.35}$	$9\overline{)0.954}$	$\begin{array}{r} 0.9 \\ \times\quad 0.27 \\ \hline \end{array}$
$\begin{array}{r} 12.4 \\ \times\quad 14.6 \\ \hline \end{array}$	$1.3\overline{)2.314}$	$\begin{array}{r} 86.35 \\ \times\qquad 7 \\ \hline \end{array}$	$0.4\overline{)1.06}$	$6\overline{)72.72}$
$1.2\overline{)0.9}$	$\begin{array}{r} 1.05 \\ \times\quad 1.05 \\ \hline \end{array}$	$2.4\overline{)8.7}$	$\begin{array}{r} 7.2 \\ \times\quad 0.06 \\ \hline \end{array}$	$75\overline{)18}$
$\begin{array}{r} 86.3 \\ \times\quad 0.4 \\ \hline \end{array}$	$16\overline{)0.04}$	$8\overline{)4.4}$	$\begin{array}{r} 5.2 \\ \times\quad 3.8 \\ \hline \end{array}$	$\begin{array}{r} 22.3 \\ \times\quad 1.8 \\ \hline \end{array}$

↓
FINISH

TOPIC 2 INTEGERS AND RATIONAL NUMBERS

? Topic Essential Question

What are integers and rational numbers? How are points graphed on a coordinate plane?

Topic Overview

Topic Vocabulary

- absolute value
- coordinate plane
- integers
- opposites
- ordered pair
- origin
- quadrants
- rational number
- *x*- and *y*-axes

Lesson Digital Resources

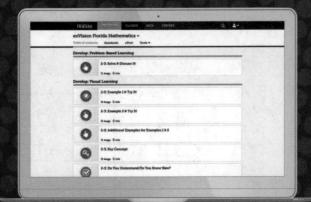

INTERACTIVE STUDENT EDITION
Access online or offline.

VISUAL LEARNING ANIMATION
Interact with visual learning animations.

ACTIVITY Use with *Solve & Discuss It, Expl*
and *Explain It* activities, and to explore Exa

VIDEOS Watch clips to support *3-Act
Mathematical Modeling Lessons* and *STEM*

Go online | **PearsonRealize.com**

The ULTIMATE THROW

▶ The Ultimate Throw

Have you ever played ultimate? It's a team sport played with a flying disc. The goal is to score the most points by passing the disc to your opponent's end zone. Ultimate is played by millions of people across the globe, from casual games to professional leagues.

There are many ways to throw a flying disc. It takes a lot of practice to learn each type of throw. If you want the disc to travel a specific path and distance, you need to try different throws with different amounts of spin and power. Think about this during the 3-Act Mathematical Modeling lesson.

PRACTICE Practice what you've learned.

TUTORIALS Get help from *Virtual Nerd*, right when you need it.

MATH TOOLS Explore math with digital tools.

GAMES Play Math Games to help you learn.

KEY CONCEPT Review important lesson content.

GLOSSARY Read and listen to English/Spanish definitions.

ASSESSMENT Show what you've learned.

Did You Know?

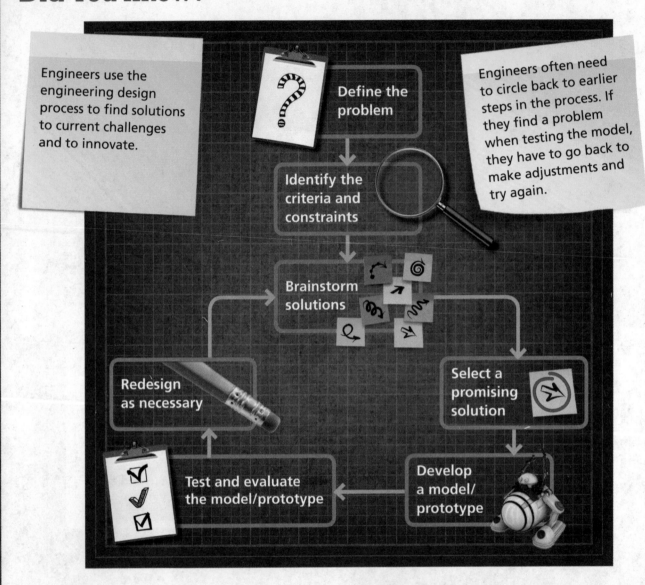

Engineers use the engineering design process to find solutions to current challenges and to innovate.

Define the problem

Identify the criteria and constraints

Brainstorm solutions

Engineers often need to circle back to earlier steps in the process. If they find a problem when testing the model, they have to go back to make adjustments and try again.

Redesign as necessary

Select a promising solution

Test and evaluate the model/prototype

Develop a model/prototype

Your Task:
Improve Your School

Now that you have defined the problem, or improvement needed, you and your classmates will apply the engineering design process to propose solutions.

Review What You Know!

Vocabulary
Choose the best term from the box to complete each definition.

decimal
denominator
fraction
numerator

1. A _____ names part of a whole, part of a set, or a location on a number line.

2. The number above the fraction bar that represents the part

of the whole is the _____ .

3. The number below the fraction bar that represents the total

number of equal parts in one whole is the _____ .

Fractions and Decimals
Write each fraction as a decimal.

4. $\frac{2}{5}$

5. $\frac{3}{4}$

6. $\frac{10}{4}$

7. $\frac{12}{5}$

8. $\frac{3}{5}$

9. $\frac{15}{3}$

Division with Decimals
Divide.

10. $1.25 \div 0.5$

11. $13 \div 0.65$

12. $12.2 \div 0.4$

Ordered Pairs
Write the ordered pair for each point shown on the graph.

13. J

14. K

15. L

16. M

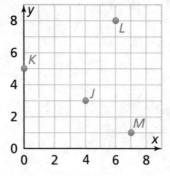

Plot each point on the coordinate plane.

17. $A(6, 2)$

18. $B(1, 3)$

19. $C(5, 7)$

20. $D(3, 4)$

Explain

21. Les said that the quotient of $3.9 \div 0.75$ is 0.52. Explain how you know Les is incorrect without completing the division.

Build Vocabulary

Use the graphic organizer to help you understand new vocabulary terms.

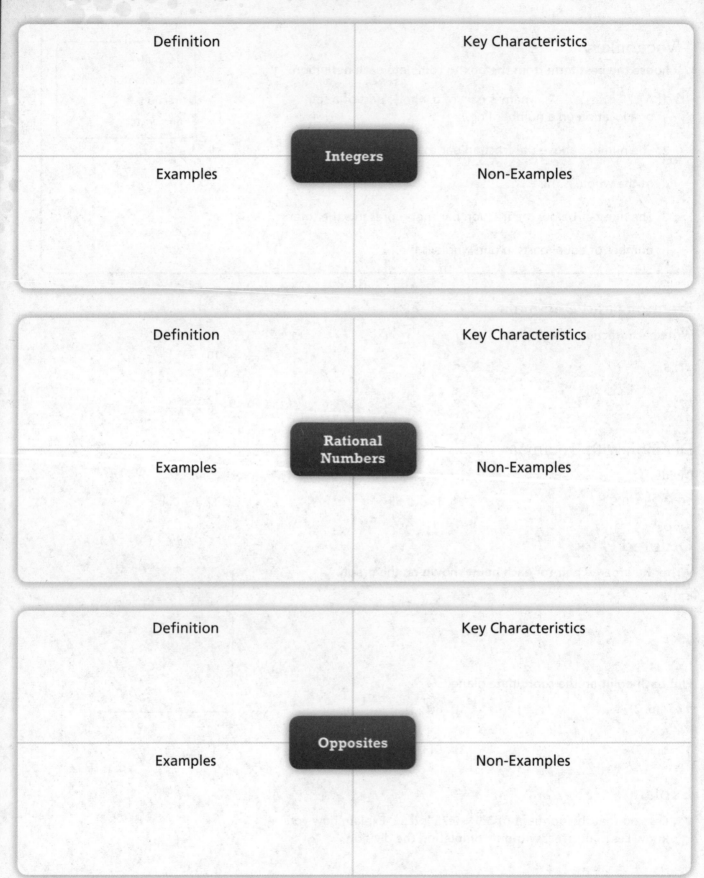

Definition	Key Characteristics
Integers	
Examples	Non-Examples

Definition	Key Characteristics
Rational Numbers	
Examples	Non-Examples

Definition	Key Characteristics
Opposites	
Examples	Non-Examples

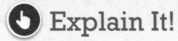

Explain It!  ACTIVITY

Sal recorded the outdoor temperature as −4°F at 7:30 A.M. At noon, it was 22°F. Sal said the temperature changed by 18°F because 22 − 4 = 18.

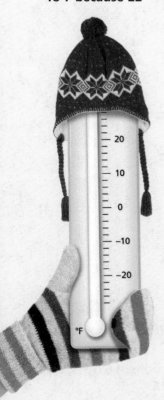

A. Critique Reasoning Is Sal right or wrong? Explain.

B. Construct Arguments What was the total temperature change from 7:30 A.M. until noon? Use the thermometer to help justify your solution.

Focus on math practices

Reasoning 0°C is the temperature at which water freezes. Which is colder, 10°C or −10°C? Explain.

? Essential Question What are integers and how are they used to represent real-world quantities?

EXAMPLE **1** **Define Integers and Opposites**

Scan for
Multimedia

The counting numbers, their opposites, and 0 are integers. Numbers that are located on opposite sides of 0 and are the same distance from 0 on a number line are opposites. What integer is the opposite of 6? What is the opposite of −6?

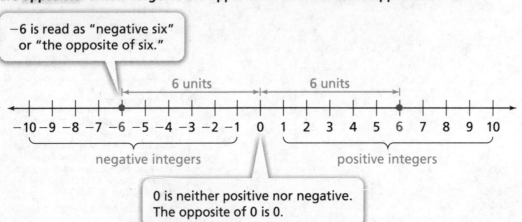

−6 is read as "negative six" or "the opposite of six."

6 units   6 units

negative integers   positive integers

0 is neither positive nor negative. The opposite of 0 is 0.

A thermometer is like a vertical number line that uses integers to show temperatures measured in degrees.

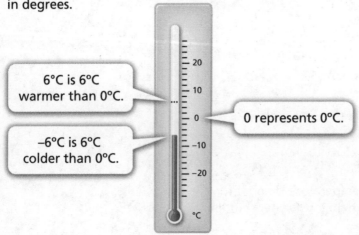

6°C is 6°C warmer than 0°C.

0 represents 0°C.

−6°C is 6°C colder than 0°C.

−6 is the opposite of 6.

The opposite of the opposite of a number is the number itself.

For example, the opposite of 6 is −6, and the opposite of −6 is 6.

Use Structure To represent the opposite of −6, write −(−6).

☑ **Try It!**

Label the integers on the number line.

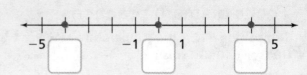

The opposite of 4 is ☐ .   The opposite of −4 is ☐ .

Convince Me! How do you know that two numbers are opposites?

EXAMPLE 2 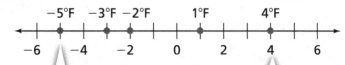 Compare and Order Integers

  ACTIVITY ASSESS

Riley recorded the temperatures for five days in January. Which day was the coldest day of Riley's data? Which was the warmest day? Write the temperatures from least to greatest.

Day	Monday	Tuesday	Wednesday	Thursday	Friday
Temperature (°F)	−5°F	−2°F	4°F	−3°F	1°F

−5°F is the integer farthest to the left on the number line, so Monday was the coldest day.

4°F is the integer farthest to the right on the number line, so Wednesday was the warmest day.

The temperatures from least to greatest are: −5°F, −3°F, −2°F, 1°F, 4°F.

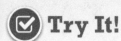 Try It!

Which number is greater, −4 or −2? Explain.

EXAMPLE 3 Use Integers to Represent Quantities

Integers describe many real-world situations including altitude, elevation, depth, temperature, and electrical charges. Zero represents a specific value in each situation. Which integer represents sea level? The airplane? The whale?

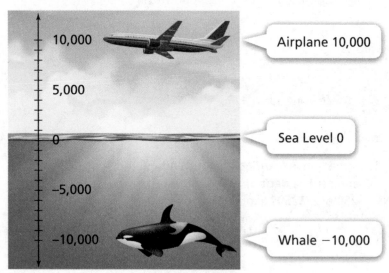

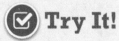 Try It!

Which integer represents each situation?

a. A $10 debt

b. Six degrees below zero

c. Deposit of $25

Integers are all of the counting numbers, their opposites, and 0.
Opposites are integers that are the same distance from 0 and on opposite sides of 0 on a number line.

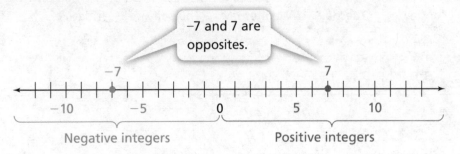

−7 and 7 are opposites.

Negative integers   Positive integers

Do You Understand?

1. 🔑 **Essential Question** What are integers and how are they used to represent real-world quantities?

2. **Reasoning** What do you know about two different integers that are opposites?

3. How do you read −17?

4. **Construct Arguments** Which amount represents a debt of two hundred fifty dollars, $250 or −$250? Explain.

5. **Generalize** When comparing two negative integers, how can you determine which integer is the greater number?

Do You Know How?

In 6–17, write the opposite of each integer.

6. 1   7. −1   8. −11

9. 30   10. 0   11. −16

12. −(−8)   13. 28   14. −(−65)

15. 98   16. 100   17. −33

In 18–20, write the integers in order from least to greatest.

18. 2, −3, 0, −4

19. 4, 12, −12, −11

20. −5, 6, −7, −8

Go Online | PearsonRealize.com

Practice & Problem Solving

Scan for
Multimedia

In 21–24, use the pictures at the right.

21. Generalize Which integer represents sea level? Explain.

Ruppell's Griffons
fly up to 37,000
feet above sea level.

22. Use a negative integer to
represent the depth to which
a dolphin may swim.

A migrating bird
flies up to 5,000 feet
above sea level.

23. Which of these animals can travel
at the greatest distance from sea level?

24. Order the elevations of the animals
as integers from least to greatest.

A dolphin can swim
to 150 feet below
sea level.

A sperm whale can
swim to 3,000 feet
below sea level.

In 25–30, plot each point on the number line below.

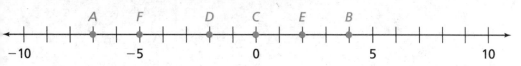

25. $G(-10)$ **26.** $H(8)$ **27.** $I(-1)$

28. $J(9)$ **29.** $K(6)$ **30.** $L(-3)$

**In 31–36, write the integer value that each point represents.
Then use the number line to help write its opposite.**

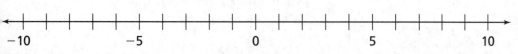

31. A **32.** B **33.** C

34. D **35.** E **36.** F

37. Write the opposite of each integer.

A. 5

B. −13

C. −(−22)

D. −31

E. −50

F. −(−66)

38. Compare the integers and write the integer with the greater value.

A. −5, 1

B. −6, −7

C. −9, 8

D. −12, −(−10)

E. −(−9), 11

F. −(−4), 3

39. The display at the right shows the daily low temperatures for several consecutive days in a New England city. Write the temperatures in order from least to greatest. On which day was it the coldest?

MON	TUE	WED	THU
4°	−5°	−7°	7°

40. In a bank account, a paid-out expense is called a *debit*, and a deposit is called a *credit*. Would you use positive or negative integers to represent credits? Debits? Explain.

41. Higher Order Thinking Atoms have negatively charged particles called *electrons* and positively charged particles called *protons*. If an atom loses an electron, it has a positive electric charge. If it gains an electron, it has a negative electric charge. Which integer would represent the electric charge of an atom that has an equal number of electrons and protons?

Assessment Practice

42. Marco goes on a recreational scuba diving expedition. What is a possible diving depth for his expedition? 🔵 6.NS.3.5

Ⓐ 0 meters

Ⓑ 40 meters

Ⓒ 400 meters

Ⓓ −40 meters

43. Fill in the bubbles to match each integer with its opposite. 🔵 6.NS.3.6a

	8	−19	−24	−(−24)
−24	Ⓐ	Ⓑ	Ⓒ	Ⓓ
19	Ⓔ	Ⓕ	Ⓖ	Ⓗ
24	Ⓘ	Ⓙ	Ⓚ	Ⓛ
−8	Ⓜ	Ⓝ	Ⓞ	Ⓟ

Explore It!

 ACTIVITY

The locations of four animals relative to sea level are shown.

Seagull $\frac{3}{4}$ yard

Dolphin $-\frac{1}{4}$ yard

Shark −0.5 yard

Sea Turtle −1 yard

Lesson 2-2
Represent Rational Numbers on the Number Line

Go Online | PearsonRealize.com

I can...
represent rational numbers using a number line.

MAFS.6.NS.3.6c Understand a rational number as a point on the number line. ... Find and position integers and other rational numbers on a horizontal or vertical number line diagram; ...
Also 6.NS.3.7a, 6.NS.3.7b

MAFS.K12.MP.2.1, MP.3.1, MP.7.1, MP.8.1

A. What can you say about the animals and their positions relative to sea level?

B. How can you use a number line to represent the locations of the animals?

Focus on math practices

Generalize How is representing the locations of negative fractions and decimals like representing the locations of positive fractions and decimals? How is it different?

71

Essential Question How can you plot, compare, and order rational numbers using a number line?

VISUAL LEARNING

EXAMPLE 1 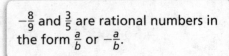 **Understand Rational Numbers**

Scan for
Multimedia

Any number that can be written as the quotient of two integers is called a **rational number**. A rational number can be written in the form $\frac{a}{b}$ or $-\frac{a}{b}$, where a and b are integers and $b \neq 0$. A rational number can be a whole number, fraction, or decimal.

How can you find and position $-\frac{4}{3}$ and -1.5 on a number line?

Generalize You can plot numbers on horizontal or vertical number lines.

$-\frac{8}{9}$ and $\frac{3}{5}$ are rational numbers in the form $\frac{a}{b}$ or $-\frac{a}{b}$.

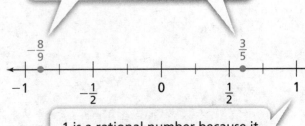

1 is a rational number because it can be written as $\frac{1}{1}$.

ONE WAY Use a horizontal number line to plot $-\frac{4}{3}$.

You can write $-\frac{4}{3}$ as a mixed number.

$$-\frac{4}{3} = -1\frac{1}{3}$$

Divide the units on the number line into thirds and find one and one-third to the left of 0.

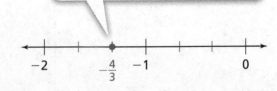

ANOTHER WAY Use a vertical number line to plot -1.5.

You can write -1.5 as a mixed number.

$$-1.5 = -1\frac{5}{10} \text{ or } -1\frac{1}{2}$$

Divide the units on the number line into halves and find one and one-half below 0.

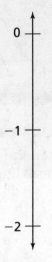

☑ **Try It!**

How can you find and position $-\frac{5}{4}$ and -1.75 on the number lines? Write $-\frac{5}{4}$ and -1.75 as mixed numbers, then plot the points on the number lines.

$-\frac{5}{4} = $ ☐ $-1.75 = $ ☐

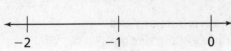

Convince Me! Why is it helpful to rename $-\frac{5}{4}$ and -1.75 as mixed numbers when plotting these points on number lines?

EXAMPLE **2**  Compare and Order
Rational Numbers

ACTIVITY   ASSESS

Haru was asked to compare and order three rational numbers. Show how he can use <, >, or = to compare $\frac{2}{3}$, 1.75, and −0.75. Then order these numbers from least to greatest.

Look for Relationships
Remember, $\frac{a}{b} = a \div b$, so $\frac{2}{3}$ means $2 \div 3 = 0.66...$ You can use this decimal form of $\frac{2}{3}$ to plot this number on a number line.

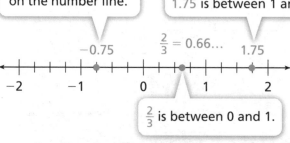

−0.75 is a negative number, so it will be farthest to the left on the number line.

1.75 is between 1 and 2.

$\frac{2}{3} = 0.66...$

$\frac{2}{3}$ is between 0 and 1.

So, $-0.75 < \frac{2}{3} < 1.75$, and their order from least to greatest is -0.75, $\frac{2}{3}$, 1.75.

 Try It!

If $\frac{1}{4}$ is ordered within the list of numbers in the example above, between which two numbers would it be placed?

EXAMPLE **3** Interpret Rational Numbers in Real-World Contexts

Sam and Rashida are scuba diving. Their locations are shown relative to sea level.

Use <, >, or = to compare the two depths and explain their relationship.

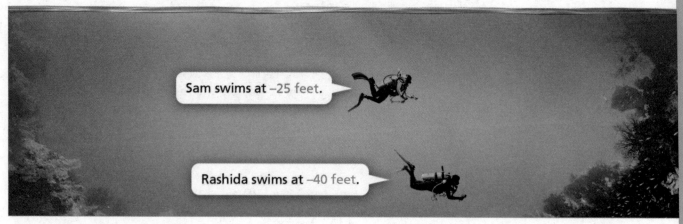

Sam swims at −25 feet.

Rashida swims at −40 feet.

−40 < −25. Rashida is at a greater depth than Sam.

 Try It!

At 10:00 P.M. one winter night, the temperature was −3°C. At midnight, the temperature was −7°C. Use <, >, or = to compare the two temperatures and explain their relationship.

A **rational number** can be expressed as a fraction in the form $\frac{a}{b}$ or $-\frac{a}{b}$, where a and b are integers and b is not 0.

> The number farthest to the left is the least number.

> The number farthest to the right is the greatest number.

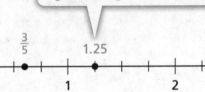

The numbers, in order from least to greatest, are: -1.75, $\frac{3}{5}$, 1.25.

Do You Understand?

1. 🔑 **Essential Question** How can you plot, compare, and order rational numbers using a number line?

2. **Generalize** Why are whole numbers rational numbers? Use 15 as an example.

3. **Vocabulary** Why are integers rational numbers? Give an example.

4. **Reasoning** Explain how the inequality $-4°C > -9°C$ describes how the temperatures are related.

Do You Know How?

In 5–7, write the number positioned at each point.

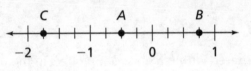

5. A 6. B 7. C

In 8–11, plot the points on the number line below.

8. P at $-1\frac{1}{4}$ 9. Q at 0.25

10. R at -0.75 11. S at $-\frac{1}{4}$

In 12–14, use the number line to help order the numbers from least to greatest.

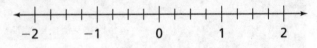

12. 1.25, $-\frac{3}{2}$, -1.25, $1\frac{1}{2}$

13. -0.5, $\frac{1}{2}$, -0.75, $\frac{3}{4}$

14. -1.5, -0.75, -1, 2

Name: _____

In 15–20, write the number positioned at each point.

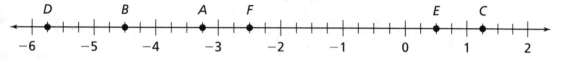

15. A   **16.** B   **17.** C

18. D   **19.** E   **20.** F

- -

21. Plot the numbers on the number line below.

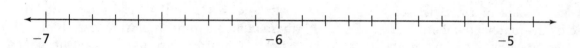

A. $-5\frac{1}{2}$ **B.** -6.3 **C.** -5.8

D. $-6\frac{7}{10}$ **E.** -4.9 **F.** $-6\frac{9}{10}$

- -

22. Use <, >, or = to compare.

A. $\frac{1}{10}$ ◯ 0.09 **B.** -1.44 ◯ $-1\frac{1}{4}$ **C.** $-\frac{2}{3}$ ◯ -0.8

D. 0.5 ◯ $\frac{2}{4}$ **E.** $-2\frac{3}{4}$ ◯ -2.25 **F.** $-\frac{3}{5}$ ◯ -0.35

- -

23. Order the numbers from least to greatest.

A. $-6, 8, -9, 13$ **B.** $-\frac{4}{5}, -\frac{1}{2}, 0.25, -0.2$ **C.** $4.75, -2\frac{1}{2}, -\frac{8}{3}, \frac{9}{2}$

D. $4, -3, -8, -1$ **E.** $-\frac{1}{4}, 0.5, \frac{3}{4}, -\frac{1}{2}$ **F.** $-\frac{4}{5}, -\frac{5}{4}, -\frac{3}{2}, 1.5$

- -

24. Make Sense and Persevere What is the least number of points you must plot to have examples of all four sets of numbers, including at least one positive integer and one negative integer? Explain.

Rational Numbers
numbers that can be expressed as a quotient of two integers $\frac{a}{b}$ ($b \neq 0$)

Integers
whole numbers and their opposites

Whole Numbers
zero and natural numbers

Natural Numbers
the set of counting numbers
1, 2, 3, 4, 5, ...

25. Reasoning Suppose you plot the locations of the animals on a number line. Which animal would be represented by the point farthest from 0 on the number line? Explain.

Animal	Possible Locations Relative to Ocean's Surface
Bloodbelly comb jelly	−0.8 km
Deep sea anglerfish	$-\frac{2}{3}$ km
Fanfin anglerfish	$-2\frac{1}{4}$ km
Gulper eel	−1.1 km
Pacific blackdragon	$-\frac{3}{10}$ km
Slender snipe eel	−0.6 km

26. Which animal is closest to a depth of −0.7 km?

27. The change in the value of a stock is represented by the rational number −5.90. Describe, in words, what this means.

28. Construct Arguments A classmate ordered these numbers from greatest to least. Is he correct? Construct an argument to justify your answer.

$$4.4,\ 4.2,\ -4.42,\ -4.24$$

29. Make Sense and Persevere Order −3.25, $-3\frac{1}{8}$, $-3\frac{3}{4}$, and −3.1 from least to greatest. Explain.

30. Higher Order Thinking Suppose $\frac{a}{b}$, $\frac{c}{d}$, and $\frac{e}{f}$ represent three rational numbers. If $\frac{a}{b}$ is less than $\frac{c}{d}$, and $\frac{c}{d}$ is less than $\frac{e}{f}$, compare $\frac{a}{b}$ and $\frac{e}{f}$. Explain.

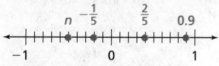

Assessment Practice

31. Which could be a value for n? 🔵 6.NS.3.6c

Ⓐ $-\frac{1}{2}$

Ⓑ $-\frac{1}{3}$

Ⓒ $-\frac{1}{4}$

Ⓓ $-\frac{1}{6}$

32. Which inequality does NOT represent the correct position of two numbers on a number line? 🔵 6.NS.3.7a

Ⓐ $4\frac{1}{2} > \frac{25}{4}$

Ⓑ $-4\frac{1}{2} > -\frac{25}{4}$

Ⓒ $-6 < -5$

Ⓓ $-\frac{1}{2} < \frac{1}{2}$

Solve & Discuss It!

🖥️ ⬤ ACTIVITY

A portion of a bank account statement is shown below. How would you interpret the value of the ending balance? Explain.

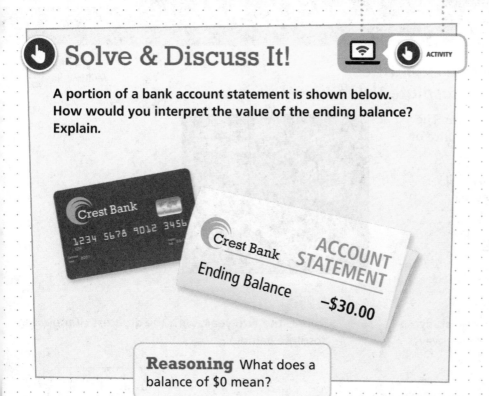

Crest Bank
1234 5678 9012 3456

Crest Bank   ACCOUNT STATEMENT
Ending Balance   –$30.00

Reasoning What does a balance of $0 mean?

I can...
find and interpret absolute value.

MAFS.6.NS.3.7c Understand the absolute value of a rational number as its distance from 0 on the number line; interpret absolute value as magnitude for a positive or negative quantity in a real-world situation. Also 6.NS.3.7d

MAFS.K12.MP.2.1, MP.3.1, MP.7.1

Focus on math practices

Reasoning What is an example of a bank account balance that represents an amount owed greater than $40?

? Essential Question How are absolute values used to describe quantities?

EXAMPLE 1 **Describe Quantities Using Absolute Value**

Scan for Multimedia

Stock prices rise and fall during the year. The table shows the overall change in the price of a company's stock from year to year.

During which two years was the overall change in the stock price the greatest?

Year	Change in Price ($)
2015	11
2014	19
2013	-34
2012	6

The **absolute value** of a number is its distance from 0 on the number line. Distance is always positive.

The absolute value of −5 is written as |−5|.

The absolute value of 5 is written |5|.

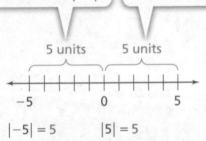

5 units   5 units

|−5| = 5 |5| = 5

Look for Relationships Opposite numbers have the same absolute values because they are the same distance from zero.

To find the two years with the greatest change, use absolute values.

−34   0 6 11 19

The absolute values of the changes in the company's stock price each year are shown below.

2015: |11| = 11
2014: |19| = 19 ·········· 2nd greatest change
2013: |−34| = 34 ·········· greatest change
2012: |6| = 6

So, the two years in which the change in stock price was the greatest were 2013 and 2014.

☑ Try It!

The students in a science class recorded the change in the water level of a local river. During which week did the water level change by the greatest amount?

Use absolute values to represent the change in the water level.

The water level changed by the greatest amount in Week ☐.

Convince Me! Can a lesser number represent a greater change in water level than a greater number? Explain.

Week	1	2	3
Change in Water Level (in.)	$-7\frac{1}{2}$	2.2	−4.38

Week 1: $\left|-7\frac{1}{2}\right|$ = ☐ in.

Week 2: |2.2| = ☐ in.

Week 3: |−4.38| = ☐ in.

EXAMPLE **2** **Find Absolute Value**

  ACTIVITY ASSESS

Find each absolute value.

A. |−4| B. |0| C. |3|

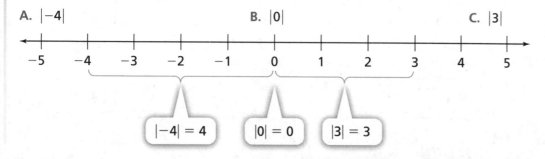

|−4| = 4 |0| = 0 |3| = 3

EXAMPLE **3** **Interpret Absolute Value**

Negative numbers sometimes represent debts. Yasmin is a business owner. The table shows three account balances that represent her gallery's debts.

A. Which account has the least balance?

B. Which account has the greatest debt?

Yasmin's Gallery

	E	F
	Account	**Balance**
	A	−$35.42
	B	−$50.99
	C	−$12.75

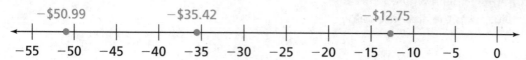

−$50.99   −$35.42   −$12.75

Because −50.99 is farther to the left on the number line than either −35.42 or −12.75, −50.99 is the least number, or the least balance.

The absolute value of each balance describes the size of each debt, or amount of money owed.

Account A	**Account B**	**Account C**
|−35.42| = 35.42	|−50.99| = 50.99	|−12.75| = 12.75

$50.99 is the greatest amount of money owed. Account B has the greatest debt.

☑ Try It!

A bank has two customers with overdrawn accounts. Which balance is the greater number? Which balance is the lesser amount owed?

Account	Balance
V. Wong	−$19.45

Account	Balance
J. Olson	−$23.76

The **absolute value** of a number is its distance from 0 on a number line. Distance is always positive. The absolute value of any number, n, is written $|n|$.

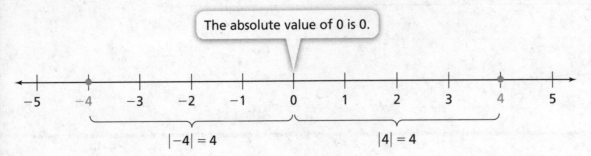

The absolute value of 0 is 0.

$|-4| = 4$ $|4| = 4$

−4 and 4 are opposites as they are the same distance from 0.

Do You Understand?

1. **Essential Question** How are absolute values used to describe quantities?

2. **Construct Arguments** Explain why −7 has a greater absolute value than the absolute value of 6.

3. **Reasoning** Give an example of a balance that has a greater integer value than a balance of −$12, but represents a debt of less than $5.

4. Of the three elevations, −2 feet, −12 feet, and 30 feet, which represents the least number? Which represents the farthest distance from sea level?

Do You Know How?

In 5–14, find each absolute value.

5. $|-9|$

6. $\left|5\frac{3}{4}\right|$

7. $|-5.5|$

8. $|82.5|$

9. $\left|-14\frac{1}{3}\right|$

10. $|-7.75|$

11. $|-19|$

12. $\left|-2\frac{1}{2}\right|$

13. $|24|$

14. $|35.4|$

In 15–17, use the absolute value of each account balance to determine which account has the greater overdrawn amount.

15. Account A: −$5.42
    Account B: −$35.76

16. Account A: −$6.47
    Account B: −$2.56

17. Account A: −$32.56
    Account B: −$29.12

Name: _____

Practice & Problem Solving

In 18–33, find each absolute value.

18. $|-46|$

19. $|0.7|$

20. $\left|-\frac{2}{3}\right|$

21. $|-7.35|$

22. $\left|-4\frac{3}{4}\right|$

23. $|-54.5|$

24. $\left|27\frac{1}{4}\right|$

25. $|-13.35|$

26. $|14|$

27. $|-11.5|$

28. $|-6.3|$

29. $|3.75|$

30. $|-8.5|$

31. $|15|$

32. $\left|-6\frac{3}{4}\right|$

33. $|-5.3|$

In 34–37, order the numbers from least to greatest.

34. $|-12|, \left|11\frac{3}{4}\right|, |-20.5|, |2|$

35. $|10|, |-3|, |0|, |-5.25|$

36. $|-6|, |-4|, |11|, |0|$

37. $|4|, |-3|, |-18|, |-3.18|$

Alberto and Rebecca toss horseshoes at a stake. Whoever's horseshoe is closer to the stake wins a point.

38. Reasoning What integer best describes the location of Alberto's horseshoe in relation to the stake? What integer best describes the location of Rebecca's horseshoe?

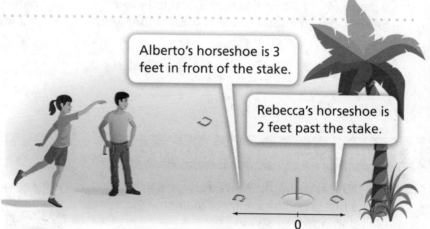

Alberto's horseshoe is 3 feet in front of the stake.

Rebecca's horseshoe is 2 feet past the stake.

39. Critique Reasoning Alberto says that −3 is less than 2, so he wins a point. Is Alberto correct? Explain.

40. Model with Math Find the distance from Alberto's horseshoe to Rebecca's horseshoe. Explain.

41. Higher Order Thinking Let a = any rational number. Is the absolute value of a different if a is a positive number or a negative number? Explain.

42. Construct Arguments Samuel and Leticia are playing a game. After the first round of the game, Samuel's score was −19, and Leticia's score was 21. The score with the greater absolute value wins each round. Who won the first round? Explain.

43. Use Structure Ana and Chuyen are exploring underwater sea life while on a helmet diving adventure. Ana's location is −30 feet below sea level, and Chuyen's location is −12 feet below sea level. Which girl is located farther from sea level?

44. Marie's account balance is −$45.62. Tom's account balance is −$42.55. Which balance represents the greater number? Which balance represents the lesser amount owed?

45. In New York, the Federal Reserve gold vault is located at a depth of $|-80|$ feet below ground. The treasure at Oak Island is believed to be at a depth of $|-134|$ feet. Which is farther below ground, the gold vault or the Oak Island treasure?

46. Two scuba divers are swimming below sea level. The locations of the divers can be represented by −30 feet and −42 feet. Which measure represents the location that is closest to sea level?

Assessment Practice

47. The table at the right shows the scores at the end of the first round of a golf tournament. The scores are relative to par. 🕐 6.NS.3.7c

Golfer	Kate	Sam	Lisa	Carlos
Score	−6	5	2	−3

PART A

Par is represented as 0. Using absolute value, show the distance each score is from par.

PART B

The golfer with the least score wins the round. Who won the first round of the tournament? Explain.

1. Vocabulary Describe the relative locations of the rational numbers $-\left(-\frac{a}{b}\right)$ and $\frac{a}{b}$ on a number line. *Lessons 2-1 and 2-2* 🌐 6.NS.3.5, 6.NS.3.6a

2. Marc deposited $175 in a new bank account. After buying some furniture, he was overdrawn by $55. Select all the true statements about Marc's account. *Lesson 2-1* 🌐 6.NS.3.5

☐ To start, Marc had a negative balance.

☐ In this situation, 0 represents an empty bank account.

☐ When Marc was overdrawn, he had a negative balance.

☐ After buying furniture, Marc had a positive balance.

☐ The lowest balance in the account was $-\$55$.

3. What number is represented on the number line? Give your answer as a decimal and as a fraction. *Lesson 2-2* 🌐 6.NS.3.6c

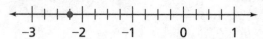

4. The absolute value of a number is 52. Select all the integers that this number could be. *Lesson 2-3* 🌐 6.NS.3.7c

☐ -52 ☐ -25 ☐ 25 ☐ $-\frac{1}{52}$ ☐ 52

5. The table shows the location of four treasure chests relative to sea level. How can you use the number line to find the treasure chest that is farthest from sea level? *Lesson 2-2* 🌐 6.NS.3.6c, 6.NS.3.7d

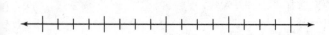

Treasure Chest	Location Relative to Sea Level
A	0.75 foot
B	$-\frac{5}{4}$ feet
C	-0.5 foot
D	1 foot

6. Three customers have accounts owing money. The table shows the account balances that represent what the customers owe. Which customer owes the least amount of money? *Lesson 2-3* 🌐 6.NS.3.7c, 6.NS.3.7d

Customer	Balance
M. Milo	$-\$85.50$
B. Barker	$-\$42.75$
S. Stampas	$-\$43.25$

How well did you do on the mid-topic checkpoint? Fill in the stars.

MID-TOPIC PERFORMANCE TASK

Warren and Natasha started a dog-walking business. During their first week, they paid $10 to make their business cards and $6 for a 4.5-pound box of doggie treats. Warren walked a dog for 15 minutes, and Natasha walked a dog for 30 minutes.

PART A

Which integers represent the dollar amounts either spent or earned during the first week Warren and Natasha were in business? Select all that apply.
🔊 6.NS.3.5

☐ $5   ☐ −$5   ☐ $10   ☐ −$10   ☐ −$6

Number of Minutes	Cost for One Dog
15	$5
30	$10
60	$20

PART B

At the end of each week, Warren records the weight in pounds of doggie treats eaten as a negative rational number. Plot the numbers of pounds eaten each week on the number line. Order the numbers from most pounds eaten to fewest pounds eaten. 🔊 6.NS.3.6c, 6.NS.3.7

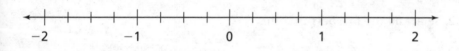

Week	Pound(s) Eaten
1	$-\frac{3}{2}$
2	$-\frac{2}{3}$
3	-0.5
4	$-\frac{5}{4}$

PART C

Find the absolute value for the number of pounds of doggie treats eaten each week. Which two weeks had the greatest number of pounds eaten? 🔊 6.NS.3.7c, 6.NS.3.7d

Solve & Discuss It!  ACTIVITY

Point *B* has the same *x*-coordinate as point *A*, but its *y*-coordinate is the opposite of the *y*-coordinate of point *A*. Plot point *B* and write its coordinates.

Make Sense and Persevere
How can you use what you know about integers and graphing points on a coordinate plane to plot point *B*?

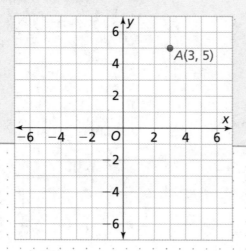

I can...
graph points with rational coordinates on a coordinate plane.

MAFS.6.NS.3.6b ... Understand signs of numbers in ordered pairs as indicating locations in quadrants of the coordinate plane; recognize that when two ordered pairs differ only by signs, the locations of the points are related by reflections across one or both axes. Also 6.NS.3.6c

MAFS.K12.MP.1.1, MP.4.1, MP.6.1, MP.7.1, MP.8.1

Focus on math practices
Generalize Two points have the same *x*-coordinate but opposite *y*-coordinates. Across which axis do they form mirror images of each other?

EXAMPLE 1 **Graph Points with Integer Coordinates**

A coordinate plane is a grid containing two number lines that intersect in a right angle at 0. The number lines, called the *x*-axis and *y*-axis, divide the plane into four quadrants. How can you graph and label points on a coordinate plane?

> **Use Structure** How can you extend what you know about grids to the coordinate plane?

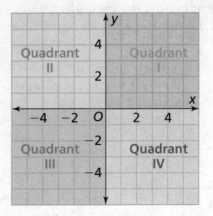

An **ordered pair** (*x*, *y*) of numbers gives the coordinates that locate a point relative to each axis. Graph the points *Q*(2, −3), *R*(−1, 1), and *S*(0, 2) on a coordinate plane.

To graph any point with coordinates (*x*, *y*):

- Start at the **origin**, (0, 0).

- Use the *x*-coordinate of the point to move right (if positive) or left (if negative) along the *x*-axis.

- Then use the *y*-coordinate of the point to move up (if positive) or down (if negative) following the *y*-axis.

- Draw a point on the coordinate plane and label the point.

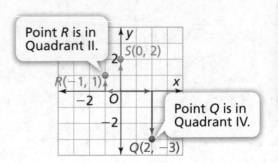

☑ **Try It!**

Graph point *P*(−2, −3) on the coordinate plane shown.

Start at the origin (☐ , ☐).

The *x*-coordinate is negative, so move ☐ units to the left.

Then use the *y*-coordinate to move ☐ units down.

Draw and label the point.

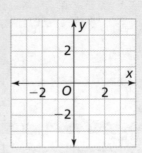

Convince Me! How do the signs of the coordinates relate to the quadrant in which a point is located? Explain for each of the four quadrants.

EXAMPLE **2**

 Locate and Identify Points with Rational Coordinates

A grid map of Washington, D.C., is shown at the right. What are the coordinates of the location of the Jefferson Memorial?

Find the Jefferson Memorial on the map.

- Follow the grid lines directly to the x-axis to find the x-coordinate, 0.5.

- Follow the grid lines directly to the y-axis to find the y-coordinate, −1.75.

The coordinates of the location of the Jefferson Memorial are (0.5, −1.75).

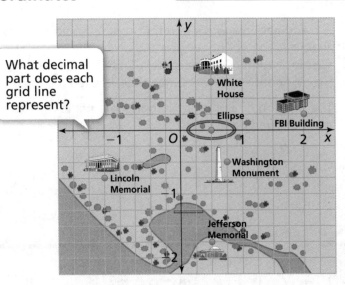

What decimal part does each grid line represent?

> **Model with Math** You can use decimals or fractions to represent rational number coordinates. Because $0.5 = \frac{1}{2}$ and $-1.75 = -1\frac{3}{4}$, the coordinates can also be written as $\left(\frac{1}{2}, -1\frac{3}{4}\right)$.

 Try It!

What landmark is located on the map at $\left(2, \frac{1}{4}\right)$?

EXAMPLE **3** **Reflect Points Across the Axes**

How are points N(−3, 2), P(3, −2), and Q(−3, −2) related to point M(3, 2)?

Point N(−3, 2) and point M(3, 2) differ only in the sign of the x-coordinate. They are reflections of each other across the y-axis.

Point P(3, −2) and point M(3, 2) differ only in the sign of the y-coordinate. They are reflections of each other across the x-axis.

Point Q(−3, −2) and point M(3, 2) differ in the signs of the x-coordinate and y-coordinate. They are reflections of each other across *both* axes.

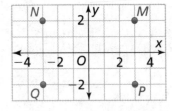

> **Be Precise** A *reflection* is a mirror image across a line.

 Try It!

The coordinates of point A are (−3, 5). What are the coordinates of point B, which is a reflection of point A across the x-axis?

A **coordinate plane** is a grid that contains number lines that intersect at right angles and divide the plane into four **quadrants**. The horizontal number line is called the **x-axis,** and the vertical number line is called the **y-axis.**

The location of a point on a coordinate plane is written as an **ordered pair** (x, y).

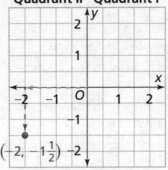

Quadrant II   Quadrant I

$\left(-2, -1\frac{1}{2}\right)$

Quadrant III   Quadrant IV

Do You Understand?

1. **Essential Question** How can you graph a point with rational coordinates on a coordinate plane?

2. What is the y-coordinate of any point that lies on the x-axis?

3. **Look for Relationships** How are the points (4, 5) and (−4, 5) related?

4. **Construct Arguments** On a larger map, the coordinates for the location of another Washington, D.C. landmark are (8, −10). In which quadrant of the map is this landmark located? Explain.

Do You Know How?

In **5–7,** graph and label each point on the coordinate plane.

5. A(−4, 1)

6. B(4, 3)

7. C(0, −2)

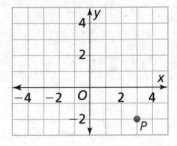

8. What ordered pair gives the coordinates of point P above?

In **9** and **10,** use the map in Example 2 and write the ordered pair of each location.

9. White House

10. Lincoln Memorial

In **11** and **12,** use the map in Example 2 and write the landmark located at each ordered pair.

11. (0.5, 0)

12. $\left(\frac{3}{4}, -\frac{1}{2}\right)$

Practice & Problem Solving

Scan for
Multimedia

In 13–20, graph and label each point.

13. $A(1, -1)$

14. $B(4, 3)$

15. $C(-4, 3)$

16. $D(5, -2)$

17. $E(-2.5, 1.5)$

18. $F(2, 1.5)$

19. $G\left(-2, -1\frac{1}{2}\right)$

20. $H\left(1\frac{1}{2}, -1\right)$

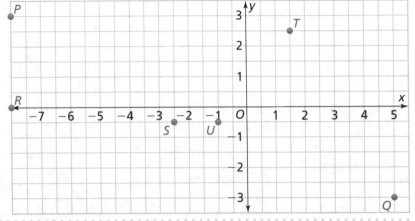

In 21–26, write the ordered pair for each point.

21. P

22. Q

23. R

24. S

25. T

26. U

In 27–30, use the map at the right.

27. Which building is located in Quadrant III?

28. Which two places have the same x-coordinate?

29. **Use Structure** The city council wants the location of the entrance to a new city park to be determined by the reflection of the school entrance across the y-axis. What are the coordinates of the entrance to the new city park on this map?

30. **Higher Order Thinking** You are at the market square (0, 0) and want to get to the doctor's office. Following the grid lines, what is the shortest route?

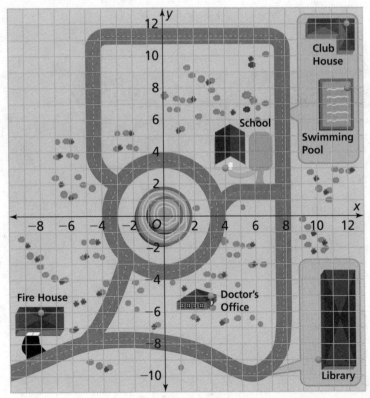

In 31–36, use the coordinate plane at the right.

31. What is located at $(-0.7, -0.2)$?

32. What is located at $\left(\frac{3}{10}, -\frac{1}{5}\right)$?

33. Be Precise Write the ordered pair to locate the end of hiking trail in two different ways.

34. What are the coordinates of the information center? Explain.

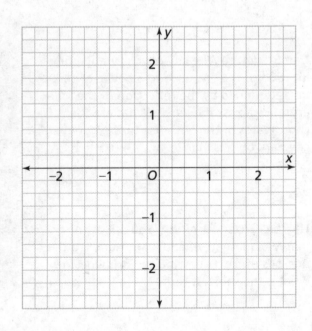

35. What are the coordinates of the point that is a reflection across the *x*-axis of the pond?

36. Use Structure Which picnic areas are located at points that are reflections of each other across one of the axes of the coordinate plane?

37. Graph and label each point on the coordinate plane at the right. 6.NS.3.6b

$A\left(\frac{3}{4}, -1\frac{1}{2}\right)$

$B(-2.75, -2.25)$

$C\left(0, 2\frac{1}{4}\right)$

$D(-1.75, 2)$

3-Act Mathematical Modeling:
The Ultimate Throw

 Go Online | PearsonRealize.com

MAFS.K12.MP.4.1 Model with mathematics.
Also MP.1.1, MP.2.1, MP.3.1, MP.5.1, MP.7.1, MP.8.1

MAFS.6.NS.3.7d Understand ordering and absolute value of rational numbers. Distinguish comparisons of absolute value from statements about order. ...
Also 6.NS.3.5

ACT 1

1. After watching the video, what is the first question that comes to mind?

2. Write the Main Question you will answer.

3. Make a prediction to answer this Main Question.

The person who threw the flying disc farther is [   ].

4. Construct Arguments Explain how you arrived at your prediction.

5. What information in this situation would be helpful to know? How would you use that information?

6. Use Appropriate Tools What tools can you use to get the information you need? Record the information as you find it.

7. Model with Math Represent the situation using the mathematical content, concepts, and skills from this topic. Use your representation to answer the Main Question.

8. What is your answer to the Main Question? Does it differ from your prediction? Explain.

Go Online | PearsonRealize.com

9. Write the answer you saw in the video.

10. **Reasoning** Does your answer match the answer in the video? If not, what are some reasons that would explain the difference?

11. **Make Sense and Persevere** Would you change your model now that you know the answer? Explain.

Reflect

12. Model with Math Explain how you used a mathematical model to represent the situation. How did the model help you answer the Main Question?

13. Make Sense and Persevere When did you struggle most while solving the problem? How did you overcome that obstacle?

SEQUEL

14. Reasoning Suppose each person walks to the other person's disc. They throw each other's discs toward the starting point. Where do you think each disc will land?

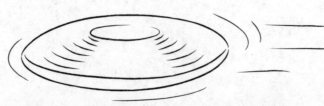

Go Online | **PearsonRealize.com**

Solve & Discuss It!  ACTIVITY

Graph the points on the coordinate plane below. What picture do you make when you connect the points in order?

(3, 3), (0, 0), (−4, −4), (−9, 0), (−4, 4), (0, 0), (3, −3), (3, 3)

Name a pair of points that are the same distance from the x-axis. Explain your choice.

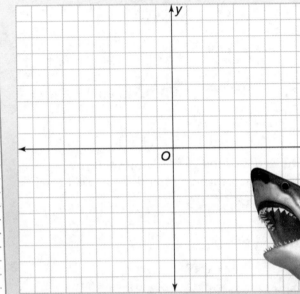

Use Structure How can you use the structure of the grid to find a pair of points that are the same distance from the x-axis?

I can...
use absolute value to find distance on a coordinate plane.

MAFS.6.NS.3.8 Solve real-world and mathematical problems by graphing points in all four quadrants of the coordinate plane. Include use of coordinates and absolute value to find distances between points with the same first coordinate or the same second coordinate.

MAFS.K12.MP.2.1, MP.7.1

Focus on math practices

Use Structure How can you use the coordinate plane to find the total length of the picture you graphed?

? **Essential Question** How can you find the distance between two points on a coordinate plane?

EXAMPLE 1 **Find Vertical Distance**

Scan for Multimedia

Tammy drew a map of her neighborhood. How far is it from Li's house to school?

> **Reasoning** How can you use absolute values to find the distances?

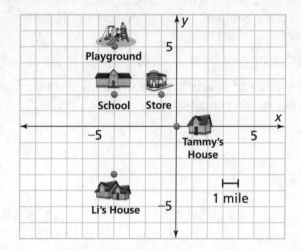

Find the coordinates of Li's house and the school.

- The coordinates for Li's house are (−4, −3).

- The coordinates for the school are (−4, 2).

The absolute values of the y-coordinates tell you the distance between each point and the x-axis.

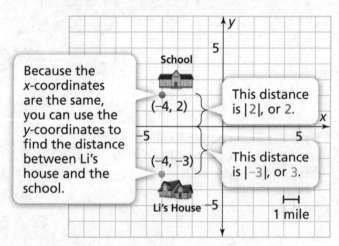

Because the x-coordinates are the same, you can use the y-coordinates to find the distance between Li's house and the school.

School
(−4, 2)

This distance is $|2|$, or 2.

(−4, −3)

This distance is $|-3|$, or 3.

Li's House

1 mile

The distance from Li's house to school is
$|2| + |-3| = 2 + 3 = 5$ miles.

☑ Try It!

What is the distance from the school to the playground? Explain how you used absolute values to find the distance.

Convince Me! To find the distance from the school to the playground, do you add or subtract the absolute values of the y-coordinates? Explain.

EXAMPLE **2** **Find Horizontal Distance**   ACTIVITY ASSESS

The Coulter family starts at their home and stops at a rest stop to eat lunch. How much farther do they need to drive to get to the water park? Use coordinates to find the distance.

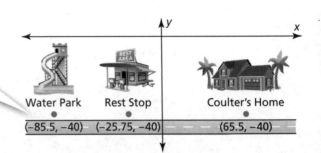

The y-coordinates are the same. Use the absolute values of the x-coordinates to find the distance. Subtract the absolute values.

Water Park   Rest Stop   Coulter's Home
(−85.5, −40) (−25.75, −40)   (65.5, −40)

Each unit represents 1 mile.

$$(-85.5, -40) \ (-25.75, -40)$$
$$|-85.5| \qquad |-25.75|$$
$$85.5 \quad - \quad 25.75$$

The remaining distance to the water park is 59.75 miles.

 Try It!

What is the total distance of the Coulters' return trip after their day at the water park?

The distance of the return trip is $|-85.5|$ ☐ $|65.5|$ = ☐ ☐ ☐ = ☐ miles.

EXAMPLE **3** **Solve Problems Using Distance**

Point B is on the x-axis and has the same x-coordinate as point A. Point C is graphed at (−2, n). The distance from point A to point C is equal to the distance from point A to point B. What is the value of n?

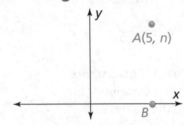

STEP 1 Find the distance from point A to point C.

The y-coordinates are the same.

$$|-2| + |5| = 2 + 5 = 7 \text{ units}$$

Add the absolute values of the x-coordinates to find the distance.

STEP 2 Find the value of n.

The ordered pair (5, 0) describes the location of point B.

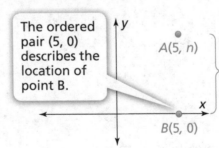

The distance from point A to point B is 7 units.
$$n - 0 = 7$$
$$n = 7$$

$B(5, 0)$

 Try It!

Point D is in Quadrant IV and is the same distance from point B as point A. What are the coordinates of point D?

You can use absolute values to find distances between points on a coordinate plane.

$|-3| + |4| = 3 + 4 = 7$

A(−3, 5)   B(4, 5)

C(−4, −1)

D(−4, −5)

$|-5| - |-1| = 5 - 1 = 4$

Do You Understand?

1. **? Essential Question** How can you find the distance between two points on a coordinate plane?

2. **Look for Relationships** To find the distance between two points using their coordinates, when do you add their absolute values and when do you subtract them?

3. **Reasoning** Can you use absolute value to find the distance between Li's house and Tammy's house in Example 1? Explain.

Do You Know How?

In 4–9, find the distance between each pair of points.

4. (−5, 2) and (−5, 6)

5. (4.5, −3.3) and (4.5, 5.5)

6. $\left(5\frac{1}{2}, -7\frac{1}{2}\right)$ and $\left(5\frac{1}{2}, -1\frac{1}{2}\right)$

7. $\left(-2\frac{1}{4}, -8\right)$ and $\left(7\frac{3}{4}, -8\right)$

8. $\left(5\frac{1}{4}, -3\frac{1}{4}\right)$ and $\left(5\frac{1}{4}, -6\frac{1}{4}\right)$

9. $\left(-1\frac{1}{2}, -6\frac{1}{2}\right)$ and $\left(-2\frac{1}{2}, -6\frac{1}{2}\right)$

Practice & Problem Solving

Scan for
Multimedia

Leveled Practice In **10–15**, find the distance between each pair of points.

10. (−2, 8) and (7, 8)

$$\left| \boxed{} \right| + \left| \boxed{} \right|$$

$$= \boxed{} + \boxed{}$$

$$= \boxed{} \text{ units}$$

11. (−6.1, −8.4) and (−6.1, −4.2)

$$\left| \boxed{} \right| - \left| \boxed{} \right|$$

$$= \boxed{} - \boxed{}$$

$$= \boxed{} \text{ units}$$

12. $\left(12\frac{1}{2}, 3\frac{3}{4}\right)$ and $\left(-4\frac{1}{2}, 3\frac{3}{4}\right)$

$$\left| \boxed{} \right| + \left| \boxed{} \right|$$

$$= \boxed{} + \boxed{}$$

$$= \boxed{} \text{ units}$$

13. (−5, −3) and (−5, −6)

14. (−5.4, 4.7) and (0.6, 4.7)

15. $\left(7\frac{1}{2}, -5\frac{3}{4}\right)$ and $\left(7\frac{1}{2}, -1\frac{1}{4}\right)$

In **16–19**, use the map at the right.

16. Find the distance from roller coaster 1 to the swings.

17. Find the distance from the Ferris wheel to roller coaster 3.

18. Find the total distance from roller coaster 2 to roller coaster 3 and then to the water slide.

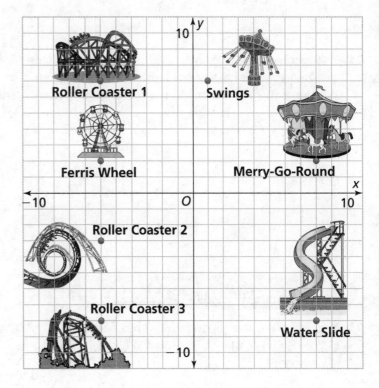

19. Higher Order Thinking Is the distance from the merry-go-round to the water slide the same as the distance from the water slide to the merry-go-round? Explain.

In 20 and 21, use the coordinate plane at the right.

The graph shows the locations of point *G* and point *H*. Point *J* is graphed at $(n, -3)$. The distance from point *H* to point *J* is equal to the distance from point *H* to point *G*.

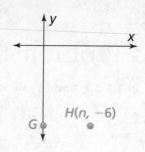

20. What is the distance from point *H* to point *J*?

21. What is the value of *n*?

22. **Use Structure** Suppose *a*, *b*, and *c* are all negative numbers. How do you find the distance between points (a, b) and (a, c)?

23. A scientist graphed the locations of the epicenter of an earthquake and all of the places where people reported feeling the earthquake. She positioned the epicenter at $(-1, 8)$ and the farthest location reported to have felt the quake was positioned at $(85, 8)$. If each unit on the graph represents 1 mile, how far from its epicenter was the earthquake felt?

24. The rectangle *ABCD* shown on the coordinate plane represents an overhead view of a piece of land. Each unit represents 1,000 feet. What are the dimensions of the rectangular piece of land, in feet?

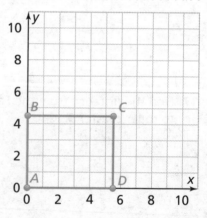

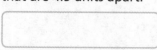

Assessment Practice

25. You are given the following ordered pairs.
$(3.5, -1)$ $(-1.5, 3)$ $(-3, 3)$ $(3.5, 2.5)$ $(-1.5, -1.5)$

🔵 6.NS.3.8

PART A

Graph the ordered pairs on the coordinate plane.

PART B

Find the two ordered pairs on the coordinate plane that are 4.5 units apart.

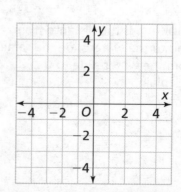

Go Online | **PearsonRealize.com**

Solve & Discuss It!  ACTIVITY

Draw a polygon with vertices at *A*(−1, 6), *B*(−7, 6), *C*(−7, −3), and *D*(−1, −3). Then find the perimeter of the polygon.

Use Structure How can you use the coordinate plane to draw the polygon and find its perimeter?

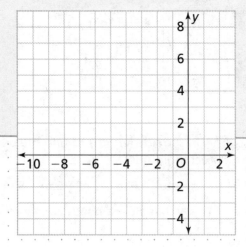

I can...
find side lengths of polygons on a coordinate plane.

MAFS.6.NS.3.8 Solve real-world and mathematical problems by graphing points in all four quadrants of the coordinate plane. Include use of coordinates and absolute value to find distances between points with the same first coordinate or the same second coordinate. **Also 6.G.1.3**

MAFS.K12.MP.2.1, MP.3.1, MP.7.1, MP.8.1

Focus on math practices
Construct Arguments What type of polygon did you draw? Use a definition to justify your answer.

Scan for Multimedia

EXAMPLE 1 **Find the Perimeter of a Rectangle**

An archaeologist used a coordinate plane to map a dig site. She marked the corners of a building with flags, as shown. How much rope does she need to go around the building?

> **Generalize** How can you use what you know about finding distances to find the perimeter of the building?

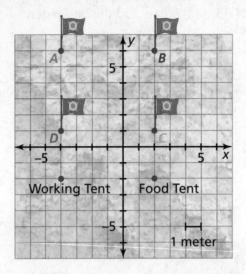

Find the length of each side of rectangle *ABCD*. Use the coordinates of the vertices of the rectangle; *A*(−4, 6), *B*(2, 6), *C* (2, 1), and *D*(−4, 1).

- *A* to *B* = |−4| + |2| = 4 + 2 = 6 m
- *B* to *C* = |6| − |1| = 6 − 1 = 5 m
- *C* to *D* = |2| + |−4| = 2 + 4 = 6 m
- *D* to *A* = |6| − |1| = 6 − 1 = 5 m

Add the side lengths to find the perimeter of rectangle *ABCD*.

Perimeter = 6 m + 5 m + 6 m + 5 m = 22 meters

The archaeologist needs 22 meters of rope.

☑ Try It!

The archaeologist later decides to extend the roped-off area so that the new perimeter goes from *A* to *B* to the food tent to the working tent and then back to *A*. How much rope does she need now?

A to *B* = ☐ m

B to food tent = ☐ m

Food tent to working tent = |2| + |☐| = 2 + ☐ = ☐ m

Working tent to *A* = |☐| + |6| = ☐ + 6 = ☐ m

The archaeologist needs ☐ meters of rope.

Convince Me! How could you use the formula for the perimeter of a rectangle to find the perimeter of the larger rectangle using two of the distances?

Go Online | **PearsonRealize.com**

EXAMPLE **2** Find the Perimeter of an Irregular Polygon

  ACTIVITY ASSESS

A rancher maps the coordinates for a holding pen for his cows. How much fencing does the rancher need to enclose the cows' holding pen?

STEP 1 Find the side lengths.

$LM = |-16.25| - |-4.5| = 16.25 - 4.5 = 11.75$

$MN = |4| + |-6| = 4 + 6 = 10$

$NO = |-4.5| + |8.25| = 4.5 + 8.25 = 12.75$

$OP = |-12| - |-6| = 12 - 6 = 6$

$PQ = |8.25| + |-16.25| = 8.25 + 16.25 = 24.50$

$QL = |-12| + |4| = 12 + 4 = 16$

STEP 2 Add the side lengths.

$11.75 + 10 + 12.75 + 6 + 24.50 + 16 = 81$

The rancher needs 81 yards of fencing.

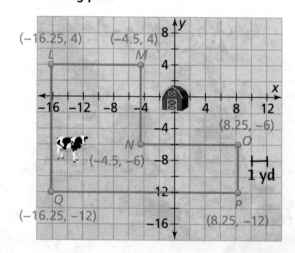

Try It!

The rancher needs to replace the fence for the holding pen for the horses. How much fencing does he need?

The rancher needs [ ] yards of fencing.

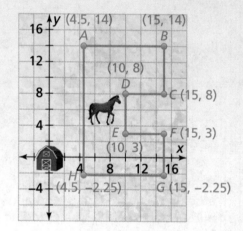

EXAMPLE **3** Apply Distance to Geometry

Are triangle *ABC* and triangle *BCD* isosceles? Explain.

Find the length of the green sides of each triangle.

The length of side $AC = |-5| + |1| = 5 + 1 = 6$ units.

The length of side $DC = |7| - |1| = 7 - 1 = 6$ units.

The length of side $BC = |8| - |2| = 8 - 2 = 6$ units.

The sides are the same length so the triangles are isosceles.

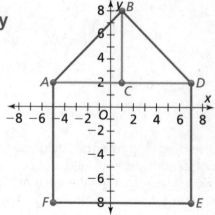

Try It!

Joaquin says that quadrilateral *ADEF* is a square. Is he correct? Explain.

You can represent polygons on a coordinate plane and solve problems by using absolute values to find side lengths.

Add or subtract absolute values to find the length of each side.

AB: $|-3| + |2| = 3 + 2 = 5$ units

BC: $|4| - |2| = 4 - 2 = 2$ units

CD: $|-3| + |2| = 3 + 2 = 5$ units

DA: $|4| - |2| = 4 - 2 = 2$ units

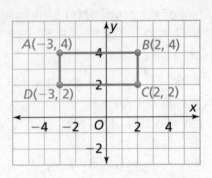

Do You Understand?

1. **Essential Question** How is distance used to solve problems about polygons in a coordinate plane?

2. **Reasoning** In Example 1, why do you add absolute values to find the distance from A to B but subtract absolute values to find the distance from B to C?

3. **Construct Arguments** Could you add or subtract the absolute values of coordinates to find the length of the diagonal AC of rectangle $ABCD$ in Example 1? Explain.

Do You Know How?

4. Find the perimeter of rectangle $MNOP$ with vertices $M(-2, 5)$, $N(-2, -4)$, $O(3, -4)$, and $P(3, 5)$.

5. Jen draws a polygon with vertices $E(-2, 3.5)$, $F(3, 3.5)$, $G(3, -1.5)$, and $H(-2, -1.5)$. Is $EFGH$ a square? Justify your answer.

6. Square $ABCD$ has vertices $A(-4.5, 4)$, $B(3.5, 4)$, $C(3.5, -4)$, and $D(-4.5, -4)$. What is the area of square $ABCD$?

Go Online | PearsonRealize.com

Practice & Problem Solving

Scan for
Multimedia

Leveled Practice In **7** and **8**, find the perimeter of each rectangle.

7. Rectangle *JKLM*: *J*(−3, 8), *K*(−3, −1), *L*(4, −1),
  M(4, 8)

$JK = |8| + |-1| =$ ☐

$KL = |-3| + |4| =$ ☐

Perimeter = ☐ units

8. Rectangle *WXYZ*: *W*(−3, −2), *X*(4, −2), *Y*(4, −5),
  Z(−3, −5)

$WX = |-3| + |4| =$ ☐

$XY = |-5| - |-2| =$ ☐

Perimeter = ☐ units

9. Triangle *JKL* has vertices *J*(0, 0), *K*(5, 0), and
  L(0, −3). Is triangle *JKL* equilateral? Justify
  your answer.

10. Polygon *WXYZ* has vertices *W*(−1.5, 1.5),
  X(6, 1.5), *Y*(6, −4.5), and *Z*(−1.5, −4.5). Is
  WXYZ a rectangle? Justify your answer.

11. What are the perimeter and area of rectangle
  ABCD?

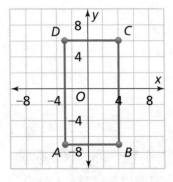

12. Mike used a coordinate plane to design the
  patio shown at the right. Each unit on the grid
  represents 1 yard. To buy materials to build the
  patio, Mike needs to know its perimeter. What is
  the perimeter of the patio?

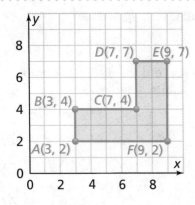

13. Jordan started at her home at point *H*. She ran to the bank (*B*), the library (*L*), the post office (*P*), the café (*C*), her school (*S*), and then back to her home, as shown. The coordinates represent the position, in miles, of each of these locations with respect to the center of town, which is located at the origin. What is the total distance that Jordan ran?

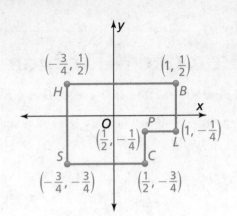

14. Use Structure Ana drew a plan for a rectangular piece of material that she will use for a quilt. The vertices are $(-1.2, -3.5)$, $(-1.2, 4.4)$, and $(5.5, 4.4)$. What are the coordinates of the fourth vertex?

15. Mr. Janas is building a pool in his backyard. He sketches the rectangular pool on a coordinate plane. The vertices of the pool are $A(-5, 7)$, $B(1, 7)$, $C(1, -1)$, and $D(-5, -1)$. If each unit represents 1 yard, how much area of the backyard is needed for the pool?

16. Vocabulary Why is absolute value used to find distances on a coordinate plane?

17. Higher Order Thinking A square on a coordinate plane has one vertex at $(-0.5, -2)$ and a perimeter of 10 units. If all of the vertices are located in Quadrant III, what are the coordinates of the other three vertices?

Assessment Practice

18. You are given the following points on a coordinate plane: $A\left(-1\frac{1}{2}, -\frac{1}{2}\right)$, $B\left(-1\frac{1}{2}, -3\right)$, and $C(4, -3)$. ✆ 6.NS.3.8

PART A

Using absolute value, find the distance (number of units) between points *A* and *B*.

PART B

Select all the coordinates that are 8 units from point *C*.

- ☐ $(12, -3)$
- ☐ $(12, -11)$
- ☐ $(4, -3)$
- ☐ $(-4, -3)$
- ☐ $(4, -11)$

Go Online | PearsonRealize.com

? Topic Essential Question

What are integers and rational numbers? How are points graphed on a coordinate plane?

Vocabulary Review

Complete each definition and then provide an example of each vocabulary word.

Vocabulary   absolute value   opposite   ordered pair   rational number

Definition	Example
1. A point on a coordinate plane is represented by a(n) _____ .	
2. The _____ of a positive integer is a negative integer.	
3. A(n) _____ is any number that can be written as the quotient of two integers.	

Use Vocabulary in Writing

Explain how the points $A\left(9, -\frac{2}{5}\right)$ and $B\left(9, \frac{2}{5}\right)$ are related. Use vocabulary words in your explanation.

Concepts and Skills Review

LESSON 2-1 Understand Integers

Quick Review

Integers are all of the counting numbers, their opposites, and 0. **Opposites** are integers located on opposite sides of 0 and the same distance from 0 on a number line.

Example

For each point on the number line, write the integer and its opposite.

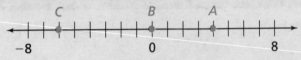

A: 4, −4   B: 0, 0   C: −6, 6

The opposite of the opposite of a number is the number itself.

Practice

For each point on the number line, write the integer and its opposite.

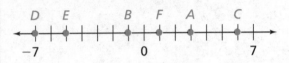

1. A

2. B

3. C

4. D

5. E

6. F

LESSON 2-2 Represent Rational Numbers on the Number Line

Quick Review

Rational numbers are numbers that can be written as a quotient $\frac{a}{b}$, where a and b are integers and b does not equal 0. You can use number lines to represent, compare, and order rational numbers.

Example

Compare and order − 0.1, 0.75, and −$\frac{1}{4}$ from least to greatest.

Plot the numbers on a number line.

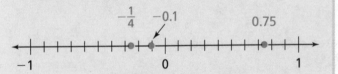

So $-\frac{1}{4} < -0.1 < 0.75$, and their order from least to greatest is $-\frac{1}{4}$, −0.1, 0.75.

Practice

In 1–3, plot each rational number on the number line.

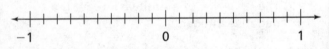

1. $\frac{3}{4}$ **2.** $-\frac{2}{5}$ **3.** 0.5

In 4–7, use <, >, or = to compare.

4. 0.25 ◯ $\frac{1}{4}$

5. $1\frac{5}{8}$ ◯ 1.6

6. 3.65 ◯ $3\frac{3}{4}$

7. $-\frac{2}{3}$ ◯ $-\frac{3}{4}$

Go Online | PearsonRealize.com

Quick Review

The **absolute value** of a number is its distance from 0 on the number line. Distance is always positive. Absolute values are never negative.

Example

Find the absolute values and order $|3|, |4|, |-2|, |-5|$ from *least* to *greatest*.

$$\left.\begin{array}{l} |3| = 3 \\ |4| = 4 \\ |-2| = 2 \\ |-5| = 5 \end{array}\right\}$$ Ordered from least to greatest: $|-2|, |3|, |4|, |-5|$

Practice

In **1–4**, find each value.

1. $|-9|$ **2.** $|-2|$

3. $|4|$ **4.** $-|-10|$

In **5–8**, order the values from least to greatest.

5. $|-3|, |-2|, |10|$ **6.** $|-7|, |0|, |-5|$

7. $|-18.5|, |18|, |-12.5|$ **8.** $|26|, |-20|, |-24.5|$

Quick Review

An **ordered pair** (x, y) of numbers gives the coordinates that locate a point on a **coordinate plane**. Coordinates can be whole numbers, fractions, mixed numbers, or decimals.

Example

Explain how to plot any point with coordinates (x, y).

- Start at the origin, $(0, 0)$.

- Use the *x*-coordinate to move right (if positive) or left (if negative) along the *x*-axis.

- Then use the *y*-coordinate of the point to move up (if positive) or down (if negative) following the *y*-axis.

- Draw and label the point on the coordinate plane.

Explain how to name the location of a point on a coordinate plane.

Follow the grid line from the point to the *x*-axis to name the *x*-coordinate, and follow the grid line from the point to the *y*-axis to name the *y*-coordinate.

Practice

In **1–6**, give the ordered pair for each point.

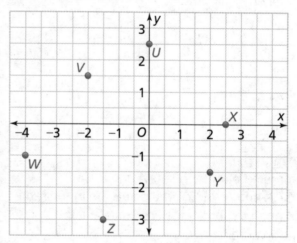

1. U **2.** V

3. W **4.** X

5. Y **6.** Z

Quick Review

You can use absolute value to find the distance between two points that share the same *x*- or *y*-coordinate. When the *y*-coordinates are the same, use the *x*-coordinates to find the distance. When the *x*-coordinates are the same, use the *y*-coordinates. If the points are in different quadrants, add their absolute values. If the points are in the same quadrant, subtract their absolute values.

You can use what you know about finding the distance between two points to find the lengths of the sides of a polygon on a coordinate plane.

Example

Find the length of side *AB*.

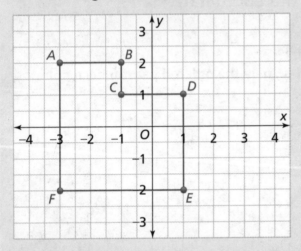

The ordered pairs for points *A* and *B* are $A(-3, 2)$ and $B(-1, 2)$. The points are in the same quadrant, so subtract the absolute values of the *x*-coordinates.

$$|-3| - |-1| = 3 - 1 = 2 \text{ units}$$

The length of side *AB* is 2 units.

Practice

In **1–6**, find the remaining side lengths of polygon *ABCDEF*. Then find the polygon's perimeter.

1. Length of *BC*

2. Length of *CD*

3. Length of *DE*

4. Length of *EF*

5. Length of *FA*

6. Perimeter of *ABCDEF*

In **7** and **8**, polygon *QRST* has vertices $Q(-4, -1)$, $R(-4, 5)$, $S(2, 5)$, and $T(2, -1)$.

7. Draw and label polygon *QRST* on the coordinate plane.

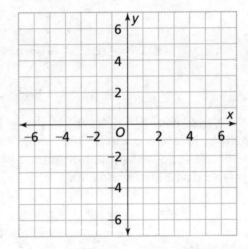

8. Construct an argument to justify whether or not polygon *QRST* is a square.

Hidden Clue

For each ordered pair, simplify the two coordinates. Then locate and label the corresponding point on the graph. Draw line segments to connect the points in alphabetical order. Use the completed picture to help answer the riddle below.

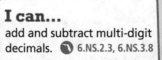

I can...
add and subtract multi-digit decimals. 6.NS.2.3, 6.NS.3.8

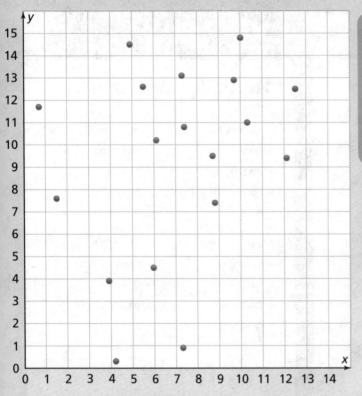

What kind of tree can you carry in your hand?

A (6.4 + 0.92, 15.74 − 2.64)

B (9.65 + 0.4, 16.058 − 1.2)

C (13.4 − 0.896, 8.6 + 4.095)

D (22.10 − 9.99, 0.251 + 9.16)

E (15.6 − 5.87, 8 + 4.95)

F (5.16 + 5.16, 15.6 − 4.6)

G (16.9 − 8.04, 5.08 + 2.27)

H (8.64 + 0.1, 19 − 9.45)

I (9.6 − 2.18, 4.8 + 6.024)

J (12.4 − 6.45, 0.808 + 3.61)

K (5.94 + 1.36, 2.76 − 1.87)

L (4.09 + 0.144, 4.012 − 3.7)

M (6.982 − 3.03, 1.5 + 2.4)

N (7.3 − 1.17, 0.54 + 9.63)

P (0.83 + 0.57, 12.65 − 4.95)

Q (9 − 3.6, 5.74 + 7.06)

R (0.18 + 0.67, 20.02 − 8.17)

S (15.6 − 10.7, 5.43 + 9.07)

? Topic Essential Question

What are expressions and how can they be written and evaluated?

Topic Overview

3-1 Understand and Represent Exponents
6.EE.1.1, MP.2.1, MP.3.1, MP.7.1, MP.8.1

3-2 Find Greatest Common Factor and Least Common Multiple
6.NS.2.4, MP.3.1, MP.7.1, MP.8.1

3-3 Write and Evaluate Numerical Expressions
6.EE.1.1, 6.EE.1.3, MP.1.1, MP.3.1, MP.4.1, MP.6.1, MP.7.1

3-4 Write Algebraic Expressions
6.EE.1.2a, 6.EE.1.2b, 6.EE.2.6, MP.1.1, MP.2.1, MP.4.1, MP.7.1

3-5 Evaluate Algebraic Expressions
6.EE.1.2c, 6.EE.2.6, MP.3.1, MP.4.1, MP.7.1

3-Act Mathematical Modeling: The Field Trip
6.EE.1.2, 6.EE.2.6, MP.1.1, MP.2.1, MP.3.1, MP.4.1, MP.5.1, MP.7.1, MP.8.1

3-6 Generate Equivalent Expressions
6.EE.1.3, 6.EE.1.4, MP.1.1, MP.3.1, MP.7.1, MP.8.1

3-7 Simplify Algebraic Expressions
6.EE.1.3, 6.EE.1.4, MP.1.1, MP.3.1, MP.6.1, MP.7.1

Topic Vocabulary

- algebraic expression
- base
- coefficient
- composite number
- equivalent expressions
- evaluate
- exponent
- factor tree
- greatest common factor (GCF)
- least common multiple (LCM)
- like terms
- numerical expression
- power
- prime factorization
- prime number
- simplify
- substitution
- term
- variable

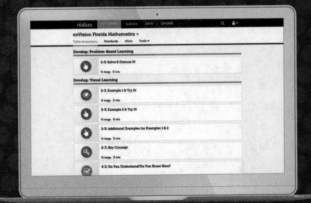

Lesson Digital Resources

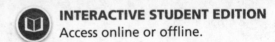

INTERACTIVE STUDENT EDITION
Access online or offline.

VISUAL LEARNING ANIMATION
Interact with visual learning animations.

ACTIVITY Use with *Solve & Discuss It, Exp* and *Explain It* activities, and to explore Exa

VIDEOS Watch clips to support *3-Act Mathematical Modeling Lessons* and *STEM*

Go online | **PearsonRealize.com**

The Field Trip

The Field Trip

When was the last time your class went on a field trip? There's one thing all field trips have in common—they cost money. Schools need to find creative ways to pay for field trips. Fundraising is a great way to generate this money while also giving students the satisfaction of helping make the trip happen.

No matter where the money comes from, it's important for the school to consider every possible cost. Think about this during the 3-Act Mathematical Modeling lesson.

PRACTICE Practice what you've learned.

TUTORIALS Get help from *Virtual Nerd*, right when you need it.

MATH TOOLS Explore math with digital tools.

GAMES Play Math Games to help you learn.

KEY CONCEPT Review important lesson content.

GLOSSARY Read and listen to English/Spanish definitions.

ASSESSMENT Show what you've learned.

enVision® STEM Project

Did You Know?

There are more than 600,000 bridges in the United States.

It took workers 14 years to build the Brooklyn Bridge.

The Mackinac Bridge in Michigan contains 1,016,600 steel bolts.

The Golden Gate Bridge, completed in 1937, has been closed due to high winds three times.

The Mike O'Callaghan-Pat Tillman Memorial Bridge at the Hoover Dam is made up of 30,000 cubic yards of concrete and 16 million pounds of steel.

Your Task: Design a Bridge ▶

Suppose the proposed maximum weight limit for a new bridge in your community is 100,000 pounds. How many and what types of vehicles can be allowed to cross the bridge? How can the weight on the bridge be controlled? You and your classmates will begin the engineering design process to understand the problem, do necessary research, and brainstorm solutions.

Review What You Know!

Vocabulary

Choose the best term from the box to complete each definition.

> composite number
> formula
> numerical expression
> prime number

1. A _____ is a rule that uses symbols to relate two or more quantities.

2. The number 12 is a _____ because it has more than two factors.

3. A _____ is a mathematical phrase that includes numbers and at least one operation.

Perimeter and Area

Use the formulas $P = 2\ell + 2w$ and $A = \ell w$, where ℓ is the length and w is the width, to find the perimeter, P, and the area, A, of each figure.

4.
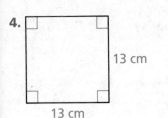
13 cm

13 cm

$P =$ _____

$A =$ _____

5.
5 in.

21 in.

$P =$ _____

$A =$ _____

6.
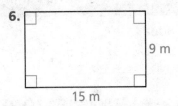
9 m

15 m

$P =$ _____

$A =$ _____

Multiples

Write the first five multiples of each number.

7. 8

8. 9

9. 10

10. 6

11. 4

12. 3

Factors

13. How can you find the factors of 12 and 15? Explain.

Operations

14. How are the terms *difference*, *sum*, *quotient*, and *product* alike?

Prepare for Reading Success

Under each lesson title, write the main idea of the lesson in one sentence. Then write one or two details that support the main idea.

Understand and Represent Exponents

Main Idea:

Details →

Find Greatest Common Factor and Least Common Multiple

Main Idea:

Details →

Write and Evaluate Numerical Expressions

Main Idea:

Details →

Write Algebraic Expressions

Main Idea:

Details →

Evaluate Algebraic Expressions

Main Idea:

Details →

Generate Equivalent Expressions

Main Idea:

Details →

Simplify Algebraic Expressions

Main Idea:

Details →

👆 Solve & Discuss It!

📶 👆 ACTIVITY

Fold a sheet of paper in half. Record the number of sections you see when it is unfolded. Continue folding the paper in half 4 more times. Record the number of sections each time. Describe any patterns you see.

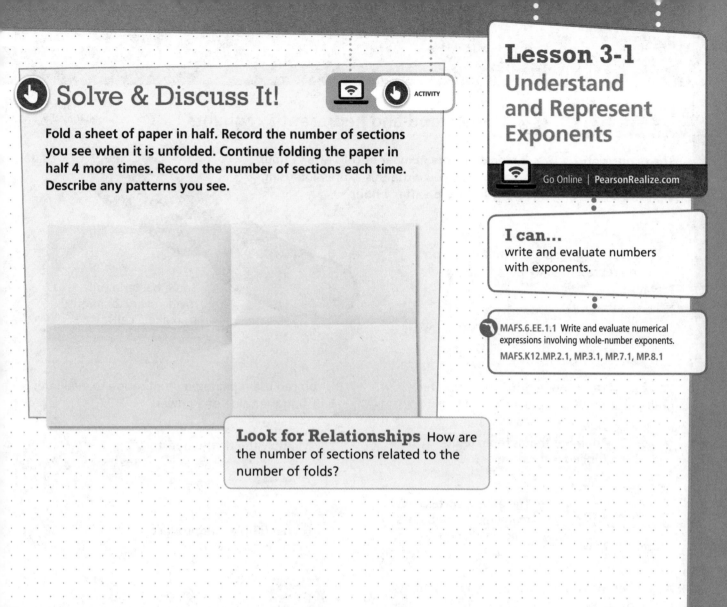

Look for Relationships How are the number of sections related to the number of folds?

I can...
write and evaluate numbers with exponents.

🔵 MAFS.6.EE.1.1 Write and evaluate numerical expressions involving whole-number exponents.
MAFS.K12.MP.2.1, MP.3.1, MP.7.1, MP.8.1

Focus on math practices

Use Structure How many sections will there be after 6 folds? 7 folds?

? **Essential Question** How can you write and evaluate numbers with exponents?

 EXAMPLE **1** **Understand and Represent Exponents**

Scan for Multimedia

The expression 2 × 2 × 2 represents the number of cells after 1 hour if there is 1 cell at the start. How can you write this expression using exponents? How many cells will there be after 1 hour?

> **Reasoning** Repeated multiplication can be represented in more than one way.

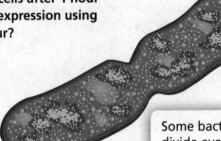

Some bacteria cells divide every 20 minutes to make 2 cells.

You can use an exponent to write repeated multiplication of a number.

> The number that is repeatedly multiplied is the **base**.

$$2 \times 2 \times 2 = 2^3$$

3 factors of 2   power

> The **exponent** tells how many times the base is used as a factor.

A number that can be written using exponents is called a **power**.

You can use repeated multiplication to **evaluate**, or find the value of a power.

> Multiply the first two factors, 2 × 2 = 4.

$$2^3 = \overbrace{2 \times 2} \times 2 = 8$$

> Then multiply that product by the last factor, 4 × 2 = 8.

Power	2^3
Value	8

There will be 8 cells after 1 hour.

☑ **Try It!**

There are 2 × 2 × 2 × 2 × 2 × 2 × 2 × 2 × 2 bacteria cells after 3 hours. Write the repeated multiplication as a power and then evaluate.

Convince Me! Why can you represent the number of cells after two hours as the power 2^6?

EXAMPLE **2** **Evaluate Exponents**

A. How can you evaluate 2^0?

The base is 2. The exponent is 0.

Make a table and look for a pattern.

Power	2^0	2^1	2^2	2^3	2^4
Value	n	2	4	8	16

Each value equals the previous value multiplied by 2.

$1 \times 2 = 2$, so the value of 2^0 is 1.

Generalize Any nonzero number raised to an exponent of zero has a value of 1.

B. How can you evaluate 1.2^4?

The base is 1.2. The exponent is 4.

Find $1.2 \times 1.2 \times 1.2 \times 1.2$.

$1.2 \times 1.2 \times 1.2 \times 1.2$ ········· Multiply the first two factors.

1.44×1.2 ············· Multiply by the third factor.

1.728×1.2 ·········· Multiply by the fourth factor.

2.0736

Power	1.2^1	1.2^2	1.2^3	1.2^4
Value	1.2	1.44	1.728	2.0736

$1.2^4 = 2.0736$

Try It!

Evaluate $\left(\frac{1}{3}\right)^3$.

EXAMPLE **3** **Evaluate Expressions with Exponents**

Julia calculated the foil as 1.9×10^5 units thick. Thom calculated the foil as 183,000 units thick. Which calculation represents the greater thickness for the foil?

Evaluate the expression: 1.9×10^5.

Power	10^1	10^2	10^3	10^4	10^5
Value	10	100	1,000	10,000	100,000

$10^5 = 10 \times 10 \times 10 \times 10 \times 10 = 100,000$

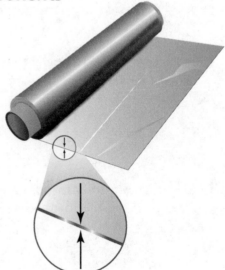

Multiply by the decimal: $1.9 \times 100,000 = \mathbf{190,000}$

Compare the numbers.

$190,000 > 183,000$

Julia's calculation represents the greater thickness for the foil.

Try It!

Rafael calculated the foil as 1.8×10^4 units thick. Evaluate Rafael's expression.

You can represent a repeated multiplication expression using an exponent.

$$5 \times 5 \times 5 \times 5 = 5^4$$

base → exponent

power

You can evaluate a power using repeated multiplication.

$$5^4 = 5 \times 5 \times 5 \times 5 = 625$$

Do You Understand?

1. ? Essential Question How can you write and evaluate numbers with exponents?

2. Look for Relationships How many times is 4 used as a factor in the expression 4^5? Write the numerical expression as repeated multiplication.

3. Be Precise What is a power that has the same value as 1^8? Explain.

4. Construct Arguments Does 2.5×10^0 equal 0, 1, 2.5, or 25? Justify your answer.

5. Model with Math How would you write $\left(\frac{1}{2}\right)^3$ as repeated multiplication?

Do You Know How?

6. Write 81 as a repeated multiplication of 3s. Then write it as a power.

7. Write 125 as a repeated multiplication of 5s. Then write it as a power.

8. What is $0.75 \times 0.75 \times 0.75 \times 0.75 \times 0.75$ written as a power?

9. What is $\frac{3}{8} \times \frac{3}{8} \times \frac{3}{8}$ written as a power?

In **10–13**, evaluate each power.

10. $\left(\frac{1}{6}\right)^2$

11. 45^0

12. 0.1^5

13. 7^3

In **14–16**, evaluate each expression.

14. 4.5×10^4

15. 0.6×10^6

16. 3.4×10^0

Go Online | PearsonRealize.com

Practice & Problem Solving

Scan for
Multimedia

In 17–20, write the exponent for each expression.

17. $9 \times 9 \times 9 \times 9$

18. 1.2^9

19. $\frac{1}{6} \times \frac{1}{6} \times \frac{1}{6}$

20. 7

Leveled Practice In 21–26, evaluate each power or expression.

21. 8^3

☐ × ☐ × ☐

$8^3 =$ ☐

22. $\left(\frac{1}{5}\right)^4$

☐ × ☐ × ☐ × ☐

$\left(\frac{1}{5}\right)^4 =$ ☐

23. 0.6^2

24. $\left(\frac{1}{4}\right)^2$

25. 58^0

26. 6.2×10^3

27. A company rents two storage units. Both units are cube-shaped. What is the difference in volume of the two storage units? Note that the volume of a cube is s^3, where s is the side length. Explain.

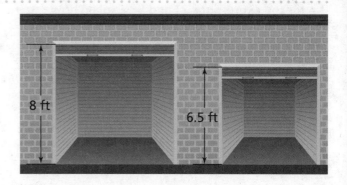

8 ft

6.5 ft

28. Jia is tiling a floor. The floor is a square with side length 12 feet. Jia wants the tiles to be squares with side length 2 feet. How many tiles does Jia need to cover the entire floor? Note that the area of a square is s^2, where s is the side length. Explain.

29. A marine biologist studies the population of seals in a research area. How many seals are in the research area?

Seal population
3.27×10^2

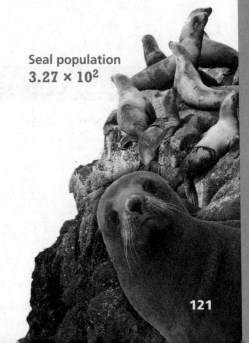

30. **Higher Order Thinking** Zach invested $50 and tripled his money in two years. Kayla also invested $50, and after two years the amount was equal to 50 to the third power. Who had more money after two years? Explain.

31. Malik read that the land area of Alaska is about 5.7×10^5 square miles. About how many square miles is the land area of Alaska?

ALASKA   CANADA

32. Explain why the expressions 10^0, 1^4, and 1×1.0^0 have the same value.

33. Solve the equation $0.3^3 = n$.

34. **Construct Arguments** The same digits are used for the expressions 2^5 and 5^2. Explain how to compare the values of the expressions.

35. **Critique Reasoning** Kristen was asked to write each of the numbers in the expression $80,000 \times 25$ using exponents. Her response was $(8 \times 10^3) \times 5^2$. Was Kristen's response correct? Explain.

36. Consider the equation $1,000,000 = 10^6$. Why is 10 used as the base to write 10^6?

37. Isabella saved 2 nickels today. If she doubles the number of nickels she saves each day, how many days, including today, will it take her to save more than 500 nickels?

Assessment Practice

38. Select all expressions equivalent to $5 \times 5 \times 5 \times 5$. 🕐 6.EE.1.1

- ☐ $5^1 \times 5^4$
- ☐ 5^4
- ☐ $5^2 \times 5^2$
- ☐ 4^5
- ☐ $4(5^1)$

39. Which expression is equivalent to $\frac{1}{36}$? 🕐 6.EE.1.1

- Ⓐ $\frac{1}{3} \times \frac{1}{6}$
- Ⓑ $\frac{1}{4} \times \left(\frac{1}{3}\right)^3$
- Ⓒ $\left(\frac{1}{2}\right)^2 \times \left(\frac{1}{3}\right)^2$
- Ⓓ $\frac{1}{2} \times \frac{1}{3} \times \frac{1}{3} \times \frac{1}{3}$

Go Online | PearsonRealize.com

Solve & Discuss It!

Mark sets the dinner table every 2 days and dries the dishes every 3 days. If he sets the table on Day 2 and dries the dishes on Day 3, on what day would Mark first perform both chores on the same day?

Look for Relationships
What is the relationship between the chores that Mark does each day?

I can...
write the prime factorization and find the greatest common factor and the least common multiple of two numbers.

MAFS.6.NS.2.4 Find the greatest common factor of two whole numbers less than or equal to 100 and the least common multiple of two whole numbers less than or equal to 12. Use the distributive property to express a sum of two whole numbers 1–100 with a common factor as a multiple of a sum of two whole numbers with no common factor. ...

MAFS.K12.MP.3.1, MP.7.1, MP.8.1

Day	Chore

Focus on math practices

Generalize On what day will Mark do both chores on the same day again? How can you find on which days Mark does both chores without making a list?

123

EXAMPLE 1 👁 **Find the Prime Factorization of a Number**

Scan for Multimedia

Whole numbers greater than 1 are either prime or composite numbers. A composite number can be written as a product of its prime factors, called its **prime factorization**.

How can you find the prime factorization of 48?

$1 \times 5 = 5$

5 is a **prime number** because the only factors of 5 are 1 and 5.

12 is a **composite number** because it has more than two factors.

$1 \times 12 = 12$
$2 \times 6 = 12$
$3 \times 4 = 12$

ONE WAY To find the prime factorization of 48, write its factors as a product.

$48 = 2 \times 24$

Start with the least prime factor. 2 is the least prime factor of 48.

$= 2 \times 2 \times 12$

Continue using prime factors.

$= 2 \times 2 \times 2 \times 6$

$= 2 \times 2 \times 2 \times 2 \times 3$

The prime factorization of 48 is $2 \times 2 \times 2 \times 2 \times 3$ or $2^4 \times 3$.

ANOTHER WAY A **factor tree** shows the prime factorization of a composite number.

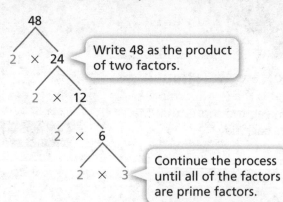

Write 48 as the product of two factors.

Continue the process until all of the factors are prime factors.

The prime factorization of 48 is $2 \times 2 \times 2 \times 2 \times 3$ or $2^4 \times 3$.

There is only one prime factorization for any number.

☑ **Try It!**

Find the prime factorization of 56. Start with the least prime factor.

$56 = 2 \times \boxed{}$

The prime factorization of 56 is $\boxed{} \times \boxed{} \times \boxed{} \times \boxed{}$

$= 2 \times \boxed{} \times \boxed{}$

or $\boxed{} \times \boxed{}$.

$= 2 \times \boxed{} \times \boxed{} \times \boxed{}$

Convince Me! A number is greater than 2 and it has 2 as a factor. Is the number prime or composite? Explain.

Keesha is putting together bags of supplies. She puts an equal number of craft sticks and an equal number of glue bottles in each bag. There are no supplies left over. What is the greatest number of bags of supplies that Keesha can make?

Identify the **greatest common factor (GCF)** of 12 and 42. The GCF is the greatest number that is a factor of two or more numbers.

$12 = 2 \times 2 \times 3$
$42 = 2 \times 3 \times 7$

Write the prime factorization of each number and identify common factors.

Multiply the common factors.

$2 \times 3 = 6$

The greatest common factor (GCF) of 12 and 42 is 6.
Keesha can make 6 bags of supplies.

12 bottles of glue
42 craft sticks

 Try It!

Keesha has 24 beads to add equally to each bag. Can she still make 6 bags and have no supplies left over? Explain.

EXAMPLE **3** **Use the Greatest Common Factor and the Distributive Property to Find the Sum of Two Numbers**

Use the GCF and the Distributive Property to find the sum of 18 and 24.

STEP 1 Find the GCF of 18 and 24.

$18 = 2 \times 3 \times 3$
$24 = 2 \times 2 \times 2 \times 3$

The greatest number that is a factor of both 18 and 24 is 2×3.

The GCF of 18 and 24 is 6.

STEP 2 Write each number as a product using the GCF as a factor.

$18 + 24 = 6 \times 3 + 6 \times 4$

$= 6(3 + 4)$ ← Apply the Distributive Property.

$= 6(7)$

$= 42$

The sum of 18 and 24 is 42.

 Try It!

Use the GCF and the Distributive Property to find the sum of 12 and 36.

EXAMPLE 4 ▶ 👆 **Find the Least Common Multiple of Two Numbers**

Grant is making picnic lunches. He wants to buy as many juice bottles as applesauce cups but no more than he needs to have an equal number of each.

How many packages of each should Grant buy?

> **Look for Relationships** How are the multiples of 6 and 8 related?

8 applesauce cups per pack

6 juice bottles per pack

The **least common multiple (LCM)** is the least multiple, not including zero, common to both numbers.

$6 = 2 \times 3$
$8 = 2 \times 2 \times 2$

> Write the prime factorization of each number.

List the greatest number of times each factor appears in either prime factorization. Multiply these factors to find the LCM.

$3 \times 2 \times 2 \times 2 = 24$

> 24 is the LCM of 6 and 8.

$6 \times 4 = 24$ $8 \times 3 = 24$

Grant should buy 4 packages of juice and 3 packages of applesauce.

☑ Try It!

Grant also buys bottled water and juice pouches for the picnic. There are 12 bottles of water in each case and 10 juice pouches in each box. Grant wants to buy the least amount but still have as many bottles of water as juice pouches. How many of each should he buy? Explain.

KEY CONCEPT 🔑

The **greatest common factor (GCF)** of two numbers is the greatest number that is a factor of both numbers.

Factors of 12: 1, 2, 3, 4, 6, 12

Factors of 40: 1, 2, 4, 5, 8, 10, 20, 40

2 and 4 are common factors of 12 and 40.

4 is the greatest common factor.

The GCF of 12 and 40 is 4.

The **least common multiple (LCM)** of two numbers is the least multiple, not including zero, common to both numbers.

Multiples of 6: 6, 12, 18, 24, 30, 36, 42, 48 . . .

Multiples of 9: 9, 18, 27, 36, 45, 54 . . .

18 and 36 are common multiples of 6 and 9.

18 is the least common multiple.

The LCM of 6 and 9 is 18.

Do You Understand?

1. **Essential Question** How can you write the prime factorization and find the greatest common factor and the least common multiple of two numbers?

2. What are two different ways in which you can use prime factorization to find the prime factors of a number?

3. **Generalize** Why is the GCF of two prime numbers always 1?

4. **Construct Arguments** In Example 4, Grant finds applesauce that comes in packages of 8, but now he finds juice bottles in only packages of 3. Will the LCM change? Explain.

5. **Critique Reasoning** Sarah says that you can find the LCM of any two whole numbers by multiplying them together. Provide a counterexample to show that Sarah's statement is incorrect.

Do You Know How?

In **6–8**, write the prime factorization of each number. If the number is prime, write *prime*.

6. 33

7. 32

8. 19

In **9–11**, find the GCF for each pair of numbers.

9. 18, 36

10. 22, 55

11. 100, 48

In **12–14**, find the LCM for each pair of numbers.

12. 2, 5

13. 8, 12

14. 8, 10

Practice & Problem Solving

Leveled Practice In **15–18**, find the prime factorization of each number. If it is prime, write *prime*.

15.

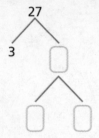

27

3

16.

30

2

17. 26

18. 47

In **19–21**, find the GCF for each pair of numbers.

19. 21, 49

20. 8, 52

21. 32, 81

In **22–24**, use the GCF and the Distributive Property to find each sum.

22. 30 + 66

23. 34 + 51

24. 15 + 36

In **25–27**, find the LCM for each pair of numbers.

25. 12, 11

26. 4, 12

27. 5, 8

28. Critique Reasoning Gabrielle and John each wrote the prime factorization of 64. Analyze their work and explain any errors.

Gabrielle's Work

64

8   8

2   4   2   4

2   2   2   2

$64 = 2 \times 2 \times 2 \times 2 \times 2 \times 2 = 2^6$

John's Work

$64 = 2 \times 32$
$= 2 \times 2 \times 16$
$= 2 \times 2 \times 2 \times 8$
$= 2 \times 2 \times 2 \times 2 \times 4$
$= 2 \times 2 \times 2 \times 2 \times 2 \times 2$

29. To celebrate its grand opening, a store is giving customers gift certificates. Which customer is the first to get two gift certificates?

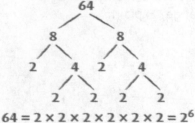

Every 8th customer gets a $50 gift certificate.

Every 6th customer gets a $10 gift certificate.

30. Model with Math The Venn diagram at the right shows the factors of 24 and 40.

a. What is the meaning of each of the three shaded regions?

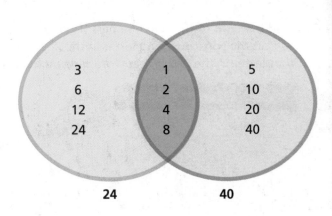

3	1	5
6	2	10
12	4	20
24	8	40

24   40

b. Explain how you use the Venn diagram to find the GCF of 24 and 40. What is the GCF of 24 and 40?

31. Reasoning You have 50 blueberry scones and 75 cranberry scones. You want to make as many identical bags as possible. Each bag should have an equal number of blueberry scones and an equal number of cranberry scones. What is the greatest number of bags you can fill? Explain.

32. Make Sense and Persevere The prime factorizations of A and B are shown. Find the value of n that needs to be listed as a prime factor of B so that the greatest common factor (GCF) of A and B is 9.

Prime factorization of A: $3 \times 3 \times 3$

Prime factorization of B: $2 \times 2 \times 3 \times n$

33. Higher Order Thinking Gena has 28 trading cards, Sam has 91 trading cards, and Tiffany has 49 trading cards. Use the GCF and the Distributive Property to find the total number of trading cards Gena, Sam, and Tiffany have.

34. Periodical cicada species emerge in large numbers from their larval stage at different yearly intervals. What is the GCF of the years?

Emerges every 13 years

Emerges every 17 years

35. People are waiting in line for a theater premiere. Every 5th person in line will receive a free theater ticket. Every 6th person will receive a gift card for $40. Which person is the first to receive both prizes?

36. Two volunteer groups plant trees. Group A plants the trees in clusters of 3. Group B plants the trees in clusters of 10. Both groups plant the same number of trees. What is the least number of clusters that Group B plants?

37. Find the LCM of the two numbers. Then use the LCM to find the corresponding letter in the key. Write that letter in the box. What word did you decode?

2 and 3	3 and 7	2 and 7

Decryption Key				
A = 1	B = 2	C = 3	D = 4	E = 5
F = 6	G = 7	H = 8	I = 9	J = 10
K = 11	L = 12	M = 13	N = 14	O = 15
P = 16	Q = 17	R = 18	S = 19	T = 20
U = 21	V = 22	W = 23	X = 24	Y = 25
Z = 26				

38. Rami has swimming lessons every 3 days and guitar lessons every 8 days. If he has both lessons on the first day of the month, in how many days will Rami have both lessons on the same day again?

39. A number is between 58 and 68. It has prime factors of 2, 3, and 5. What is the number?

40. A college offers shuttle service from Dickson Hall or Lot B to its campus quad. Both shuttles first depart their locations at 9:10 A.M. They run from each location to campus and back at the intervals shown. When is the next time both shuttles will depart for campus at the same time? Explain.

College Shuttle
Departs from:
Lot B
Every 10 minutes
Dickson Hall
Every 12 minutes

SHUTTLE STOP

First shuttles leave at 9:10 A.M.

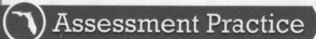
Assessment Practice

41. Match each pair of numbers with the pair(s) of numbers that has the same LCM. 🕐 6.NS.2.4

	Same LCM as 6, 12	Same LCM as 2, 9	Same LCM as 3, 9	Same LCM as 4, 6	Same LCM as 9, 12
6, 9	☐	☐	☐	☐	☐
3, 4	☐	☐	☐	☐	☐

42. Which expression is equivalent to 48 + 60? 🕐 6.NS.2.4

Ⓐ 12(4 + 5)

Ⓑ 12(8 + 5)

Ⓒ 6(6 + 10)

Ⓓ 6(8 + 12)

Go Online | PearsonRealize.com

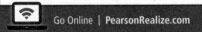
 ## Solve & Discuss It!  ACTIVITY

An airline company charges additional fees for bags that do not meet the weight and size limits. For one flight, fees were charged for a total of 50 bags that were over the weight limit and 6 oversized bags. Find the total amount of fees collected for that flight.

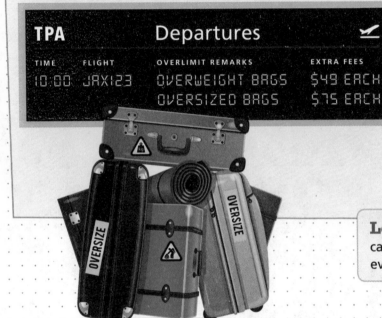

TPA	Departures	✈
TIME	**FLIGHT**	**OVERLIMIT REMARKS**	**EXTRA FEES**
10:00	JAX123	OVERWEIGHT BAGS	$49 EACH
		OVERSIZED BAGS	$75 EACH

> **I can...**
> use the order of operations to evaluate numerical expressions.

> MAFS.6.EE.1.1 Write and evaluate numerical expressions involving whole-number exponents. Also 6.EE.1.3
> MAFS.K12.MP.1.1, MP.3.1, MP.4.1, MP.6.1, MP.7.1

> **Look for Relationships** You can use the order of operations to evaluate numerical expressions.

Focus on math practices

Model with Math Tamara was charged for two bags that were over the weight limit and another bag that was over the size limit. Write and evaluate a numerical expression to find the additional fees Tamara was charged for her bags.

? **Essential Question** How do you write and evaluate numerical expressions?

  VISUAL LEARNING ASS

 EXAMPLE **1** **Use the Order of Operations to Evaluate Numerical Expressions**

Scan for Multimedia

Some expressions look difficult because they include parentheses and brackets. You can think of brackets as "outside" parentheses.

Evaluate the following numerical expression.

$$\frac{1}{2} \times 4^2 - [2 + (3.6 \div 0.9)]$$

A **numerical expression** is a math expression that contains numbers and at least one operation. $3 + 4$, $(5)\left(\frac{3}{4}\right)$, and $8 \div 2 + 0.5$ are numerical expressions.

Order of Operations

1 Evaluate parentheses and brackets from inside out.

2 Evaluate powers.

3 Multiply and divide from left to right.

4 Add and subtract from left to right.

(1) Evaluate parentheses and brackets from inside out.

$\frac{1}{2} \times 4^2 - [2 + (3.6 \div 0.9)]$ ··· Evaluate inside the parentheses.

$= \frac{1}{2} \times 4^2 - [2 + 4]$ ·········· Evaluate inside the brackets.

$= \frac{1}{2} \times 4^2 - 6$

(2) Evaluate powers.

$= \frac{1}{2} \times 4^2 - 6$ ················ Evaluate the power.

$= \frac{1}{2} \times 16 - 6$

(3) Multiply and divide from left to right.

$\frac{1}{2} \times 16 - 6 = \frac{1}{2} \times \frac{16}{1} - 6$ ················ Multiply or divide from left to right.

$= 8 - 6$

(4) Add and subtract from left to right.

$= 8 - 6$ ················ Add or subtract from left to right.

$= 2$

✓ Try It!

Evaluate the numerical expression at the right.

Convince Me! Why is it important to follow the order of operations?

$\frac{1}{8}[6^3 + (48 \div 6)] - 20$

$= \frac{1}{8}[6^3 + \boxed{}] - 20$

$= \frac{1}{8}[\boxed{} + \boxed{}] - 20$

$= \frac{1}{8}[\boxed{}] - 20$

$= \boxed{} - 20$

$= \boxed{}$

Evaluate the numerical expression $2.5^2 + [(6 - \frac{3}{4}) \div 2] \times 2^5$.

$2.5^2 + [(6 - \frac{3}{4}) \div 2] \times 2^5$ ·········· Evaluate inside the parentheses.

$= 2.5^2 + [5\frac{1}{4} \div 2] \times 2^5$ ·········· Evaluate inside the brackets.

$= 2.5^2 + 2\frac{5}{8} \times 2^5$ ·········· Evaluate the powers.

$= 6.25 + 2\frac{5}{8} \times 32$ ·········· Multiply from left to right.

$= 6.25 + 84$ ·········· Add from left to right.

$= 90.25$

The value of the numerical expression is 90.25.

EXAMPLE **3** **Insert Grouping Symbols in a Numerical Expression**

Insert grouping symbols in the expression so that it has a value of 10.

$40 - 7 + 33 \times \frac{3}{4}$

Place parentheses around $40 - 7$ and evaluate.

$(40 - 7) + 33 \times \frac{3}{4}$ ◁ Evaluate inside the parentheses.

$= 33 + 33 \times \frac{3}{4}$ ◁ Multiply.

$= 33 + 24\frac{3}{4}$

$= 57\frac{3}{4}$

$57\frac{3}{4} \neq 10$, so place the grouping symbols in another location.

$40 - 7 + 33 \times \frac{3}{4}$

Place parentheses around $7 + 33$ and evaluate.

$40 - (7 + 33) \times \frac{3}{4}$ ◁ Evaluate inside the parentheses.

$= 40 - 40 \times \frac{3}{4}$ ◁ Multiply.

$= 40 - 30$

$= 10$

Inserting grouping symbols around $7 + 33$ gives the numerical expression a value of 10.

> **Be Precise** When you use math symbols correctly, you are being precise.

Try It!

A. Evaluate the numerical expression: $3.2^2 - [(9 \times 4) + 9] \times \left(\frac{1}{3}\right)^2$.

B. Insert grouping symbols so that the numerical expression has a value of 80.

$6 + 12 \times \left(\frac{2}{3}\right)^2 \times 3 + 7$

The order of operations is a set of rules used to evaluate expressions that include more than one operation.

Order of Operations

1 Evaluate inside grouping symbols, such as parentheses or brackets.

2 Evaluate powers.

3 Multiply or divide from left to right.

4 Add or subtract from left to right.

Do You Understand?

1. **? Essential Question** How do you write and evaluate numerical expressions?

2. **Make Sense and Persevere** Explain why grouping symbols can change the value of a numerical expression. Then insert grouping symbols to show four different values for the following expression.
$80 \div 8 \times 5 + 4^2$

3. In the expression $(21 - 3) \times (7 + 2) \div (12 - 4)$, what operation should you perform last? Explain.

4. **Critique Reasoning** Charles says that $2 \times 3 - 2$ is 4, and Seth says that $2 \times 3 - 2$ is 2. Who is correct? Explain.

Do You Know How?

In **5–9**, evaluate each expression.

5. $5^2 + (6.7 - 3.1)$

6. $(8.2 + 5.3) \div 5$

7. $(1.5 - 0.5^2) \div [(3 + 2) \times 2]$

8. $36.8 \div [11.5 - (2.5 \times 3)]^2$

9. $6 + 4 \times 5 \div 2 - 8 \times 1.5$

In **10–12**, insert grouping symbols so that the expression has the given value.

10. $12 \times 3^2 + 36$ Target value: 540

11. $32 \div 2^3 - 4$ Target value: 8

12. $2.3^2 + 9 \times 4 \div 2$ Target value: 28.58

Practice & Problem Solving

Scan for
Multimedia

Leveled Practice In **13–18**, use the order of operations to evaluate.

13. $4^2 - (3.1 + 6.4) + 4.5$

$= 4^2 - \boxed{} + 4.5$

$= \boxed{} - \boxed{} + 4.5$

$= \boxed{} + 4.5$

$= \boxed{}$

14. $(8.7 + 3.3) \times \left(\frac{1}{2}\right)^2$

$= \boxed{} \times \left(\frac{1}{2}\right)^2$

$= \boxed{} \times \boxed{}$

$= \boxed{}$

15. $157.8 - (3^2 + 6) \times 3$

$= 157.8 - (\boxed{} + 6) \times 3$

$= 157.8 - \boxed{} \times 3$

$= 157.8 - \boxed{}$

$= \boxed{}$

16. $4.3 + (8.4 - 5.1)$

17. $1.25 \times 4 + 3 \times 2 \div \left(\frac{1}{2}\right)^3$

18. $[2^3 \times (152 \div 8)] - 52$

In **19–21**, insert grouping symbols so that the expression has the given value.

19. Target value: 32

$2 \times 9 + 7$

20. Target value: 6

$\frac{1}{3} \times 21 - 3$

21. Target value: 43

$2.5 + 5 \times 6 - 2$

22. Cory bought some baseball equipment. He used a coupon for $\frac{1}{2}$ off the price of the bat and glove. Write and evaluate a numerical expression to find the total cost of the bat, the glove, and 3 baseballs.

$69

$75

Baseballs
$5.50
each

23. Make Sense and Persevere Write a numerical expression, with at least three operations, that has the same value as the following expression. Justify your answer.

$5 + (8 - 4) \div 2 + 3$

24. Use Structure How do you know which part of the numerical expression to evaluate first? Explain.

$(26 + 2.5) - [(8.3 \times 3) + (1^3 - 0.25)]$

25. Construct Arguments Evan says that the value of the numerical expression $0.2^2 + 12 \div (1.5 \times 4)$ is 32.04. Do you agree? Explain.

26. The width of the rectangular drawing is one-third the length plus 3 inches. What is the perimeter of the drawing? Write and evaluate an expression to solve the problem.

12 in.

27. Higher Order Thinking Frederick evaluates the numerical expression $[(53.7 + 37.2) - (3^3 + 3.8)] - 8.6$ and records the answer as 51.5. Lana evaluates the numerical expression $53.7 + 37.2 - 3^3 + 3.8 - 8.6$ and records the answer as 59.1. The expressions have the same numbers and operations. Explain how Frederick and Lana can both be correct.

28. Model with Math Lillian went to the gift shop on the boardwalk and bought four bags of dyed seashells at $3.99 each. She had a coupon for $1 off. Her mom paid for half of the remaining cost. Write and evaluate a numerical expression to find how much Lillian paid toward the purchase of the seashells.

29. In an ecosystem, some animals get energy by eating plants. Write and evaluate an expression to find how many pounds of plants a herd of 18 elk can eat in one week.

An elk can eat 20 pounds of plants each day.

30. Select all expressions that are equivalent to $2^4 \div [(3.2 \times 0.8) + 1.44]$. ✪ 6.EE.1.1

☐ $2^4 \div [(4 \times 0.64) + 1.44]$

☐ $16 \div [(2^2 \times 0.64) + (0.72 \times 2)]$

☐ $8 \div [(3.2 \times 0.8) + (0.48 \times 3)]$

☐ $2^4 \div [2.56 + (0.48 \times 4)]$

☐ $4^2 \div [2.56 + (0.48 \times 4)]$

31. Which value is equivalent to the expression $18.9 \times [(2 \times 2.7) - 4.6] - 2^2$? ✪ 6.EE.1.1

Ⓐ 1,112

Ⓑ 111.2

Ⓒ 11.12

Ⓓ 1.112

1. **Vocabulary** Describe the relationship between the base and the exponent in 4^3. *Lesson 3-1* 🔵 6.EE.1.1

2. What is the GCF of 14 and 42? *Lesson 3-2* 🔵 6.NS.2.4

3. Which pair of numbers has a GCF of 5? *Lesson 3-2* 🔵 6.NS.2.4

   Ⓐ 15 and 30   Ⓑ 5 and 21

   Ⓒ 45 and 9   Ⓓ 20 and 55

4. What is the LCM of 12 and 9? *Lesson 3-2* 🔵 6.NS.2.4

5. Evaluate the numerical expression. *Lesson 3-3* 🔵 6.EE.1.3

   $$0.5^2 \times (20 - 2^2 \times 3) \times \left(\frac{2}{5} \times 25\right)$$

6. Select all the expressions that are equal to $\left(\frac{2}{3}\right)^2$. *Lesson 3-1* 🔵 6.EE.1.1

   ☐ $\frac{4}{9}$ ☐ $\frac{4}{3}$ ☐ $\frac{1}{3} \times \frac{1}{3}$ ☐ $\frac{1}{9} \times 4$ ☐ $\frac{2}{3} \times \frac{2}{3}$

7. Liam bought 2 vintage movie posters, 2 rock posters, and 1 rap poster. He applied a $35 gift card to the total purchase and a $\frac{1}{2}$-off coupon to the rap poster. Write and evaluate a numerical expression to show how much Liam paid for the posters. *Lesson 3-3* 🔵 6.EE.1.3

Poster Prices	
Vintage Movie	$28.50
B Movie	$18.25
Rock	$29.75
Rap	$19.50

8. Eva counts up by 3s, while Jin counts up by 5s. What is the smallest number that they both say? *Lesson 3-2* 🔵 6.NS.2.4

How well did you do on the mid-topic checkpoint? Fill in the stars. ☆☆☆

MID-TOPIC PERFORMANCE TASK

Monique and Raoul are helping teachers make gift bags and gather supplies for a student celebration day at Pineville Middle School.

PART A

Raoul has 72 wristbands and 96 movie passes to put in gift bags. The greatest common factor for the number of wristbands and the number of movie passes is equal to the number of gift bags Raoul needs to make. Find the number of gift bags Raoul needs to make. Then find how many wristbands and how many movie passes Raoul can put in each gift bag if he evenly distributes the items. 🎾 6.NS.2.4

PART B

Monique wants to have an equal number of cups and napkins. What is the least number of packages of cups and the least number of packages of napkins Monique should buy to have an equal number of cups and napkins? Justify your answer. 🎾 6.NS.2.4

Big Sale!

Cups	$3.50	12 per packa
Napkins	$4.25	10 per packa

PART C

Which numerical expressions show the equal number of both cups and napkins that Monique will have in Part B? Select all that apply. 🎾 6.EE.1.3

- ☐ $2^1 \times 30$
- ☐ $10^2 \times 60$
- ☐ $2^2 \times 15$
- ☐ 460^0
- ☐ $4^0 \times 60$

PART D

The teachers have $25 to buy supplies. Write and evaluate a numerical expression to show how much more money they will need to buy the cups and napkins. 🎾 6.EE.1.3

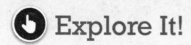 Explore It!

 ACTIVITY

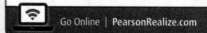
The table shows the number of games the Hornets won and the number of games the Lynx won.

GAMES WON

HORNETS	LYNX
3	5
6	8
9	11
n	

I can...
use variables to write algebraic expressions.

MAFS.6.EE.1.2a Write, read, and evaluate expressions in which letters stand for numbers. Write expressions that record operations with numbers and with letters standing for numbers. ...
Also 6.EE.1.2b, 6.EE.2.6

MAFS.K12.MP.1.1, MP.2.1, MP.4.1, MP.7.1

A. What pattern do you see in the data in the table? Explain how the pattern relates to the number of games won.

B. Look for Relationships Write numerical expressions to relate the number of games won by the Lynx to the number of games won by the Hornets.

Hornets	Lynx
3	3 + 2
6	
9	

C. Explain how to complete the table above for the Lynx if the Hornets won n games.

Focus on math practices

Reasoning Suppose the Lynx won g games. What mathematical expression could you write to show how many games the Hornets won? How is this expression related to the expression you wrote to find the number of games the Lynx won when the Hornets won n games? Explain.

EXAMPLE 1 ▶ 👁 **Write an Algebraic Expression Using a Pattern**

Scan for Multimedia

Darius bought some comic books. How can you write an algebraic expression to represent the total cost of the comic books?

Use a variable to write an algebraic expression.

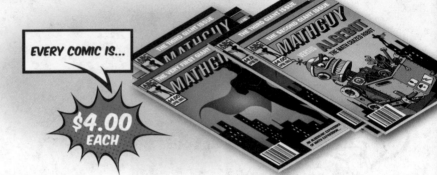

EVERY COMIC IS...

$4.00 EACH

Let n = the number of comic books. Each comic book costs $4.

Number of Comic Books	Total Cost ($)
1	4×1
2	4×2
3	4×3
4	4×4
⋮	
n	$4 \times n$

A **variable** is a letter or symbol that represents an unknown quantity.

The total cost of n comic books can be represented by the expression $4 \times n$.

An **algebraic expression** is a type of math expression that has at least one variable and at least one operation.

You can use a solid dot (·), parentheses, or no symbol at all to write the expression $4 \times n$.

$4 \cdot n$ or $4(n)$ or $4n$

Model with Math $4 \times n$, $4 \cdot n$, $4(n)$, and $4n$ are all ways to write the same expression.

☑ Try It!

Darius's sister Rachel bought m mystery books for $6.50 each. Show three ways to write an algebraic expression that represents the total cost of the mystery books.

Convince Me! How do you know that the expressions you wrote for the cost of the mystery books are algebraic expressions?

EXAMPLE **2** **Write Algebraic Expressions**

  ACTIVITY ASSESS

How can an algebraic expression represent a given situation?

An algebraic expression can use variables and operations to represent given situations.

A. five minutes **more than** time t

addition

$t + 5$

B. ten erasers **decreased by** a number n

subtraction

$10 - n$

C. n nectarines **shared equally** by three

division

$n \div 3$ or $\frac{n}{3}$

D. 4 **times** the quantity x **plus** 8

multiplication   addition

$4(x + 8)$

Try It!

Write an algebraic expression that represents "8 minus the quantity b divided by 6."

EXAMPLE **3** **Identify Parts of an Expression**

Each part of an expression that is separated by a plus sign or a minus sign is called a term. How many terms does the expression $12r + \frac{r}{2} - 19$ have? Describe the parts of the expression.

Remember that a fraction bar also means divide.

$12r + \frac{r}{2} - 19$ has three terms.

$$\underbrace{12r + \frac{r}{2} - 19}_{\text{terms}}$$

The terms are $12r$, $\frac{r}{2}$, and 19.

The first term, $12r$, is a product of two factors.

A **coefficient** is the number that is multiplied by a variable.

12 is the coefficient of r.

$$\underset{\text{coefficient}}{\underbrace{12r}}$$

The second term, $\frac{r}{2}$, is written as a fraction and represents the quotient of r divided by 2.

$$\text{quotient} - \left[\frac{r}{2}\right] \begin{array}{l} \text{dividend} \\ \text{divisor} \end{array}$$

The third term, 19, is a constant numerical value.

Try It!

How many terms does the expression $r \div 9 + 5.5$ have? Explain.

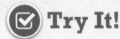

A variable, written as a letter, represents a quantity that can change. You can use a variable to write an algebraic expression that has at least one operation.

Word Phrase	Variable	Operation	Algebraic Expression
the **sum** of 8 and a number a	a	Addition	$8 + a$
five **less than** a number b	b	Subtraction	$b - 5$
the **product** of 8 and a number c	c	Multiplication	$8c$
the quotient of a number d **divided by** 2	d	Division	$\dfrac{d}{2}$

Do You Understand?

1. **Essential Question** How can you write an algebraic expression?

2. **Be Precise** Identify the variable and the operation in the algebraic expression $\frac{6}{x}$.

3. **Vocabulary** Explain why $15 + \frac{1}{2}n$ is an algebraic expression.

4. **Reasoning** Could you describe the expression $2(3 + 4)$ as a product of two factors? Explain.

5. Which part of the expression $2(3 + 4)$ is the sum of two terms? Explain.

Do You Know How?

In **6** and **7**, write an algebraic expression for each situation.

6. five less than y

7. six times the quantity two x plus three y

In **8–10**, use the expression $\frac{w}{4} + 12.5 - 7z$.

8. How many terms does the expression have? Explain.

9. Which term has a coefficient? Explain.

10. Which term is a constant numerical value?

Go Online | PearsonRealize.com

Practice & Problem Solving

In 11–14, write an algebraic expression for each situation.

11. 12 times a number g

12. p pennies added to 22 pennies

13. 22 divided by a number s

14. $12\frac{3}{4}$ less than the product of 7 and a number x

---

In 15–18, tell how many terms each expression has.

15. $5 - g$

16. $3 + \frac{1}{2}b$

17. $\frac{v}{3} + 2 \cdot 5$

18. $16.2 - (3 \cdot 4) + (14 \div 2)$

In 19 and 20, use the expression $5.3t - (20 \div 4) + 11$.

19. Which part of the expression is a quotient? Describe its parts.

20. Which part of the expression is a product of two factors? Describe its parts.

In 21 and 22, use the table at the right.

21. Model with Math Write an expression to show how much longer the round-trip to San Diego is than the round-trip to San Jose. How many terms does the expression have?

22. Make Sense and Persevere Last month, a truck driver made 5 round-trips to Los Angeles and some round-trips to San Diego. Write an expression that shows how many miles he drove in all. Identify and describe the part of the expression that shows how many miles he drove and trips he made to San Diego.

Sacramento to ...	Round-Trip Distance (miles)
San Jose	236
Los Angeles	770
San Diego	1,012

23. Use the expression $y \div 3(4 - 2) + 5.5$ to complete the table. Identify the parts of the expression that correspond to the descriptions.

Description of Part	Part
Variable	
Difference	
Product	
Constant numerical value	

24. The floats in the Orlando Citrus parade may use as many citrus fruits as a small orchard produces in 6 years. If f is the number of citrus fruits a small orchard produces in 1 year, write an algebraic expression to represent the number of citrus fruits the floats in the parade may use.

25. Critique Reasoning Anthony says that the expression abc has three terms because it uses three different variables. Critique Anthony's reasoning and explain whether he is correct.

26. Yuri walked p poodles and b bulldogs on Monday. He walked the same number of poodles and bulldogs each day Tuesday through Friday as he did on Monday. Write an algebraic expression to represent how many total dogs were walked in this 5-day period.

27. Higher Order Thinking Some students equally share 2 baskets of oranges. Each basket has 12 oranges. Write an algebraic expression to represent this situation. Then explain how you chose which variable and operations to use.

28. Model with Math The figure at the right is a regular octagon with side length s. Write two algebraic expressions that use different operations to represent the perimeter of the figure.

STOP

Assessment Practice

29. Which algebraic expression represents the phrase *Four more than the product 3 times the number of* c *cats*? 🔖 6.EE.1.2a

- (A) $4 + 3c$
- (B) $(4 + 3)c$
- (C) $3 + 4c$
- (D) $4 \times 3 \times c$

30. Select all of the phrases that could be represented by the algebraic expression $\frac{w}{4} - 4$. 🔖 6.EE.1.2a

- ☐ four less than the quotient of a number w and four
- ☐ the difference between a number w and 4
- ☐ four less than w divided by 4
- ☐ four less than a number w
- ☐ the quotient of four and a number w

Go Online | PearsonRealize.com

👆 Solve & Discuss It!  📶 👆 ACTIVITY

A bike shop charges by the hour to rent a bike. Related items are rented for flat fees. Write an expression that represents how much it will cost to rent a bike and helmet for *h* hours. How much would it cost to rent a bike and a helmet for 3 hours?

BOB'S BIKE RENTALS
THE BEST IN FLORIDA SINCE 1960

RENTAL	COST
Bike	$12.50/h
Helmet	$5.25
Lock	$1.75
Basket	$2.25

I can...
evaluate an algebraic expression with whole numbers, decimals, and fractions.

MAFS.6.EE.1.2c Evaluate expressions at specific values of their variables. Include expressions that arise from formulas used in real-world problems. Perform arithmetic operations, including those involving whole-number exponents, in the conventional order when there are no parentheses to specify a particular order (Order of Operations). ... Also 6.EE.2.6

MAFS.K12.MP.3.1, MP.4.1, MP.7.1

Model with Math You can write an algebraic expression with decimals in the same way you do with whole numbers.

Focus on math practices

Use Structure Write an expression that represents renting a bike, a lock, and a basket for *h* hours. What is the cost of renting this equipment for 4 hours?

VISUAL LEARNING

EXAMPLE 1 **Evaluate Algebraic Expressions with Whole Numbers**

Scan for Multimedia

Erik collects miniature cars. He has one large case that has 20 cars. He also has 3 same-size, smaller cases filled with cars.

Let n = the number of cars in each smaller case.

How many miniature cars does Erik have if each smaller case holds 10 cars? 12 cars? 14 cars?

$20 + 3n$ represents the total number of cars that Erik has.

Use Structure Follow the order of operations when you evaluate an expression.

To evaluate an algebraic expression, use **substitution** to replace the variable with a number.

Evaluate $20 + 3n$ when n equals 10, 12, or 14.

$20 + 3n$
$20 + 3(10)$ — Substitute 10 for n.
$= 20 + 30$
$= 50$

If each smaller case holds 10 cars, Erik has 50 cars.

$20 + 3n$
$20 + 3(12)$ — Substitute 12 for n.
$= 20 + 36$
$= 56$

If each smaller case holds 12 cars, Erik has 56 cars.

$20 + 3n$
$20 + 3(14)$ — Substitute 14 for n.
$= 20 + 42$
$= 62$

If each smaller case holds 14 cars, Erik has 62 cars.

The table summarizes the values of $20 + 3n$ for each number of cars in a smaller case.

n	$20 + 3n$
10	50
12	56
14	62

☑ Try It!

Evaluate the expression $50 - t$ when t equals 10, 20, or 25. Then complete the table to show the values.

$50 - t$ $50 - t$ $50 - t$

$50 - \boxed{}$ $50 - \boxed{}$ $50 - \boxed{}$

$= \boxed{}$ $= \boxed{}$ $= \boxed{}$

t	10	20	25
$50 - t$	$\boxed{}$	$\boxed{}$	$\boxed{}$

Convince Me! What does it mean to use substitution to evaluate an algebraic expression?

Go Online | PearsonRealize.com

EXAMPLE **2**

EXAMPLE 2 Evaluate Algebraic Equations with Decimals

Julie's family took a 4-day trip. Julie's mother wrote an equation to calculate their gas mileage, m, in miles per gallon. Let d = the number of total miles driven on the trip. Let g = the total number of gallons of gas used for the trip.

$m = \dfrac{d}{g}$

What was the gas mileage for the 4-day trip?

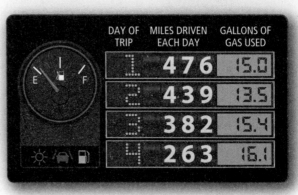

DAY OF TRIP	MILES DRIVEN EACH DAY	GALLONS OF GAS USED
1	476	15.0
2	439	13.5
3	382	15.4
4	263	16.1

STEP 1 Identify the values of the variables d and g.

$d = 476 + 439 + 382 + 263 = 1{,}560$

$g = 15 + 13.5 + 15.4 + 16.1 = 60$

STEP 2 Substitute the values of the variables into the equation and evaluate.

$m = \dfrac{1{,}560}{60} = 26$

The gas mileage was 26 miles per gallon.

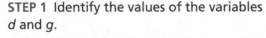 **Try It!**

Evaluate the expression $3.4 + 12a \div 4$ for $a = 10$.

 EXAMPLE 3 Evaluate Algebraic Expressions with Fractions

Mr. Grant wants to tile a 27-square-foot area with square tiles. Let s = the side length, in feet, of a square tile. Use the expression $27 \div s^2$ to find the number of tiles Mr. Grant needs to buy.

$s = \dfrac{1}{3}$ ft

Substitute $\dfrac{1}{3}$ for s.

$27 \div s^2$

$= 27 \div \left(\dfrac{1}{3} \cdot \dfrac{1}{3} \right)$

$= 27 \div \dfrac{1}{9}$

Evaluate the expression.

$27 \div \dfrac{1}{9}$
 To divide by $\dfrac{1}{9}$, multiply by the reciprocal.

$= 27 \cdot \dfrac{9}{1}$

$= 243$

Mr. Grant needs to buy 243 tiles.

Try It!

Suppose Mr. Grant decides to buy square tiles that have side lengths of $\dfrac{3}{4}$ foot. How many of these tiles will he need to buy?

To evaluate an expression, use substitution to replace a variable with its numerical value. Then use the order of operations to simplify.

$a = 9, b = 6, c = 3, d = 5$

$5a + 2b \div c + d^2$

$= 5(9) + 2(6) \div 3 + 5^2$ ← Replace each variable with its specific value.

$= 74$

Do You Understand?

1. **? Essential Question** How can you evaluate an algebraic expression?

2. **Construct Arguments** Why is it important to use the order of operations to evaluate algebraic expressions?

3. How is evaluating an expression with fractions like evaluating an expression with whole numbers? How is it different?

4. **Reasoning** Annalise earns $4 an hour walking pets in her neighborhood. She evaluates the expression $4h$, where h represents the number of hours, to find the amount she earns. Can any number be substituted for h? Explain.

Do You Know How?

In **5–8**, evaluate each expression for $t = 8$, $w = \frac{1}{2}$, and $x = 3$.

5. $3t - 8$

6. $6w \div x + 9$

7. $t^2 - 12w \div x$

8. $5x - 2w + t$

In **9–14**, evaluate each expression for the value given.

9. $z \div 4; z = 824$

10. $6t \div 9 - 22; t = 60$

11. $r \div 2.4; r = 16.8$

12. $9.85 \times s; s = 4$

13. $x \div 12; x = \frac{2}{3}$

14. $\frac{3}{4} + 4y \div 3; y = 1\frac{1}{2}$

Practice & Problem Solving

In **15–17**, evaluate each expression for $w = 5$, $x = 3$, $y = 4$, and $z = 8$.

15. $9x$

16. $3y + 6 \div 2x$

17. $w^2 + 2 + 48 \div 2z$

In **18–20**, evaluate each expression for $x = 1.8$, $x = 5$, and $x = 6.4$.

18. $x \div 4$

19. $x(3.35)$

20. $2x + 3.1$

In **21–23**, evaluate each expression for the value given.

21. $j + \frac{3}{8}; j = \frac{3}{4}$

22. $8 - g \div \frac{7}{8}; g = \frac{5}{6}$

23. $3m \div \frac{2}{5}; m = \frac{2}{3}$

24. Evaluate the expression for the values of b.

b	8.9	5.1	0.2
$b(3) + 20.4$			

25. Evaluate the expression for the values of j.

j	$\frac{1}{2}$	$\frac{4}{5}$	$1\frac{3}{4}$
$2j + \frac{3}{5}$			

In **26–28**, use the table at the right.

26. Model with Math Ms. White wants to rent a small car for a week. It will cost the weekly fee plus $0.30 per mile driven.

a. Let m = the number of miles Ms. White drives during the week. Write an expression that shows the amount she will pay for the car.

b. Evaluate the expression you wrote to find how much Ms. White will pay if she drives 100 miles.

ABC Car Rentals: Rates

Vehicle	Week	Day
Small car	$250	$100
Medium car	$290	$110
Luxury car	$325	$120
Small van	$350	$150
Large van	$390	$170

27. Mr. Black rents a luxury car for one week and a few days, d. He does not pay a per-mile fee. Evaluate the expression $325 + 120d$ to find how much Mr. Black will pay for an 11-day rental.

28. For any of the vehicles listed in the table, how many days can you rent the vehicle before it would be less expensive to rent for the week?

In **29** and **30**, use the table at the right.

29. **Model with Math** Tamara is making a medium-length necklace. Write an expression that shows how much it will cost Tamara for the chain, pendant, and *b* beads that cost $0.25 each. Then find the total cost of the necklace if Tamara uses 30 beads.

Necklace Length	Cost of Chain	Cost of Pendant
Long	$2.25	$4.50
Medium	$1.80	$3.72
Short	$1.15	$2.39

30. **Higher Order Thinking** Ronnie is making short and long necklaces with only one chain and one pendant per necklace. Write an expression that shows how much it will cost Ronnie to make *s* short necklaces and *n* long necklaces. Then find the cost for 3 short necklaces and 2 long necklaces.

31. **Critique Reasoning** Katrina says that the expression $5{,}432 + 4{,}564 + 13{,}908 \div 61n$ can be evaluated by adding $5{,}432 + 4{,}564 + 13{,}908$ and then dividing by the value of $61n$. Do you agree? Explain.

32. The density, *d*, of an object can be found by using the formula $d = \frac{m}{v}$, where *m* is the mass of the object and *v* is its volume. What is the density of an object that has a mass of 73,430 kilograms and a volume of 7 m³?

33. The formula $V = s^3$ can be used to find the volume of a cube. Use the formula to find the volume, *V*, of a cube-shaped bin with side length *s* of $\frac{2}{3}$ yard.

34. Katie is evaluating the expression $15.75 \div p + 3p$ when $p = 3.15$. Explain each step that she should follow.

Assessment Practice

35. An equation is shown.

    $5x + (x \div 3) = 38.4$

    Which value of *x* makes the equation true? 🎧 6.EE.1.2c

    Ⓐ $x = 5.1$

    Ⓑ $x = 5.2$

    Ⓒ $x = 6.1$

    Ⓓ $x = 7.2$

Go Online | PearsonRealize.com

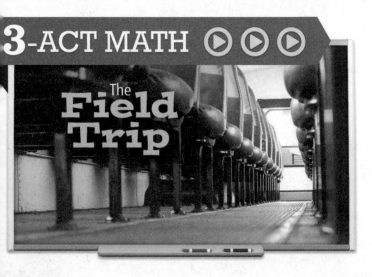
The Field Trip

MAFS.K12.MP.4.1 Model with mathematics. Also MP.1.1, MP.2.1, MP.3.1, MP.5.1, MP.7.1, MP.8.1

MAFS.6.EE.1.2 Write, read, and evaluate expressions in which letters stand for numbers. Also 6.EE.2.6

ACT 1

1. After watching the video, what is the first question that comes to mind?

2. Write the Main Question you will answer.

3. Construct Arguments Make a prediction to answer this Main Question. Explain your prediction.

4. On the number line below, write a number that is too small to be the answer. Write a number that is too large.

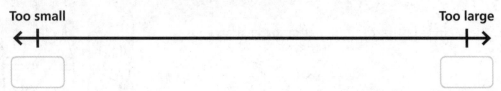

Too small   Too large

5. Plot your prediction on the same number line.

6. What information in this situation would be helpful to know? How would you use that information?

7. **Use Appropriate Tools** What tools can you use to get the information you need? Record the information as you find it.

8. **Model with Math** Represent the situation using the mathematical content, concepts, and skills from this topic. Use your representation to answer the Main Question.

9. What is your answer to the Main Question? Is it higher or lower than your prediction? Explain why.

Go Online | PearsonRealize.com

10. Write the answer you saw in the video.

11. Reasoning Does your answer match the answer in the video? If not, what are some reasons that would explain the difference?

12. Make Sense and Persevere Would you change your model now that you know the answer? Explain.

Reflect

13. Model with Math Explain how you used a mathematical model to represent the situation. How did the model help you answer the Main Question?

14. Critique Reasoning A classmate said your model works for any number of students and adults. Do you agree? Justify your reasoning or explain your classmate's error.

15. Generalize Suppose the entire grade goes on the field trip: 283 students and 10 teachers. Each bus holds 72 people and costs $610 for transport. How much money is needed? Explain how you reused your model.

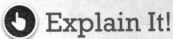 Explain It!

Juwon says all three expressions are equivalent.

$$8n + 6$$
$$2(4n + 3)$$
$$\underline{14n}$$

I can...
identify and write equivalent algebraic expressions.

MAFS.6.EE.1.3 Apply the properties of operations to generate equivalent expressions. ...
Also 6.EE.1.4

MAFS.K12.MP.1.1, MP.3.1, MP.7.1, MP.8.1

A. Find the value of each expression for $n = 1$.

$8n + 6$	$2(4n + 3)$	$14n$
$8(\boxed{}) + 6$	$2(4 \cdot \boxed{} + 3)$	$14(\boxed{})$
$= \boxed{} + 6$	$= 2(\boxed{} + 3)$	$= \boxed{}$
$= \boxed{}$	$= 2 \cdot \boxed{}$	
	$= \boxed{}$	

B. Find the value of each expression for $n = 2$.

$8n + 6$	$2(4n + 3)$	$14n$

C. Critique Reasoning Do you agree with Juwon that all three expressions are equivalent? Explain.

Focus on math practices

Generalize When a number is substituted for the same variable in two expressions, how many times must those two expressions have different values before you know they are not equivalent? Explain.

VISUAL LEARNING

EXAMPLE 1 Use Properties of Operations to Write Equivalent Expressions

Scan for Multimedia

Equivalent expressions have the same value regardless of the value that is substituted for the same variable in the expressions.

Use properties of operations to write equivalent expressions for $3(4x - 1)$ and $2x + 4$.

Use Structure Think about how you can use these properties of operations for any numbers *a*, *b*, or *c*.

Properties of Operations

1. **Commutative Property**
   of Addition $a + b = b + a$
   of Multiplication $a \times b = b \times a$
2. **Associative Property**
   of Addition $(a + b) + c = a + (b + c)$
   of Multiplication $(a \times b) \times c = a \times (b \times c)$
3. **Distributive Property**
   across Addition $a(b + c) = a(b) + a(c)$
   across Subtraction $a(b - c) = a(b) - a(c)$

Use the Distributive and Associative Properties to write an expression that is equivalent to $3(4x - 1)$.

$3(4x - 1) = 3(4x) - 3(1)$ ·········· Distributive Property

$= (3 \cdot 4)x - 3$ ·········· Associative Property of Multiplication

$= 12x - 3$

$12x - 3$ and $3(4x - 1)$ are equivalent expressions.

Equivalent expressions can be written in more than one way.

Use the Distributive Property in reverse order to write an expression that is equivalent to $2x + 4$.

Look for a common factor of both terms that is greater than 1.

$2x + 4 = 2(x) + 2(2)$ ·········· Distributive Property

$= 2(x + 2)$ ················ 2 is a common factor.

So, $2(x + 2)$ is equivalent to $2x + 4$.

☑ Try It!

Write an expression that is equivalent to $3y - 9$.

A common factor of 3 and 9 is ☐.

$3y - 9 = $ ☐ $(y) - $ ☐ $($ ☐ $)$

$= $ ☐ $($ ☐ $- $ ☐ $)$

So, $3y - 9$ is equivalent to ☐.

Convince Me! Why can you use properties of operations to write equivalent expressions?

Go Online | PearsonRealize.com

Which of the expressions below are equivalent?

$8x - 4$ $4x$ $4(2x - 1)$

> **Use Structure** You can use properties of operations to determine whether expressions are equivalent.

Use the Distributive Property to simplify $4(2x - 1)$.

$4(2x - 1) = 4(2x) - 4(1)$

$\qquad = 8x - 4$

So, $4(2x - 1)$ and $8x - 4$ are equivalent expressions.

Properties of operations cannot be used to write either $8x - 4$ or $4(2x - 1)$ as $4x$.

$8x - 4 \neq 4x$

$4(2x - 1) \neq 4x$

So, neither $8x - 4$ nor $4(2x - 1)$ is equivalent to $4x$.

 **Try It!**

Which of the following expressions are equivalent? Explain.

$$10y + 5 \quad 15y \quad 5(2y + 1)$$

EXAMPLE **3** **Use Substitution to Justify Equivalent Expressions**

Are $6(n + 3) - 4$ and $6n + 14$ equivalent expressions?

Use properties of operations to simplify $6(n + 3) - 4$.

$6(n + 3) - 4 = 6(n) + 6(3) - 4$

$\qquad = 6n + 18 - 4$ *Use the Distributive Property.*

$\qquad = 6n + 14$

> **Generalize** When two expressions name the same number regardless of the value of the variable, they are equivalent.

Substitute 3 for n to justify that the expressions are equivalent.

$6(n + 3) - 4 = 6(3) + 6(3) - 4$ $6n + 14 = 6(3) + 14$

$\qquad = 18 + 18 - 4$ $\qquad = 18 + 14$

$\qquad = 32$ $\qquad = 32$

So, $6(n + 3) - 4$ and $6n + 14$ are equivalent expressions.

 **Try It!**

Are $2(x - 3) + 1$ and $2x + 6$ equivalent expressions? Use substitution to justify your work.

Two algebraic expressions are equivalent if they have the same value when any number is substituted for the variable.

You can use the properties of operations to write equivalent expressions.

Properties of Operations

1 Commutative Property
of Addition $\quad a + b = b + a$
of Multiplication $\quad a \times b = b \times a$

2 Associative Property
of Addition $\quad (a + b) + c = a + (b + c)$
of Multiplication $\quad (a \times b) \times c = a \times (b \times c)$

3 Distributive Property
across Addition $\quad a(b + c) = a(b) + a(c)$
across Subtraction $\quad a(b - c) = a(b) - a(c)$

Do You Understand?

1. **Essential Question** How can you identify and write equivalent expressions?

2. **Use Structure** Which property of operations could you use to write an equivalent expression for $y + \frac{1}{2}$? Write the equivalent expression.

3. **Generalize** Are z^3 and $3z$ equivalent expressions? Explain.

4. Are the expressions $3(y + 1)$ and $3y + 3$ equivalent for $y = 1$? $y = 2$? $y = 3$?

5. **Construct Arguments** Are the expressions $3(y + 1)$ and $3y + 3$ equivalent for any value of y? Explain.

Do You Know How?

In **6–8**, use properties of operations to complete the equivalent expressions.

6. $2(r + 3) = \boxed{} r + \boxed{}$

7. $6(4s - 1) = \boxed{} s - \boxed{}$

8. $8t + 2 = 2(\boxed{} t + \boxed{})$

9. Complete the table below.

x	12x − 6	3x + 3	6(2x − 1)
1			
2			
3			

10. In Exercise 9, which expressions in the table are equivalent?

Go Online | PearsonRealize.com

Practice & Problem Solving

Scan for
Multimedia

Leveled Practice In **11–20**, write equivalent expressions.

11. $3(m + 3) = \boxed{}\,m + \boxed{}$

12. $20n - 4m = 4(\boxed{}\,n - \boxed{}\,m)$

13. $3(x - 6)$

14. $2x + 10$

15. $8\left(2y + \frac{1}{4}\right)$

16. $5.7 + (3z + 0.3)$

17. $5w - 15$

18. $2x + 4y$

19. $10(y^2 + 2.45)$

20. $\frac{3}{4} \cdot (z^3 \cdot 4)$

In **21–24**, write the letters of the expressions that are equivalent to the given expression.

21. $5(2x + 3)$

  a. $10x + 15$

  b. $5x + 15 + 5x$

  c. $10x + 8$

22. $4x - 8$

  a. $2(2x - 6)$

  b. $2(2x - 4)$

  c. $x - 8 + 3x$

23. $12x - 16$

  a. $9.6x - 16 + 2.4x$

  b. $3(3x - 5)$

  c. $4(3x - 4)$

24. $2\left(6x + \frac{1}{2}\right)$

  a. $12x + 2$

  b. $12x + 1$

  c. $6x + \frac{1}{2} + 6x + \frac{1}{2}$

In **25–27**, use the signs at the right.

25. Write an algebraic expression that represents each purchase.

  a. Mr. Tonkery bought x number of soccer balls and 3 baseballs.

Soccer Balls
$15 each

Baseballs
$6 each

Sweat Socks
$5 per pair

  b. Dennis, Eddie, and Felix are on a baseball team. They each bought a baseball and x pairs of sweat socks.

26. Make Sense and Persevere Suppose x has the same value in both of the expressions you wrote for Exercise 25. Are the two expressions you wrote equivalent? Explain.

27. Critique Reasoning Wendy says that soccer balls cost $2\frac{1}{2}$ times as much as baseballs. Do you agree? Explain.

28. Use Structure Write an algebraic expression to represent the area of the rectangular rug. Then use properties of operations to write an equivalent expression.

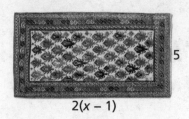

5

$2(x - 1)$

29. Critique Reasoning Jamie says that the expressions $6x - 2x + 4$ and $4(x + 1)$ are not equivalent because one expression has a term that is subtracted and the other does not. Do you agree? Explain.

30. Are the two expressions shown below equivalent? Explain.

$4(n + 3) - (3 + n)$ and $3n + 9$

31. Critique Reasoning Chris says that the expression $4n - 2$ can be written as $2(2n - 1)$. Do you agree? Explain.

32. Higher Order Thinking Write an expression that has only one term and is equivalent to the expression below.

$(f \cdot g^2) + 5 - (g^2 \cdot f)$

33. Construct Arguments A Florida college golf team with 14 members is planning an awards banquet. To find the total cost of the meals, the team uses the expression $5(g + 14)$, where g is the number of guests attending the banquet. A team member says that an equivalent expression is $5g + 14$. Do you agree? Explain.

$5 per meal

34. Select each expression that is equivalent to $8.5 + (2s + 0.5)$. 🔘 6.EE.1.3

☐ $(8.5 + 2s) + 0.5$

☐ $(8.5 + 0.5) + 2s$

☐ $9 + 2$

☐ $2(4.5 + s)$

☐ $8.5(2s + 0.5)$

35. Select each expression that is equivalent to $5(n + 4)$. 🔘 6.EE.1.3

☐ $5n + 4$

☐ $5n + 20$

☐ $15 + 5n + 5$

☐ $5(n + 3) + 5$

☐ $5n + 54$

Solve & Discuss It!

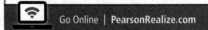

ACTIVITY

Write an expression equivalent to $x + 5 + 2x + 2$.

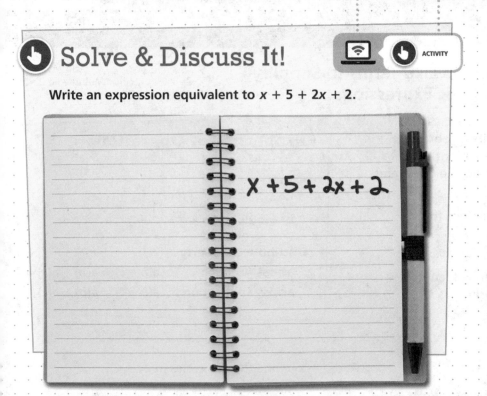

$$x + 5 + 2x + 2$$

Make Sense and Persevere Use what you know about algebraic expressions and properties of operations to make sense of the problem.

I can...
combine like terms in algebraic expressions.

MAFS.6.EE.1.3 Apply the properties of operations to generate equivalent expressions. ...
Also 6.EE.1.4
MAFS.K12.MP.1.1, MP.3.1, MP.6.1, MP.7.1

Focus on math practices

Be Precise How do you know that the expression you wrote is equivalent to $x + 5 + 2x + 2$?

EXAMPLE 1 **Combine Like Terms to Simplify Algebraic Expressions**

Scan for Multimedia

Terms that have the same variable part, such as y and $2y$, are like terms. To simplify algebraic expressions, use properties of operations to write equivalent expressions that have no like terms and no parentheses.

Write simplified equivalent expressions for $x + x + x$ and $2y - y$.

> **Use Structure** You can use the Identity Property of Multiplication to write x as $1x$.

Properties of Operations

Identity Property
    of Addition $a + 0 = a = 0 + a$
    of Multiplication $a \times 1 = a = 1 \times a$

Distributive Property
    across Addition $a(b + c) = a(b) + a(c)$
    across Subtraction $a(b - c) = a(b) - a(c)$

Combine the like terms in $x + x + x$.

$x + x + x$ .... All three terms are like terms.

$= 1x + 1x + 1x$ .... Identity Property of Multiplication

$= (1 + 1 + 1)x$ .... Distributive Property

$= 3x$

> Add the coefficients, and write the common variable.

So, $3x$ is equivalent to $x + x + x$.

Combine the like terms in $2y - y$.

$2y - y$ .... $2y$ and y are like terms.

$= 2y - 1y$ .... Identity Property of Multiplication

$= (2 - 1)y$ .... Distributive Property

$= 1y$ or y

> Subtract the coefficients, and write the common variable.

So, y is equivalent to $2y - y$.

✓ Try It!

Simplify the expression $4z - z + z - 2z$.

$4z - z + z - 2z$

$= 4z - 1z + \boxed{} - \boxed{}$ .... Use the Identity Property of Multiplication.

$= (4 - 1 + \boxed{} - \boxed{})\boxed{}$ .... Use the Distributive Property.

$= \boxed{}$

The simplified expression is $\boxed{}$.

Convince Me! How do you know that the expression $2x + 4y$ is not equivalent to $6xy$?

EXAMPLE **2**

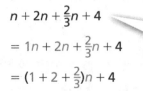 Simplify Algebraic Expressions with Fractions

A new hiking trail includes three sections of an old trail. There is a flat section, a hilly section, and a winding section. The park ranger marked the sections of the trail in relation to the length of the flat stretch of the trail, which is *n* kilometers. What is the simplified expression that describes the length of the new trail?

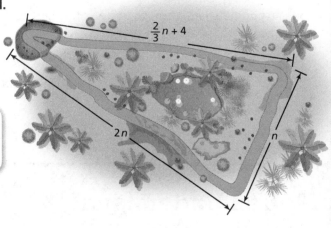

$n + 2n + \frac{2}{3}n + 4$

> Write an expression that represents the total length of the trail and simplify.

$= 1n + 2n + \frac{2}{3}n + 4$

$= (1 + 2 + \frac{2}{3})n + 4$

$= 3\frac{2}{3}n + 4$

$3\frac{2}{3}n + 4$ is equivalent to $n + 2n + \frac{2}{3}n + 4$.

Try It!

Park rangers add another section to the trail, represented by the expression $\frac{1}{2}n + n + \frac{1}{2}$. Write an expression for the new total length of the trail. Then write a simplified equivalent expression.

 EXAMPLE **3** Simplify Algebraic Expressions with Parentheses and Decimals

This summer Vanna wants to charge 2.5 times as much for mowing and raking, but her expenses ($10 per weekend) will also increase 2.5 times. The expression below can be used to find how much Vanna will make this summer mowing and raking *x* lawns in a weekend.

$2.5(20.50x + 5.50x - 10)$

How can you use properties of operations to write a simplified equivalent expression without parentheses?

Use the Distributive Property.

$2.5(20.50x + 5.50x - 10) = 2.5(26x - 10)$

$= 2.5(26x) - 2.5(10)$

$= 65x - 25$

> Simplifying expressions can make the expressions easier to evaluate.

$65x - 25$ is equivalent to $2.5(20.50x + 5.50x - 10)$.

Try It!

Suppose Vanna increases her rate by 3.5 times and her expenses also increase by 3.5 times this summer. Write two equivalent expressions to represent how much she can earn mowing and raking grass.

You can combine like terms to write equivalent expressions. Like terms have the same variable part.

$2x + 6 + 5x + 4$ ···················· Identify like terms.

$= 2x + 5x + 6 + 4$ ··············· Commutative Property of Addition

$= 7x + 10$

$2x + 6 + 5x + 4 = 7x + 10$

Do You Understand?

1. **? Essential Question** How can you simplify algebraic expressions?

2. Explain how you know which terms to combine when combining like terms.

3. **Construct Arguments** Explain why the expression $2y - y$ can be written as y.

4. Explain why the expressions $\frac{1}{2}x + \frac{1}{2}x$ and x are equivalent.

5. **Critique Reasoning** Henry wrote $4z^2 - z^2$ as 4. Are $4z^2 - z^2$ and 4 equivalent expressions? Explain.

Do You Know How?

In 6–15, simplify each expression.

6. $x + x + x + x$

7. $4y - y$

8. $7y - 4.5 - 6y$

9. $4x + 2 - \frac{1}{2}x$

10. $3 + 3y - 1 + y$

11. $x + 6x$

12. $0.5w + 1.7w - 0.5$

13. $12\frac{1}{3}b + 6\frac{2}{3} - 10\frac{2}{3}b$

14. $\frac{3}{4}x + 2 + 3x - \frac{1}{2}$

15. $3.2x + 6.5 - 2.4x - 4.4$

Practice & Problem Solving

Scan for
Multimedia

Leveled Practice In **16–26**, combine like terms to simplify each expression.

16. $2.1x^2 + 3 - 0.5x^2 - 1$

$= ($ ☐ $x^2 - $ ☐ $x^2) + (3 - 1)$

$= $ ☐ $x^2 + $ ☐

17. $\frac{2}{3}n + 6 + 3n - \frac{2}{3}$

$= ($ ☐ $n + $ ☐ $n) + ($ ☐ $- $ ☐ $)$

$= $ ☐ $n + $ ☐

18. $5 + 3w + 3 - w$

19. $5w - 5w$

20. $2x + 5 + 3x + 6$

21. $\frac{3}{4}z^3 + 4 - \frac{1}{4}z^3$

22. $3.4m + 2.4m$

23. $4.2n + 5 - 3.2n$

24. $q^5 + q^5 + q^5$

25. $3x + \frac{1}{4} + 2y + \frac{1}{4} + 7x - y$

26. $1.5z^2 + 4.5 + 6z - 0.3 - 3z + z^2$

27. Use Structure Use the table at the right. Yolanda is planning a party that will take place in three rooms.

a. Write an expression that can be used to represent the total amount Yolanda will need to rent all three rooms and the sound system for t hours.

Room	Rental Fee (per hour)	Sound System Fee
1	$25	$15
2	$20	$10
3	$50	no charge

b. How can you use a property to write a simplified equivalent expression?

In 28–30, use the diagram at the right.

28. Write an algebraic expression for the perimeter of the swimming pool.

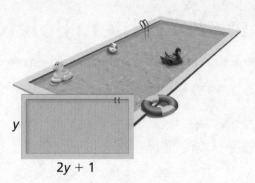

y

$2y + 1$

29. **Use Structure** Write a new expression equivalent to the expression you wrote for Exercise 28.

30. Justify that the two expressions are equivalent.

31. Rodney rewrote the expression $\frac{1}{2}(2x + 7)$ as $x + 3\frac{1}{2}$. Which property of operations did Rodney use?

32. **Construct Arguments** Annie said that she simplified the expression $6.5(x + 0.5x + 1)$ by writing the equivalent expression $6.5x + 3.25x + 6.5$. Do you agree? Explain.

33. **Critique Reasoning** Thea said that the expressions $4x - 3x + 2$ and $x + 2$ are equivalent. Is Thea correct? Explain.

34. **Higher Order Thinking** Write an equivalent expression for the expression shown below.

$$\frac{a}{3} + \frac{a}{3} + \frac{a}{3}$$

35. Select all expressions that are equivalent to $8x + 3 + 5x - 2x$. 🔵 6.EE.1.3

☐ $13x + 3 - 2x$

☐ $11x + 3x$

☐ $11 + 3x$

☐ $14x$

☐ $11x + 3$

36. Select which expression is equivalent to or NOT equivalent to the given expression. 🔵 6.EE.1.4

	Equivalent to $2x + 7 + 6x - x$	NOT Equivalent to $2x + 7 + 6x - x$
$2x + 13$	☐	☐
$7 + 7x$	☐	☐
$14x$	☐	☐
$7x + 7$	☐	☐

Go Online | PearsonRealize.com

? Topic Essential Question

What are expressions and how can they be written and evaluated?

Vocabulary Review

Complete each definition with a vocabulary word.

> **Vocabulary** algebraic expression   coefficient   exponent
> factor tree   like terms   variable

1. A(n) _____ tells the number of times the base is used as a factor.

2. A letter or symbol that represents an unknown quantity is a(n) _____.

3. A diagram that shows the prime factors of a composite number is a(n) _____.

Draw a line from each pair of numbers in Column A to the *least common multiple* (*LCM*) of the numbers in Column B.

Column A	Column B
4. 9, 6	36
5. 9, 12	56
6. 8, 7	18

7. Look at the variables in each expression below. Write **Y** if the terms of each expression are *like terms*. Write **N** if they are NOT *like terms*.

    a. $3a + 3z$ b. $\frac{x}{3} + \frac{x}{4}$ c. $4j - j + 3.8j$

Use Vocabulary in Writing

Explain one way to simplify the expression $4(3q - q)$. Use vocabulary words in your explanation.

Concepts and Skills Review

Understand and Represent Exponents

Quick Review

An exponent is a way to show repeated multiplication.

Example

Use an exponent to write the expression $6 \times 6 \times 6$. Then evaluate the expression.

6 is used as a factor 3 times.

6 is the base and 3 is the exponent.

$6 \times 6 \times 6 = 6^3 = 216$

Find 6^0.

A number with an exponent of 0 is always equal to 1.

$6^0 = 1$

Practice

Write each expression using an exponent.

1. $8 \times 8 \times 8 \times 8 \times 8 \times 8 \times 8$

2. 4

3. $10 \times 10 \times 10 \times 10$

Evaluate each expression.

4. 9^2

5. 99^1

6. $3,105^0$

7. 22^2

8. 2^7

9. 3^4

Find Greatest Common Factor and Least Common Multiple

Quick Review

You can use prime factorization to find the greatest common factor and the least common multiple of two numbers.

Example

Find the greatest common factor (GCF) and the least common multiple (LCM) of 12 and 6.

List the prime factors of both numbers.

12: ②× 2 ×③
6: ②×③   Identify the common factors, then multiply.

GCF: $2 \times 3 = 6$

12: ②×②× 3
6: 2 ×③   Identify the greatest number of times each factor appears, then multiply.

LCM: $2 \times 2 \times 3 = 12$

Practice

Find the GCF for each pair of numbers. Use the GCF and the Distributive Property to find the sum of each pair of numbers.

1. 30, 100

2. 8, 52

3. 28, 42

4. 37, 67

5. 12, 24

6. 8; 12

Find the LCM for each pair of numbers.

7. 4, 9

8. 3, 6

9. 8, 10

10. 3, 5

11. 12, 5

12. 4, 11

Go Online | PearsonRealize.com

Quick Review

Use the order of operations to evaluate numerical expressions.

Example

Evaluate the expression $3^2 + 2[(21 - 9) \div 4]$.

$3^2 + 2[(21 - 9) \div 4]$ .... Evaluate inside the parentheses.

$= 3^2 + 2[12 \div 4]$ .... Evaluate inside the brackets.

$= 3^2 + 2 \times 3$ .... Evaluate the power.

$= 9 + 2 \times 3$ .... Multiply.

$= 9 + 6$ .... Add.

$= 15$

The value of $3^2 + 2[(21 - 9) \div 4]$ is 15.

Practice

Evaluate each expression.

1. $80 - 4^2 \div 8$

2. $92.3 - (3.2 \div 0.4) \times 2^3$

3. $\left[(2^3 \times 2.5) \div \frac{1}{2}\right] + 120$

4. $[20 + (2.5 \times 3)] - 3^3$

5. $\left[(2 \times 10^0) \div \frac{1}{3}\right] + 8$

Quick Review

An algebraic expression can be written to represent a situation with an unknown quantity. Use a variable to represent the unknown quantity. An algebraic expression can be evaluated by substituting a value for the variable and performing the operations.

Example

Write an algebraic expression for 9 times the difference of 12 and *a* divided by 2. Then evaluate the expression for *a* = 4.

"9 times the difference of 12 and *a* divided by 2" is represented by $9 \times (12 - a) \div 2$.

Evaluate $9 \times (12 - a) \div 2$ when $a = 4$.

$9 \times (12 - a) \div 2$

$9 \times (12 - 4) \div 2$ ◁ Use substitution to replace the variable with its value.

$= 9 \times 8 \div 2$

$= 72 \div 2$

$= 36$

Practice

Write an algebraic expression to represent each situation.

1. 22 less than 5 times a number *f*

2. 48 times a number of game markers, *g*

3. A number of eggs, *e*, divided by 12

4. 3 times the sum of *m* and 7

Evaluate each expression for *n* = 7, *x* = 4, *y* = 8, and *z* = 1.

5. $12x - 7$

6. $x^2 \div y$

7. $5z + 3n - z^3$

8. $y^2 \div 2x + 3n - z$

Generate Equivalent Expressions

Quick Review

Equivalent expressions are expressions that have the same value. The properties of operations and substitution can be used to write and identify equivalent expressions.

Example

Are the expressions $5x + 20$, $5(x + 4)$, and $x + 4$ equivalent?

For algebraic expressions to be equivalent, each expression must name the same value no matter what value is substituted for the variable.

x	$5x + 20$	$5(x + 4)$	$x + 4$
1	25	25	5
2	30	30	6
3	35	35	7

Use the Distributive Property to write $5x + 20$ as $5(x + 4)$.

$$5x + 20 = 5 \cdot x + 5 \cdot 4$$
$$= 5(x + 4)$$

Properties of operations cannot be used to write $5x + 20$ or $5(x + 4)$ as $x + 4$.

$5x + 20$ and $5(x + 4)$ are equivalent expressions.

Practice

Complete the table. Then circle the expressions that are equivalent.

1.

y	$5(2.2y + 1) - 3$	$11y + 5 - y$	$11y + 2$
1			
2			
3			

In 2–4, write Yes or No to indicate whether the expressions are equivalent.

2. $10x - 3 + 2x - 5$ and $4(3x - 2)$

3. $3y + 3$ and $9\left(y + \frac{1}{3}\right)$

4. $6(3x + 1)$ and $9x + 6 + 9x$

In 5–7, use properties of operations to complete the equivalent expressions.

5. $2(x + 4)$ and _____ $x +$ _____

6. $5x - 45$ and $5($ _____ $-$ _____ $)$

7. $3(x + 7)$ and _____ $x +$ _____

Simplify Algebraic Expressions

Quick Review

Combine like terms to simplify algebraic expressions.

Example

Simplify the expression $3x + 7 + 6x$.

$3x + 7 + 6x$ .... Identify the like terms, $3x$ and $6x$.

$= 3x + 6x + 7$ .... Use the Commutative Property of Addition.

$= 9x + 7$ .... Simplify.

The expression $9x + 7$ is equivalent to $3x + 7 + 6x$.

Practice

Simplify each expression.

1. $9y + 4 - 6y$

2. $3x + 5 + 7x$

3. $8x + 13 - 3x + 9$

4. $y^2 + 3y^2$

5. $4x + 15 - 3x + 10$

6. $10x + 2x - 12x$

Go Online | PearsonRealize.com

Crisscrossed

Find each product or quotient. Write your answers in the cross-number puzzle below. Each digit and decimal point of your answer goes in its own box.

I can...
multiply and divide multi-digit decimals.

6.NS.2.3

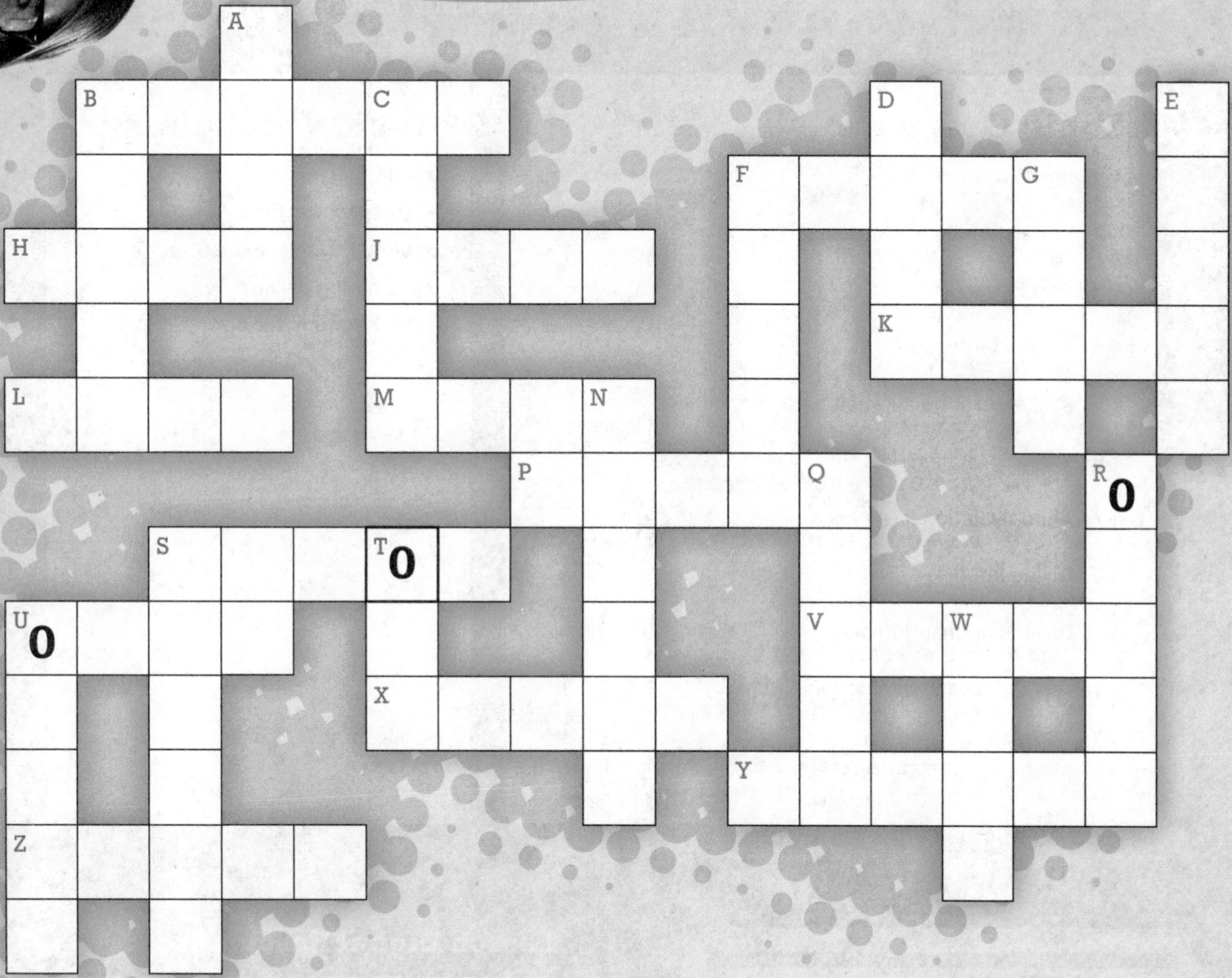

ACROSS

B 18.25 × 20.2

F 945.12 ÷ 6.6

H 7.11 ÷ 0.1

J 2.2 × 1.2

K 9.75 ÷ 1.2

L 64.2 ÷ 3

M 27.1 × 0.2

P 28.713 ÷ 0.3

S 95.3 × 0.02

U 0.009 ÷ 0.9

V 3.3456 ÷ 0.4

X 50.048 ÷ 0.08

Y 8.284 × 5.5

Z 19.698 ÷ 0.06

DOWN

A 240.5 ÷ 5

B 10.1 × 0.31

C 2.15 × 2.9

D 18.45 × 4

E 2.58 × 1.3

F 5.735 ÷ 0.5

G 5.45 × 0.4

N 62.54 ÷ 0.025

Q 0.742 ÷ 0.4

R 12.3 × 0.04

S 16.1 × 6.7

T 2.04 ÷ 3.4

U 3.3 × 0.07

W 8.85 ÷ 2.5

TOPIC 4

RATIONAL NUMBER OPERATIONS

? Topic Essential Question

How can the properties of operations be used to solve problems involving integers and rational numbers?

Topic Overview

Topic Vocabulary

- additive inverse
- complex fraction
- multiplicative inverse
- repeating decimal
- terminating decimal

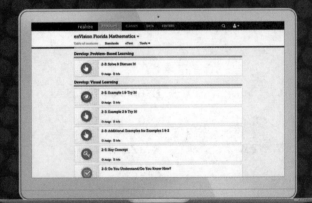

Lesson Digital Resources

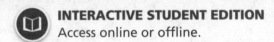

INTERACTIVE STUDENT EDITION
Access online or offline.

VISUAL LEARNING ANIMATION
Interact with visual learning animations.

ACTIVITY Use with *Solve & Discuss It, Explo* and *Explain It* activities, and to explore Exam

VIDEOS Watch clips to support *3-Act Mathematical Modeling Lessons* and *STEM F*

Go online | **PearsonRealize.com**

Win Some, Lose Some

▶ Win Some, Lose Some

Are you the kind of person who has a lot of knowledge about history, literature, or science? What about pop culture, music, sports, and current events? Some schools have an academic bowl team that competes in tournaments against other schools. The teams are made up of members with strengths in different subject areas.

In any quiz competition, it's important to understand the rules and scoring. Think about this during the 3-Act Mathematical Modeling lesson.

PRACTICE Practice what you've learned.

KEY CONCEPT Review important lesson content.

TUTORIALS Get help from *Virtual Nerd*, right when you need it.

GLOSSARY Read and listen to English/Spanish definitions.

MATH TOOLS Explore math with digital tools.

ASSESSMENT Show what you've learned.

GAMES Play Math Games to help you learn.

enVision® STEM Project

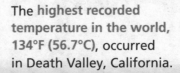

Did You Know?

The **lowest recorded temperature in the world**, –136°F (–93.2°C), occurred in Antarctica.

The **highest recorded temperature in the world**, 134°F (56.7°C), occurred in Death Valley, California.

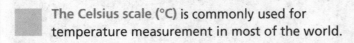

The **Celsius scale (°C)** is commonly used for temperature measurement in most of the world.

Only a small number of nations, including the United States, **regularly use the Fahrenheit scale (°F)**.

Windchill, based on the rate of heat loss from exposed skin, can make it feel colder outside than the actual air temperature indicates. Wind chills in some places of the world can **dip into the –100°F range**.

Your Task: How Cold is Too Cold?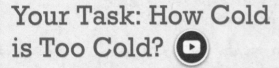

There are many regions of the world with cold temperatures and extreme conditions. How do the inhabitants of these regions adapt and thrive? Do conditions exist that make regions too cold for human living? You and your classmates will explore and describe the habitability of regions with low temperatures.

Review What You Know!

GET READY!

Vocabulary

Choose the best term from the box. Write it on the blank.

absolute value
Associative Property
Commutative Property
Distributive Property
integers
rational number

1. The _____ explains why $a \times b = b \times a$ and $a + b = b + a$.

2. The _____ of -6 is 6, because it is 6 units from zero on the number line.

3. The number $\frac{5}{3}$ is a _____ because 5 and 3 are integers and $3 \neq 0$.

4. The set of _____ consists of the counting numbers, their opposites, and zero.

5. The sum of $(a + b) + c$ is equal to the sum of $a + (b + c)$ as explained by the _____.

6. If you evaluate $n \times (y + z)$ by writing it as $(n \times y) + (n \times z)$, you have used the _____.

Add and Subtract Fractions and Decimals

Add or subtract.

7. $2\frac{1}{3} + 6\frac{3}{5}$

8. $9\frac{1}{10} - 4\frac{3}{4}$

9. $19.86 + 7.091$

10. $57 - 10.62$

Multiply and Divide Fractions and Decimals

Multiply or divide.

11. 4.08×29.7

12. $15,183.3 \div 473$

13. $\frac{15}{16} \times 9\frac{1}{5}$

14. $4\frac{7}{9} \div 1\frac{7}{12}$

15. Byron has $1\frac{7}{10}$ kilograms of black pepper. He uses $\frac{7}{8}$ of the pepper and splits it between 7 pepper shakers. How much pepper will be in each shaker?

Ⓐ $\frac{119}{80}$ kg

Ⓒ 1.4125 kg

Ⓑ $\frac{1}{8}$ kg

Ⓓ $\frac{17}{80}$ kg

Prepare for Reading Success

Use the following questions to help you understand the new ideas in Topic 4.

Questions Before Reading

What do I know about integers and rational numbers?

What do I know about fractions and decimals?

What does it mean when two things are opposites?
How can numbers be opposites?

Questions During Reading

Why might a number be positive or negative?

Who uses positive and negative numbers?
How are integers and rational numbers used in real life?

Where are opposite numbers located on a number line?

Questions After Reading

When might I use integers and rational numbers in real life?

Why is it important to know whether a number is positive or negative?

How is adding a positive number to a negative number different
from adding two positive numbers or two negative numbers?

 Solve & Discuss It! ACTIVITY

When preparing for a rocket launch, the mission control center uses the phrase "T minus" before liftoff.

...T minus 3, T minus 2, T minus 1, ...

After the rocket has launched, "T plus" is used while the rocket is in flight.

...T plus 1, T plus 2, T plus 3, ...

When does the rocket launch?
What could "T" represent?

Reasoning What integers can you use to represent this situation?

I can...
relate integers, their opposites, and their absolute values.

MAFS.7.NS.1.1a Describe situations in which opposite quantities combine to make 0.
MAFS.K12.MP1.1, MP2.1, MP.3.1, MP.4.1

Focus on math practices
Reasoning How are "T minus 4" and "T plus 4" related?

VISUAL LEARNING

EXAMPLE 1 ◉ **Combine Opposite Quantities to Make 0**

Scan for Multimedia

Alexis was shopping on the ground floor of the mall when she realized she had left her phone in her car. She walks down 6 floors to her car in the underground parking garage.

How far will Alexis walk to get back to the ground floor? Use integers to explain.

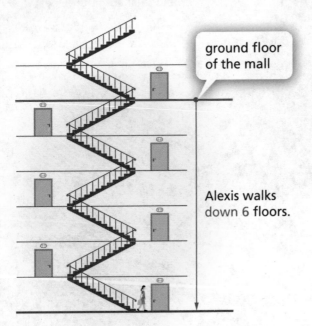

ground floor of the mall

Alexis walks down 6 floors.

Use integers on a number line to represent the situation.

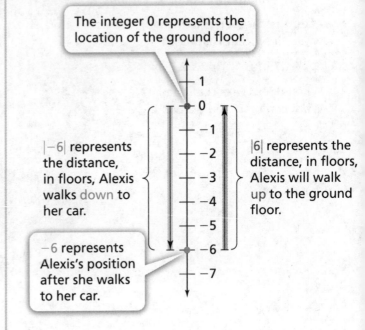

The integer 0 represents the location of the ground floor.

|−6| represents the distance, in floors, Alexis walks down to her car.

|6| represents the distance, in floors, Alexis will walk up to the ground floor.

−6 represents Alexis's position after she walks to her car.

$$|-6| = |6| = 6$$

−6 and 6 are opposites. Opposite quantities combine to make 0.

Alexis will walk the same distance, 6 floors, in the opposite direction to get back to the ground floor.

☑ Try It!

Xavier climbs 9 feet up into an apple tree. What integer represents the direction and how far he will climb to get back down to the ground? What does the integer 0 represent in this situation?

The integer ☐ represents Xavier's climb down.

The integer 0 represents ☐ .

Convince Me! How are the absolute values of opposite integers related?

Go Online | PearsonRealize.com

EXAMPLE **2** 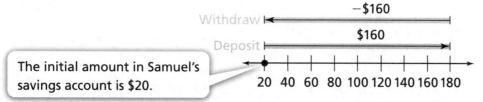 Combine Opposite Quantities ACTIVITY ASSESS

Samuel has $20 in his savings account before he makes a deposit of $160. After 2 weeks, he withdraws $160. How did Samuel's savings account balance change?

−$160
Withdraw

$160
Deposit

The initial amount in Samuel's savings account is $20.

20 40 60 80 100 120 140 160 180

The amounts deposited and withdrawn are opposite quantities and combine to make 0. Samuel's account balance did not change because the amounts deposited and withdrawn combine to make 0.

 **Try It!**

The temperature was 75°. At noon, the temperature increased 7°. By evening, the temperature decreased by 7°. How did the temperature change?

EXAMPLE **3** Represent Change Using Integers

One winter morning, the temperature was −2°C. By 11:00 A.M., the temperature had decreased by 3°. At 4:00 P.M., the temperature reached 0°C. What integer represents the temperature change from 11:00 A.M. to 4:00 P.M.?

7am	11am	4pm

Cloudy −2°C	Cloudy ?°C	Cloudy 0°C

Start at −2. The integer −3 represents the temperature decrease, so move 3 units left. The temperature has a change of −3.

Next, move 5 units right to show the temperature increase to 0°C. The temperature has a change of 5.

Increase of 5°

Decrease of 3°

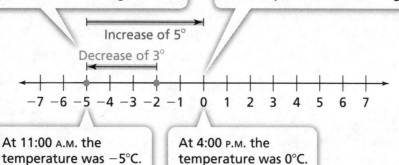

−7 −6 −5 −4 −3 −2 −1 0 1 2 3 4 5 6 7

At 11:00 A.M. the temperature was −5°C.

At 4:00 P.M. the temperature was 0°C.

The integer 5 represents the temperature change from 11:00 A.M. to 4:00 P.M.

 **Try It!**

Shaniqua has $45 in her wallet. She spends $4 on snacks and $8 on a movie ticket. What integer represents the change in the amount of money in Shaniqua's wallet? How much money does she have left?

An integer, n, and its opposite, $-n$, combine to make 0.

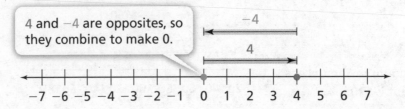

4 and -4 are opposites, so they combine to make 0.

Do You Understand?

1. **Essential Question** How are integers and their opposites related?

2. **Reasoning** In order for an atom to have a zero charge, every proton, which has a charge of $+1$, must be matched with an electron, which has a charge of -1. A helium atom has 2 protons and 2 electrons. Explain why a helium atom has a zero charge.

3. **Model with Math** Explain how to use a number line to show that opposite quantities combine to make 0.

Do You Know How?

4. Marcus dives from the surface of the ocean to a reef 18 meters below sea level. What integer represents Marcus's location relative to the surface? How far does Marcus have to go to return to the surface?

5. The temperature of the water in Emily's fish tank was 78°F on Sunday. The water temperature changed by $-3°$ on Monday, and then by $3°$ on Tuesday. What integer represents the temperature change of the water from Sunday to Tuesday? What was the water temperature on Tuesday?

6. The scores of players on a golf team are shown in the table. The team's combined score was 0. What was Travis's score?

Golfer	Score
CELIA	−3
JANINE	3
SAMI	1
TED	4
TRAVIS	

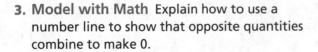

Practice & Problem Solving

Leveled Practice In 7–9, write the integer that represents the situation.

7. Max spent $53 and now has no money left. He had $ [   ] before his purchase.

8. The temperature was 8°F. It dropped so that the temperature was 0°F.

   [   ] °F represents the change in temperature.

9. An airplane descended 4,000 feet before landing. The integer that represents how many feet the airplane was above the ground before

   its descent is [   ] .

10. Carolyn says that point A and point B represent opposite integers.

    a. What is the opposite of the integer represented by point A?
       By point B?

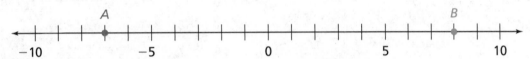

    b. **Construct Arguments** Do you agree with Carolyn? Explain.

11. A football team lost 9 yards during a play. The team had a combined gain or loss of 0 yards after the next play. What integer represents the yards gained or lost on the next play? Show this on the number line.

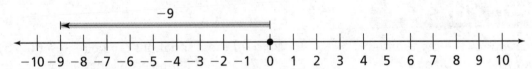

12. A roller coaster car goes above and below ground. Use the number line to show its changes in height. What is the height of the car at the end of the ride?

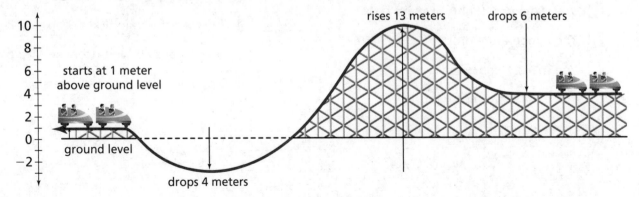

13. Dimitri is buying a car. He chooses Option 1 to add a new sound system to his car. What integer represents the change from the base price of the car to its final price?

Used Car
DEALER
Price Sticker

	Base Price
Sale	−$700.00
Opt.1	+$1,400.00
Markdown	−$1,100.00
	?

14. **Make Sense and Persevere** What values do x and y have if $|x| = 16$, $|y| = 16$, and when x and y are combined they equal 0? Explain your reasoning.

15. Write a situation that can be represented by the opposite of −42.

16. **Higher Order Thinking** Three friends all live on the same street that runs west to east. Beth lives 5 blocks from Ann. Carl lives 2 blocks from Beth. If the street is represented by a number line and Ann's house is located at 0, what are the possible locations for Carl's house? Assume that each unit on the number line represents 1 block.

Assessment Practice

17. Which of these situations can be represented with an integer that when combined with −9 makes 0? Select all that apply.
    🟦 7.NS.1.1a

    ☐ You walk down 9 flights of stairs.

    ☐ You climb up 9 flights of stairs.

    ☐ The temperature drops 9°F.

    ☐ You spend $9 on a book.

    ☐ You earn $9 from your job.

18. Which of these situations can be represented by the opposite of 80? Select all that apply.
    🟦 7.NS.1.1a

    ☐ An airplane descends 80 m.

    ☐ An elevator ascends 80 m.

    ☐ The cost of a train ticket drops by $80.

    ☐ You remove 80 songs from an MP3 player.

    ☐ Suzy's grandmother is 80 years old.

Solve & Discuss It!  ACTIVITY

Calvin wants to customize his surfboard so that it is wider than the 82 model but narrower than the 92 model. What measurement could be the width of his surfboard? Explain.

I can...
recognize rational numbers and write them in decimal form.

MAFS.7.NS.1.2d Convert a rational number to a decimal using long division; know that the decimal form of a rational number terminates in 0s or eventually repeats.

MAFS.K12.MP.1.1, MP.2.1, MP.6.1, MP.7.1

Be Precise
Between which two numbers is the custom width located?

Model	82	92	102
	$22\frac{1}{2}$" wide	$23\frac{1}{4}$" wide	24" wide
	$3\frac{1}{4}$" thick	$3\frac{1}{2}$" thick	$3\frac{5}{8}$" thick

Focus on math practices

Use Structure Lindy's surfboard is $23\frac{1}{3}$ inches wide. Between which two surfboard models is her custom surfboard's width? How do you know?

EXAMPLE **1** 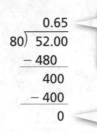 **Write Rational Numbers in Decimal Form: Terminating Decimals**

Scan for Multimedia

Juanita is reporting on pitching statistics. Pedro's fastball statistic is $\frac{52}{80}$. How can Juanita write the fastball statistic in decimal form?

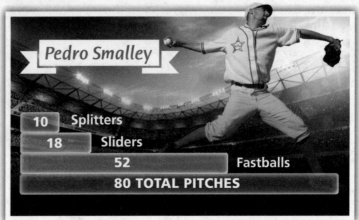

Pedro Smalley

10	Splitters
18	Sliders
52	Fastballs
80 TOTAL PITCHES	

Make Sense and Persevere
How can you write a rational number as a decimal?

Make a bar diagram to show how the quantities are related.

| 52 Fastballs |
| 80 TOTAL PITCHES |

$\frac{52}{80}$

Divide the numerator by the denominator to convert the rational number $\frac{52}{80}$ to decimal form.

$$
\begin{array}{r}
0.65 \\
80\overline{)52.00} \\
-480 \\
\hline
400 \\
-400 \\
\hline
0
\end{array}
$$

A **terminating decimal** is a decimal that ends in zero.

The remainder is 0, so the decimal form of $\frac{52}{80}$ is a terminating decimal.

Juanita can write $\frac{52}{80}$ as 0.65.

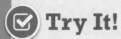 **Try It!**

In the next several games, the pitcher threw a total of 384 pitches and used a fastball 240 times. What decimal should Juanita use to update her report?

| 240 Fastballs |
| 384 TOTAL PITCHES |

Juanita should use the decimal ☐ to update her report.

Convince Me! How do you know that the answer is a terminating decimal?

$$
\begin{array}{r}
\square\ \square\ \square\ \square\ .\ \square \\
384\overline{)2\ 4\ 0\ .\ 0\ 0\ } \\
-2\ 3\ 0\ 4 \\
\hline
9\ 6\ 0 \\
-7\ 6\ 8 \\
\hline
\square\ \square\ \square\ \square \\
-1\ 9\ 2\ 0 \\
\hline
\square
\end{array}
$$

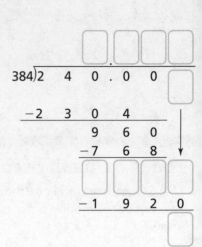

A class votes on whether to change their school mascot. How can you express the number of students in favor of a new mascot in decimal form?

In a class of **18** students, **5** voted to change their mascot.

Divide to write $\frac{5}{18}$ in decimal form.

```
      0.277
18)5.000
   -3 6
     1 4 0
    -1 2 6
       1 4 0
      -1 2 6
         1 4
```

A **repeating decimal** has a decimal expansion that repeats the same digit, or block of digits, without end.

The products and differences repeat. The remainder will never be 0.

The decimal form of $\frac{5}{18}$ is 0.277... or $0.2\overline{7}$.

The ... means the decimal does not terminate.

A line over one or more digits indicates that those digits repeat.

 Try It!

What is the decimal form of $\frac{100}{3}$, $\frac{100}{5}$, and $\frac{100}{6}$? Determine whether each decimal repeats or terminates.

EXAMPLE 3 **Recognize Rational Numbers in Decimal Form**

Explain whether each of the following is a rational number.

a. −6.382

The decimal terminates, so this is a rational number.

b. $1.539\overline{81}$

The digits 8 and 1 repeat infinitely, so this is a rational number.

c. 0.43524982...

The decimal does not terminate and the digits do not repeat, so this is **NOT** a rational number.

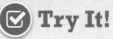 **Try It!**

Is $-0.\overline{3}$ a rational number? Is 3.14144144414444... a rational number? Explain your reasoning.

To convert from the fraction form of a rational number to its decimal form, divide the numerator by the denominator. The decimal form of a rational number either terminates in 0s or eventually repeats.

Terminating Decimal	Repeating Decimal
$\frac{3}{4}$	$\frac{1}{6}$
$\begin{array}{r} 0.75 \\ 4{\overline{)3.00}} \end{array}$	$\begin{array}{r} 0.1\overline{6} \\ 6{\overline{)1.00}} \end{array}$

Do You Understand?

1. **? Essential Question** How are rational numbers written as decimals?

2. **Reasoning** How can you use division to find the decimal equivalent of a rational number?

3. **Be Precise** What is the difference between a terminating decimal and a repeating decimal?

Do You Know How?

4. What is the decimal equivalent of each rational number?

   a. $\frac{7}{20}$

   b. $-\frac{23}{20}$

   c. $\frac{1}{18}$

   d. $-\frac{60}{22}$

5. There are 5,280 feet in a mile. What part of a mile, in decimal form, will you drive until you reach the exit?

   EXIT 1,000 FEET

Practice & Problem Solving

Leveled Practice In **6–8**, write the decimal equivalent for each rational number. Use a bar over any repeating digits.

6. $\frac{2}{3}$

7. $\frac{3}{11}$

8. $8\frac{4}{9}$

---

9. Is $1.02\overline{27}$ a rational number? Explain.

10. Which should Aaron use to convert a fraction to a decimal?

Ⓐ numerator$\overline{)\text{denominator}}$

Ⓑ $\frac{\text{denominator}}{\text{numerator}} \cdot 100$

Ⓒ denominator$\overline{)\text{numerator}}$

Ⓓ $\frac{\text{numerator}}{\text{denominator}} \cdot 100$

---

11. Is the fraction $\frac{1}{3}$ equivalent to a terminating decimal or a decimal that does not terminate?

12. Determine whether the given number belongs to each set.

	Whole Numbers	Integers	Rational Numbers
−34			

---

13. Ariel incorrectly says that $2\frac{5}{8}$ is the same as 2.58.

a. Convert $2\frac{5}{8}$ to a decimal.

b. What was Ariel's likely error?

14. Use Structure Consider the rational number $\frac{3}{11}$.

a. What are the values of a and b in $a\overline{)b}$ when you use division to find the decimal form?

b. What is the decimal form for $\frac{3}{11}$?

---

15. At a grocery store, Daniel wants to buy $3\frac{1}{5}$ lb of ham. What decimal should the digital scale show?

Write $3\frac{1}{5}$ as a fraction and then divide.

The scale should read ☐ lb.

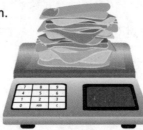

16. **Reasoning** At a butcher shop, Hilda bought beef and pork. She left with $18\frac{8}{25}$ pounds of meat. Express the number of pounds of pork she bought using a decimal.

17. **Be Precise** Is 9.373 a repeating decimal? Is it rational? Explain your reasoning.

18. **Reasoning** Aiden has one box that is $3\frac{3}{11}$ feet tall and a second box that is 3.27 feet tall. If he stacks the boxes, about how tall will the stack be?

19. You are adding air to a tire. The air pressure in the tire should be $32\frac{27}{200}$ pounds per square inch. What decimal should you watch for on the digital pressure gauge?

20. **Higher Order Thinking** Dion has a pizza with a diameter of $10\frac{1}{3}$ in. Is the square box shown big enough to fit the pizza inside? Justify your answer.

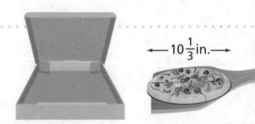

←—10$\frac{1}{3}$in.—→

←—— 10.38 in. ——→

Assessment Practice

21. Which of the following mixed numbers has the same decimal value as $110\frac{147}{168}$? 🔵 7.NS.1.2d

    Ⓐ $110\frac{49}{56}$ Ⓑ $110\frac{170}{180}$ Ⓒ $110\frac{56}{72}$ Ⓓ $110\frac{247}{268}$

22. Select all the true statements about the negative fractions $-\frac{4}{5}$ and $-\frac{5}{6}$. 🔵 7.NS.1.2d

    ☐ $-\frac{4}{5}$ can be expressed as a repeating decimal.

    ☐ $-\frac{5}{6}$ can be expressed as a repeating decimal.

    ☐ Both fractions can be expressed as repeating decimals.

    ☐ The digit that repeats is 3.

    ☐ The digit that repeats is 8.

Explore It!

ACTIVITY

Rain increases the height of water in a kiddie pool, while evaporation decreases the height. The pool water level is currently 2 inches above the fill line.

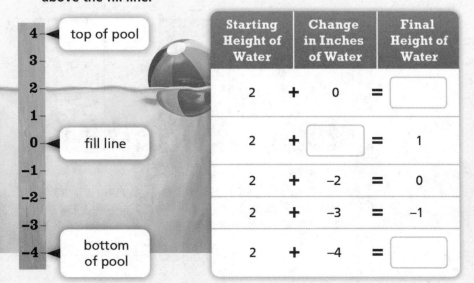

Starting Height of Water		Change in Inches of Water		Final Height of Water
2	+	0	=	
2	+		=	1
2	+	−2	=	0
2	+	−3	=	−1
2	+	−4	=	

4 — top of pool
3 —
2 —
1 —
0 — fill line
−1 —
−2 —
−3 —
−4 — bottom of pool

I can...
add integers.

MAFS. 7.NS.1.1b Understand $p + q$ as the number located a distance $|q|$ from p, in the positive or negative direction depending on whether q is positive or negative. Show that a number and it's opposite have a sum of 0 (are additive inverses). Interpret sums of rational numbers by describing real-world contexts. Also 7.NS.1.1d

MAFS.K12.MP2.1, MP.3.1, MP.4.1, MP.5.1, MP.7.1

A. Look for patterns in the equations in the table so you can fill in the missing numbers. Describe any relationships you notice.

B. Will the sum of 2 and (−6) be a positive or negative number? Explain.

Focus on math practices

Look for Relationships Suppose the water level of the pool started at 2 inches below the fill line. Make a table to show the starting height of the water, the change in inches, and the new final height of the water.

VISUAL LEARNING
 ASS

EXAMPLE 1 **Add Two Negative Integers**

Scan for
Multimedia

Nita wants to straighten a photo.
She uses an app to adjust the tilt.
What was the total tilt adjustment?

> **Reasoning** Why is the total tilt adjustment negative?

Set at 0.

Adjust by
−4 degrees.

Adjust by another
−6 degrees.

Use a number line to represent the total tilt adjustment.

> Start at 0.
> Move 4 units
> left to show
> an adjustment
> of −4.

> Then move 6 units left to show
> an adjustment of −6. The total
> adjustment was −10.

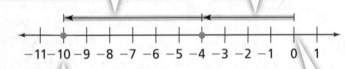

> The sum of −4 and −6 is located
> 6 units to the left of −4.

> The tilt starts
> at 0 degrees.

Add integers to find the total tilt adjustmen

$$-4 + (-6)$$

Because you moved 4 units and then
6 units in the **same direction** on the
number line, **add** the absolute values
to find the amount of tilt.

$$|-4| + |-6|$$
$$4 + 6 = 10$$

> 10 represents the
> amount of tilt.

Because you moved to the **left** twice,
the sum is negative.

$$-4 + (-6) = -10$$

> Both adjustments
> are negative, so
> the tilt is negative.

The total tilt adjustment was −10.

✅ Try It!

Dana recorded a temperature drop of 2° and a second temperature drop
of 3°. What is the total change in temperature?

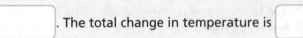

☐ + ☐ = ☐

The sign of the sum is ☐ . The total change in temperature is ☐° .

Convince Me! Would the sum of two positive integers be positive or negative? Explain.

EXAMPLE **2** **Add Integers with Different Signs** ACTIVITY ASSESS

Kara entered her chili recipe into the neighborhood cook-off. Nine judges rated each recipe with a thumbs up (+ 1) or thumbs down (−1). What was the final rating for Kara's recipe?

Reasoning There were more thumbs-down votes, so the final rating is negative.

Use a number line to represent Kara's final rating.

Start at 0. Move 5 units left for −5. Move 4 units right for 4. The final rating is −1.

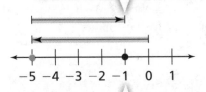

The sum of −5 and 4 is located 4 units to the right of −5.

Add integers to find Kara's final rating.

$-5 + 4$

Because you moved in **different directions** on the number line, **subtract** the absolute values.

$|-5| - |4|$

$5 - 4 = 1$

There is 1 more thumbs down vote than thumbs up.

Because you moved a **greater distance** to the left than to the right, the sum is negative.

$-5 + 4 = -1$

The sum is negative because $|-5|$ is greater than $|4|$.

The final rating for Kara's recipe was −1.

EXAMPLE **3** **Identify Additive Inverses and Opposite Integers**

Playing golf, Mike got a +2 on the first hole and − 2 on the second hole. What is his combined score for the first two holes?

$2 + (-2)$

$|2| = 2$ and $|-2| = 2$

$2 - 2 = 0$

So, $2 + (-2) = 0$.

When the signs of the addends are different, subtract the absolute values.

Two numbers that have a sum of 0 are called **additive inverses**, or opposites.

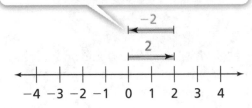

Mike's combined score for the first two holes is 0.

☑ **Try It!**

Find the sum for each expression.

a. $-66 + 42$ b. $-57 + 57$ c. $29 + (-28)$

When adding integers with the **same** sign, find the **sum** of the absolute values.

$(-36) + (-12)$

$|-36| = 36$ and $|-12| = 12$
$36 + 12 = 48$

So, $(-36) + (-12) = -48$ | Use the **same** sign as the addends.

When adding integers with **different** signs, find the **difference** of the absolute values.

$18 + (-14)$

$|18| = 18$ and $|-14| = 14$
$18 - 14 = 4$

So, $18 + (-14) = 4$ | Use the sign of the greater absolute value.

Do You Understand?

1. **? Essential Question** How do you use what you know about absolute value to add integers?

2. **Reasoning** How can you tell the sign of the sum of a positive and negative integer without doing any calculations?

3. **Model with Math** How would you use a number line to determine the sum of two negative integers?

Do You Know How?

4. Sarah bought a bike that cost $260. She had a coupon that was worth $55 off the cost of any bike. Use the expression $260 + (-55)$ to find how much Sarah paid for her bike.

5. A shark is swimming 60 feet below the surface of the ocean. There is a fish that is 25 feet deeper in the water. Use the expression $(-60) + (-25)$ to describe the fish's location relative to the surface of the ocean.

60 feet

25 feet

6. The high temperature one day was 30°F. Then the temperature dropped 23 degrees during the night. Does the expression $30 + (-23)$ represent the temperature at night? Explain.

Practice & Problem Solving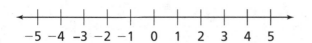

Leveled Practice For 7–9, use a number line to help find the sum.

7. $5 + (-3)$ is [ ] units from 5, in the [ ] direction.

Use the number line to find $5 + (-3)$.

```
<--+--+--+--+--+--+--+--+--+--+--+-->
  -5 -4 -3 -2 -1  0  1  2  3  4  5
```

8. $-1 + (-3)$ is [ ] units from -1, in the [ ] direction.

```
<--+--+--+--+--+--+--+--+--+--+--+-->
  -5 -4 -3 -2 -1  0  1  2  3  4  5
```

9. In City A, the temperature rises 9° from 8 A.M. to 9 A.M. Then the temperature drops 8° from 9 A.M. to 10 A.M. In City B, the temperature drops 5° from 8 A.M. to 9 A.M. Then the temperature drops 4° from 9 A.M. to 10 A.M.

[ ]   [ ]

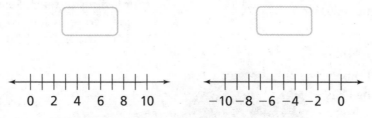

```
<--+-+-+-+-+-+-+-+-+-+-->        <--+-+-+-+-+-+-+-+-+-+-->
   0   2   4   6   8  10         -10 -8  -6  -4  -2   0
```

a. What expression represents the change in temperature for City A?

b. What integer represents the change in temperature for City A?

c. What expression represents the change in temperature for City B?

d. What integer represents the change in temperature for City B?

e. Which city has the greater change in temperature from 8 A.M. to 10 A.M.?

10. An airplane flying at an altitude of 30,000 feet flies up to avoid a storm. Immediately after passing the storm, the airplane returns to its original altitude.

a. What integer represents the airplane's change in altitude to avoid the storm?

b. What integer represents the airplane's change in altitude immediately after passing the storm?

c. Use Appropriate Tools Draw a number line to represent the airplane's change in altitude.

The airplane flies up to 38,000 feet to avoid a storm.

```
<--+--+--+--+--+--+--+--+--+--+-->
   30,000      34,000      38,000
```
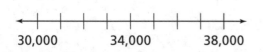

11. A deep-sea diver dives 81 feet from the surface. He then dives 14 more feet. The diver's depth can be represented by $-81 + (-14)$. What is the diver's present location?

12. Rena's rowboat drifts 23 feet from shore, followed by 9 more feet. The rowboat's current position can be represented by $-23 + (-9)$. What integer represents the rowboat's position?

13. Critique Reasoning A submarine traveling 200 meters below the surface of the ocean increases its depth by 45 meters. Adam says that the new location of the submarine is -155 meters. Describe an error Adam could have made that would result in the answer he gave.

14. Kim has $45 to spend for a day at the zoo. She pays $17 for admission, $8 for lunch, and $4 for a snack.

   a. Model with Math Use integers to write an addition expression that represents the amount of money Kim has left.

   b. Kim goes to the gift shop and finds a T-shirt she likes for $19. Does she have enough money to buy the T-shirt? Explain.

15. Higher Order Thinking Samantha has $300 for guitar lessons to learn her favorite song. Mrs. Jones charges $80 per lesson and requires three lessons to teach Samantha the song. Mr. Beliz charges $62 per lesson and will require four lessons to teach Samantha the song. Use integers to represent what each teacher charges. Which is the better deal for Samantha?

Assessment Practice

16. A fish swims at 10 ft below sea level, and then swims another 10 ft deeper to avoid a shark. Write an addition expression that represents this situation. 🔊 7.NS.1.1b

17. The temperature drops 10 degrees and then rises 10 degrees. Write an addition expression that represents this situation. 🔊 7.NS.1.1b

Solve & Discuss It!

ACTIVITY

A library database shows the total number of books checked out at any given time as a negative number. What are the possible numbers of books that were checked out and checked in on Monday? Explain.

MONDAY
Morning (–37)
Evening (–45)

Make Sense and Persevere How can you use the data to understand what happened during the day?

Go Online | PearsonRealize.com

I can...
subtract integers.

MAFS.7.NS.1.1c Understand subtraction of rational numbers as adding the additive inverse, $p - q = p + (-q)$. Show that the distance between two rational numbers on the number line is the absolute value of their difference, and apply this principle in real-world contexts. Also 7.NS.1.1d

MAFS.K12.MP.1.1, MP.1.2, MP.1.3

Focus on math practices

Reasoning Suppose the library database showed 0 for Monday evening. What do you know about the number of books checked out and checked in that day?

? Essential Question How is subtracting integers related to adding integers?

VISUAL LEARNING   ASS

 EXAMPLE 1 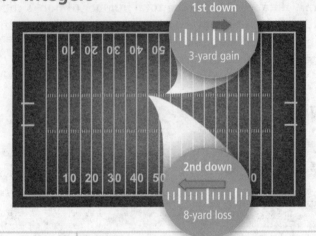 **Subtract Positive Integers**

Scan for Multimedia

A football team gains 3 yards on first down. On second down, they lose 8 yards. What is the total change in yards after the first two downs?

Look for Relationships You can use what you know about adding integers to subtract integers.

1st down
3-yard gain

2nd down
8-yard loss

Use a number line to represent the team's total change in yards.

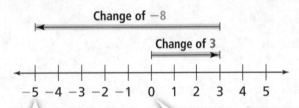

Change of −8

Change of 3

−5 −4 −3 −2 −1 0 1 2 3 4 5

The team's final position represents a 5-yard loss.

0 represents the team's starting position.

Use a subtraction expression to represent the teams' change in yards.

$3 - 8$

$= 3 + (-8)$

Subtraction is the same as adding the opposite. To subtract 8, add its opposite, −8.

Now add.

$|3| = 3$ and $|-8| = 8$

$8 - 3 = 5$

$3 - 8 = -5$

The total change in yards after the first two downs is represented by −5.

☑ Try It!

On the next play, the team gained 5 yards and then lost 6 yards. What is the total change in yards?

$5 - \boxed{}$

$= 5 + \boxed{}$

$= \boxed{}$

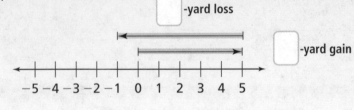

$\boxed{}$-yard loss

$\boxed{}$-yard gain

−5 −4 −3 −2 −1 0 1 2 3 4 5

The total change in yards is $\boxed{}$, so they had a total loss of $\boxed{}$ yard.

Convince Me! Is the additive inverse of an integer always negative? Explain.

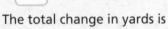

EXAMPLE **2** **Subtract Integers with Different Signs**

  ACTIVITY ASSESS

Ian's football team lost 2 yards on a running play. Then they received a 5-yard penalty. What is the team's total change in yards?

Write a subtraction expression to represent the change in yards.

$-2 - 5$

$= (-2) + (-5)$ ◀ Write an equivalent addition expression.

Add.

$|-2| = 2$ and $|-5| = 5$

$2 + 5 = 7$

$(-2) + (-5) = -7$

$-2 - 5 = -7$

> Move 5 units to the left from −2.

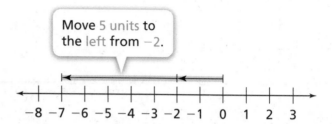

The team's total change in yards is represented by -7, so they lost 7 yards.

EXAMPLE **3** **Subtract Negative Integers**

Find $-7 - (-8)$.

Write $-7 - (-8)$ as an equivalent addition expression. Then add.

$-7 + (8)$

$|-7| = 7$ and $|8| = 8$ ◀ The signs of the addends are different, so find the difference of the absolute values. The sum has the same sign as the greater absolute value.

$8 - 7 = 1$

$-7 + (8) = 1$

$-7 - (-8) = 1$

> Subtracting −8 is the same as adding the opposite of −8, or +8.

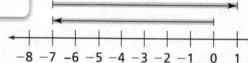

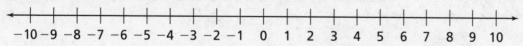 **Try It!**

Subtract. Use a number line to help you find the answer.

a. $-4 - 6$ **b.** $-6 - (-4)$ **c.** $4 - (-6)$

d. $6 - 4$ **e.** $4 - 6$ **f.** $-4 - (-6)$

When subtracting integers, such as $a - b$, you can use the additive inverse to write subtraction as an equivalent addition expression.

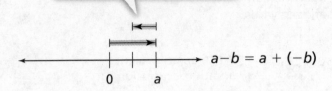

Subtracting b is the same as adding the opposite of b.

$$a - b = a + (-b)$$

Do You Understand?

1. **Essential Question** How is subtracting integers related to adding integers?

2. **Reasoning** Explain how to simplify the expression $-98 - 31$ using the additive inverse.

3. **Model with Math** How can you use a number line to represent the subtraction between two integers?

Do You Know How?

4. It was 12°C when Preston got home from school. The weather report shows a storm front moving in that will drop the temperature by 17°C. What is the expected temperature?

5. Complete the equation.

$$-67 - \boxed{} = 0$$

6. Find the difference.

   a. $41 - 275$

   b. $-15 - 47$

   c. $-72 - (-151)$

   d. $612 - (-144)$

Practice & Problem Solving

Leveled Practice In 7–8, fill in the boxes to solve.

7. What subtraction expression does the number line model show?

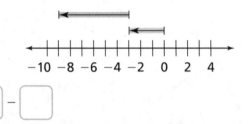

☐ – ☐

8. What is the value of the expression $-9 - (-5)$?

$$-9 - (-5)$$

$$= -9 \ \boxed{} \ 5$$

$$= \boxed{}$$

9. The temperature at the beginning of the day was 6°F. The temperature dropped 9°F by the end of the day. Use the number line to find the temperature at the end of the day.

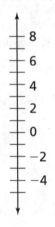

10. Murphy and Naryam do their math homework together. When they find $9 - (-8)$, they get different answers. Murphy claims the difference is 17. Naryam claims the difference is -1.

a. Who is correct?

b. What error likely led to the incorrect answer?

11. The news reports that today's high temperature is 16°F colder than yesterday's high temperature. Yesterday's high temperature was -2°F.

a. Write an expression to represent today's high temperature.

b. Reasoning Is today's high temperature positive or negative? Why?

12. Max sprints forward 10 feet and then stops and sprints back 15 feet. Use subtraction to explain where Max is relative to where he started.

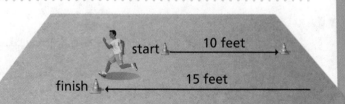

13. Higher Order Thinking Use the number line at the right.

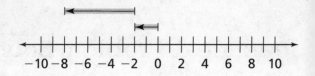

a. What subtraction equation does the number line represent?

b. Use the number line to represent a different subtraction equation that has the same difference shown in the number line. Write the subtraction equation.

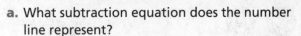

---

14. A crane lifts a pallet of concrete blocks 8 feet from the back of a truck. The truck drives away and the crane lowers the pallet 13 feet. What is the final position of the pallet relative to where it started in the back of the truck?

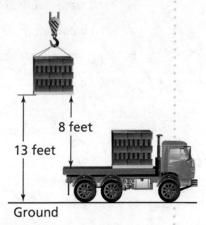

8 feet

13 feet

Ground

15. Make Sense and Persevere At its highest point, the elevation of a county is 5,762 feet above sea level. At its lowest point, the elevation of the county is 9 feet below sea level.

a. Write an expression using integers to represent the difference between the elevations.

b. Will the answer be written as a positive or negative integer?

c. What is the difference between the highest and lowest points of the county?

---

16. Which number line model shows the subtraction 2 − 4? 🅣 7.NS.1.1c

Ⓐ
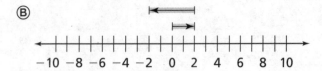

Ⓒ
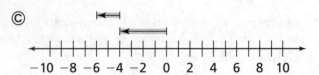

Ⓑ
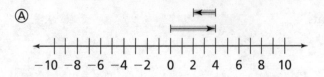

Ⓓ
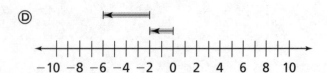

Solve & Discuss It!  ACTIVITY

Malik hikes Castle Trail from point A to point B. The elevation at point A is below sea level. What are possible beginning and ending elevations of Malik's hike?

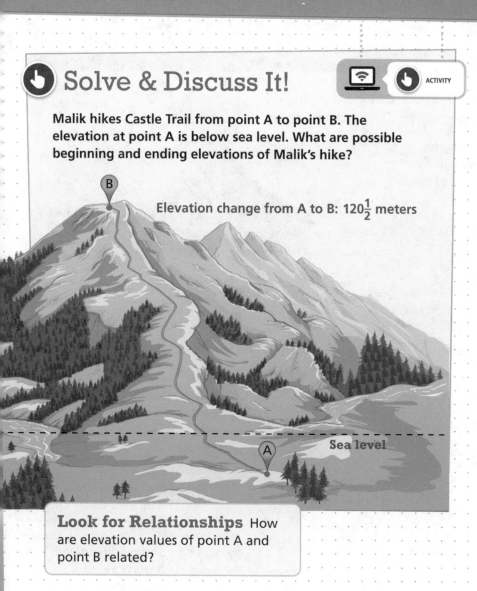

Elevation change from A to B: $120\frac{1}{2}$ meters

Sea level

Look for Relationships How are elevation values of point A and point B related?

I can...
add and subtract rational numbers.

MAFS.7.NS.1.1c ... Show that the distance between two rational numbers on the number line is the absolute value of their difference, and apply this principle in real-world contexts.
Also 7.NS.1.1b, 7.NS.1.1d
MAFS.K12.MP.2.1, MP.3.1, MP.4.1, MP.7.1, MP.8.1

Focus on math practices
Reasoning What would be different about the hike from point B to point A?

VISUAL LEARNING   ASS

EXAMPLE 1 Add and Subtract Rational Numbers with Different Signs

Scan for Multimedia

Lava flows from an active volcano's magma reservoir located below sea level through the magma conduit. How far is the summit of the volcano from sea level?

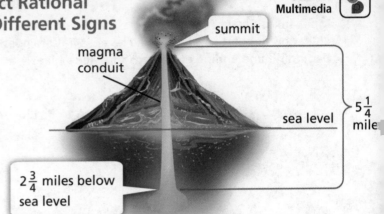

summit

magma conduit

sea level

$5\frac{1}{4}$ mile

Generalize You can use the rules for adding integers to add all other rational numbers.

$2\frac{3}{4}$ miles below sea level

Use a number line to represent the distances.

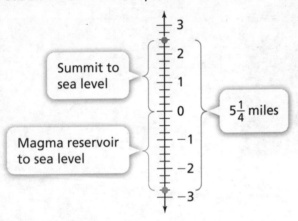

Summit to sea level

Magma reservoir to sea level

$5\frac{1}{4}$ miles

You can use the rules for adding integers to add any other rational numbers.

$\left(-2\frac{3}{4}\right) + 5\frac{1}{4}$ — Write an expression to represent the distance.

$\left|-2\frac{3}{4}\right| = 2\frac{3}{4}$ and $\left|5\frac{1}{4}\right| = 5\frac{1}{4}$

$5\frac{1}{4} - 2\frac{3}{4} = 2\frac{1}{2}$ — When the signs are different, find the difference.

$-2\frac{3}{4} + 5\frac{1}{4} = 2\frac{1}{2}$ — Use the sign of the addend with the greater absolute value.

The summit of the volcano is $2\frac{1}{2}$ miles above sea level.

☑ Try It!

A dolphin is at the surface of the water and then descends to a depth of $4\frac{1}{2}$ feet. Then the dolphin swims down another $2\frac{3}{4}$ feet. What is the location of the dolphin relative to the surface of the water?

$-4\frac{1}{2} - \boxed{}$

$-4\frac{1}{2} + \boxed{} = \boxed{}$

The location of the dolphin relative to the surface of the water is $\boxed{}$ feet.

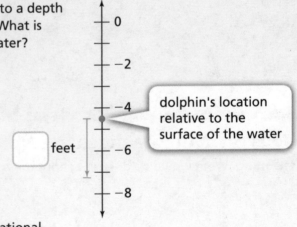

dolphin's location relative to the surface of the water

$\boxed{}$ feet

Convince Me! How are adding and subtracting two rational numbers with different signs related to adding and subtracting two integers with different signs?

EXAMPLE **2**  ACTIVITY ASSESS

Use Properties of Operations to Add and Subtract

The force of gravity added to the force of thrust is the combined force at work on a model rocket. What is the combined force, in newtons, on the rocket?

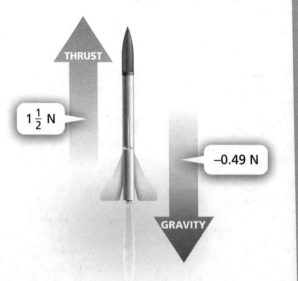

$$-0.49 + 1\frac{1}{2}$$

Use the Commutative Property and additive inverses as a strategy to add.

$$= 1\frac{1}{2} + (-0.49)$$

$$= 1\frac{1}{2} - 0.49$$

$$= 1.5 - 0.49$$

$$= 1.01$$

The combined force on the rocket is 1.01 newtons.

THRUST

$1\frac{1}{2}$ N

−0.49 N

GRAVITY

 Try It!

Find the sum or difference of the rational numbers.

a. $-2.5 + \left(-5\frac{6}{10}\right)$ **b.** $-4.4 - \left(-1\frac{1}{2}\right)$ **c.** $-135.4 + 78\frac{1}{2}$

EXAMPLE **3** 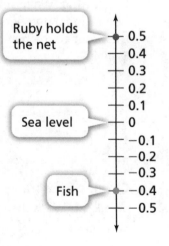 **Find Distances on a Number Line**

Ruby looks over the edge of her boat and sees fish 0.4 meter below the surface of the water. If Ruby holds a 1-meter-long net at 0.5 meter above sea level, can she reach the fish? Explain.

ONE WAY

$$|0.5 - (-0.4)|$$

To find the distance between any two points on a number line, find the absolute value of their difference.

$$= |0.5 + 0.4|$$

$$= |0.9|$$

$$= 0.9$$

ANOTHER WAY

$$|-0.4 - 0.5|$$

$$= |-0.4 + (-0.5)|$$

$$= |-0.9|$$

$$= 0.9$$

Ruby holds the net — 0.5, 0.4, 0.3, 0.2, 0.1

Sea level — 0, −0.1, −0.2, −0.3

Fish — −0.4, −0.5

Yes. The fish are 0.9 meter below where Ruby holds the net, so Ruby can reach the fish with a 1-meter-long net.

 Try It!

Two divers are swimming at different depths below sea level. One diver is at −25.5 feet. The other diver is at −40.75 feet. How much farther below sea level is the diver who is farthest below sea level?

The rules for adding and subtracting all rational numbers are the same as those for adding and subtracting integers.

The distance between any two rational numbers p and q on a number line is the absolute value of their difference.

> The distance between p and q can be written as $|p - q|$ or $|q - p|$.

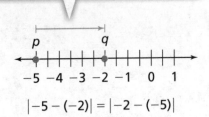

$$|-5 - (-2)| = |-2 - (-5)|$$

Do You Understand?

1. **Essential Question** How are adding and subtracting integers related to adding and subtracting other rational numbers?

2. **Reasoning** When finding the distance between two rational numbers on a number line, does the order of the numbers you subtract matter? Explain.

3. **Critique Reasoning** Gwen says that the sum of $-1\frac{3}{4}$ and $2\frac{1}{2}$ is the same as the difference between $2\frac{1}{2}$ and $1\frac{3}{4}$. Is Gwen correct? Explain why or why not.

Do You Know How?

4. What is the distance between the top of the fishing pole and the fish?

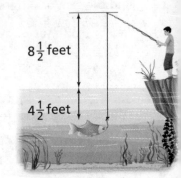

$8\frac{1}{2}$ feet

$4\frac{1}{2}$ feet

5. A shark began at 172.5 meters below sea level and then swam up 137.1 meters. Where is the shark's location now in relation to sea level?

6. Find the sum or difference.

   a. $-12\frac{1}{2} + 4\frac{1}{2}$

   b. $-0.35 - (-0.25)$

Practice & Problem Solving

Scan for
Multimedia

Leveled Practice In **7–8**, complete the expressions to find the sum or difference.

7. $3.2 - (-5.7)$

$= 3.2 + \boxed{}$

$= \boxed{}$

8. $\frac{12}{13} + \left(\frac{-1}{13}\right)$

$= \boxed{} - \boxed{}$

$= \boxed{}$

9. Reasoning When Tom simplified the expression $-2.6 + (-5.4)$, he got 2.8. What mistake did Tom likely make?

10. The temperature in a town is 36.6°F during the day and −12.6°F at night. What is the temperature change from day to night?

11. Simplify each expression.

a. $50\frac{1}{2} + (-12.3)$

b. $-50\frac{1}{2} + (-12.3)$

c. $-50\frac{1}{2} + 12.3$

12. At the beginning of the day, the stock market goes up $30\frac{1}{2}$ points. At the end of the day, the stock market goes down $120\frac{1}{4}$ points. What is the total change in the stock market from the beginning of the day to the end of the day?

13. A dolphin is swimming 18 feet below the surface of the ocean. There is a coast guard helicopter 75.5 feet above the surface of the water that is directly above the dolphin. What is the distance between the dolphin and the helicopter?

14. A bird flies from its nest to the bottom of the canyon. How far did the bird fly?

$528\frac{1}{5}$ feet — nest

sea level

$-89\frac{3}{5}$ feet — canyon floor

15. A scuba diving instructor takes a group of students to a depth of 54.96 feet. Then they ascend 22.38 feet to see some fish. Where are the fish in relation to the surface?

16. Model with Math Write an addition expression that is represented by the number line.

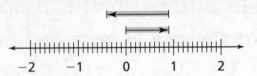

17. The roots of a plant reach down $3\frac{3}{4}$ inches below ground. How many inches is the plant above the ground?

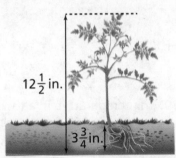

$12\frac{1}{2}$ in.

$3\frac{3}{4}$ in.

18. Higher Order Thinking

a. Simplify the expression $(-13.2) + 8.1$.

b. How are $(-13.2) + 8.1$ and $13.2 + (-8.1)$ related? Explain without computing.

c. Using a property of operations, what can you say about the sum of the two expressions?

Assessment Practice

19. The temperatures at sunrise and sunset are shown in the table. 🔊 7.NS.1.1d

	Temperature at Sunrise (°F)	Temperature at Sunset (°F)
Day 1	−11.31	13.49
Day 2	−7.69	25.25

PART A

Write an expression that represents the change in temperature for Day 1. Show how you can use properties of operations to find the value of the expression.

PART B

On which day did the temperature change more? Explain your reasoning.

20. Mischa dives from a platform that is 5 meters above water. Her dive takes her 2.1 meters below the surface of the water. Which expression could represent the distance, in meters, that Mischa dives? Select all that apply. 🔊 7.NS.1.1c

- ☐ $|5 - (-2.1)|$
- ☐ $|-(2.1) - (-5)|$
- ☐ $|2.1 - 5|$
- ☐ $|-(2.1) - 5|$
- ☐ $|5 + (-2.1)|$

1. Vocabulary How do you find the additive inverse of a number? Give an example of a number and its additive inverse. *Lesson 4-3*
🐊 7.NS.1.1d

2. A plastic toy submarine is held 15 centimeters below the water surface in a bath tub. The submarine is let go and rises 15 centimeters. What integer represents the toy submarine's position with respect to the surface of the water? *Lesson 4-1* 🐊 7.NS.1.1a

3. The temperature in the late afternoon was $-7.5°C$. It dropped 5 degrees by early evening and then dropped another 8.5 degrees by midnight. What was the temperature at midnight? *Lessons 4-3, 4-4, and 4-5*
🐊 7.NS.1.1b, 7.NS.1.1d

4. The floor of an elevator in a building is 30 feet above ground level. It travels down to the lower level of the building, where the floor is 10 feet below ground level. What distance has the elevator's floor traveled? *Lessons 4-4 and 4-5* 🐊 7.NS.1.1c

5. Greg says that $3.\overline{3}$ is a rational number. Kari says $3.\overline{3}$ is not a terminating decimal. Who is correct and why? *Lesson 4-2* 🐊 7.NS.1.2d

6. Cece is hiking on a mountain and stops at $15\frac{5}{8}$ feet above sea level. The base of the mountain is 10.2 feet below sea level. What is the vertical distance between Cece and the base of the mountain? *Lesson 4-5*
🐊 7.NS.1.1c, 7.NS.1.1d

Ⓐ 5.425 feet

Ⓑ 25.825 feet

Ⓒ $25\frac{3}{8}$ feet

Ⓓ $5\frac{1}{4}$ feet

How well did you do on the mid-topic checkpoint? Fill in the stars.

MID-TOPIC PERFORMANCE TASK

An oceanographer, Dr. Price, is studying the types of sea life at various depths.

Location	Sea Life	Depth Relative Sea Level (m)
A	Eels	−895.9
B	Eels	$-1{,}098\frac{3}{20}$
C	Shrimp	−2,784.75
D	Shrimp	$-3{,}259\frac{5}{8}$

PART A

Dr. Price uses a table to organize the types of sea life and the positions relative to sea level of each location. 🔵 7.NS.1.1d

Complete each sentence.

The difference between Location A and Location B is _____ meters.

The difference between Location B and Location C is _____ meters.

The difference between Location C and Location D is _____ meters.

PART B

After observing Location B, Dr. Price returns to Location A before descending to Location C. What is the total distance she travels? 🔵 7.NS.1.1c, 7.NS.1.1d

PART C

Dr. Price descends to Location D to observe shrimp. She then ascends and stops to observe sea life that is halfway between Location B and Location C. What is the total distance between Location D and where Dr. Price stopped to observe? 🔵 7.NS.1.1b, 7.NS.1.1d

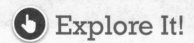

A popular beach erodes 4 inches per year on average.

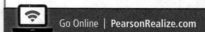
I can...
multiply integers.

MAFS.7.NS.1.2a Understand that multiplication is extended from fractions to rational numbers by requiring that operations continue to satisfy the properties of operations, particularly the distributive property, leading to products such as $(-1)(-1) = 1$ and the rules for multiplying signed numbers. Interpret products of rational numbers by describing real world contexts. Also 7.NS.1.2c

MAFS.K12.MP.1.1, MP.2.1, MP.3.1, MP.4.1, MP.6.1, MP.7.1, MP.8.1

A. How many years will it take for the coastline to erode one foot?

B. The number line below shows the expected change in the coastline as years pass. How could you use the number line to show the erosion after 10 years?

Coastline this year

-8 -4 0

Focus on math practices
Be Precise What expression could you use to represent the change in the coastline in 5 years?

VISUAL LEARNING   ASS

EXAMPLE 1 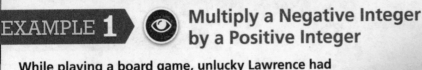 Multiply a Negative Integer by a Positive Integer

Scan for Multimedia

While playing a board game, unlucky Lawrence had to move back 2 spaces for 4 turns in a row. What integer represents his change in position?

Model with Math What integer can you use to represent the number of spaces Lawrence had to move back each turn?

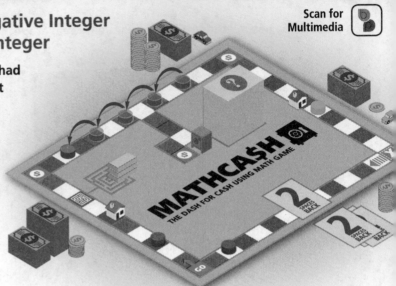

Use a number line to represent the change in position on the game board.

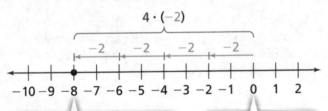

$4 \cdot (-2)$

$-2 \quad -2 \quad -2 \quad -2$

−10 −9 −8 −7 −6 −5 −4 −3 −2 −1 0 1 2

−8 represents the change in position on the board.

0 represents the starting position.

The total change in position on the board is -8. Lawrence had to move back 8 spaces.

Use multiplication and properties of operations to show why $4 \cdot (-2) = -8$.

$4 \cdot (-2 + 2) = 0$

$4 \cdot (-2) + 4 \cdot 2 = 0$

Use additive inverses and the Zero Property of Multiplication to write a multiplication problem.

$4 \cdot (-2) + 8 = 0$

$? \ + 8 = 0$

You know that opposites add to 0, so $-8 + 8 = 0$.

So, $4 \cdot (-2) = -8$.

Generalize A rule for multiplication of integers is: positive • negative = negative.

☑ Try It!

A race car game takes 6 points from a player each time the player hits a cone. What integer represents the change in total points if the player hits 10 cones?

$10 \cdot \boxed{} = \boxed{}$

The change in total points is $\boxed{}$.

Convince Me! Could the product of a positive integer and a negative integer be positive? Explain.

EXAMPLE **2**

  ACTIVITY ASSESS

Multiply a Positive Integer by a Negative Integer

What is the balloon's change in elevation in 3 minutes?

−500 • 3

Write an expression to represent the change in elevation.

$= 3 \cdot (-500)$

$= -1,500$

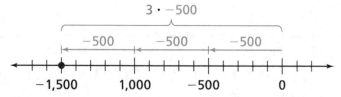

The change in elevation for the balloon is −1,500 feet.

> **Generalize** A rule for multiplication of integers is: negative • positive = negative.

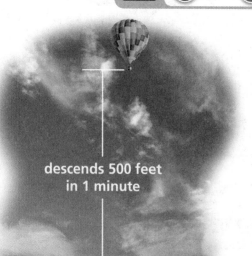

descends 500 feet in 1 minute

EXAMPLE **3**
 Multiply a Negative Integer by a Negative Integer

a. Use a number line to represent $-3 \cdot (-10)$.

$-(3 \cdot (-10))$ is the opposite of $3 \cdot (-10)$. So, $-3 \cdot (-10) = 30$.

$3 \cdot (-10) = -30$

```
  -10  -10  -10
 ├────┼────┼────┤
────┼────┼────┼────┼────┼────┼────┼──
  -30  -20  -10   0   10   20   30
```

Opposites are the same distance from 0, but on opposite sides of 0.

b. Use multiplication and properties of operations to show why
$-3 \cdot (-10) = 30$.

$-3 \cdot (-10 + 10) = 0$

Use additive inverses and the Zero Property of Multiplication to write a multiplication problem.

$-3 \cdot (-10) + -3 \cdot 10 = 0$

$-3 \cdot (-10) + (-30) = 0$

$\quad ? \quad + (-30) = 0$

So, $-3 \cdot (-10) = 30$.

You know that opposites add to 0, so $30 + (-30) = 0$.

> **Generalize** A rule for multiplication of integers is: negative • negative = positive.

☑ Try It!

Find each product.

a. $-7 \cdot (-2)$ **b.** $7 \cdot (-13)$ **c.** $-6 \cdot 8$ **d.** $(-1) \cdot (-1)$

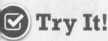

When multiplying two integers, the sign of the product depends on the sign of the factors.

If the signs of the factors are the *same*, the product is positive.

$$7 \cdot 3 = 21 \qquad\qquad -7 \cdot (-3) = 21$$

If the signs of the factors are *different*, the product is negative.

$$-4 \cdot 5 = -20 \qquad\qquad 4 \cdot (-5) = -20$$

Do You Understand?

1. **Essential Question** How do the signs of factors affect their product?

2. **Construct Arguments** What is the sign of the product if you multiplied three negative integers? Explain your answer.

3. **Reasoning** Explain why the product of two negative integers is not negative. Use $(-1)(-1)$ as an example.

4. **Use Structure** Is the product the same when multiplying $22 \times (-5)$ and multiplying $(-5) \times 22$? Explain.

Do You Know How?

5. Represent $2 \cdot (-3)$ on the number line.

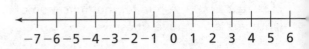

6. Which of these products is negative? Select all that apply.

   ☐ $-8 \cdot (-3)$

   ☐ $-2 \cdot 8$

   ☐ $0 \cdot (-2)$

   ☐ $15 \cdot (-5)$

   ☐ $-8 \cdot (-9)$

7. Find each product.

   a. $-9 \cdot (-4)$ b. $-7 \cdot 12$

   c. $8 \cdot (-8)$ d. $9 \cdot 15$

8. A game show contestant starts a game by answering two questions incorrectly. Each incorrect answer costs the contestant $600. Use a product of two integers to show the point total that would appear for the contestant.

Practice & Problem Solving

In 9–14, multiply.

9. $(-6) \cdot (-2)$

10. $4 \cdot (-8)$

11. $7 \cdot (-5)$

12. $-5 \cdot 2$

13. $-1 \cdot (-24)$

14. $(5) \cdot (-9) \cdot (-2)$

15. A football team lost the same number of yards on each of 3 consecutive plays. What is the total change in yards from where the team started?

16. a. Find the product.

$-41 \cdot (-1)$

b. Construct Arguments Describe how you use the properties of multiplication to find the product.

17. Alex is working to simplify $5 \cdot (-8) \cdot 2$.

a. What is the product?

b. Suppose Alex found the opposite of the correct product. Describe an error he could have made that resulted in that product.

18. Which product is greater, $(-4) \cdot (-6)$ or $(-7) \cdot (-8)$? Explain.

19. Make Sense and Persevere While playing a board game, Cecilia had to move back 6 spaces 9 times. What integer represents Cecilia's movement on the board for those 9 turns?

20. Anya makes withdrawals from and deposits into her bank account.

   a. What integer represents the change in the amount in her account if Anya withdraws \$12 once each day for four days?

   b. What integer represents the change in the amount in her account if Anya deposits \$12 once each day for four days?

   c. Look for Relationships Explain the difference between the integer for the withdrawals and the integer for the deposits.

21. Higher Order Thinking A gold mine has two elevators, one for equipment and one for miners. One day, the equipment elevator begins to descend. After 28 seconds, the elevator for the miners begins to descend. What is the position of each elevator relative to the surface after another 14 seconds? At that time, how much deeper is the elevator for the miners?

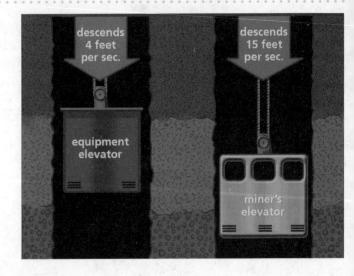

descends 4 feet per sec.

descends 15 feet per sec.

equipment elevator

miner's elevator

22. A number line is shown.

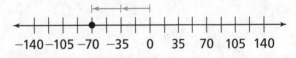

−140 −105 −70 −35 0 35 70 105 140

Write a multiplication equation that is represented by the number line. 🔊 7.NS.1.2a

23. Which of these expressions have the same product as $(-6) \cdot 7$? Select all that apply. 🔊 7.NS.1.2c

☐ $(-3) \cdot 14$

☐ $16 \cdot (-3)$

☐ $-6 \cdot (-7)$

☐ $7 \cdot (-6)$

☐ $14 \cdot (-3)$

Solve & Discuss It!  ACTIVITY

Stella is making the United States flag. She has blue fabric, red fabric, and white fabric. Choose a length for the flag. What length of blue fabric would Stella need to make this flag? Explain your thinking.

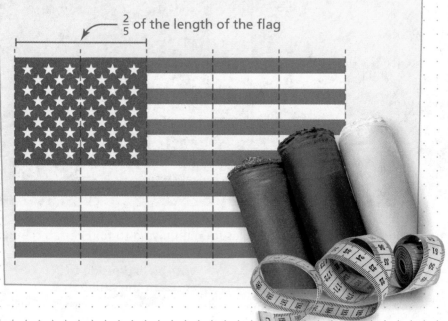

$\frac{2}{5}$ of the length of the flag

I can...
multiply rational numbers.

MAFS.7.NS.1.2a Understand that multiplication is extended from fractions to rational numbers by requiring that operations continue to satisfy the properties of operations, particularly the distributive property, leading to products such as $(-1)(-1) = 1$ and the rules for multiplying signed numbers. Interpret products of rational numbers by describing real-world contexts. Also 7.NS1.2c

MAFS.K12.MP.4.1, MP.6.1, MP.8.1

Focus on math practices

Be Precise The blue region of the flag is $\frac{7}{13}$ the width and $\frac{2}{5}$ the length of the flag. What part of the total area is the blue region of the flag?

EXAMPLE 1 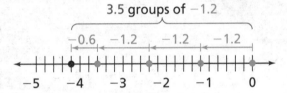 Multiply a Negative Number by a Positive Rational Number

Scan for Multimedia

Two hikers descend from the summit of a mountain. What is Petra's change in elevation?

Petra's change in elevation is 3.5 times as great as Ben's change in elevation.

−1.2 m change in elevation

Ben

Petra

Use a number line to represent Petra's change in elevation.

3.5 groups of −1.2

−0.6 −1.2 −1.2 −1.2

−5   −4   −3   −2   −1   0

Petra's change in elevation is −4.2 meters.

Use the rules for multiplying to find Petra's change in elevation.

$3.5 \cdot (-1.2)$ — Write an expression to represent the situation.

$= -4.2$

Petra's change in elevation is −4.2 meters.

> **Generalize** The rules for multiplying integers apply to all rational numbers.
>
> positive · negative = negative

☑ Try It!

Meghan's bank account is charged $9.95 per month for an online newspaper subscription. How could you represent the change in her account balance after three months of charges?

☐ groups of ☐

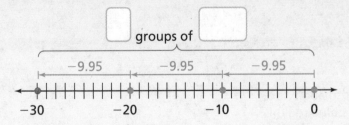

−30   −20   −10   0

☐ · −9.95 = ☐

After three months, the change in her account balance is $ ☐ .

Convince Me! Meghan's bank account is charged 3 times. Without calculating, how can you determine whether this is a negative or positive change to her account? Explain.

EXAMPLE **2**

 Multiply a Positive Number by a Negative Rational Number

Find the product of $-\frac{5}{6}$ and $\frac{2}{5}$.

$-\frac{5}{6} \cdot \frac{2}{5}$

$= \frac{-5 \cdot 2}{6 \cdot 5}$

$= \frac{-10}{30} = -\frac{1}{3}$ ← Multiply the numerators and the denominators and then simplify.

So, $-\frac{5}{6} \cdot \frac{2}{5} = -\frac{1}{3}$.

Plot the negative value and then find $\frac{2}{5}$ of that length.

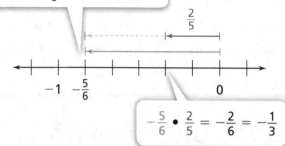

$-\frac{5}{6} \cdot \frac{2}{5} = -\frac{2}{6} = -\frac{1}{3}$

EXAMPLE **3** **Multiply a Negative Number by a Negative Rational Number**

Find the product of -0.3 and $-\frac{11}{30}$.

$-0.30 \cdot \left(-\frac{11}{30}\right)$

$= \frac{-3}{10} \cdot \left(-\frac{11}{30}\right)$ ← Convert one of the rational numbers so that they are both fractions or both decimals.

$= \frac{-3 \cdot (-11)}{10 \cdot 30}$

$= \frac{33}{300}$ or 0.11

So, $-0.3 \cdot \left(-\frac{11}{30}\right) = 0.11$ or $\frac{11}{100}$.

Generalize The rules for multiplying integers apply to all rational numbers.

negative · negative = positive

☑ Try It!

Find each product.

a. $-5.3 \cdot (-2.6)$

b. $-\frac{3}{5} \cdot 4\frac{1}{6}$

c. $0.2 \cdot (-1.78)$

d. $-2.5 \cdot \left(-\frac{7}{10}\right)$

The same rules for multiplying integers apply to multiplying all rational numbers.

When multiplying two rational numbers:

- If the signs of the factors are the *same*, the product is *positive*.
- If the signs of the factors are *different*, the product is *negative*.

Do You Understand?

1. **Essential Question** How is multiplying rational numbers like multiplying integers?

2. How do you multiply a decimal greater than 0 and a fraction less than 0?

3. **Model with Math** How does this number line represent multiplication of a negative number by a positive number? Explain.

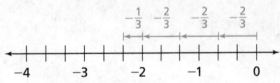

Do You Know How?

4. Use the number line to find the product $3 \cdot \left(-1\frac{1}{2}\right)$.

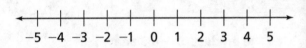

5. Which of these products is positive? Select all that apply.

   ☐ $-0.2 \cdot (12.5)$

   ☐ $-\frac{1}{12} \cdot \left(-6\frac{1}{2}\right)$

   ☐ $3.2 \cdot \left(-\frac{1}{900}\right)$

   ☐ $-3\frac{1}{2} \cdot 0$

   ☐ $-4.7 \cdot (-1)$

6. Find the product.

   a. $-3.1 \cdot (-2.9)$

   b. $1\frac{1}{2} \cdot \left(-\frac{5}{3}\right)$

   c. $-3\frac{1}{2} \cdot 0.5$

   d. $-\frac{4}{5} \cdot -\frac{1}{8}$

Practice & Problem Solving

In 7–14, multiply.

7. $(-2.655) \cdot (18.44)$

8. $-1\frac{5}{6} \cdot 6\frac{1}{2}$

9. $-2\frac{1}{2} \cdot \left(-1\frac{2}{3}\right)$

10. $-3\frac{7}{8} \cdot \left(-5\frac{3}{4}\right)$

11. $-7.5 \cdot -2\frac{3}{4}$

12. $-0.6 \cdot (-0.62)$

13. $-0.2 \cdot -\frac{5}{6}$

14. $-\frac{5}{6} \cdot \frac{1}{8}$

- -

15. At the beginning of the season, Jamie pays full price for a ticket to see the Panthers, her favorite baseball team.

The Panthers currently have 33 wins and 31 losses.

a. Represent the total change in the cost of a ticket given their losses.

b. What is the cost of a ticket for the next game they play?

Ticket prices decrease $0.41 for every game the Panthers lose this season!

GAME ONE

VIP   ZONE: C4   SEAT: 280   C1

STADIUM   STANDARD Price $49.64   VIP
C1   Standard

16. The price per share of ENVX stock is dropping at a rate of $1.45 each hour.

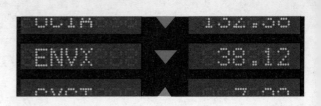

    a. Write the rate as a negative number.

    b. What rational number represents the change in the price per share after 5 hours?

    c. What is the price per share after 5 hours?

17. Ming incorrectly says that this product is $\frac{4}{63}$.

$$-\left(-\frac{4}{9}\right) \cdot \left(-\frac{1}{7}\right)$$

    a. What is the correct product?

    b. What error could Ming have made?

18. Higher Order Thinking Place the products in order from least to greatest.

$$4\frac{4}{7} \cdot 4\frac{4}{7}$$

$$5\frac{6}{7} \cdot \left(-6\frac{6}{7}\right)$$

$$-5\frac{1}{8} \cdot \left(-2\frac{1}{4}\right)$$

Assessment Practice

19. Suppose there is a 1.3°F drop in temperature for every thousand feet that an airplane climbs into the sky. The temperature on the ground is −2.8°F.   🔊 7.NS.1.2a

PART A

Write a multiplication equation to represent the change in temperature after the plane ascends 10,000 feet.

PART B

What will the temperature be when the plane reaches an altitude of 10,000 feet?

    Ⓐ −15.8

    Ⓑ −10.2

    Ⓒ 10.2

    Ⓓ 15.8

 Explain It!

The shapes below are used to show the relationship between each of the four equations in the same fact family.

$8 \times 3 = 24$ ◼ × ⬤ = ★

$3 \times 8 = 24$ ⬤ × ◼ = ★

$24 \div 3 = 8$ ★ ÷ ⬤ = ◼

$24 \div 8 = 3$ ★ ÷ ◼ = ⬤

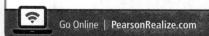
Go Online | PearsonRealize.com

I can...
divide integers.

MAFS.7.NS.1.2b understand that integers can be divided, provided that the divisor is not zero, and every quotient of integers with (with non-zero divisor) is a rational number. If p and q are integers, then $-\left(\frac{p}{q}\right) = \frac{(-p)}{q} = \frac{p}{(-q)}$. Interpret quotients of rational numbers by describing real-world contexts. Also 7.NS.1.2c

MAFS.K12.MP.2.1, MP.4.1, MP.7.1, MP.8.1

A. Suppose the star represents −24. What values could the other shapes represent?

B. What do you know about the square and circle if the star represents a negative number?

C. What do you know about the star if the square and circle both represent a negative number?

Focus on math practices

Use Structure Suppose the square represents −8 and the circle represents 3. Use what you know about integer multiplication and the relationship between multiplication and division to write the complete fact family.

? Essential Question How does dividing integers relate to multiplying integers?

Scan for Multimedia

EXAMPLE 1 Divide Integers with Different Signs

A machine drill is used to access water under the ground. If the machine drills the same distance each day, what is the change in the location of the bottom of the hole each day?

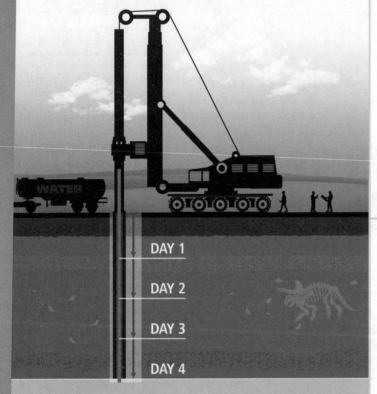

DAY 1
DAY 2
DAY 3
DAY 4

water at 160 feet below ground level

Use a number line to represent the change each day.

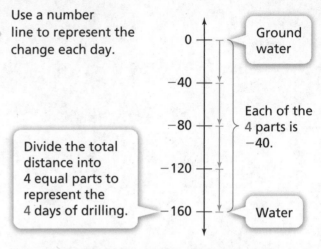

0 — Ground water
−40
−80 — Each of the 4 parts is −40.
−120
−160 — Water

Divide the total distance into 4 equal parts to represent the 4 days of drilling.

The location of the bottom of the hole changed −40 feet, or 40 feet lower each day.

Use the inverse relationship between multiplication and division.

$-160 \div 4 = ?$

$4 \cdot ? = -160$ ← Write a related multiplication equation.

$4 \cdot (-40) = -160$

So, $-160 \div 4 = -40$.

When dividing integers with different signs, the quotient will be negative.

The location of the bottom of the hole changed by −40 feet, or decreased by 40 feet, each day.

☑ Try It!

Suppose the machine drilled the same distance into the ground for 3 days and reached water at 84 feet below ground level. What was the change in the location of the bottom of the hole each day?

Each day, the location of the bottom of the hole changed by ☐ feet, or decreased by ☐ feet.

Convince Me! Explain why the quotient of two integers with different signs is negative.

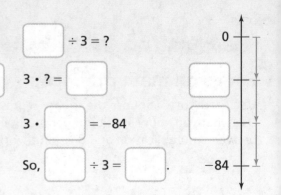

☐ ÷ 3 = ?

3 · ? = ☐

3 · ☐ = −84

So, ☐ ÷ 3 = ☐ .

0

−84

EXAMPLE **2** **Divide Integers with the Same Sign**

  ACTIVITY ASSESS

Simplify $-27 \div (-3)$.

ONE WAY Use a related multiplication fact.

$-27 \div (-3) = ?$

$-3 \cdot ? = -27$ ← Write division as a product with a missing factor.

$-3 \cdot 9 = -27$

So, $-27 \div (-3) = 9$.

When dividing integers with the same sign, the quotient will be positive.

ANOTHER WAY Write the division expression as a fraction and use properties of operations.

$\dfrac{-27}{-3}$

$= \dfrac{-1 \cdot 27}{-1 \cdot 3}$ ← Write negative numbers as a product, and then write as a product of fractions.

$= \dfrac{-1}{-1} \cdot \dfrac{27}{3}$

$= 1 \cdot 9$

$= 9$

So, $-27 \div (-3) = 9$.

 Try It!

Simplify.

a. $-40 \div (-5)$

b. $40 \div (-5)$

c. $0 \div -40$

EXAMPLE **3** **Write Equivalent Quotients of Integers**

Are the following quotients equivalent? Justify your answer.

$-\left(\dfrac{18}{4}\right)$ $\qquad$ $\dfrac{-18}{4}$ $\qquad$ $\dfrac{18}{-4}$

$-\left(\dfrac{18}{4}\right) = -(18 \div 4)$ $\qquad$ $\dfrac{-18}{4} = -18 \div 4$ $\qquad$ $\dfrac{18}{-4} = 18 \div -4$

$\quad = -(4.5)$ $\qquad\qquad\quad = -4.5$ $\qquad\qquad\quad = -4.5$

$\quad = -4.5$

Yes, each expression is equivalent to -4.5.

Generalize The value of $-\left(\dfrac{p}{q}\right)$ is equivalent to $\dfrac{-p}{q}$ and $\dfrac{p}{-q}$.

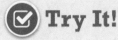 **Try It!**

Which of the following are equivalent to -5?

$\dfrac{55}{11}$ $\quad$ $-\left(\dfrac{55}{11}\right)$ $\quad$ $\dfrac{-55}{11}$ $\quad$ $\dfrac{-55}{-11}$ $\quad$ $\dfrac{55}{-11}$ $\quad$ $-\left(\dfrac{-55}{-11}\right)$

The rules for dividing integers are related to the rules for multiplying integers.

If the signs of the dividend and the divisor are the same, the quotient is positive.	If the signs of the dividend and the divisor are different, the quotient is negative.
$24 \div 4 = 6 \qquad -24 \div (-4) = 6$	$-15 \div 3 = -5 \qquad 15 \div (-3) = -5$

Do You Understand?

1. **Essential Question** How does dividing integers relate to multiplying integers?

2. **Reasoning** Why is the quotient of two negative integers positive?

3. Helen wrote the following facts to try to show that division by 0 results in 0. Explain her error.

$$0 \times (-7) = 0$$
$$\text{So, } (-7) \div 0 = 0 \quad \times$$

Do You Know How?

4. Find each quotient.

   a. $-\dfrac{18}{3}$

   b. $\dfrac{-5}{-1}$

   c. $\dfrac{24}{-6}$

   d. $\dfrac{-10}{-1}$

   e. $\dfrac{-25}{5}$

   f. $-\dfrac{8}{2}$

5. A scuba diver descends 63 feet in 18 seconds. What integer represents the change in the diver's position in feet per second?

6. Which of the following are equivalent to -7?

   ☐ $\dfrac{-49}{-7}$

   ☐ $\dfrac{0}{-7}$

   ☐ $\dfrac{49}{-7}$

   ☐ $\dfrac{-21}{3}$

   ☐ $\dfrac{21}{3}$

Practice & Problem Solving

Scan for
Multimedia

Leveled Practice In 7–8, fill in the boxes to find each quotient.

7. $-16 \div 4 = ?$

$4 \cdot ? = \boxed{}$

$4 \cdot \boxed{} = \boxed{}$

So, $-16 \div 4 = \boxed{}$.

8. $-56 \div -7 = ?$

$\boxed{} \cdot ? = \boxed{}$

$\boxed{} \cdot \boxed{} = \boxed{}$

So, $-56 \div -7 = \boxed{}$.

9. Classify the quotient $-50 \div 5$ as positive, negative, zero, or undefined.

10. Is the expression $\frac{42}{-7}$ undefined? If not, find the quotient.

11. A company loses $780 as a result of a shipping delay. The 6 owners of the company must share the loss equally.

a. Write an expression to show the change in profit for each owner.

b. Evaluate the expression.

12. Which of the quotients are equivalent to 2.5? Select all that apply.

☐ $\frac{10}{-4}$ ☐ $\frac{-5}{-2}$

☐ $\frac{10}{4}$ ☐ $\frac{-5}{2}$

☐ $\frac{-10}{-4}$ ☐ $\frac{5}{2}$

13. Use Structure The price of a stock steadily decreased by a total of $127 over 15 months. Which expression shows the change in the stock's value?

Ⓐ $\frac{-\$127}{-15 \text{ months}}$ Ⓒ $\frac{-\$127}{15 \text{ months}}$

Ⓑ $\frac{\$127}{15 \text{ months}}$ Ⓓ $\frac{\$15}{127 \text{ months}}$

14. Zak goes parachuting and descends at the rate shown. If he maintains a steady descent, what integer represents Zak's change in elevation in feet per second?

24 feet in 2 seconds

15. Model with Math Find each quotient and plot it on the number line. Which of the expressions are undefined?

$-8 \div 4$ $\frac{-21}{-7}$ $-4 \div 0$ $-25 \div (-5)$ $\frac{36}{-9}$ $\frac{9}{0}$ $0 \div (-8)$

<−−−+−−+−−+−−+−−+−−+−−+−−+−−+−−+−−>
  −5 −4 −3 −2 −1   0   1   2   3   4   5

16. Use Structure The temperature in a town increased 16°F in 5 hours. The temperature decreased 31°F in the next 8 hours. Which of the expressions shows the rate of the total change in temperature?

Ⓐ $\dfrac{-15°F}{13\ hours}$

Ⓑ $\dfrac{47°F}{13\ hours}$

Ⓒ $\dfrac{15°F}{10\ minutes}$

Ⓓ $\dfrac{47°F}{-13\ hours}$

17. Camille takes a rock-climbing class. On her first outing, she rappels down the side of a boulder in three equal descents. What integer represents Camille's change in altitude in feet each time she descends?

Elevation 165 Feet

18. Higher Order Thinking If the fraction $\dfrac{396}{x-10}$ is equivalent to −22, find the value of x. Show your work.

19. Which of the quotients is equivalent to $-\dfrac{5}{8}$? Select all that apply. 🖩 7.NS.1.2b

☐ $\dfrac{-5}{8}$

☐ $\dfrac{5}{8}$

☐ $\dfrac{5}{-8}$

☐ $-\left(\dfrac{5}{-8}\right)$

☐ $\dfrac{-5}{-8}$

20. Which of the following pairs of quotients are equivalent? 🖩 7.NS.1.2b

Ⓐ $\dfrac{-4}{5}$ and $-\left(\dfrac{20}{25}\right)$

Ⓑ $-\left(\dfrac{2}{-3}\right)$ and $\dfrac{-4}{6}$

Ⓒ $\dfrac{-5}{7}$ and $\dfrac{35}{-40}$

Ⓓ $\dfrac{1}{5}$ and $-\left(\dfrac{-2}{-10}\right)$

21. An elevator descends 36 feet in 3 seconds. What integer represents the elevator's change in elevation in feet per a second? 🖩 7.NS.1.2b

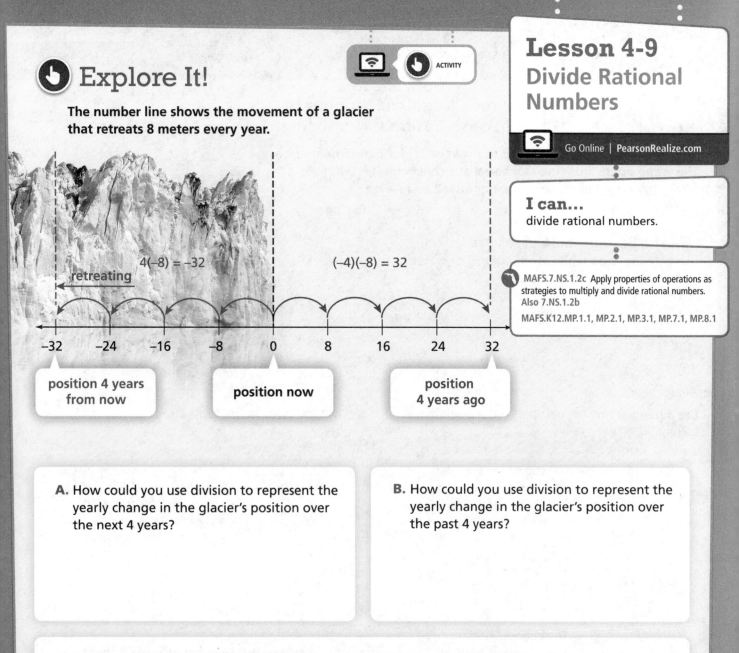
Explore It!

The number line shows the movement of a glacier that retreats 8 meters every year.

retreating

$4(-8) = -32$ $(-4)(-8) = 32$

| -32 | -24 | -16 | -8 | 0 | 8 | 16 | 24 | 32 |

position 4 years from now

position now

position 4 years ago

ACTIVITY

I can...
divide rational numbers.

MAFS.7.NS.1.2c Apply properties of operations as strategies to multiply and divide rational numbers. Also 7.NS.1.2b

MAFS.K12.MP.1.1, MP.2.1, MP.3.1, MP.7.1, MP.8.1

A. How could you use division to represent the yearly change in the glacier's position over the next 4 years?

B. How could you use division to represent the yearly change in the glacier's position over the past 4 years?

C. Suppose the glacier retreated 8.25 meters every year. Draw a number line to represent this movement.

Focus on math practices

Reasoning If the number of meters the glacier retreats each year changes, does it affect the signs of each part of the division statement in Part A? Explain.

Essential Question How is dividing rational numbers like dividing integers?

  VISUAL LEARNING   ASSESS

EXAMPLE 1 Divide a Negative Number by a Positive Rational Number

Scan for Multimedia

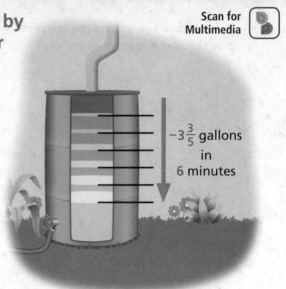

Yumiko has a drip hose attached to a rain barrel for her garden. The water drains from the rain barrel at a constant rate. What is the change in the volume of water after 1 minute?

$-3\frac{3}{5}$ gallons in 6 minutes

Make Sense and Persevere Start by estimating the change in the volume of water after 1 minute.

Use a number line to represent the change in the volume.

Divide the given change in volume into 6 equal parts.

$-3\frac{3}{5} \div 6$

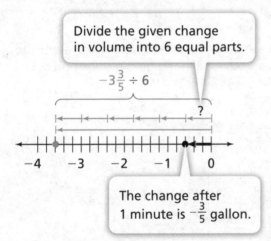

The change after 1 minute is $-\frac{3}{5}$ gallon.

Use the rules for multiplication.

$$-3\frac{3}{5} \div 6$$

$$= -\frac{18}{5} \div \frac{6}{1}$$

Two numbers whose product is 1 are **multiplicative inverses**, or reciprocals.

$$= -\frac{18}{5} \cdot \frac{1}{6}$$

$$= -\frac{18}{30} = -\frac{3}{5}$$

So, the change in the volume of water after 1 minute is $-\frac{3}{5}$ gallon.

Generalize You can extend what you know about multiplying rational numbers and dividing integers to division of rational numbers.

✓ Try It!

Suppose that the volume of water in the rain barrel decreased by $4\frac{5}{8}$ gallons in 4 minutes. What will be the change in the volume of water after 1 minute?

The rain barrel will lose ☐ gallons in 1 minute.

Convince Me! How are multiplicative inverses used in division with rational numbers?

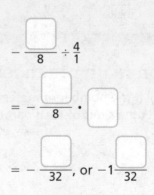

$$-\frac{\boxed{}}{8} \div \frac{4}{1}$$

$$= -\frac{\boxed{}}{8} \cdot \boxed{}$$

$$= -\frac{\boxed{}}{32}, \text{ or } -1\frac{\boxed{}}{32}$$

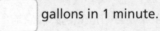 Go Online | PearsonRealize.com

Simplify $\dfrac{3\frac{2}{3}}{-\frac{2}{3}}$.

A **complex fraction** has a fraction in the numerator, the denominator, or both.

$3\frac{2}{3} \div \left(-\frac{2}{3}\right)$

$= \dfrac{11}{3} \div \left(-\dfrac{2}{3}\right)$

$= \dfrac{11}{3} \cdot \left(-\dfrac{3}{2}\right)$

The multiplicative inverse of $-\frac{2}{3}$ is $-\frac{3}{2}$ because $-\frac{3}{2} \cdot -\frac{2}{3} = 1$.

$= \dfrac{11 \cdot (-3)}{3 \cdot 2}$

$= -\dfrac{33}{6} = -\dfrac{11}{2}$

$= -5\dfrac{1}{2}$

✅ Try It!

Find each quotient.

a. $\dfrac{1\frac{2}{5}}{-\frac{1}{5}}$

b. $-0.4 \div 0.25$

c. $\dfrac{7}{8} \div -\dfrac{3}{4}$

d. $0.7 \div -1\dfrac{1}{6}$

EXAMPLE **3** **Divide Rational Numbers with the Same Sign**

The location of a submarine changes by -0.06 kilometer each minute. How much time does it take to get to the sea bottom?

$-\dfrac{3}{4} \div (-0.06)$ ··········· Divide the location of the sea bottom by the change in the location of the submarine.

$= -0.75 \div (-0.06)$

$= 12.5$

The rules for dividing integers apply to all rational numbers.
negative ÷ negative = positive

$-\dfrac{3}{4}$ km

It takes 12.5 minutes to reach the sea bottom.

✅ Try It!

Find each quotient.

a. $-1\dfrac{1}{3} \div (-1.6)$

b. $\dfrac{-\frac{2}{3}}{-\frac{1}{4}}$

c. $-\dfrac{9}{10} \div \left(-\dfrac{3}{10}\right)$

d. $-0.5 \div \left(-\dfrac{3}{13}\right)$

The same rules for dividing integers apply to dividing rational numbers. When dividing two rational numbers:

- If the signs of the dividend and divisor are the same, the quotient is positive.

- If the signs of the dividend and divisor are different, the quotient is negative.

Do You Understand?

1. **? Essential Question** How is dividing rational numbers like dividing integers?

2. **Use Structure** How do you know the sign of the quotient $-\frac{4}{5} \div \frac{1}{6}$?

3. **Reasoning** When -4 is divided by a rational number between 0 and 1, where would the quotient be located on the number line? Why?

Do You Know How?

4. Find each quotient.

   a. $-\frac{7}{12} \div \frac{1}{7}$

   b. $-0.05 \div \left(-\frac{5}{8}\right)$

   c. $6\frac{1}{4} \div \left(-\frac{5}{16}\right)$

   d. $-1 \div \left(-\frac{10}{13}\right)$

5. Simplify the complex fraction.

   a. $\dfrac{-\frac{2}{7}}{1\frac{1}{3}}$

   b. $\dfrac{-\frac{3}{5}}{2\frac{1}{4}}$

   c. $\dfrac{-\frac{9}{10}}{1\frac{3}{5}}$

Name: _____

Practice & Problem Solving

Leveled Practice In 6–7, fill in the boxes to find the quotient.

6. Find the quotient $\frac{5}{7} \div \left(-\frac{11}{5}\right)$.

$$\frac{5}{7} \div \left(-\frac{11}{5}\right) = \frac{5}{7} \cdot \boxed{}$$

$$= -\frac{\boxed{}}{\boxed{}}$$

7. Simplify the complex fraction $\dfrac{-\frac{4}{5}}{\frac{3}{10}}$.

Rewrite the complex fraction: $\boxed{} \div \boxed{}$

Write the division as multiplication: $\boxed{} \cdot \boxed{}$

The product is $\boxed{}$.

8. Which multiplication expression is equivalent to the division expression $-\frac{7}{17} \div \frac{13}{34}$?

Ⓐ $-\frac{17}{7} \times \frac{13}{34}$ Ⓒ $-\frac{17}{7} \times \frac{34}{13}$

Ⓑ $-\frac{7}{17} \times \frac{13}{34}$ Ⓓ $-\frac{7}{17} \times \frac{34}{13}$

9. Derek says that the quotient $-\frac{2}{7} \div \left(-\frac{2}{21}\right)$ is $-\frac{1}{3}$.

a. What is the correct quotient?

b. What mistake did Derek likely make?

10. The water level of a lake fell by $1\frac{1}{2}$ inches during a $1\frac{2}{3}$-week-long dry spell. Simplify the complex fraction below to find the average rate at which the water level changed every week.

$\dfrac{-1\frac{1}{2}}{1\frac{2}{3}}$ inches/week

Water level dropped $1\frac{1}{2}$ inches

11. Complete the table. Simplify expressions.

	Dividend	Divisor	Quotient
a.	$-\frac{3}{4}$	$\frac{2}{5}$	
b.	-0.75	0.4	
c.	$\frac{3}{4}$	$-\frac{2}{5}$	

12. a. Find the reciprocal of $-1\frac{1}{17}$.

b. Find the reciprocal of $-\frac{17}{18}$.

c. Reasoning Explain why the answer for part a is the multiplicative inverse of the answer for part b.

13. Use numbers $-\frac{7}{13}$, $1\frac{6}{7}$, $-1\frac{6}{7}$, $\frac{7}{13}$

   a. Which is the reciprocal of $1\frac{6}{7}$?

   b. Which is the reciprocal of $\frac{7}{13}$?

   c. **Reasoning** What do you notice about the reciprocals of $1\frac{6}{7}$ and $\frac{7}{13}$?

14. A water tank in Stewart's home had a small, steady leak.

Loss of $1\frac{3}{5}$ mL in 10 min.

   a. Use a complex fraction to represent the change in the volume of water in 1 minute.

   $$\frac{\boxed{}}{10 \text{ minutes}} \text{ milliliters}$$

   b. Simplify the complex fraction to find the change in the volume of water in the tank in 1 minute.

15. Find the quotient. Express your answer as a simplified fraction.

   $$\frac{3}{10} \div 3.8$$

16. **Higher Order Thinking** Between 10 P.M. and 7:45 A.M., the water level in a swimming pool decreased by $\frac{13}{16}$ inch.

   Assuming that the water level decreased at a constant rate, how much did it drop each hour?

   The water level decreased by $\boxed{}$ inch each hour.

17. **Critique Reasoning** Kayla wants to find $2\frac{2}{3} \div \left(-1\frac{3}{7}\right)$. She first rewrites the division as $\left(2\frac{2}{3}\right)\left(-1\frac{7}{3}\right)$. What is wrong with Kayla's reasoning?

🌴 Assessment Practice

18. Which is an equivalent multiplication expression for $\dfrac{-\frac{3}{8}}{\left(-\frac{7}{54}\right)}$? 🔵 7.NS.1.2c

   Ⓐ $-\frac{3}{8} \cdot \left(\frac{7}{54}\right)$

   Ⓑ $-\frac{3}{8} \cdot \left(-\frac{54}{7}\right)$

   Ⓒ $-\frac{3}{8} \cdot \left(\frac{54}{7}\right)$

   Ⓓ $-\frac{8}{3} \cdot \left(-\frac{7}{54}\right)$

19. Which is NOT a step you perform to divide $-2\frac{1}{8} \div 6\frac{4}{5}$. Select all that apply. 🔵 7.NS.1.2b, 7.NS.1.2c

   ☐ Rewrite the mixed numbers as fractions.

   ☐ Divide 8 by 4.

   ☐ Multiply by the multiplicative inverse of $\frac{34}{5}$.

   ☐ Multiply by the multiplicative inverse of $\frac{17}{8}$.

   ☐ Multiply 8 and 34.

Go Online | PearsonRealize.com

Solve & Discuss It!

 ACTIVITY

Stefan estimates the income and expenses for renting a phone accessory store in the mall. He enters the amounts in the table below. Should Stefan rent a phone accessory store? Explain.

Estimated Income and Expenses

Type	Amount	Frequency
Sales	$950	Each week
Services	$2,875	Each month
Rent	−$4,500	Each month
Travel	−$7.50	Each day
Merchandise	−$1,650	Each month

Focus on math practices

Reasoning How can you assess the reasonableness of your solution using mental math or estimation strategies?

Lesson 4-10
Solve Problems with Rational Numbers

 Go Online | PearsonRealize.com

I can...
solve problems with rational numbers.

MPFS.7.NS.1.3 Solve real-world and mathematical problems involving the four operations with rational numbers. Also 7.EE.2.3

MAFS.K12.MP.1.1, MP.2.1, MP.3.1, MP.4.1, MP.7.1

233

VISUAL LEARNING   ASSESS

Scan for
Multimedia

EXAMPLE 1 **Decide Which Operations to Use to Solve Problems**

Water drains steadily out of a lock to lower a boat from one level to another. What is the boat's change in position each minute?

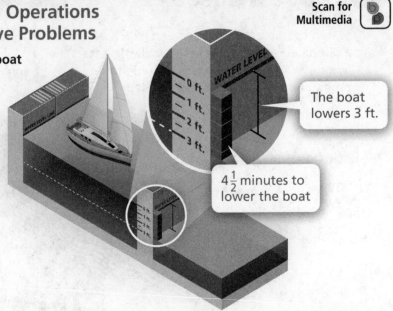

The boat lowers 3 ft.

$4\frac{1}{2}$ minutes to lower the boat

Reasoning Which operation can you use to find the boat's change in position in 1 minute?

STEP 1 Use a bar diagram to represent the time it takes the boat to lower 3 feet in the lock.

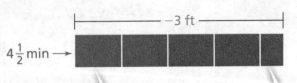

$4\frac{1}{2}$ min →

—3 ft—

Each whole box represents the boat's change in position in 1 minute.

This $\frac{1}{2}$ box represents the boat's change in position in $\frac{1}{2}$ minute.

STEP 2 Decide which operation to use to find the boat's change in position in 1 minute.

$\dfrac{-3}{4\frac{1}{2}}$

Divide to find the boat's change in position in 1 minute.

$= -3 \div \frac{9}{2}$

$= -3 \cdot \frac{2}{9}$

$= -\frac{6}{9} = -\frac{2}{3}$

So, the boat's change in position each minute is $-\frac{2}{3}$ feet. The boat lowers $\frac{2}{3}$ feet each minute.

☑ Try It!

A weather balloon ascended from an elevation of 18 feet below sea level to an elevation of $19\frac{1}{2}$ feet above sea level. What distance did the weather balloon rise?

The distance between two points is the absolute value of their ☐ .

So, $|-18 \bigcirc 19\frac{1}{2}| = $ ☐ .

The weather balloon rose a distance of ☐ feet.

Convince Me! How can you decide which operation to use to solve a problem?

 Go Online | PearsonRealize.com

EXAMPLE **2**

 Use Properties of Operations with Rational Numbers

Kevin played a trivia game. Each correct answer is worth $2\frac{1}{4}$ points, and each incorrect answer is worth $-\frac{1}{2}$ point. What was Kevin's score?

Kevin's Statistics

TOTAL CORRECT: 15 ✔

TOTAL INCORRECT: 15 ✘

> **Use Structure** How are the two methods of solving the problem alike? How are they different?

ONE WAY

$(15)2\frac{1}{4} + (15)\left(-\frac{1}{2}\right)$

$= \frac{9}{4}(15) + \left(-\frac{1}{2}\right)(15)$ ⟵ Multiply first. Then add.

$= \frac{135}{4} + \left(-\frac{15}{2}\right)$

$= \frac{135}{4} + \left(-\frac{30}{4}\right)$

$= \frac{105}{4} = 26\frac{1}{4}$

Kevin's score was $26\frac{1}{4}$ points.

ANOTHER WAY

$(15)2\frac{1}{4} + (15)\left(-\frac{1}{2}\right)$

$= 15\left[2\frac{1}{4} + \left(-\frac{1}{2}\right)\right]$

$= 15\left(1\frac{3}{4}\right)$

$= 15\left(\frac{7}{4}\right)$

$= \frac{105}{4} = 26\frac{1}{4}$

Kevin's score was $26\frac{1}{4}$ points.

> Since Kevin had the same number of correct and incorrect answers, use the Distributive Property.

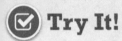 **Try It!**

Rashida had 18 correct answers and 12 incorrect answers. What was Rashida's score?

 EXAMPLE **3**   **Solve Multi-Step Problems with Rational Numbers**

The temperature at 4:00 P.M. was 2.5°F. It dropped 0.75°F each hour for the next 4 hours. What was the temperature at 8:00 P.M.?

STEP 1 Multiply to find the total change in temperature.

$-0.75 \times 4 = -3$

The total change in temperature was −3 degrees.

STEP 2 Add the total change in temperature to the initial temperature.

$2.5 + (-3) = -0.5$

The temperature at 8:00 P.M. was −0.5°F.

> **Reasoning** Use multiplication if a value is given per hour and you need to find the value after several hours.

Try It!

The temperature at 10:00 A.M. was −3°F and increased 2.25°F each hour for the next 5 hours. What was the temperature at 3:00 P.M.?

You can solve a problem with rational numbers by making sense of the problem and deciding which operations to use.

Do You Understand?

1. **Essential Question** How do you decide which rational number operations to use to solve problems?

2. **Reasoning** A truck's position relative to a car's position is −60 feet. The car and the truck move in the same direction, but the car moves 5 feet per second faster for 8 seconds. What operations could be used to find the truck's relative position after 8 seconds? Explain.

3. **Construct Arguments** Emilio used addition of two rational numbers to solve a problem. Jim used subtraction to solve the same problem. Is it possible that they both solved the problem correctly? Use a specific example to explain.

Do You Know How?

4. Kara had a savings account balance of $153 on Monday. On Tuesday, she had six withdrawals of $15.72 and a deposit of $235.15. What was her account balance after these transactions?

5. A scuba diver is swimming at the depth shown, and then swims 0.5 foot toward the surface every 3 seconds. What is the location of the scuba diver, relative to the surface, after 15 seconds?

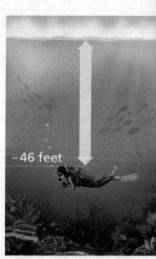

−46 feet

6. The temperature of a cup of coffee changed by −54°F over $22\frac{1}{2}$ minutes. What was the change in temperature each minute?

Practice & Problem Solving

7. Suppose there is a 1.1°F drop in temperature for every thousand feet that an airplane climbs into the sky. If the temperature on the ground is 59.7°F, what will be the temperature at an altitude of 11,000 ft?

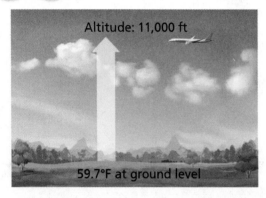

Altitude: 11,000 ft

59.7°F at ground level

8. A farmer sells an average of $15\frac{3}{5}$ bushels of corn each day. What integer represents the change in bushels of corn in his inventory after 6 days?

9. A certain plant grows $1\frac{1}{6}$ inches every week. How long will it take the plant to grow $6\frac{1}{6}$ inches?

10. An object is traveling at a steady speed of $8\frac{2}{3}$ miles per hour. How long will it take the object to travel $5\frac{1}{5}$ miles?

11. Brianna works as a customer service representative. She knows that the amount of her yearly bonus is $155, but $2.50 is taken away for each customer complaint about her during the year. What is her bonus if there are 12 complaints about her in the year?

12. Make Sense and Persevere There are ten birdbaths in a park. On the first day of spring, the birdbaths are filled. Several weeks later, the overall change in the water level is found. The results are shown in the table. What is the range of the data?

Changes in Water Level (inches)									
2.4	1.4	−2.3	2.9	2.3	−1.2	−1.4	−1.8	2.5	0.9

13. **Model with Math** Marcelo played a carnival game at the Interstate Fair 6 times. He spent 3 tokens to play each game, and he won 7 tokens each game. Write two different expressions that can be used to find the total profit in tokens that Marcelo made.

14. The temperature of a pot of water is shown. The temperature of the water changed −2.5°F per minute.

   a. What was the temperature after 20 minutes?

   b. **Make Sense and Persevere** How many minutes did it take to cool to 100.3°F?

15. **Higher Order Thinking** The table shows the relationship between a hedgehog's change in weight and the number of days of hibernation.

   a. What number represents the change in weight for each day of hibernation?

   b. What number represents the change in weight in ounces for the hedgehog in 115 days of hibernation?

Weight Loss of Hedgehog

Days of Hibernation	Change in Weight (oz)
8	−0.24
28	−0.84
75	−2.25
93	−2.79

Assessment Practice

16. A basketball team played six games. In those games, the team won by 7 points, lost by 20, won by 8, won by 11, lost by 3, and won by 9. Which was the mean amount by which the team won or lost over the six games? 7.NS.1.3, 7.EE.2.3

   Ⓐ −3 points

   Ⓑ 2 points

   Ⓒ 3 points

   Ⓓ 6 points

17. In digging a hole, the construction crew records the location of the bottom of the hole relative to ground level. After 3 hours the hole is 8.25 feet deep. 7.NS.1.3

   PART A

   What number represents the change in location in feet after 1 hour?

   PART B

   If the crew were to continue digging at the same rate, what number would they record for the location in feet after 8 hours?

Go Online | PearsonRealize.com

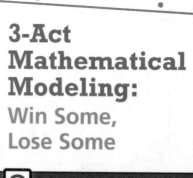
CT 1

MAFS.K12.MP.4.1 Model with mathematics.
Also MP.1.1, MP.2.1, MP.3.1, MP.5.1, MP.7.1, MP.8.1

MAFS.7.NS.1.1 Apply and extend previous understandings of addition and subtraction to add and subtract rational numbers; represent addition and subtraction on a horizontal or vertical number line diagram. Also 7.NS.1.3

1. After watching the video, what is the first question that comes to mind?

2. Write the Main Question you will answer.

3. Make a prediction to answer this Main Question.

The person who will win is [   ].

4. Construct Arguments Explain how you arrived at your prediction.

5. What information in this situation would be helpful to know? How would you use that information?

6. Use Appropriate Tools What tools can you use to get the information you need? Record the information as you find it.

7. Model with Math Represent the situation using the mathematical content, concepts, and skills from this topic. Use your representation to answer the Main Question.

8. What is your answer to the Main Question? Does it differ from your prediction? Explain.

Go Online | PearsonRealize.com

9. Write the answer you saw in the video.

10. Reasoning Does your answer match the answer in the video? If not, what are some reasons that would explain the difference?

11. Make Sense and Persevere Would you change your model now that you know the answer? Explain.

Reflect

12. Model with Math Explain how you used a mathematical model to represent the situation. How did the model help you answer the Main Question?

13. Reasoning How is each person's starting score related to their final score?

14. Construct Arguments If there were one final round where each contestant chooses how much to wager, how much should each person wager? Explain your reasoning.

$100	$200	$300	$400
$500	$100	$400	$300
$400	$500	$200	$500
	$300		$100

How can the properties of operations be used to solve problems involving integers and rational numbers?

Vocabulary Review

Complete each definition and then provide an example of each vocabulary word.

| **Vocabulary** | additive inverses | complex fraction | terminating decimal | repeating decimal |

Definition	Example
1. A _____ is a fraction $\frac{a}{b}$ where a and/or b are fractions and b is not equal to 0.	
2. A decimal that ends is a(n) _____ .	
3. Two numbers that have a sum of 0 are _____ .	

Use Vocabulary in Writing

Explain how you could determine whether $\dfrac{\frac{21}{3}}{\frac{120}{12}}$ and $\frac{7}{9}$ have the same decimal equivalent. Use vocabulary words in your explanation.

Concepts and Skills Review

Relate Integers and Their Opposites

Quick Review

Integers are the counting numbers, their opposites, and 0. Opposite integers are the same distance from 0 in opposite directions. Opposite quantities combine to make 0.

Example

A climber descends 3 miles into a canyon. What integer represents the descent of her climb? How far does she have to climb to return to her starting point?

The descent of her climb is represented by -3. She has to climb 3 miles to return to her starting point.

Practice

1. On a cold winter morning, the temperature was $-4°F$. By noon, the temperature increased $4°$. What was the temperature at noon?

2. Audrey deposits $27 in her account. Then she makes two withdrawals, one for $15 and one for $12. What is the total change to the balance of Audrey's account? Explain.

Understand Rational Numbers

Quick Review

All rational numbers have an equivalent decimal form. The decimal equivalent will be either a terminating decimal or a repeating decimal. A terminating decimal ends in repeating zeros. A repeating decimal has a never-ending pattern of the same digits.

Example

Write the decimal equivalents for $\frac{5}{8}$ and $\frac{8}{11}$. Are the decimals terminating or repeating?

The decimal equivalent for $\frac{5}{8} = 0.625$, which is a terminating decimal.

The decimal equivalent for $\frac{8}{11} = 0.7272... = 0.\overline{72}$, which is a repeating decimal.

Practice

1. Which fractions have a decimal equivalent that is a repeating decimal? Select all that apply.

   ☐ $\frac{13}{65}$ ☐ $\frac{141}{47}$

   ☐ $\frac{11}{12}$ ☐ $\frac{19}{3}$

2. Greg bought $19\frac{11}{16}$ gallons of gas. What decimal should the meter on the gas pump read?

3. What is the decimal equivalent of each rational number?

   a. $\frac{9}{11}$ b. $\frac{4}{5}$

   c. $-\frac{17}{5}$ d. $\frac{5}{9}$

Quick Review

To add integers with the same sign, add the absolute value of each integer. The sign of the sum will be the same as the sign of the addends. To add integers with different signs, find the difference of the absolute value of each integer. The sign of the sum will be the same as the sign of the greater addend.

Example

Find the sum of $(-28) + (-19)$.

$|-28| + |-19| = 28 + 19 = 47$

The sum of $(-28) + (-19) = -47$.

Find the sum of $(-28) + 19$.

$|-28| - |19| = 28 - 19 = 9$

The sum of $(-28) + 19 = -9$, because $|-28| > |19|$.

Practice

1. Jonah's cell phone came with 64 GB of memory. He has used 15 GB. He then uses 5 GB of memory to record photos and videos from a trip. Use the addition expression $64 + (-15) + (-5)$ to find how much memory is left on his phone.

2. Stella walks down a flight of stairs to the basement. Then she walks back up the stairs and up another flight of stairs to the second floor of her house. Each flight of stairs represents a change of 12 feet in height. How far is Stella above the ground?

3. Find the sum.
   a. $64 + (-15)$ b. $-121 + (-34)$
   c. $-86 + 92$ d. $109 + (-162)$

Quick Review

To subtract integers, use the additive inverse to write an equivalent addition expression. Then follow the rules for addition. When the signs are the same, find the sum of the absolute values. When the signs are different, find the difference. Use the sign of the number with the greater absolute value.

Example

Find $-7 - (8)$.

$-7 + (-8) = -15$

The signs are the same, so the sum has the same sign as the addends.

Find $-7 - (-8)$.

$-7 + 8 = 1$

The signs are different, so the sign of the difference is the same sign as the integer (8) with the greater absolute value, which is positive.

Practice

1. The temperature is 1°F at dusk. It is 8 degrees colder at dawn. What is the temperature at dawn?

2. Kyle and Nadim are on the same space on a board game they are playing. Kyle moves back 2 spaces in one turn and moves back 3 more spaces in his second turn. Nadim has remained in the same place. What integer represents Kyle's location relative to Nadim's location on the game board?

3. Find the difference.
   a. $82 - (-14)$ b. $-18 - (-55)$
   c. $-17 - 44$ d. $70 - (-101)$

Add and Subtract Rational Numbers

Quick Review

Positive and negative rational numbers and decimals can be added and subtracted following the same rules as adding and subtracting integers.

Example

Find $-5\frac{1}{2} - 1.75$.

Convert 1.75 to an equivalent fraction, $1\frac{3}{4}$.

$-5\frac{1}{2} - 1\frac{3}{4}$

$= -5\frac{2}{4} + \left(-1\frac{3}{4}\right)$

$= -6\frac{5}{4}$

$= -7\frac{1}{4}$

Practice

1. Doug digs a hole that is 1.7 feet below ground level. He plants a bush that is $3\frac{2}{10}$ feet tall from the bottom of the root to the top branch. How much of the bush is above the ground?

2. Penelope has a birdhouse that is $4\frac{9}{10}$ feet above the roof of her garage. She has a second birdhouse that is 5.36 feet below the roof of her garage. What is the distance between the birdhouses?

3. Find the sum or difference.

   a. $-2.63 + 3\frac{1}{4}$ b. $-4\frac{1}{2} - (-1.07)$

   c. $0.74 + \left(-\frac{3}{5}\right)$ d. $-\frac{1}{8} - 0.356$

Multiply Integers

Quick Review

Multiply integers the same way you multiply whole numbers. If the signs of the factors are the same, the product is positive. If the signs of the factors are different, the product is negative.

Example

$-9 \cdot -8 = 72$
$-9 \cdot 8 = -72$

Practice

1. Marisa buys 4 books at $13 per book. What integer represents the total change in the amount of money Marisa has?

2. Which expressions have a product of -18? Select all that apply.

   ☐ $-2 \cdot -9$ ☐ $-6 \cdot 3$

   ☐ $-3 \cdot 6$ ☐ $-9 \cdot 2$

3. Find the product.

   a. $-7 \cdot -14$ b. $-15 \cdot 12$

   c. $9 \cdot -20$ d. $-11 \cdot -16$

Go Online | PearsonRealize.com

Quick Review

The same rules for multiplying integers apply to multiplying rational numbers. If the signs of the factors are the same, the product will be positive. If the signs of the factors are different, the product will be negative.

Example

$-9.6 \cdot 1.8 = -17.28$

$-9.6 \cdot -1.8 = 17.28$

Practice

1. Jason spends $2.35 to buy lunch at school. If he buys a lunch on 9 days, what number represents the total change in the amount of money Jason has?

Multiply.

2. $-2\frac{2}{3} \cdot -4\frac{3}{7}$

3. $-3\frac{4}{9} \cdot 5\frac{2}{5}$

4. $6\frac{2}{3} \cdot -4\frac{1}{5}$

Quick Review

Divide integers the same way you divide whole numbers. The quotient is positive if the signs of the dividend and divisor are the same. The quotient is negative if the signs of the dividend and divisor are different.

Example

$-39 \div 3 = -13$

$-39 \div -3 = 13$

Practice

1. Which expressions have a quotient of -4? Select all that apply.

   ☐ $\frac{-24}{6}$ ☐ $-36 \div -9$

   ☐ $-72 \div 18$ ☐ $\frac{84}{-21}$

2. Whitney rolls a ball down a ramp that is 18 feet long. If the ball rolls down 2 feet each second, what integer represents the amount of time, in seconds, the ball takes to reach the end of the ramp?

3. Find the quotient.

   a. $\frac{81}{-9}$ b. $-123 \div -4$

   c. $-\frac{94}{4}$ d. $65 \div (-5)$

Divide Rational Numbers

Quick Review

The same rules for dividing integers apply to dividing all rational numbers. The quotient is positive when the numbers being divided have the same signs. The quotient is negative when the numbers being divided have different signs. **Complex fractions** have a fraction in the numerator, the denominator, or both. To divide by a fraction, rewrite as multiplication by its **multiplicative inverse**, or reciprocal.

Example

Simplify $\dfrac{-\frac{3}{4}}{\frac{15}{24}}$.

$$-\frac{3}{4} \div \frac{15}{24} = -\frac{3}{4} \cdot \frac{24}{15} = -\frac{72}{60} = -\frac{6}{5} = -1\frac{1}{5}$$

Practice

Find the quotient.

1. $\dfrac{8}{9} \div -1\dfrac{4}{15}$

2. $-3.6 \div 2\dfrac{1}{7}$

3. A boat drops an anchor 17.5 feet to the bottom of a lake. If the anchor falls at a rate of 0.07 feet each second, how long will it take the anchor to reach the bottom of the lake?

Solve Problems with Rational Numbers

Quick Review

You can use rational numbers to solve problems in the same way that you use whole numbers. Be sure to make sense of the problem you are solving to help you choose the correct operations and determine which values will be positive and which will be negative.

Example

During a 15-day dry spell, the water level in a lake changed by $-2\frac{3}{8}$ inches. What rational number represents the average change in the water level per day?

$$-2\frac{3}{8} \div 15$$

$$= -\frac{19}{8} \cdot \frac{1}{15}$$

$$= -\frac{19}{120} \text{ inch}$$

Practice

1. In 5 rounds of a game, Jill scored -3, 8, 9, -7, and 13. What integer represents her average score for the 5 rounds?

2. Peter signed up for a program that costs $10.50 per month to stream movies to his computer. He decided to cancel his service after $\frac{5}{6}$ month. He only has to pay for the amount of time he used the service. What number represents the total change in the amount of money Peter has after paying for the service?

3. Maggie spent $4.05 on cheese and fruit at the farmer's market. She bought $\frac{1}{8}$ pound of apples, $\frac{1}{4}$ pound of pears, and 1.25 pounds of bananas. If fruit cost $0.80 per pound, how much did Maggie spend on cheese?

Crisscrossed

Find each sum, difference, product, or quotient. Write your answers in the cross-number puzzle below. Each digit and negative sign in your answers goes in its own box.

I can...
add, subtract, multiply, and divide integers.
7.NS.1.1, 7.NS.1.2

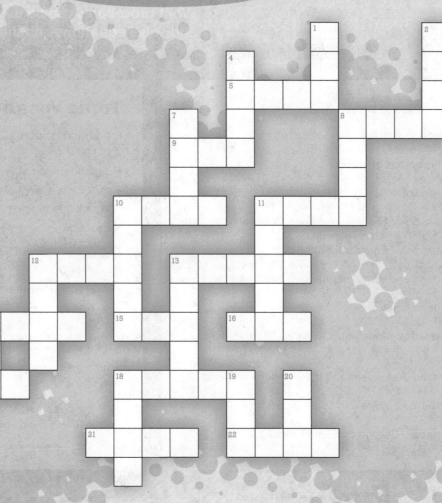

Across

2. $248 + (-1,027)$
5. $818 - (-1,021)$
6. $-516 + 774$
8. $242 + (-656)$
9. $2,087 + (-1,359)$
10. $631 - 897$
11. $-342 + 199$
12. $-49 \cdot -27$
13. $-321 - 987$
14. $2,988 \div -3$
15. $2,580 \div 6$
16. $4,592 \div -82$
17. $48 \cdot -27$
18. $-24 \cdot 83$
21. $-118 + 1,201$
22. $-45 \cdot -59$

Down

1. $246 + 173$
2. $22 \cdot -22$
3. $726 - (-219)$
4. $501 - 699$
7. $-10,740 \div 15$
8. $6,327 \div -9$
10. $144 \cdot -16$
11. $15 \cdot -67$
12. $7,164 \div 4$
13. $-33 \cdot 63$
14. $-2,695 \div 55$
17. $-1,032 - (-285)$
18. $512 - 720$
19. $-729 + 951$
20. $-17 \cdot -25$

REPRESENT AND SOLVE EQUATIONS AND INEQUALITIES

? Topic Essential Question

What procedures can be used to write and solve equations and inequalities?

Topic Overview

Topic Vocabulary

- Addition Property of Equality
- dependent variable
- Division Property of Equality
- equation
- independent variable
- inequality
- inverse relationship
- Multiplication Property of Equality
- solution of an equation
- Subtraction Property of Equality

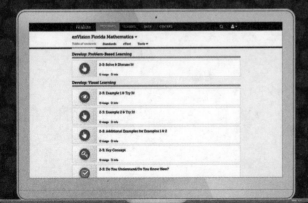

Lesson Digital Resources

INTERACTIVE STUDENT EDITION
Access online or offline.

VISUAL LEARNING ANIMATION
Interact with visual learning animations.

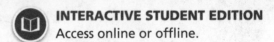

ACTIVITY Use with *Solve & Discuss It, Explo* and *Explain It* activities, and to explore Exar

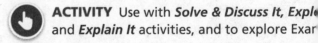

VIDEOS Watch clips to support *3-Act Mathematical Modeling Lessons* and *STEM*

Go online | **PearsonRealize.com**

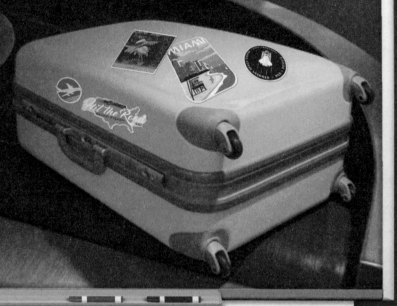

Checking a Bag

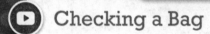
Checking a Bag

A large plane flying across the ocean can weigh almost 1 million pounds! The heavier an airplane is, the more fuel it needs for a flight. The cost of fuel has led many airlines to add a weight restriction on luggage.

If you were to fly somewhere, what would you bring? What would you leave at home to minimize the weight of your luggage? Packing light is important, not only to avoid a fee but also to do your part to conserve fuel. Think about this during the 3-Act Mathematical Modeling lesson.

 PRACTICE Practice what you've learned.

 TUTORIALS Get help from *Virtual Nerd*, right when you need it.

 MATH TOOLS Explore math with digital tools.

 GAMES Play Math Games to help you learn.

 KEY CONCEPT Review important lesson content.

 GLOSSARY Read and listen to English/Spanish definitions.

 ASSESSMENT Show what you've learned.

enVision® STEM Project

VIDEO

Did You Know?

The design of a bridge depends on factors such as the distance the bridge will cover, the expected number of vehicles that will cross the bridge daily, and the geographic conditions.

Beam

Beam bridges contain a horizontal beam supported at each end by piers.

Arch

Arch bridges have a curved design with supports, or abutments, on each end.

Cantilever

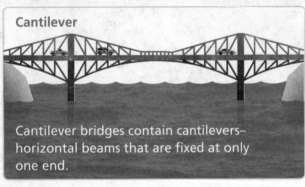

Cantilever bridges contain cantilevers–horizontal beams that are fixed at only one end.

Truss

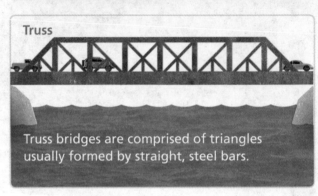

Truss bridges are comprised of triangles usually formed by straight, steel bars.

Suspension

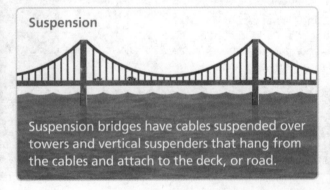

Suspension bridges have cables suspended over towers and vertical suspenders that hang from the cables and attach to the deck, or road.

Cable-stayed

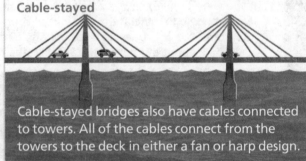

Cable-stayed bridges also have cables connected to towers. All of the cables connect from the towers to the deck in either a fan or harp design.

Your Task: Design a Bridge ▶

Now that you have defined the problem, identified the criteria and constraints, and performed some data collection, it is time to focus on the solution. You and your classmates will continue to be engineers as you brainstorm solutions and develop prototypes for your bridge.

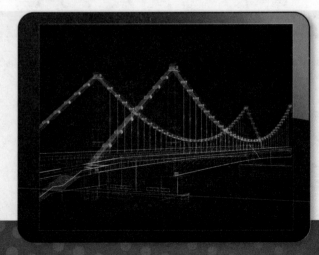

Review What You Know!

Vocabulary

Choose the best term from the box to complete each definition.

> algebraic expression
> coefficient
> equation
> evaluate
> variable

1. In $6x$, x is a(n) _____.

2. $x + 5$ is an example of a(n) _____.

3. _____ an expression to find its value.

4. The expressions on each side of the equal sign in a(n) _____ are equal.

Equality

Tell whether the equation is true or false.

5. $6 + 2 = 2 + 6$

6. $2.5 - 1 = 1 - 2.5$

7. $\frac{1}{2} \times 3 = 3 \times \frac{1}{2}$

8. $\frac{3}{4} \div 5 = \frac{3}{4} \times \frac{1}{5}$

9. $5 \div \frac{1}{3} = \frac{5}{3}$

10. $\frac{2}{3} \times 5 = \frac{10}{15}$

Expressions

Evaluate each expression.

11. $x - 2$ for $x = 8$

12. $2b$ for $b = 9$

13. $3\frac{3}{4} + y$ for $y = \frac{5}{6}$

14. $\frac{15}{x}$ for $x = 3$

15. $5.6t$ for $t = 0.7$

16. $4x$ for $x = \frac{1}{2}$

Order of Operations

17. Explain the order in which you should compute the operations in the expression below. Then evaluate the expression.

$[(33 \div 3) + 1] - 2^2$

Graphing in the Coordinate Plane

18. Describe how to plot point $A(-6, 2)$ on a coordinate plane.

Build Vocabulary

Use the graphic organizer to help you understand new vocabulary terms.

Addition Property of Equality

Definition

Example

Subtraction Property of Equality

Definition

Example

Properties of Equality

Multiplication Property of Equality

Definition

Example

Division Property of Equality

Definition

Example

Go Online | **PearsonRealize.com**

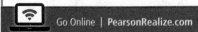
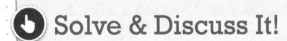

Solve & Discuss It!

 ACTIVITY

Unit cubes are placed on a pan balance. There are 3 cubes on one pan and 9 cubes on the other pan. What can you do to make the pans balance?

Model with Math A pan balance can be used to represent the relationship between two quantities. You can write an equation with a variable to show this relationship.

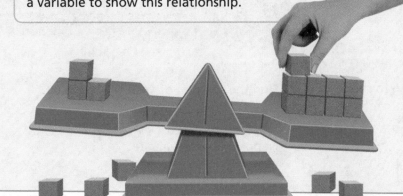

I can...
determine if a value for a variable makes an equation true.

MAFS.6.EE.2.5 Understand solving an equation... as a process of answering a question: which values from a specified set, if any, make the equation... true? Use substitution to determine whether a given number in a specified set makes an equation... true.

MAFS.K12.MP.2.1, MP.3.1, MP.4.1, MP.7.1

Focus on math practices

Use Structure Suppose that you added 10 cubes to the pan with 3 cubes and then added 4 cubes to the pan with 9 cubes. Would the pans balance? Write an equation to show this relationship.

VISUAL LEARNING ASSE

 EXAMPLE 1 Determine Whether a Value is a Solution of an Equation

Scan for Multimedia

Jordan received a $15.00 gift card for phone apps. He has used $4.50 of the value and wants to buy one more app to use up the balance. Which app should Jordan buy?

12:30 PM

PHONE APPS

🍴 RECIPES $9.50

W02 SPORTS $10.50

REMOTE DESKTOP $12.00

> **Model with Math** How can you use a bar diagram to help write an equation?

Draw a bar diagram and write an equation to show how the quantities are related.

$15.00

| $4.50 | x |

$4.50 + x = $15.00

> An **equation** is a mathematical sentence that uses an equal sign to show that two expressions are equal.

> A **solution of an equation** is a value for the variable that makes the equation true.

Find the solution of $4.50 + x = $15.00.

> Substitute the cost of each app for x and evaluate.

Try x = $9.50:

$4.50 + $9.50 = $14.00   Not a solution

Try x = $10.50:

$4.50 + $10.50 = $15.00   Solution

Try x = $12.00:

$4.50 + $12.00 = $16.50   Not a solution

The solution is $10.50, so Jordan should buy the W02 Sports app.

✅ **Try It!**

Tracy received a $21.00 gift card for phone apps. She has used $9.00 of the value and wants to buy one more app from the list above to use up the balance. Complete the bar diagram and use the equation $21.00 = x + $9.00 to determine which app she should buy.

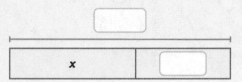

| x | |

The solution is ▢ , so Tracy should buy the ▢ app.

Convince Me! What do you notice about the expression on the left side of an equation compared to the expression on the right side when a value is substituted for the variable? How do you know which value is a solution?

Go Online | PearsonRealize.com

Maya has a total of 1,190 marbles and 5 boxes. She puts an equal number of marbles in each box.

A. Which of Maya's three friends, if any, correctly guessed the number of marbles, x, Maya has in each box?

1,190 marbles

x	x	x	x	x

$$5x = 1,190$$

Substitute each guess for x and evaluate.

Try $x = 234$: $5 \times 234 \neq 1,190$ Not a solution

Try $x = 242$: $5 \times 242 \neq 1,190$ Not a solution

Try $x = 240$: $5 \times 240 \neq 1,190$ Not a solution

Of Maya's three friends, none correctly guessed the number of marbles in each box. No solution is given in the set of values.

B. How many marbles did Maya place in each box?

There are 1,190 marbles equally divided into 5 boxes.
$1,190 \div 5 = 238$, so $5 \times 238 = 1,190$.

Maya put 238 marbles in each box.

An equation may have a solution that is not given in the set of possible values.

☑ Try It!

Anthony has a total of y marbles and 4 boxes. He puts 13 marbles in each box and has none left over. Which of his friends, if any, correctly guessed how many marbles Anthony has in all? Use the equation $y \div 4 = 13$.

y marbles

13	13	13	13

Substitute each guess for y and evaluate.

Try $y = 48$: $\boxed{} \div 4 = \boxed{}$

Try $y = 60$: $\boxed{} \div 4 = \boxed{}$

Try $y = 120$: $\boxed{} \div 4 = \boxed{}$

Friend	Guess
Julianne	48 marbles
Nikos	60 marbles
Quincy	120 marbles

Of Anthony's three friends, $\boxed{}$ correctly guessed the number of marbles he has in all.

No solution is given in the set of values.

Anthony has $\boxed{}$ marbles in all.

A **solution of an equation** is a value for the variable that makes the equation true. Substitute values from a given set for the variable and evaluate.

$x - 4 = 12$ $x = 9, 16$

$$x - 4 = 12$$

| 9 is not a solution of this equation because $9 - 4 \neq 12$. | 16 is a solution of this equation because $16 - 4 = 12$. |

Do You Understand?

1. **? Essential Question** How can you determine whether a given number makes an equation true?

2. When is an equation true?

3. **Reasoning** Ben says that $n = 5$ is the solution of the equation $7n = 45$. How can you check whether Ben is correct?

4. A pan balance has 3 cubes on one pan and 11 cubes on the other pan. Lucy thinks she should add 7, 8, 9, or 10 cubes to make the pans balance. How can you use the equation $3 + c = 11$ to find the number of cubes Lucy should add?

Do You Know How?

In **5–8**, substitute each given value of the variable to find which, if any, is a solution of the equation.

5. $d + 9 = 35$ $d = 16, 22, 26, 36$

6. $14n = 35$ $n = 2, 3, 3.5, 4$

7. $13.4 - g = 8.1$ $g = 4.3, 5.3, 5.5, 6.5$

8. $4 = 36 \div m$ $m = 4, 6, 8, 9$

In **9–12**, tell whether each equation is true or false for $n = 8$.

9. $n = 54 - 36$ 10. $5n = 40$

11. $152 \div n = 21$ 12. $n + 46 = 54$

Go Online | PearsonRealize.com

Practice & Problem Solving

Scan for
Multimedia

In 13–16, tell which given value, if any, is a solution of the equation.

13. $t - 2.1 = 0$ $t = 2.1, 2.4, 2.6, 2.8$

14. $49 = 7r$ $r = 3, 6, 7, 9$

15. $\$4.10 = \$6.25 - y$ $y = \$2.15, \$2.95, \$3.05, \$3.15$

16. $24 \div h = 6$ $h = 1, 3, 6, 8$

17. In the past, Marcie's father rode his bike 108 miles in 7.5 hours. Her mother rode the same distance in 8 hours. Marcie plans to ride her bike 108 miles at a steady rate of 18 mph for y hours. Will she match her father's or mother's time? Use the equation $108 \div y = 18$ to justify your answer.

18. Write if $b = 6$ is a *solution* or is *not a solution* of each equation.

   a. $8b = 48$

   b. $11 - b = 6$

   c. $b + 3 = 9$

   d. $54 \div b = 9$

19. A group of 4 friends is planning a fun day trip. The equations in the table represent the number of people n who can participate in each activity for $29.

Activity	Cost ($)
Raft Trip	$6n + 5 = 29$
Amusement Park	$14n = 29$
Balloon Ride	$30n - 40 = 29$

Which activity should the friends choose if they want to spend exactly $29?

20. There are 27 pennies on one pan of a pan balance and 18 pennies on the other. To make the pans balance, Hillary thinks 5 pennies should be added to the higher pan. Sean thinks 8 pennies should be added, and Rachel thinks 9 pennies should be added. Use the equation $27 = 18 + p$ to determine who is correct.

21. Construct Arguments Gerard spent $5.12 for a drink and a sandwich. His drink cost $1.30. Did he have a ham sandwich for $3.54, a tuna sandwich for $3.82, or a turkey sandwich for $3.92? Use the equation $s + 1.30 = 5.12$ to justify your answer.

22. Higher Order Thinking Write an equation that has a solution of 12. Show how you know that 12 is the solution.

23. Gina's family is driving 255 miles to visit Tallahassee. After driving for a while, they pass a sign that reads "Tallahassee: 124 miles." Substitute the values $m = 111$, 121, 131, and 141 in the equation $255 - m = 124$ to find the number of miles the family has already driven.

24. Lisa is making a quilt that uses a pattern of triangles like the one shown. Write an equation that represents the missing side length if the perimeter is 19 centimeters.

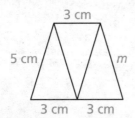

25. Alisa's family planted 7 palm trees in their yard. The park down the street has 147 palm trees. Alisa guessed that the park has either 11 or 31 times as many palm trees as her yard has. Is either of Alisa's guesses correct? Use the equation $7n = 147$ to justify your answer.

Assessment Practice

26. Trish has $26.00 to spend at a craft store. She buys fabric that costs $18.62. She also wants to buy knitting needles for $7.32, silk flowers for $7.38, or oil paints for $8.48.

Use the equation $\$18.62 + c = \$26.00$, where c is the item cost, to find the most expensive item Trish can buy. Explain how you found your answer. �@ 6.EE.2.5

Go Online | PearsonRealize.com

Solve & Discuss It! 🖥 ACTIVITY

Start with the equation 4 + 8 = 12 and complete each computation listed below. Do each computation individually. Which of the computations keeps the equation true? Explain.

I can...
use the properties of equality to write equivalent equations.

MAFS.6.EE.1.4 Identify when two expressions are equivalent (i.e., when the two expressions name the same number regardless of which value is substituted into them). ... Also 6.EE.2.7
MAFS.K12.MP.2.1, MP.3.1, MP.4.1, MP.7.1

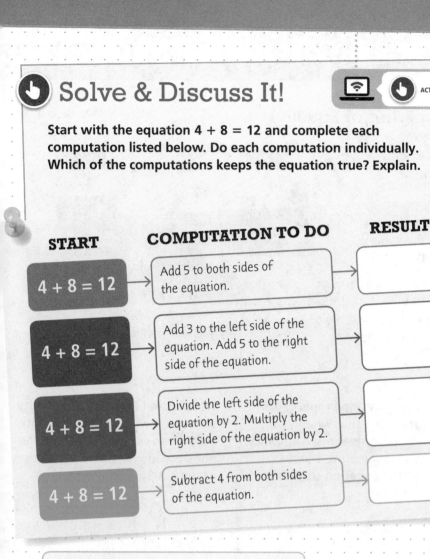

START	COMPUTATION TO DO	RESULT
4 + 8 = 12	Add 5 to both sides of the equation.	
4 + 8 = 12	Add 3 to the left side of the equation. Add 5 to the right side of the equation.	
4 + 8 = 12	Divide the left side of the equation by 2. Multiply the right side of the equation by 2.	
4 + 8 = 12	Subtract 4 from both sides of the equation.	

Reasoning How can you determine whether an equation is true?

Focus on math practices

Use Structure Complete the equation 7 + ☐ = 10 − ☐ by filling in the missing numbers. Describe at least two other operations with numbers that you can do to each side of the completed equation to keep it true.

EXAMPLE **1** **Define Properties of Equality**

Scan for Multimedia

Recall that an equation uses an equal sign to show that two expressions have the same value.

$$5 + 3 = 8$$

The **Addition Property of Equality** states that the two sides of an equation stay equal when the same amount is added to both sides of the equation.

> **Model with Math** An equation is like a balance. To keep the equation balanced, you must do the same thing to both sides.

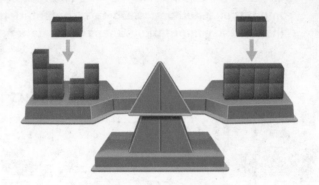

$$(5 + 3) + 2 = 8 + 2$$

The **Subtraction Property of Equality** states that when you subtract the same amount from both sides of an equation, the two sides of the equation stay equal.	The **Multiplication Property of Equality** states that when you multiply both sides of an equation by the same amount, the two sides of the equation stay equal.	The **Division Property of Equality** states that when you divide both sides of an equation by the same non-zero amount, the two sides of the equation stay equal.
$5 + 3 = 8$	$5 + 3 = 8$	$5 + 3 = 8$
$(5 + 3) - 2 = 8 - 2$	$(5 + 3) \times 2 = 8 \times 2$	$(5 + 3) \div 2 = 8 \div 2$

☑ Try It!

If $5y = 25$, which property of equality was used to keep the equation $5y - 7 = 25 - 7$ equal?

Convince Me! What other properties of equality could you apply to keep the equation $5y = 25$ equal? Give an example of each.

The scale balances with 1 blue x-block on one side and 4 green blocks on the other side. Franklin put some more green blocks on the right side and now the scale is not balanced. What can you do to make the scale balance? Which Property of Equality justifies this?

Multiply the left side of the balance by 3 to balance the scale.

$x = 4$

$3 \cdot x = 4 \cdot 3$

> The quantity 4 is multiplied by 3 on the right side of the balance.

> The Multiplication Property of Equality says that you can multiply each side of an equation by the same amount and the two sides will be equal.

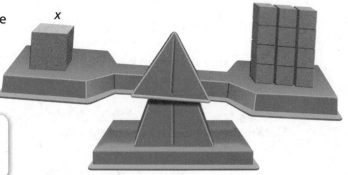

x

EXAMPLE **3** Apply Addition and Subtraction Properties of Equality

Merijoy says, "You can add 12 to each side of the equation $y - 12 = 30$ and the equation will still be true."

George says, "You can subtract 5 from each side of the equation $y - 12 = 30$ and the equation will still be true."

Who is correct? Explain.

$y - 12 + 12 = 30 + 12$

$y - 12 - 5 = 30 - 5$

> The Addition Property of Equality says you can add the same amount to each side of an equation and the two sides will still be equal.

> The Subtraction Property of Equality says you can subtract the same amount from each side of an equation and the two sides will still be equal.

Both Merijoy and George are correct.

✅ Try It!

A. A scale balances with four blue x-blocks on one side and 36 green blocks on the other side. Complete the equation to balance the scale with only one blue x-block.

$4 \cdot x = 36$

$(4 \cdot x) \div \boxed{} = 36 \div \boxed{}$

$x = 9$

B. If $25 + d = 36$, does $25 + d - 25 = 36 - 20$? Explain.

You can use the properties of equality to write equivalent equations.

Addition Property of Equality	**Subtraction Property of Equality**
$7 + 3 = 10$	$7 + 3 = 10$
$(7 + 3) + a = 10 + a$	$(7 + 3) - a = 10 - a$
Add the same amount to each side to keep the equation balanced.	Subtract the same amount from each side to keep the equation balanced.

Multiplication Property of Equality	**Division Property of Equality**
$7 + 3 = 10$	$7 + 3 = 10$
$(7 + 3) \times a = 10 \times a$	$(7 + 3) \div a = 10 \div a$
Multiply each side of the equation by the same amount to keep the equation balanced.	Divide each side of the equation by the same non-zero amount to keep the equation balanced.

Do You Understand?

1. **Essential Question** How can you use the properties of equality to write equivalent equations?

2. A pan balance shows $7 + 5 = 12$. If 4 units are removed from one side, what needs to be done to the other side to keep the pans balanced?

3. If one side of the equation $23 + 43 = 66$ is multiplied by 3, what needs to be done to the other side of the equation to keep the sides equal?

4. **Reasoning** If one side of the equation $x + 5 = 8$ has 9 added to it and the other side has $(4 + 5)$ added to it, will the equation stay equal?

Do You Know How?

In **5** and **6**, answer yes or no and explain why or why not.

5. If $23 + 37 = 60$, does $23 + 37 + 9 = 60 + 9$?

6. If $16 + 1 = 17$, does $(16 + 1) - 1 = 17 - 2$?

7. Apply the Multiplication Property of Equality to write an equation equivalent to $7n = 28$.

8. **Critique Reasoning** Tomas says that if one side of the equation $6m = 9$ is divided by 2 and the other side is divided by 3, the equation will stay equal because the result will be $3m = 3$. Is Tomas correct? Explain.

Practice & Problem Solving

Scan for
Multimedia

In 9–12, tell which property of equality was used.

9. $5m + 4 = 19$

    $5m + 4 - 3 = 19 - 3$

10. $3t = 20$

    $3t \div 2 = 20 \div 2$

11. $\frac{n}{6} = 9$

    $\left(\frac{n}{6}\right) \times 5 = 9 \times 5$

12. $5b - 6 = 14$

    $(5b - 6) + 2 = 14 + 2$

13. If $r + 9 = 42$, does $r + 9 - 9 = 42 + 9$? Why or why not?

14. If $6s = 24$, does $6s \div 6 = 24 \div 6$? Why or why not?

15. This scale was balanced. Find the number to add that makes the scale become balanced again. Then complete the equation to make it true.

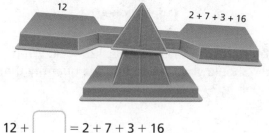

    $12 + \boxed{} = 2 + 7 + 3 + 16$

16. This scale balanced with 3 green blocks on one side and 1 blue x-block on the other side. Find the number to multiply by that makes the scale balance. Then complete the equation to make it true.

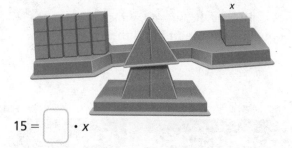

    $15 = \boxed{} \cdot x$

17. You start with the equation $8x = 24$. Your friend changes the equation as follows.

$$8x = 24 \div 4$$

How can you make your friend's equation equivalent to the original equation?

18. A scale balanced with 1 blue x-block and 20 green blocks on the left side and 40 green blocks on the right side. A student bumped into the scale and knocked some blocks off so that only 1 blue x-block and 3 green blocks remained on the left side. How many blocks do you need to remove from the right side to make the scale balance?

19. Bobbie wrote $y + 6 = 15$. Then she wrote $(y + 6) \div 3 = 15$. Explain why the second equation is not equivalent to the first. What can Bobbie do to make the two equations equivalent?

20. **Construct Arguments** John wrote that $5 + 5 = 10$. Then he wrote that $5 + 5 + n = 10 + n$. Are the equations John wrote equivalent? Explain.

21. **Reasoning** Scientists often use a pan balance to measure mass when doing experiments. The equation $4 + 3 - 1 = 7 - 1$ represents a scientist taking away one unit of mass from each side of a pan balance. Construct an argument to explain how the scientist knows that the pans are still in balance.

22. Bryce wrote the equation $n - 3 = 4$. Lexi used a property of equality to write an equivalent equation. Write an equation Lexi could have written. Explain how you know the equations are equivalent.

23. **Higher Order Thinking** Emil has $1 and a quarter. Jade has 5 quarters. If Emil gives Jade $1 and Jade gives Emil 4 quarters, will they each still have the same amount of money? Explain.

Emil's money

Jade's money

24. **Vocabulary** If $7w = 49$, which property of equality was used to find the equivalent equation $7w \div 7 = 49 \div 7$?

25. You start with the equation $12b = 24$. What step should you take to find the quantity that equals $4b$?

Assessment Practice

26. Which equation is equivalent to $n + 4 = 11$?
    🔵 6.EE.1.4

    Ⓐ $(n + 4) \times 2 = 11$

    Ⓑ $(n + 4) \times 2 = 11 \div 2$

    Ⓒ $(n + 4) \times 2 = 11 \times 4$

    Ⓓ $(n + 4) \times 2 = 11 \times 2$

27. Which of the equations is **NOT** equivalent to $8p = 12$? Select all that apply. 🔵 6.EE.1.4

    ☐ $8p \div 8 = 12 \div 8$

    ☐ $8p \div 8 = 12 \div 12$

    ☐ $8p + 4 = 12 + 4$

    ☐ $8p - 2 = 12 - 2$

    ☐ $8p \times 8 = 12 \times 12$

Solve & Discuss It!

ACTIVITY

A group of students were on a school bus. How many students were on the bus before the last stop?

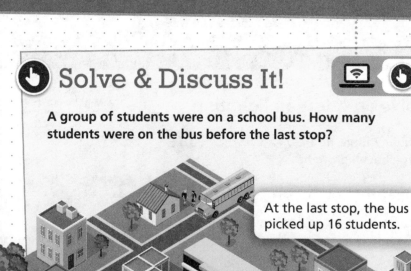

At the last stop, the bus picked up 16 students.

The bus arrived at school with 25 students.

Lesson 5-3
Write and Solve Addition and Subtraction Equations

Go Online | PearsonRealize.com

I can...
write and solve an addition or subtraction equation.

MAFS.6.EE.2.7 Solve real-world and mathematical problems by writing and solving equations of the form $x + p = q$... for cases in which p, q, and x are all non-negative rational numbers. Also 6.EE.2.6

MAFS.K12.MP.2.1, MP.4.1, MP.5.1

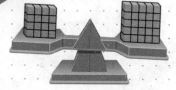

Use Appropriate Tools
You use a pan balance to help solve for the unknown.

Focus on math practices
Reasoning How does using cubes on the pan balance demonstrate the Addition and Subtraction Properties of Equality?

267

? **Essential Question** How can you write and solve an addition or subtraction equation?

VISUAL LEARNING

ASSE

EXAMPLE 1 Write and Solve an Addition Equation

Scan for Multimedia

George had some plastic figures. After he bought 7 more figures, he had 25. How many plastic figures did George have before he bought more?

Model with Math You can use a bar diagram, a balance, or an equation to represent this situation.

George bought 7 more figures.

ONE WAY You can find the value of *n* by getting it alone on one side of the equation.

Take 7 away from each side. That will leave the *n* alone.

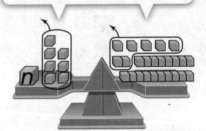

n is 18.

ANOTHER WAY Draw a bar diagram to represent the situation.

Total number of figures
25

n	7

Let *n* represent the number of plastic figures George had before he bought more.

He bought 7 more figures.

$$n + 7 = 25$$

To solve the equation, you find the value of *n* that makes the equation true.

Solve the addition equation.

$$n + 7 = 25$$

$$n + 7 - 7 = 25 - 7$$

$$n = 18$$

Operations that undo each other have an **inverse relationship**. Subtracting 7 is the inverse of adding 7.

To check, substitute 18 for *n*.

$$n + 7 = 25$$

$$18 + 7 = 25$$

$$25 = 25 \quad \text{It checks.}$$

George started with 18 figures.

☑ **Try It!**

Cabrini had some markers. After she bought 12 more markers, she had 16. How many markers did Cabrini have at the start?

Let *n* represent the number of markers Cabrini had at the start.

Convince Me! Which property of equality is used to solve the equation $n + 12 = 16$? Could one of the other properties of equality have also been used? Explain.

Solve the addition equation.

$$n + 12 = 16$$

$$n + 12 \boxed{} = 16 \boxed{}$$

$$n = \boxed{}$$

Cabrini had $\boxed{}$ markers at the start.

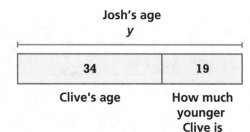

Write and Solve a Subtraction Equation

Clive is 19 years younger than Josh. Clive is 34. Write and solve a subtraction equation to find Josh's age, y.

Josh's age
y

34	19

Clive's age | How much younger Clive is

$y - 19 = 34$

$y - 19 + 19 = 34 + 19$

$y = 53$

Josh is 53 years old.

Substitute 53 for y to check your work.

$y - 19 = 34$

$53 - 19 = 34$

$34 = 34$

Solve Problems Using Equations

Andy had some basketball cards. After he bought 12 more, he had 48 cards. How many cards did Andy have at the start?

Draw a bar diagram to represent the situation.

Total cards Andy has
48

n	12

Cards Andy originally had | Cards Andy bought

ONE WAY Write and solve an addition equation.

$n + 12 = 48$

$n + 12 - 12 = 48 - 12$

$n = 36$

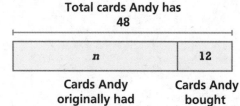
Original number + Cards bought = Total cards

Andy had 36 cards at the start.

ANOTHER WAY Write and solve a subtraction equation.

$n = 48 - 12$

$n = 36$

Original number = Total cards – Cards bought

Andy had 36 cards at the start.

Try It!

Vivian read 14 fewer pages than she was assigned to read. She read 60 pages. Write and solve an equation to find how many pages, p, Vivian was assigned to read.

You can use inverse relationships and the properties of equality to solve equations.

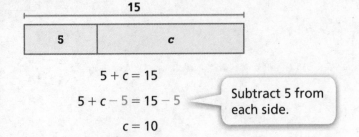

$$5 + c = 15$$
$$5 + c - 5 = 15 - 5$$

Subtract 5 from each side.

$$c = 10$$

$$m - 20 = 16$$
$$m - 20 + 20 = 16 + 20$$

Add 20 to each side.

$$m = 36$$

Do You Understand?

1. **? Essential Question** How can you write and solve an addition or subtraction equation?

2. Explain how you can use the inverse relationship of addition and subtraction to solve the equation $n + 7 = 25$.

3. **Model with Math** Clare had t seashells. After she bought 8 more seashells, she had 24 seashells. Write and solve an equation to find the number of seashells Clare started with.

4. **Model with Math** The outside temperature dropped 20°F from the time Arianna ate breakfast until the time she ate dinner. When she ate dinner the temperature was 35°F. Write and solve an equation to find the outside temperature t when Arianna ate breakfast.

Do You Know How?

In **5–10**, solve each equation.

5. $24 + m = 49$

6. $12 = y - 11$

7. $22 = 13 + a$

8. $t - 40 = 3$

9. $d + 11 = 15$

10. $32 = s - 19$

Go Online | PearsonRealize.com

Practice & Problem Solving

Scan for
Multimedia

Leveled Practice In **11–16**, solve each equation.

11.
$$y - 12 = 89$$

$$y - 12 + \boxed{} = 89 + 12$$

$$y = \boxed{}$$

12.
$$80 + r = 160$$

$$80 + r - \boxed{} = 160 - \boxed{}$$

$$r = \boxed{}$$

13.
$$60 = x - 16$$

$$60 + \boxed{} = x - 16 + \boxed{}$$

$$\boxed{} = x$$

14. $20 = y + 12$

15. $x + 2 = 19$

16. $z - 313 = 176$

---

17. You have some baseball trading cards. You give 21 baseball cards to a friend and have 9 left for yourself. How many baseball cards were in your original deck? Write and solve an equation to find t, the number of baseball cards in your original deck.

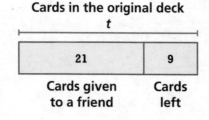

Cards in the original deck
t

21	9

Cards given
to a friend

Cards
left

---

18. Model with Math Joy added 26 new contacts to her phone list. She now has a total of 100 contacts. Let c represent how many contacts Joy had on her phone list before she updated it. Write an equation and solve for c.

19. Reasoning Jeremy bought a sandwich and a drink that cost him $7. His drink cost $1.75. Solve the equation $7 = s + 1.75$ to find s, the cost of Jeremy's sandwich.

20. A triathlon is about 51 kilometers. One participant completed two of the three legs of the race and traveled 42 kilometers. Solve the equation $42 + d = 51$ for the distance, d, of the third leg of the race.

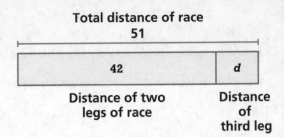

Total distance of race
51

42	d

Distance of two legs of race | Distance of third leg

---

21. What operation should be used to solve the equation $153 = g + 45$? Solve the equation.

22. Higher Order Thinking In the equation $6 + 3y = 4y + 2$ the variable y represents the same value. Is $y = 2, 3, 4,$ or 5 the solution of this equation? Explain.

---

23. A traffic helicopter descends to hover 477 meters above the ground. Let h be the original height of the helicopter. What is a subtraction equation that represents the problem? What was the original height of the helicopter?

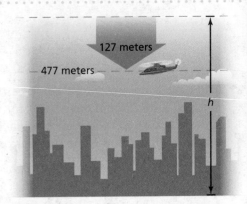

127 meters

477 meters

h

---

24. The drama club sold all the tickets for its annual production in three days. The club sold 143 tickets the first day and 295 tickets the second day. If the drama club sold 826 tickets, how many tickets were sold on the third day of sales? Solve the equation $438 + t = 826$ for the number of tickets, t, sold on the third day of ticket sales.

25. In a bag of mixed nuts, there are 35 almonds, 34 pecans, 32 walnuts, and p pistachios. The bag has a total of 134 nuts. Find the total number of almonds, pecans, and walnuts. Then write and solve an equation to find the number of pistachios in the bag.

Assessment Practice

26. Which equation has $g = 6$ as the solution? 🔵 6.EE.2.7

Ⓐ $g + 2 = 10$

Ⓑ $g - 1 = 10$

Ⓒ $58 + g = 60$

Ⓓ $44 - g = 38$

27. Select all the equations that have the same solution as $36 = x + 32$. 🔵 6.EE.2.7

☐ $42 = 38 + x$

☐ $x + 15 = 19$

☐ $18 = x - 2$

☐ $36 = x - 32$

☐ $52 - x = 46$

Solve & Discuss It!

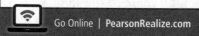

A school group is planning a trip to Jacksonville, Florida. There are 29 people going on the trip. They agreed to share the total cost of the trip equally. Let *s* equal each person's share of the cost. What is each person's share of the cost?

I can...
write and solve a multiplication or division equation.

MAFS.6.EE.2.7 Solve real-world and mathematical problems by writing and solving equations of the form... $px = q$ for cases in which p, q, and x are all non-negative rational numbers. Also 6.EE.2.6

MAFS.K12.MP.1.1, MP.3.1, MP.4.1, MP.8.1

TRIP COSTS

Bus	$7,830
Hotels	$10,034
Meals	$812
Special Events Tickets	$435
TOTAL COST	$19,111

Generalize How can you use what you know about dividing lesser numbers to write equations and solve problems involving greater numbers?

Focus on math practices

Construct Arguments Can you use the same strategy that you used above to find each person's share of the hotel bill? Explain.

? Essential Question How can you write and solve a multiplication or division equation?

> **EXAMPLE 1** **Write and Solve a Multiplication Equation**

Scan for Multimedia

Juan charged the same amount for each painting. How much did he charge for each painting?

> **Make Sense and Persevere**
> How do the quantities represented in the bar diagram and balance correspond to the equation?

3 paintings sold for $45.

ONE WAY You can use a balance to represent the equation.

> Divide both sides into 3 equal groups.

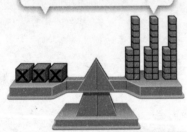

> *x* is 15.

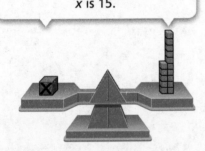

ANOTHER WAY Draw a bar diagram to represent the situation.

45

| x | x | x |

Let **x** = the amount charged for each painting.

3x = 45

> To solve the equation, find the value of x that makes the equation true.

Solve for x.

$$3x = 45$$
$$3x \div 3 = 45 \div 3$$
$$x = 15$$

> Use inverse operations to solve.

To check, substitute 15 for x.

$$3x = 45$$
$$3(15) = 45$$
$$45 = 45$$

Juan charged $15 for each painting.

☑ Try It!

Theresia picked the same number of tomatoes each day. In 4 days she picked 52 tomatoes. How many tomatoes did Theresia pick each day?

Let *n* represent the number of tomatoes Theresia picked each day.

Convince Me! Which property of equality can you use to solve Theresia's equation? Explain.

$$4n = 52$$
$$4n \div 4 = 52 \,\boxed{}$$
$$n = \boxed{}$$

Theresia picked $\boxed{}$ tomatoes each day.

 Go Online | PearsonRealize.com

EXAMPLE **2** Write and Solve for the Dividend in a Division Equation

  ACTIVITY ASSESS

The 15 members of the Adventure Club go on a group underwater diving trip. Student groups receive a special rate on snorkeling tickets that is half off the daily rate. Write and solve an equation to find, *t*, the total cost of snorkeling tickets.

Student Group Rate $\frac{1}{2}$ off $79 Ticket

Total cost of tickets
t

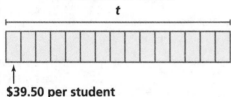

↑
$39.50 per student

$$t \div 15 = 39.50$$
$$t \div 15 \times 15 = 39.50 \times 15$$
$$t = 592.50$$

> Multiplying by 15 on both sides is the inverse of dividing by 15.

The total cost of the snorkeling tickets is $592.50.

 EXAMPLE **3** Write and Solve for the Divisor in a Division Equation

Helen puts 2,292 stickers in an album. Each page in the album holds 24 stickers. How many pages, *p*, did Helen fill?

Draw a bar diagram to represent the situation.

2,292 stickers

| 24 | *p* pages filled |

↑
Stickers on each page

$$\frac{2,292}{24} = p \quad \text{or} \quad 24p = 2,292$$

> You can use a multiplication or a division equation to represent this situation.

ONE WAY Solve the division equation $\frac{2,292}{24} = p$.

Divide to solve for *p*.

```
        95R12
24)2292
    -216
     132
    -120
      12
```

Helen filled 95 album pages.

ANOTHER WAY Solve the multiplication equation $24p = 2,292$.

$$\frac{24p}{24} = \frac{2,292}{24}$$
$$p = 95.5$$

Check.

$$24p = 2,292$$
$$24(95.5) = 2,292$$

> Evaluate the equation for *p* = 95.5.

Helen filled 95 album pages.

☑ Try It!

Meghann is reading a 630-page book. She reads 18 pages each day. Write and solve a division equation to find the number of days, *d*, it will take Meghann to finish her book.

You can multiply or divide both sides of an equation by the same number and it will remain balanced.

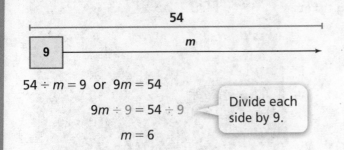

$54 \div m = 9$ or $9m = 54$

$9m \div 9 = 54 \div 9$ Divide each side by 9.

$m = 6$

$p \div 8 = 7$

$p \div 8 \times 8 = 7 \times 8$ Multiply each side by 8.

$p = 56$

Do You Understand?

1. **? Essential Question** How can you write and solve a multiplication or division equation?

2. Which property of equality would you use to solve the equation $8n = 16$?

3. Which property of equality would you use to solve the equation $a \div 9 = 2$?

4. There are 30 students in the drama club. They are carpooling in 5 vans to perform a play. They want each van to carry an equal number of students. Let s be the number of students in each van. Write and solve a multiplication equation to find the number of students in each van.

Do You Know How?

In 5–8, explain how to solve each equation.

5. $18m = 36$

6. $t \div 3 = 10$

7. $12 = 2y$

8. $22 = a \div 5$

In 9–12, solve each equation.

9. $23d = 2{,}392$

10. $74f = 6{,}179$

11. $y \div 11 = 987$

12. $r \div 187 = 9$

Practice & Problem Solving

Scan for
Multimedia

In 13–16, explain how to get the variable alone in each equation.

13. $8y = 56$

14. $t \div 15 = 3$

15. $u \div 8 = 12$

16. $31y = 310$

In 17–20, solve each equation.

17. $d \div 2 = 108$

18. $7{,}200 = 800s$

19. $x \div 3 = 294$

20. $99 = 3x$

**In 21 and 22, write a division equation and a multiplication equation
to represent each problem.**

21. Lolo typed 1,125 words in 15 minutes. Let w
represent the number of words typed each minute.
If Lolo typed the same number of words each
minute, how many words did she type in 1 minute?

22. In 12 weeks Felipé earns $4,500 doing yard work.
He earns the same amount each week. Let m
stand for the amount earned each week. How
much does Felipé make in 1 week?

23. **Model with Math** Abel has 3,330 toothpicks. He wants
to use them all to make a floor mat with 18 equal rows.
Use the bar diagram to write a division equation. Then
solve the equation to find how many toothpicks Abel
should use in each row.

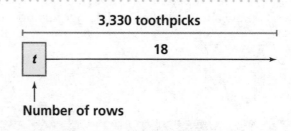

3,330 toothpicks

18

t

↑
Number of rows

24. **Model with Math** Emily took an airplane trip. Her plane
flew an equal number of miles each hour. Let m stand for
the miles flown each hour. Write an equation to represent
one way you can find how many miles Emily's plane flew
each hour.

In 25 and 26, use the triangle.

25. The area of the isosceles triangle is 44 square centimeters. Use the equation $\frac{1}{2}(8h) = 44$ to find the height of the triangle.

26. If the perimeter of the triangle is 32 centimeters, what is the length of each of the two sides? Write and solve an equation.

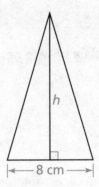

8 cm

27. Kelsey and her 4 sisters spent an equal amount of time cleaning their home. Their parents added their times. They found that each of the 5 girls spent 3 hours cleaning. Let c be the total number of hours the girls spent cleaning. Write and solve a division equation to find the total number of hours the girls spent cleaning.

28. **Higher Order Thinking** Veronica traveled 562 miles to Venice, Florida. She drove 85 miles every day. On the last day of her trip she only drove 52 miles. Write and solve an equation to find the number of days Veronica traveled. Explain each step of your problem-solving strategy.

29. **Generalize** A movie theater sells 11,550 tickets for 50 sold-out showings of the same movie. Write a division equation that you can use to find the number of people who bought tickets for each showing. Use what you know about dividing with larger numbers to solve the equation.

A-Z Theatres
A-Z Theatres
Admit One
11/21 8:00 PM
Theatre 03
General Admission

🔺 **Assessment Practice**

30. In October, Calvin's school used 4,920 pounds of sand to protect the building against flooding during different tropical storms. One bag contains 40 pounds of sand.

    Which of the following equations can be used to find how many bags of sand, b, Calvin's school used in October? 🔘 6.EE.2.7

    Ⓐ $4{,}920b = 40$

    Ⓑ $b \div 40 = 4{,}920$

    Ⓒ $40b = 4{,}920$

    Ⓓ $b \div 4{,}920 = 40$

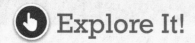 **Explore It!** ACTIVITY

The cost of T-shirts for four different soccer teams are shown below.

| $12.50 | $11.95 | $8.75 | $14.80 |

Team **A**   Team **B**   Team **C**   Team **D**

I can...
write and solve equations that
involve rational numbers.

MAFS.6.EE.2.7 Solve real-world and mathematical
problems by writing and solving equations of the
form $x + p = q$ and $px = q$ for cases in which p, q,
and x are all non-negative rational numbers.
Also 6.EE.2.6

MAFS.K12.MP.1.1, MP.3.1, MP.4.1, MP.7.1, MP.8.1

A. Lorna is on Team A. Ben is on another team. They paid a total of $21.25
for both team T-shirts. Write an equation to represent the cost of Ben's shirt.

B. Dario also plays soccer and he says that, based on the price of Ben's
T-shirt, Ben is on Team B. Is Dario correct? Explain.

Focus on math practices

Generalize How is solving for unknowns involving money like solving for
unknowns involving whole numbers?

? Essential Question How can you write and solve equations involving rational numbers?

   VISUAL LEARNING

EXAMPLE 1 Solve Addition Equations with Fractions

Scan for Multimedia

A 6-foot piece of fruit snack is cut into two pieces. What is the length of the shorter piece of fruit snack?

$3\frac{3}{4}$ feet

Use a bar diagram to show how the quantities are related and to write an equation.

Length of fruit snack

6	
$3\frac{3}{4}$	x

Length of longer piece — Length of shorter piece

$$3\frac{3}{4} + x = 6$$

Solve for x.

$$3\frac{3}{4} + x = 6$$

$$3\frac{3}{4} + x - 3\frac{3}{4} = 6 - 3\frac{3}{4}$$

> Use inverse relationships and properties of equality.

$$x = 5\frac{4}{4} - 3\frac{3}{4}$$

$$x = 2\frac{1}{4}$$

The shorter piece is $2\frac{1}{4}$ feet long.

☑ Try It!

Suppose you cut the shorter piece of fruit snack from the example above into two pieces. The longer of the two pieces is $1\frac{3}{8}$ feet long. Complete the bar diagram to represent the equation. Then find the length of the shorter piece.

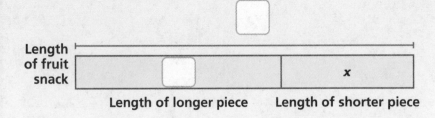

Length of fruit snack

Length of longer piece Length of shorter piece

$$1\frac{3}{8} + x = 2\frac{1}{4}$$

$$1\frac{3}{8} + x - \boxed{} = 2\frac{1}{4} - \boxed{}$$

$$x = 1\frac{10}{8} - \boxed{}$$

$$x = \boxed{}$$

The shorter piece is $\boxed{}$ foot long.

Convince Me! How does the equation change if you know the length of the shorter piece is $\frac{7}{8}$ foot and you want to know the length of the longer of the two pieces?

ACTIVITY ASSESS

Use inverse relationships to solve each equation.

A.
$$y - \frac{4}{9} = 5\frac{1}{3}$$
$$y - \frac{4}{9} + \frac{4}{9} = 5\frac{1}{3} + \frac{4}{9}$$
$$y = 5\frac{7}{9}$$

B.
$$\frac{3}{8}n = \frac{3}{4}$$
$$\left(\frac{8}{3}\right)\frac{3}{8}n = \left(\frac{8}{3}\right)\frac{3}{4}$$
$$n = \frac{8}{3} \times \frac{3}{4}$$
$$n = \frac{24}{12} \text{ or } 2$$

Multiplying by $\frac{8}{3}$ is the same as dividing by $\frac{3}{8}$.

C.
$$\frac{p}{5} = 8$$
$$\frac{5}{1} \cdot \frac{1}{5}p = \frac{5}{1} \cdot 8$$
$$p = 5 \cdot 8$$
$$p = 40$$

Multiply by the reciprocal of $\frac{1}{5}$, or $\frac{5}{1}$.

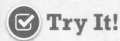 **Try It!**

Solve $\frac{5}{9}y = 25$ for y.

EXAMPLE **3** **Solve Multiplication Equations with Decimals**

Molly bought these oranges for $7.15. She paid the same amount for each orange. Write and solve an equation to find m, the cost of each orange.

Draw a bar diagram to represent the situation.

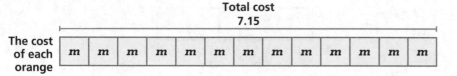

Total cost
7.15

The cost of each orange

| m | m | m | m | m | m | m | m | m | m | m | m | m |

$$13m = 7.15$$
$$13m \div 13 = 7.15 \div 13$$
$$m = 0.55$$

Molly paid $0.55 for each orange.

Oranges

Use Structure How can you use the operations in an equation to determine how to solve the equation?

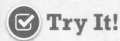 **Try It!**

Molly also buys a bag of 8 apples for $3.60. Write and solve an equation to find how much Molly paid for each apple.

EXAMPLE 4 Solve Addition, Subtraction, and Division Equations with Decimals

Use inverse relationships to solve each equation.

A.
$$m + 5.43 = 9.28$$
$$m + 5.43 - 5.43 = 9.28 - 5.43$$
$$m = 3.85$$

B.
$$y - 6.2 = 2.9$$
$$y - 6.2 + 6.2 = 2.9 + 6.2$$
$$y = 9.1$$

C.
$$x \div 2.5 = 40$$
$$x \div 2.5 \times 2.5 = 40 \times 2.5$$
$$x = 100$$

Try It!

Carmen spent $12.50 for a new notebook and a compass. The notebook cost $6.35. Write and solve an equation to find c, the cost of the compass.

KEY CONCEPT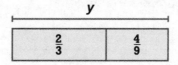

You can solve equations using properties of equality and inverse relationships.

Addition Equation

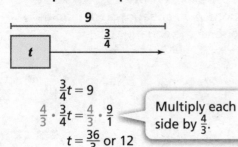

$$5.2 + c = 13.6$$
$$5.2 + c - 5.2 = 13.6 - 5.2$$
$$c = 8.4$$

Subtract 5.2 from each side.

Subtraction Equation

$$y - \frac{2}{3} = \frac{4}{9}$$
$$y - \frac{2}{3} + \frac{2}{3} = \frac{4}{9} + \frac{2}{3}$$
$$y = 1\frac{1}{9}$$

Add $\frac{2}{3}$ to each side.

Multiplication Equation

$$\frac{3}{4}t = 9$$
$$\frac{4}{3} \cdot \frac{3}{4}t = \frac{4}{3} \cdot \frac{9}{1}$$
$$t = \frac{36}{3} \text{ or } 12$$

Multiply each side by $\frac{4}{3}$.

Division Equation

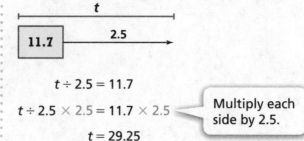

$$t \div 2.5 = 11.7$$
$$t \div 2.5 \times 2.5 = 11.7 \times 2.5$$
$$t = 29.25$$

Multiply each side by 2.5.

 Go Online | PearsonRealize.com

Do You Understand?

1. **Essential Question** How can you write and solve equations involving rational numbers?

2. **Construct Arguments** Why are inverse relationships important for solving equations?

3. **Critique Reasoning** Johnny says that he solved the equation $x - 3.5 = 7.2$ by adding 3.5 to the left side of the equation. Explain whether Johnny is correct.

4. **Generalize** When solving an equation involving a mixed number, such as $y + \frac{3}{4} = 4\frac{1}{2}$, what do you need to do to the mixed number?

5. **Construct Arguments** How is solving an equation with fractions like solving an equation with whole numbers? How is it different?

Do You Know How?

In **6–14**, solve each equation.

6. $t - \frac{2}{3} = 25\frac{3}{4}$

7. $\frac{f}{2} = \frac{5}{8}$

8. $13.27 = t - 24.45$

9. $r \div 5.5 = 18.2$

10. $\frac{7}{10} = x - \frac{3}{5}$

11. $1.8x = 40.14$

12. $17.3 + v = 22.32$

13. $9 = \frac{3}{8}y$

14. $1\frac{3}{4} + z = 2\frac{2}{3}$

Practice & Problem Solving

Leveled Practice In **15–22**, solve each equation.

15. $w - 3.2 = 5.6$

$w - 3.2 + \boxed{} = 5.6 + \boxed{}$

$w = \boxed{}$

16. $9.6 = 1.6y$

$9.6 \div \boxed{} = 1.6y \div \boxed{}$

$\boxed{} = y$

17. $48.55 + k = 61.77$

$48.55 + k - \boxed{} = 61.77 - \boxed{}$

$k = \boxed{}$

18. $m \div 3.54 = 1.5$

$m \div 3.54 \times \boxed{} = 1.5 \times \boxed{}$

$m = \boxed{}$

19. $7\frac{1}{9} = 2\frac{4}{5} + m$

20. $a + 3\frac{1}{4} = 5\frac{2}{9}$

21. $\frac{1}{8} \cdot y = 4$

22. $k - 6\frac{3}{8} = 4\frac{6}{7}$

23. Mr. Marlon buys these tickets for his family to visit the water park. The total cost is \$210. Write and solve an equation to find the cost of each ticket.

24. Higher Order Thinking Without solving, tell which equation below has a greater solution. Explain.

$\frac{5}{8}m = 2\frac{3}{4}$ $\frac{5}{9}m = 2\frac{3}{4}$

25. Make Sense and Persevere A high school track team's long jump record is 21 feet $2\frac{1}{4}$ inches. This year, Tim's best long jump is 20 feet $9\frac{1}{2}$ inches. If long jumps are measured to the nearest quarter inch, how much farther must Tim jump to break the record?

Go Online | PearsonRealize.com

26. **Make Sense and Persevere** About how many gallons of fuel does it take to move the space shuttle 3 miles from its hangar to the Vehicle Assembly Building?

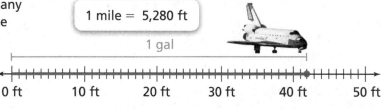

1 mile = 5,280 ft

1 gal

```
0 ft        10 ft        20 ft        30 ft        40 ft        50 ft
```

27. Is the solution of $b \times \frac{5}{6} = 25$ greater than or less than 25? How can you tell before computing?

28. What is the width of a rectangle with a length of $\frac{3}{7}$ ft and an area of 2 ft²? Write an equation to show your work.

29. **Model with Math** Helen is filling the pool shown for her little brother. She can carry $1\frac{7}{8}$ gallons of water each trip. Write and solve an equation to find how many trips Helen needs to make.

Holds $10\frac{1}{2}$ gallons

30. After the pool was full, Helen's little brother and his friend splashed g gallons of water out of the pool. There are $7\frac{7}{8}$ gallons still left in the pool. Write and solve an equation to find how much water was splashed out of the pool.

31. Grace solved the equation $2\frac{1}{2}y = \frac{5}{8}$. Her steps for the solution are shown in the table but are all mixed up. Write her steps in the correct order on the right side of the table.

Scrambled Steps	Solution Steps in Order
$2\frac{1}{2}y = \frac{5}{8}$	
$y = \frac{10}{40}$ or $\frac{1}{4}$	
$\frac{5}{2}y = \frac{5}{8}$	
$y = \frac{5}{8} \cdot \frac{2}{5}$	

32. The scientific name for the little bumps on your tongue is *fungiform papillae*. Each bump can contain many taste buds. The number of taste buds a person has varies. There are three general classifications of taste: supertaster, medium taster, and nontaster. Suppose a supertaster has 8,640 taste buds. Solve the equation $4.5n = 8,640$ to find the number of taste buds, n, a nontaster may have.

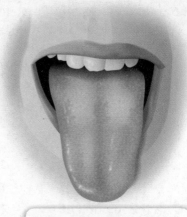

33. **Model with Math** In one study, the number of women classified as supertasters was 2.25 times the number of men classified as supertasters. Suppose 72 women were classified as supertasters. Write an equation that represents the number of men, m, who were classified as supertasters. Then solve the equation. How many men were classified as supertasters?

A supertaster may have 4.5 times as many taste buds as a nontaster.

34. **Use Structure** A fraction, f, multiplied by 5 equals $\frac{1}{8}$. Write an algebraic sentence to show the equation. Then solve the equation and explain how you solved it.

35. Yelena needs to swim a total of 8 miles this week. So far, she swam $5\frac{3}{8}$ miles. Use the equation $5\frac{3}{8} + m = 8$ to find how many more miles Yelena needs to swim.

36. Can any equation that is written using addition be written as an equivalent equation using subtraction? Explain your reasoning and give an example containing decimals that shows your reasoning.

37. **Critique Reasoning** Oscar is 12 years old and his little sister is 6. Oscar uses a to represent his age. He says that he can use the expression $a \div 2$ to always know his sister's age. Do you agree? Explain.

 Assessment Practice

38. Which value for y makes the equation $0.26y = 0.676$ true? 🌐 6.EE.2.7

    Ⓐ $y = 0.17576$

    Ⓑ $y = 0.26$

    Ⓒ $y = 2.6$

    Ⓓ $y = 26$

39. Which value for x makes the equation $0.435 + x = 0.92$ true? 🌐 6.EE.2.7

    Ⓐ $x = 1.355$

    Ⓑ $x = 0.595$

    Ⓒ $x = 0.495$

    Ⓓ $x = 0.485$

1. **Vocabulary** Describe the relationship between equations and the properties of equality. *Lessons 5-1 and 5-2* 🌐 6.EE.2.5, 6.EE.2.7

In 2–4, write an equation for the situation. Then solve the equation.

2. A fraction f multiplied by 4 equals $\frac{1}{2}$. *Lesson 5-5* 🌐 6.EE.2.7

3. When 832 is divided by n, the result is 16. *Lesson 5-4* 🌐 6.EE.2.7

4. When 10 is subtracted from x, the result is 6. *Lesson 5-3* 🌐 6.EE.2.7

5. Select all the equations that are equivalent to $n - 9 = 12$. *Lesson 5-2* 🌐 6.EE.1.4

   ☐ $n - n - 9 = 12 - n$ ☐ $n - 9 + 12 = 12 - 9$ ☐ $n - 9 + 9 = 12 + 9$

   ☐ $n - 9 - n = 12 - n$ ☐ $n - 9 + 9 = 12 - 12$

6. Select all the values for d that make the equation $9 = 18 \div d$ true. *Lesson 5-1* 🌐 6.EE.2.5

   ☐ 2 ☐ 0.5 ☐ $\frac{10}{5}$ ☐ 162 ☐ $\frac{1}{4}$

7. The area, A, of a triangle is 15.3 square centimeters. Its base, b, is 4.5 centimeters. The formula for finding the area of a triangle is $A = \frac{1}{2}bh$. Write and solve an equation to find the height, h, of the triangle. *Lessons 5-4 and 5-5* 🌐 6.EE.2.6, 6.EE.2.7

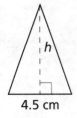

4.5 cm

How well did you do on the mid-topic checkpoint? Fill in the stars.

MID-TOPIC PERFORMANCE TASK

Ronald carved $3\frac{3}{8}$ feet of a totem pole. He says that the totem pole is $\frac{3}{4}$ complete.

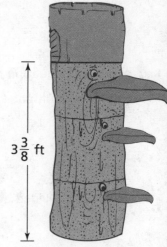

$3\frac{3}{8}$ ft

PART A

If h represents the height, in feet, of the finished totem pole, then $\frac{3}{4}h = 3\frac{3}{8}$ represents this situation. Which equations show the use of a reciprocal to write an equivalent equation that can be used to solve for h? Select all that apply. ☑ 6.EE.2.7

☐ $\frac{3}{4}h + \frac{3}{4} = 3\frac{3}{8} + \frac{3}{4}$

☐ $\frac{3}{4}h \times \frac{4}{3} = 3\frac{3}{8} \times \frac{4}{3}$

☐ $\frac{3}{4}h \times \frac{3}{4} = 3\frac{3}{8} \times \frac{3}{4}$

☐ $\frac{3}{4}h - \frac{3}{4} = 3\frac{3}{8} - \frac{3}{4}$

☐ $\frac{3}{4}h \times \frac{4}{3} = 3\frac{3}{8} \times \frac{3}{4}$

PART B

Use the equation in Part A to determine the height of the finished totem pole. Then write and solve an equation to find the height, s, of the section that has not been carved. ☑ 6.EE.2.7

PART C

Ronald spent $10.50 on tools and x dollars on the wood for the totem pole. His total cost for the totem pole is $19.35. The equation $10.50 + x = $19.35 represents this situation. What is the cost of the wood Ronald used? ☑ 6.EE.2.7

PART D

To make the same totem pole with wood that costs y dollars, Ronald would have to spend a total of $35.19. Explain which property of equality Ronald could use to solve the equation $10.50 + y = $35.19 and why that property can be used. Then show how to use that property to solve for y. ☑ 6.EE.2.7

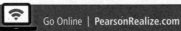
Solve & Discuss It!

ACTIVITY

The record time for the girls' 50-meter freestyle swimming competition is 24.49 seconds. Camilla has been training and wants to break the record. What are some possible times Camilla would have to swim to break the current record?

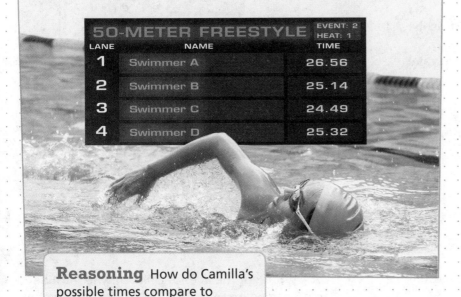

Reasoning How do Camilla's possible times compare to 24.49 seconds?

I can...
understand and write an inequality that describes a real-world situation.

MAFS.6.EE.2.8 Write an inequality of the form $x > c$ or $x < c$ to represent a constraint or condition in a real-world or mathematical problem. Recognize that inequalities of the form $x > c$ or $x < c$ have infinitely many solutions; represent solutions of such inequalities on number line diagrams.
Also 6.EE.2.5

MAFS.K12.MP.2.1, MP.4.1, MP.6.1, MP.8.1

Focus on math practices

Be Precise Fran won a blue ribbon for growing the heaviest pumpkin. It weighed 217 pounds. What could be the weights of other pumpkins in the contest? How could you show the weights of the other pumpkins using a mathematical statement? Explain.

VISUAL LEARNING   ASSES

EXAMPLE 1 👁 **Understand Inequalities**

Scan for Multimedia

BEACH WATER SLIDE

NOTICE: CHILDREN UNDER THE AGE OF 8 MUST BE ACCOMPANIED BY AN ADULT

An inequality is a mathematical sentence that contains < (less than), > (greater than), ≤ (less than or equal to), ≥ (greater than or equal to), or ≠ (not equal to).

How can you write an inequality to describe the ages of the children who must be accompanied by an adult at the beach water slide?

Model with Math How can you use an inequality to represent more than one value?

What are some ages of children who must be accompanied by an adult?

You can show some of the ages on a number line.

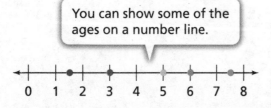

0 1 2 3 4 5 6 7 8

Let a represent the ages of children who must be accompanied by an adult. Use the *less than* symbol (<) to write the inequality.

$$a < 8$$

This inequality is read as "a is less than 8."

✅ **Try It!**

Use the number line to show some of the ages of people who do not need to be accompanied by an adult. Write an inequality to represent the ages of people, n, who do not need to be accompanied by an adult.

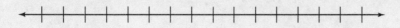

Convince Me! How do you know to which group an 8-year-old belongs, those who must be accompanied by an adult or those who do not need to be accompanied by an adult? Explain.

EXAMPLE 2 Write Inequalities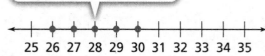

Write an inequality to represent each situation.

A. The length of a piece of wire, *l*, is longer than $20\frac{1}{4}$ feet.

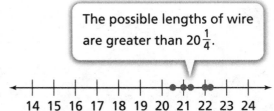

The possible lengths of wire are greater than $20\frac{1}{4}$.

14 15 16 17 18 19 20 21 22 23 24

$$l > 20\frac{1}{4}$$

B. The number of students, *s*, is at most 30.

The possible numbers of students are less than or equal to 30.

25 26 27 28 29 30 31 32 33 34 35

$$s \leq 30$$

C. The cost of the pizza, *c*, will be at least $8.00.

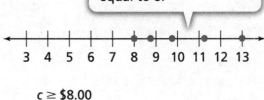

The possible costs of the pizza are greater than or equal to 8.

3 4 5 6 7 8 9 10 11 12 13

$$c \geq \$8.00$$

D. Zoe's age, *z*, is not 11 years old.

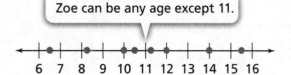

Zoe can be any age except 11.

6 7 8 9 10 11 12 13 14 15 16

$$z \neq 11$$

Be Precise The *not equal to* symbol ($\neq$) tells you that the values on the two sides of the inequality are not equal, but it does not tell you which quantity is greater.

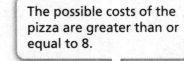

Try It!

Write an inequality to represent each situation.

a. Harry is taller than 60 inches.

b. Sherry is not 4 years old.

c. Hank has at least $7.50.

Inequality symbols can be used to describe situations that have more than one possible solution.

Inequality Symbols

Symbol	Meaning
<	less than
≤	less than or equal to
>	greater than
≥	greater than or equal to
≠	not equal to

This symbol contains a less than sign and part of an equal sign.

This symbol contains a greater than sign and part of an equal sign.

Do You Understand?

1. **? Essential Question** How can you write an inequality to describe a situation?

2. **Generalize** What is the difference between an equation with a variable and an inequality with a variable?

3. Would it be more efficient to use an inequality or to list all of the quantities less than 6? Explain.

4. **Generalize** How are the symbols for *greater than* (>) and *greater than or equal to* (≥) related?

Do You Know How?

In 5–12, write an inequality for each situation.

5. A number, n, is greater than 22.

6. The value, v, does not equal $2\frac{1}{2}$.

7. Sally's age, a, is at most 15.

8. The width of the picture, w, is shorter than 8.5 inches.

9. Steve's height, h, is at least 48 inches.

10. Vera's baby brother's age, b, is not 24 months.

11. The number of quarters, q, in the jar is less than 75.

12. The length of the fish a fisherman catches, f, must be at least 10 inches for him to keep it.

Practice & Problem Solving

In 13–22, write an inequality for each situation.

13. Up to 12 people, *p*, can ride in the van.

14. A number of days, *d*, of sunshine is not 28.

15. The distance of the race, *r*, is farther than 6.2 miles.

16. The value, *v*, of the bracelet is less than $85.25.

17. The number of people, *p*, that a restaurant can seat at one time is no more than 171.

18. The time, *t*, a customer has left on a parking meter is at least 25 minutes.

19. The bill, *b*, was less than $45.

20. The girls live *b* blocks apart; they do not live $7\frac{1}{2}$ blocks apart.

21. The speed of the truck, *s*, must be no less than 34 miles per hour.

22. The number of baseball games, *x*, that Karen went to last year is more than 5.

23. Mia is taller than Gage. If *m* represents Mia's height and *g* represents Gage's height, write an inequality that shows the relationship between their heights.

24. Taryn sold gift-wrapping paper for a school fund-raiser. She sold at least 15 rolls of paper. Write an inequality to represent the amount of money, *d*, she earned for the fund-raiser.

$8.00 per roll

25. A city in New England just experienced its greatest 1-day snowfall. Write an inequality to represent a snowfall that would beat this record.

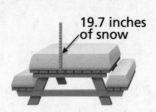
19.7 inches of snow

26. The first bookcase, *a*, in a library can hold 1 less book than the second bookcase. The second bookcase holds 2,492 books. Write an inequality to represent the number of books the first bookcase can hold.

27. A certain airplane must carry no more than 134 passengers during a flight. Write an inequality to represent the number of passengers, *p*, that would **NOT** be allowed during this flight.

28. Higher Order Thinking To ride a certain roller coaster, a rider must be at least 42 inches tall. To represent this situation, Elias wrote $h \geq 42$ and Nina wrote $h > 42$. Who is correct? Explain.

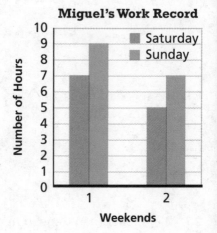
42" | STOP | YOU MUST BE THIS TALL TO GO ON THIS RIDE

29. Miguel earns extra money working two weekends with his dad. He is saving to buy a new bike that costs $140.

Heather says that Miguel needs to earn more than $6 for each hour that he works to have enough money to buy the bike. Her work is shown below. Write an inequality to explain why she is incorrect. 🐢 6.EE.2.8

> Heather's Solution
>
> Weekend 1:   16 hours
> Weekend 2: + 7 hours
> _____
>   23 hours
>
> $140 ÷ 23 hours > $6.00 per hour
>
> Miguel has to earn more than $6.00 per hour.

Miguel's Work Record

■ Saturday
■ Sunday

Number of Hours

Weekends

Solve & Discuss It!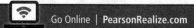

ACTIVITY

Henry is thinking of a number that is less than 17.
What number could he be thinking of?

Go Online | PearsonRealize.com

I can...
write and represent solutions
of inequalities.

MAFS.6.EE.2.5 Understand solving an... inequality
as a process of answering a question: which values
from a specified set, if any, make the... inequality
true? Use substitution to determine whether a given
number in a specified set makes an... inequality true.
Also 6.EE.2.8

MAFS.K12.MP.2.1, MP.4.1, MP.5.1, MP.6.1, MP.8.1

Use Appropriate Tools How can
you use a number line to show all the
numbers that are less than 17?

Focus on math practices
Reasoning Could Henry be thinking of 17? Explain.

VISUAL LEARNING   ASSES

EXAMPLE 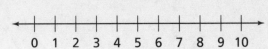 Graph the Solutions of an Inequality

Scan for
Multimedia

An inequality uses >, <, ≥, ≤, or ≠ to compare two expressions. Graph all the solutions of x > 5.

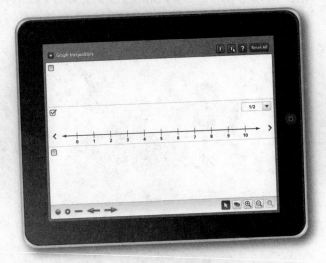

STEP 1 To graph x > 5, draw an open circle at 5 on a number line.

> The open circle shows that 5 is **NOT** a solution.

```
┼─┼─┼─┼─┼─⊕─┼─┼─┼─┼─┼
0 1 2 3 4 5 6 7 8 9 10
```

STEP 2 Find some solutions and plot them on a number line.

> 7 and 9 are solutions because 7 > 5 and 9 > 5.

```
┼─┼─┼─┼─┼─⊕─┼─●─┼─●─┼
0 1 2 3 4 5 6 7 8 9 10
```

STEP 3 Start at the open circle and shade the solutions you found.

> Draw an arrow to show that the solutions go on forever.

```
┼─┼─┼─┼─┼─⊕─┼─●─┼─●─►
0 1 2 3 4 5 6 7 8 9 10
```

Be Precise Inequalities have *infinitely many* solutions. This means that there is an unlimited number of solutions.

 **Try It!**

Graph all of the solutions of x < 8.

To graph x < 8, draw a(n) ☐ circle at 8 on the number line.

```
┼─┼─┼─┼─┼─┼─┼─┼─┼─┼─┼
0 1 2 3 4 5 6 7 8 9 10
```

7 and 4 are two of the many possible solutions of the inequality.

Shade the solutions to the ☐ of the ☐ circle you drew at 8.

Convince Me! How does the graph of the inequality change when the *less than* sign is changed to a *greater than* sign? How does it stay the same?

 Go Online | PearsonRealize.com

EXAMPLE **2** **Graph to Solve an Inequality**

 ACTIVITY ✓ ASSESS

The **Barbeque Beef dinner entrée** is the most expensive menu item. Some of the costs of the entrées are shown at the right. What are all the possible costs of the menu items?

Write and graph an inequality.

The possible costs of the menu items, m, are less than or equal to $12.25.

$m \le 12.25$ — There are too many possible costs to list, so it is more efficient to show the costs on a graph.

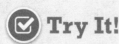

0 1 2 3 4 5 6 7 8 9 10 11 12 13 14

The closed circle shows that 12.25 is a solution of the inequality.

FLAMINGO
RESTAURANT

DINNER ENTRÉES

The Burger................. $8.75

Barbeque Beef........... $12.25

Pasta...................... $7.50

Chicken Taco............. $10.00

✓ Try It!

There are no menu items on the children's menu at the Flamingo Restaurant that cost more than $8.50. What are all the possible costs of the items on the children's menu?

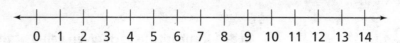

0 1 2 3 4 5 6 7 8 9 10 11 12 13 14

EXAMPLE **3** **Substitute to Solve an Inequality**

A long jumper who jumps at least 18 feet qualifies for the finals. Which athletes, if any, qualify for the finals?

Write an inequality to represent the situation.
$y \ge 18$

Amir: $22\frac{1}{3} \ge 18$ Solution

Jake: $16 \not\ge 18$ Not a solution

Tyrell: $18\frac{1}{2} \ge 18$ Solution

Ryan: $20\frac{1}{2} \ge 18$ Solution

Amir, Tyrell, and Ryan qualify for the finals because $22\frac{1}{3}$, $18\frac{1}{2}$, and $20\frac{1}{2}$ are solutions.

Long Jump Results	
Amir	$22\frac{1}{3}$ ft
Jake	16 ft
Tyrell	$18\frac{1}{2}$ ft
Ryan	$20\frac{1}{2}$ ft

✓ Try It!

Which athletes, if any, would qualify for the finals if the length of a jump that qualifies for the finals were at least $20\frac{1}{2}$ feet?

An inequality uses these symbols: $<$, $>$, $\leq$, or $\geq$ to compare two expressions.

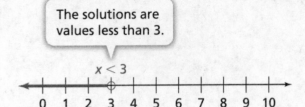

The solutions are values less than 3.

$x < 3$

```
0  1  2  3  4  5  6  7  8  9  10
```

The solutions are values greater than or equal to 5.

$y \geq 5$

```
0  1  2  3  4  5  6  7  8  9  10
```

Do You Understand?

1. **Essential Question** How can you represent the solutions of an inequality?

2. In Example 1, why is 9 a solution of $x > 5$?

3. Explain why 2 is **NOT** a solution of $x > 5$.

4. How many solutions does the inequality $x > 12$ have? Explain.

5. **Generalize** How do the graphs of the solutions of inequalities involving *greater than* ($>$) and *greater than or equal to* ($\geq$) compare?

Do You Know How?

In **6** and **7**, write the inequality that each graph represents.

6.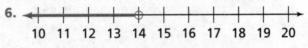

```
10  11  12  13  14  15  16  17  18  19  20
```

z

7.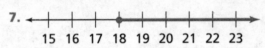

```
15  16  17  18  19  20  21  22  23
```

d

In **8–11**, substitute each given value of the variable to find which, if any, is a solution of the inequality.

8. $w < 8$ $w = 4.3, 5.3, 8.3, 9$

9. $t > 25$ $t = 24, 25, 25.1, 27$

10. $g \leq 4$ $g = 0, 4, 5, 6$

11. $y \geq 8$ $y = 4, 5, 6, 7$

Go Online | PearsonRealize.com

Practice & Problem Solving

Scan for
Multimedia

In 12–15, write the inequality that each graph represents.

12.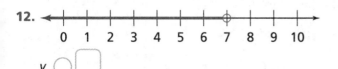

y ◯ ▢

13.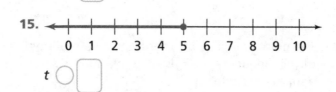

b ◯ ▢

14.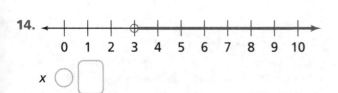

x ◯ ▢

15.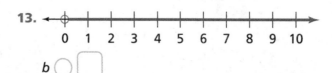

t ◯ ▢

. . . .

In 16–19, graph each inequality on a number line.

16. $h \geq 9$

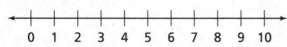

17. $p < 3$

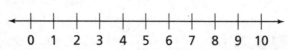

18. $t \leq 6$

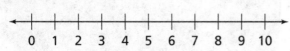

19. $s > 1$

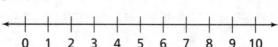

. . . .

In 20–27, name three solutions of each inequality.

20. $x > 10.5$ **21.** $r < 19$ **22.** $y \geq 200$ **23.** $m \leq 82$

24. $x \geq 12$ **25.** $q \leq 3.5$ **26.** $v > 35$ **27.** $m < 2.5$

. . . .

28. The inequality $w \leq 1,500$ describes the maximum weight in pounds, w, allowed by law in a freight elevator. Is a total weight of either 1,505 pounds or 1,600 pounds allowed in a freight elevator? Explain.

29. Reasoning Graph the inequalities $x > 2$ and $x < 2$ on the same number line. What value, if any, is not a solution of either inequality? Explain.

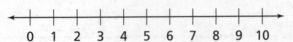

30. Model with Math Death Valley is the hottest place in the United States. The highest temperature ever recorded there was 134°F. The lowest temperature recorded there was 15°F. Write two inequalities that would describe the temperature, in degrees Fahrenheit, in Death Valley at any time since temperatures have been recorded.

31. The number line below represents the solutions of the inequality $x > 7$. Is 7.1 a solution? Is 7.01 a solution? Explain.

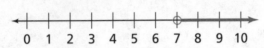

32. The temperature in a greenhouse should be 65 degrees or higher. Write an inequality to describe the allowable temperature in the greenhouse.

33. Higher Order Thinking Francine received a gift card to buy cell phone apps. She says that the card's value is enough to buy any of the apps shown at the right. Let v be the dollar value of the gift card. Write an inequality that best describes the value of the gift card.

34. The maximum load on a small plane is 400 pounds. Let w represent the weight on the plane. Write an inequality to describe the allowable weight on the plane.

35. Jillian is thinking of a whole number that is greater than 21. What numbers, if any, make the inequality $n > 21$ true for $n = 0, 1, 2, 3, 4, \ldots$?

Assessment Practice

36. Select all the given values of y that make the inequality $3y < 25$ true. 6.EE.2.5

- [ ] 6.5
- [ ] 7
- [ ] 8
- [ ] 8.5
- [ ] 9

37. Tania started a graph to show the inequality $y < 3.7$. Finish labeling the number line and draw the graph. 6.EE.2.8

3.0 3.1   4.0

Go Online | PearsonRealize.com

Checking
a **Bag**

MAFS.K12.MP.4.1 Model with mathematics.
Also MP.1.1, MP.2.1, MP.3.1, MP.5.1, MP.6.1,
MP.7.1, MP.8.1

MAFS.6.EE.2.5 Understand solving an equation
or inequality as a process of answering a question:
which values from a specified set, if any, make the
equation or inequality true? Use substitution to
determine whether a given number in a specified set
makes an equation or inequality true.
Also 6.EE.2.6, 6.EE.2.8

ACT 1

1. After watching the video, what is the first question that comes to mind?

2. Write the Main Question you will answer.

3. Construct Arguments Predict an answer to this Main Question.
Explain your prediction.

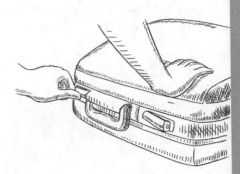

4. On the number line below, write a number that is too small to be the
answer. Write a number that is too large.

Too small   **Too large**

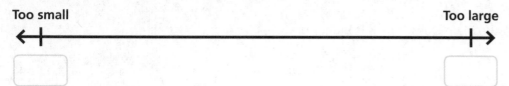

5. Plot your prediction on the same number line.

6. What information in this situation would be helpful to know? How would you use that information?

7. **Use Appropriate Tools** What tools can you use to get the information you need? Record the information as you find it.

8. **Model with Math** Represent the situation using the mathematical content, concepts, and skills from this topic. Use your representation to answer the Main Question.

9. What is your answer to the Main Question? Is it higher or lower than your prediction? Explain why.

Go Online | PearsonRealize.com

10. Write the answer you saw in the video.

11. Reasoning Does your answer match the answer in the video? If not, what are some reasons that would explain the difference?

12. Make Sense and Persevere Would you change your model now that you know the answer? Explain.

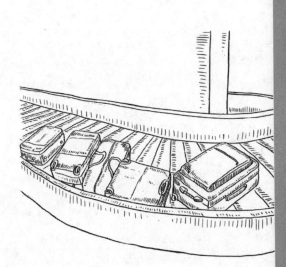

Reflect

13. Model with Math Explain how you used a mathematical model to represent the situation. How did the model help you answer the Main Question?

14. Was an *equation* or an *inequality* more useful to answer the Main Question? Explain.

15. Be Precise A different airline has a weight limit of 40 pounds for a checked bag. Explain how the answer would change for this airline.

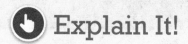

Explain It!

Max is shipping a present to his grandmother.

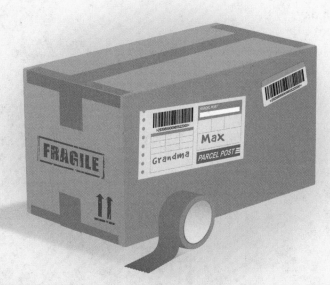

I can...
identify dependent and independent variables.

MAFS.6.EE.3.9 Use variables to represent two quantities in a real-world problem that change in relationship to one another; write an equation to express one quantity, thought of as the dependent variable, in terms of the other quantity, thought of as the independent variable. ...

MAFS.K12.MP.2.1, MP.3.1, MP.4.1

A. What are three factors that will affect the weight of the box? What are three factors that will not affect the weight of the box?

B. How might the size of the box and the contents of the box affect the weight of the box?

Focus on math practices

Model with Math Describe another situation in which changing one factor results in changes to another factor.

? **Essential Question** What does it mean for one variable to be dependent on another variable?

  VISUAL LEARNING ASSES

EXAMPLE 1 **Dependent and Independent Variables**

Scan for Multimedia

An orchard sells apples by the pound. Each day, *p* pounds of apples are sold and the amount of money taken in, *m*, is recorded. Which variable, *p* or *m*, depends on the other variable?

Reasoning When you think about how total cost is dependent on the amount and price of items sold, you are reasoning quantitatively.

Fresh-Picked APPLES

A **dependent variable** changes in response to another variable.

The amount of money, *m*, taken in depends on the number of pounds, *p*, so *m* is the dependent variable.

An **independent variable** causes the dependent variable to change.

The number of apples sold, *p*, affects the amount of money taken in, *m*, so *p* is the independent variable.

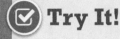 **Try It!**

A baker used a certain number of cups of batter, *b*, to make *p* pancakes. Which variable, *p*, pancakes or *b*, batter is the dependent variable? Explain.

Convince Me! If the baker doubles the number of cups of batter used, *b*, what would you expect to happen to the number of pancakes made, *p*? Explain.

EXAMPLE 2 Multiple Independent or Dependent Variables

ACTIVITY   ASSESS

A bike shop rents beach cruiser bikes and mountain bikes. Customers can rent these items by the day or the week. What are the independent and dependent variables involved in the cost of rental?

Joe's Bikes — Bike Rental Prices

	Price Per Day	Price Per Week
Beach cruiser	$18	$50
Mountain bike	$30	$90

STEP 1

Identify the variables involved in the cost of rental.

Beach cruiser, b	Mountain bike, m	Length of rental, l
Price per day, d	Price per week, w	Total rental cost, t

STEP 2

Determine whether the variables are independent or dependent.

Beach cruiser, b	Mountain bike, m	Length of rental, l	Price per day, d	Price per week, w	Total rental cost, t
Dependent on the rate per day or week	Dependent on the rate per day or week	Independent and causes the total rental cost to change	Independent and causes the total rental cost to change	Independent and causes the total rental cost to change	Dependent on the bike and length of time rented

Try It!

Jenna wants to rent a mountain bike by the week. Identify the independent variables that affect the total rental cost.

KEY CONCEPT

A **dependent variable** changes in response to another variable, called an independent variable. An **independent variable** causes the change in a dependent variable. It is *independent* because its value is not affected by other variables.

The distance a car travels, d, is dependent on the speed, s, at which it travels. Speed is the independent variable, and distance is the dependent variable.

Do You Understand?

1. **Essential Question** What does it mean for one variable to be dependent on another variable?

2.

Jake and Viola record the number of miles, *m*, they bike to help track the number of calories, *c*, they burn in an hour.

Critique Reasoning Viola says the number of calories, *c*, they burn is the dependent variable. Do you agree? Explain.

3. **Reasoning** In the biking problem above, identify at least one other independent variable that could affect the dependent variable.

Do You Know How?

In **4–11**, identify the independent variable and the dependent variable.

4. The amount of money, *m*, earned if *t* raffle tickets are sold

5. The number of hours, *h*, worked and the amount of money, *m*, earned

6. The number of shelves, *s*, in a bookcase and the number of books, *b*, the bookcase can hold

7. The number of pages, *p*, you read in your book in *h* hours

8. The number of gallons, *g*, of water a garden hose produces after running for *m* minutes

9. The number of peaches, *y*, a farmer harvests in *x* bushels

10. The number of hours, *h*, you spend driving at a speed of *r* miles per hour

11. Name at least two independent variables that could result in a change in a monthly electric bill.

Go Online | PearsonRealize.com

Practice & Problem Solving

In 12–15, identify the independent variable and the dependent variable.

12. The pages, *p*, in a book and the weight, *w*, of the book

13. The number of hamburgers, *h*, sold and the dollar amount of sales, *s*, taken in

14. The pounds, *p*, of flour you buy and the number of bread loaves, *b*, you want to make

15. The temperature, *t*, of water and the number of minutes, *m*, the water is in the freezer

16. Write your own situation. Identify the independent and dependent variables.

17. Name at least two independent variables that could result in a change in the price of a basket of grapefruits.

18. Critique Reasoning You spend *c* dollars for *p* identical pairs of pants. A friend claims that because *c* increases if you increase *p*, and *p* increases if you increase *c*, either *c* or *p* could be the independent variable. Is your friend right or wrong? Explain.

19. The number of oranges in a bag and the cost of the bag of oranges are related. What is the independent variable in this relationship? Explain.

20. The dependent variable *g* represents the growth of a plant. What variables can represent independent variables in this situation?

In 21 and 22, use the table at the right.

21. The table shows distances driven by the Williams family each day of their vacation. What is an independent variable that would affect the total distance they drove each day?

Family Vacation

Day	Distance
1	480 mi
2	260 mi
3	40 mi
4	150 mi
5	100 mi
6	320 mi

22. Name at least two dependent variables that could affect the amount of money the Williams family spends on meals during their vacation.

23. The cost of a salad at a restaurant depends on many factors. List at least two independent variables that could affect the cost of a salad.

24. Julian drove from New York to Florida. List at least two independent variables that could affect the number of days Julian took to make the trip.

25. The number of incorrect answers and the score on a math test are related. What is the dependent variable in this relationship? Explain.

26. **Higher Order Thinking** Write a situation in which time, t, is an independent variable. Then write a situation in which time, t, is a dependent variable.

Assessment Practice

27. Jonas is concerned about the amount of water he uses to wash his laundry. He made a table to show the number of gallons of water used by different washing machines to complete a load of laundry.

🔵 6.EE.3.9

Type of Washing Machine	Age of Washing Machine (years)	Gallons of Water
Older Top Loading	6	42
New Standard Model	4	28
Energy Efficient	2	14

PART A

Use variables to represent the independent and dependent quantities shown in the table.

PART B

Use variables to represent the dependent variable and the independent variable in this sentence.

Jonas records the total cost of the water he uses and the number of gallons of water he uses.

Go Online | PearsonRealize.com

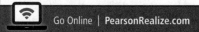
Solve & Discuss It!

 ACTIVITY

The table below shows how many candles are in different numbers of boxes. Find a pattern that explains the relationship between the values of *c* and *b*. Use words and numbers to describe the pattern. How many candles will there be in 10 boxes?

Number of Candles, *c*	Number of Boxes, *b*
8	2
12	3
16	4

Look for Relationships How can you get from each value in the left column to its matching value in the right column?

I can...
use patterns to write and solve equations with variables.

MAFS.6.EE.3.9 Use variables to represent two quantities in a real-world problem that change in relationship to one another; write an equation to express one quantity, thought of as the dependent variable, in terms of the other quantity, thought of as the independent variable. ...

MAFS.K12.MP.1.1, MP.2.1, MP.7.1

Focus on math practices

Use Structure Write a rule that explains how you get from the values in the right column of the table above to the values in the left column.

? **Essential Question** How can you use a pattern to write and solve an equation?

 EXAMPLE 1   👁 Find a Pattern to Write an Equation

The table shows the cost of weekend tickets to the Slide and Splash Water Park. Find a pattern that relates the number of tickets, n, and the cost, c, of the tickets. How much would 6 tickets cost?

> **Use Structure** How does finding the cost of 1 ticket help you find a pattern that relates the variables?

Slide and Splash Water Park

Number, n	Cost, c
3	$16.50
4	$22.00
5	$27.50
6	

Look for a pattern in the table that relates c, the dependent variable and n, the independent variables.

n		c
3	3 × 5.50	16.50
4	4 × 5.50	22.00
5	5 × 5.50	27.50

> 5.5 times the value of n equals the value of c.

Write an equation to describe the relationship.

5.5 times the value of n = the value of c

$$5.5n = c$$

or

$$c = 5.5n$$

Find the cost of 6 tickets.

$c = 5.5n$

$c = 5.5(6)$ ← Substitute 6 for n.

$c = 33$

The cost of 6 tickets is $33.00.

☑ **Try It!**

The table shows the number of yards, y, that a professional bicyclist rides in s seconds. Find a pattern that relates the variables. If the cyclist maintains this speed, how far would the cyclist ride in 8 seconds?

Seconds, s	Yards, y
2	24.4
3	36.6
5	61
6	73.2

Convince Me! How do you know that the equation you wrote describes the pattern in the table?

EXAMPLE 2

Make and Analyze a Table to Write an Equation

Ethan owes his mother $75. He repays his mother a set amount each week. How much will Ethan owe his mother after 12 weeks?

Make a table and look for a pattern that relates the variables.

Week, w	Pattern	Amount Owed, a
0	$75 - 5(0)$	75
1	$75 - 5(1)$	70
2	$75 - 5(2)$	65
3	$75 - 5(3)$	60
4	$75 - 5(4)$	55

To find the pattern, start with the amount owed. The amount owed decreases by $5 each week.

Write an equation to describe the relationship.

Amount still owed	Loan amount	Amount paid after w weeks
a	=	$75	−	$5w$

Let a stand for the amount still owed.

Let w stand for the number of weeks.

Find how much Ethan will owe after 12 weeks.

$a = 75 - 5w$

$a = 75 - 5(12)$

$a = 75 - 60$

$a = 15$

Ethan will owe $15 after 12 weeks.

 **Try It!**

If Ethan continues to pay $5 per week, how many more weeks will he need to pay his mother after 12 weeks? Explain.

You can use patterns in a table to write an equation that relates the independent and dependent variables.

j	1	4	7	8	9
m	3	12	21	24	27

The dependent variable m is 3 times the independent variable j: $m = 3j$.

Do You Understand?

1. **Essential Question** How can you use a pattern to write and solve an equation?

2. **Make Sense and Persevere** How do you find a pattern that relates the values in a table?

3. **Reasoning** In Example 2, what happens to the value of the dependent variable, a, the amount still owed, when the value of the independent variable, w, the number of weeks Ethan pays $5, is increased by 1?

4. **Look for Relationships** Use the pattern in the table below to write an equation.

x	y
1	7
2	12
3	17
4	22

Do You Know How?

5. The table shows Brenda's age, b, when Talia's age, t, is 7, 9, and 10. Find the pattern and then write a rule and an equation that represents the pattern. Then find Brenda's age when Talia is 12.

Talia's Age, t	Brenda's Age, b
7	2
9	4
10	5
12	b

In 6 and 7, use the table below.

x	4	5	6	7	8
y	1	3	5		

6. Use the equation $y = 2x - 7$ to complete the table.

7. State the rule for the pattern in words.

Practice & Problem Solving

Scan for
Multimedia

In **8** and **9**, write a rule and an equation that represents the pattern in each table.

8.

x	1	2	3	4	5
y	33	34	35	36	37

9.

m	0	1	2	3	4
n	0	3	6	9	12

In **10** and **11**, write a rule and an equation that represents the pattern in each table. Then complete the table.

10.

g	32	37	42	47	52
k	17	22	27	☐	☐

11.

x	0	9	18	27	36
y	0	1	2	☐	☐

12. To celebrate its 125th anniversary, a company produced 125 expensive teddy bears. These "125 Karat Teddy Bears" are made of gold thread and have diamonds for eyes. The table shows the approximate cost of different numbers of these bears. Write an equation that can be used to find c, the cost of n bears.

Cost of "125 Karat Teddy Bears"

Number, n	Cost, c
4	$188,000
7	$329,000
11	$517,000

13. Andrea attends the county fair. The fair charges for admission and for each ride.

a. Use the pattern in the table to the find the cost for Andrea to ride 5 rides or 8 rides. Then write an equation for the pattern.

b. Find the cost, c, for 12 rides.

Rides, r	Cost, c
3	$15.50
4	$18.00
5	☐
6	$23.00
8	☐

In 14 and 15, write an equation that best describes the pattern in each table.

14.

w	2	4	6	8	10
z	0	2	4	6	8

15.

x	0	$\frac{1}{2}$	1	$1\frac{1}{2}$	2	$2\frac{1}{2}$
y	0	2	4	6	8	10

In 16–19, use the equation to complete each table.

16. $t = 5d + 5$

d	0	1	2	3	4
t	5	10	15		

17. $y = \frac{1}{2}x - 1$

x	2	4	6	8	10
y	0	1	2		

18. $y = 2x + 1$

x	0	1	2	3
y	1	3		

19. $b = \frac{a}{2} - 2$

a	17	14	11	8	5
b					

20. Higher Order Thinking Maya wrote the equation $h = d + 22$ to represent the relationship shown in the table. Is this equation correct? Explain.

h	3	5	7	9
d	33	55	77	99

21. The table below shows the total cost for the number of movie tickets purchased. Write an equation that represents the relationship between these two quantities. Use the equation to find the cost of 6 tickets. 🔵 6.EE.3.9

Number of Tickets	3	5	7	9
Cost	$26.25	$43.75	$61.25	$78.75

Solve & Discuss It!

ACTIVITY

Nancy walks 4 blocks to Maria's house. Together, they continue the walk. The walk can be described as $n = m + 4$, where n is the number of blocks Nancy walks and m is the number of blocks Maria walks. Describe how the equation, data table, and graph reflect the walk.

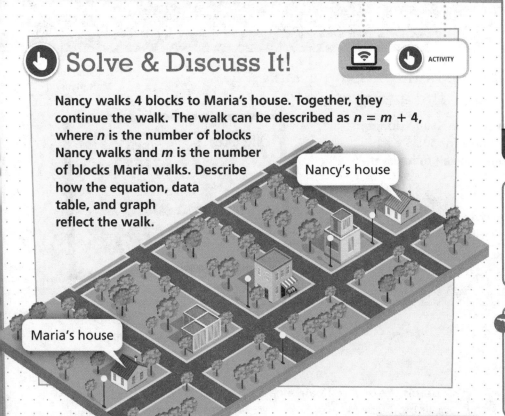

Nancy's house

Maria's house

I can...
analyze the relationship between dependent and independent variables in tables, graphs, and equations.

MAFS.6.EE.3.9 Use variables to represent two quantities in a real-world problem that change in relationship to one another; ... Analyze the relationship between the dependent and independent variables using graphs and tables, and relate these to the equation. ...

MAFS.K12.MP.2.1, MP.3.1, MP.4.1, MP.7.1

Look for Relationships How can you use the values in one row of the data table to describe the relationship shown in the equation, data table, and graph?

Number of blocks Nancy walks, n

$n = m + 4$	
m	n
1	5
2	6
3	7

Number of blocks Maria walks, m

Focus on math practices

Model with Math Draw a line through the points on the graph. What ordered pair on the line includes $m = 5$? Explain what that ordered pair represents.

? **Essential Question** How can you analyze the relationship between dependent and independent variables using tables, graphs, and equations?

EXAMPLE 1 **Relate Quantities Using a Table, a Graph, and an Equation**

Scan for Multimedia

The booster club members want to raise $50 to donate to a local charity. They buy pom poms for $0.55 each. How many pom poms do they need to sell to reach their fundraising goal?

Look for Relationships How can you use a table, a graph, and an equation to analyze the relationship between independent and dependent variables?

The booster club raises $0.45 for each pom pom they sell.

STEP 1 Make a table to relate the number of pom poms sold, n, to the amount of money raised, r.

The amount raised depends on the number of pom poms sold.

n	r
10	$4.50
50	$22.50
110	$49.50

STEP 2 Graph the ordered pairs on the coordinate plane.

Money raised, r

This point represents the number of pom poms sold to raise $50.

Number of pom poms sold, n

STEP 3 Write an equation that describes the relationship.

The amount of money raised, r, is 0.45 times the number of pom poms sold, n.

$$r = 0.45n$$

Substitute $r = 50$ and solve for n.

$$50 = 0.45n$$

$$50 \div 0.45 = 0.45n \div 0.45$$

$$111.11 \approx n$$

The booster club must sell at least 112 pom poms to raise $50.

☑ **Try It!**

The booster club now raises $0.41 for each pom pom they sell. Complete the table and graph. Write and solve an equation to find how many pom poms they need to sell to raise $50.

Convince Me! How does finding three values for x and y help you represent the relationship between x and y?

n	r
50	$20.50
100	$41.00
150	

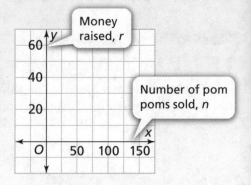

Money raised, r

Number of pom poms sold, n

EXAMPLE 2

Relate an Equation with Two Operations to a Table and a Graph

 ACTIVITY ASSESS

The temperature was 6°C at 8 A.M. and increased 2°C each hour for 6 hours one spring day. What was the temperature after 6 hours?

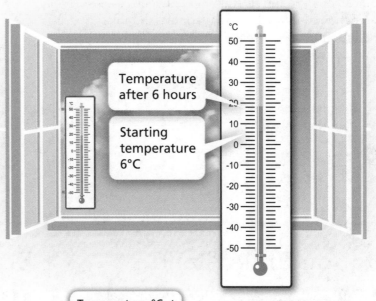

Temperature after 6 hours

Starting temperature 6°C

STEP 1 Make a table to relate the number of hours, n, to the temperature, t.

The temperature, t, depends on the number of hours passed, n.

n	t
0	6
2	10
4	14
6	18

STEP 2 Graph the ordered pairs on the coordinate plane.

STEP 3 Write an equation that describes the relationship.

$t = 6 + 2n$

Substitute $n = 6$ and solve for t.

$t = 6 + 2(6)$

$t = 6 + 12$

$t = 18$

The temperature was 18°C after 6 hours.

Temperature °C, t

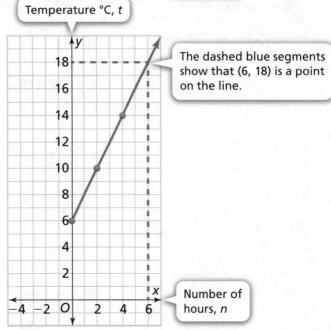

The dashed blue segments show that (6, 18) is a point on the line.

x

Number of hours, n

✅ Try It!

A company makes decorations for pens. All the supplies cost $5, and the company plans to sell the decorations for $2 apiece. Analyze the relationship between the number of decorations sold and the profit by completing the table and the graph. Use the table and the graph to write and solve an equation to find the number of decorations that must be sold for the company to make a $15 profit.

Independent variable

Dependent variable

Profit, y

x	y
3	

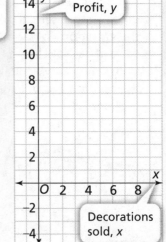

Decorations sold, x

You can analyze the relationship between independent and dependent variables in tables and graphs. You can relate tables and graphs to an equation.

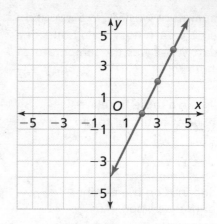

Do You Understand?

1. **Essential Question** How can you analyze the relationship between dependent and independent variables using tables, graphs, and equations?

2. **Reasoning** Using the relationship in Example 1, how many pom poms must the booster club sell to raise $75 for charity? Explain.

3. **Construct Arguments** For every 4 bananas a grocery store sells, it sells 2 apples. Mary wrote the equation $4b \times 2 = a$, where $b =$ the number of bananas sold and $a =$ the number of apples sold. Does Mary's equation correctly represent the relationship of bananas sold to apples sold? Explain.

Do You Know How?

In 4–6, use the equation $d = 4t$.

4. Complete the table.
   $d =$ distance
   $t =$ time

d = 4t	
t	d
1	
2	
3	

5. Name four ordered pairs found on the line plotted using this equation.

6. Describe the relationship between the variables.

In 7, complete the table and graph to show the relationship between the variables in the equation $d = 5 + 5t$.

7. $d =$ distance
   $t =$ time

d = 5 + 5t	
t	d
0	
2	

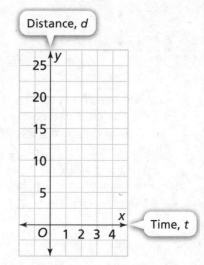

PRACTICE   TUTORIAL

Practice & Problem Solving

Scan for
Multimedia

In **8** and **9**, complete the table and graph to show the relationship between the variables in each equation.

8. A rectangle is $\frac{1}{2}$ inch longer than it is wide.

Let w = width.
Let ℓ = length.
Graph $\ell = w + \frac{1}{2}$.

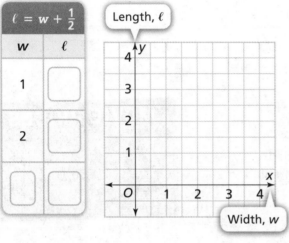

9. The sale price is $5 less than the regular price.

Let s = the sale price.
Let r = the regular price.
Graph $s = r - 5$.

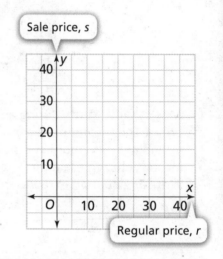

10. The points (2, 4) and (−2, −4) are plotted on the coordinate plane using the equation $y = a \cdot x$. How can you use the coordinates to find the value of a?

11. Without using a table or graph, identify three other points that a graph of the equation in Exercise 10 will pass through.

12. Reasoning The Jackson family is planning a weekend vacation. They plan to rent a car from the ABC Car Rental Company. Let m represent the number of miles the family will drive. Let c represent the cost for renting a car. Write an equation that shows what the cost for renting a car will be.

EXIT 32

ABC
CAR RENTAL
COMPANY
NEXT EXIT

Weekend Special
$40 + $0.10 per mile

In 13, write an equation. Complete the table and graph to solve the problem.

13. A puppy weighs 1 pound. What does the puppy weigh after 4 weeks?

Puppy gains $\frac{1}{2}$ pound each week.

x	y
0	
2	

Weight, in pounds, y

Number of weeks, x

14. **Model with Math** During a movie matinee, the film projector broke. The theater manager refunded the ticket price to everyone attending. Let *n* represent the number of people watching the movie. Let *r* represent the total amount of money refunded. Write an equation to represent the amount of money refunded.

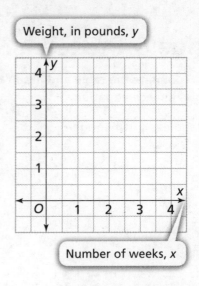

MOVIE PRICES

ADULTS $8.50

CHILDREN AND SENIORS $7.00

MATINEES: ALL AGES $5.00

15. **Higher Order Thinking** Write an algebraic equation that matches the values shown in the table at the right. Explain how you solved the problem.

x	y
1	8
2	11
3	14
4	17

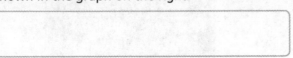

Assessment Practice

16. For every hour Sonia worked, she hand made 2 seashell necklaces for her gift shop. 🜚 6.EE.3.9

PART A

Write an equation that describes the relationship shown in the graph on the right.

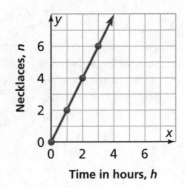

Time in hours, *h*

PART B

Describe the relationship between the variables in the graph and the equation.

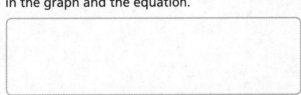

? Topic Essential Question

What procedures can be used to write and solve equations and inequalities?

Vocabulary Review

Complete each definition with a vocabulary word.

> **Vocabulary**   dependent variable   independent variable   inequality   equation

1. In the equation $y = x + 9$, the variable x is the _____.

2. A(n) _____ has an infinite number of solutions.

3. In the equation $y = x - 9$, the variable y is the _____.

Draw a line from each equation to the property of equality it illustrates.

4. $(6 + 3) - 3 = 9 - 3$ Addition Property of Equality

5. $(6 + 3) \times 3 = 9 \times 3$ Division Property of Equality

6. $(6 + 3) + 3 = 9 + 3$ Multiplication Property of Equality

7. $(6 + 3) \div 3 = 9 \div 3$ Subtraction Property of Equality

Use Vocabulary in Writing

Describe how to solve $\frac{3}{7}n = 27$. Use vocabulary words in your explanation.

Concepts and Skills Review

LESSON 5-1 **Understand Equations and Solutions**

Quick Review

The **solution of an equation** makes the equation true. Substitute each of the given values into the equation for the variable to determine which value, if any, is a solution of the equation.

Example

Which value of x is a solution of the equation?

$x + 4.8 = 19$ $x = 13, 14.2, 15.8$

Try $x = 13$: $13 + 4.8 \neq 17.8$ ✗
Try $x = 14.2$: $14.2 + 4.8 = 19$ ✔
Try $x = 15.8$: $15.8 + 4.8 \neq 20.6$ ✗

Practice

Tell which value of the variable, if any, is a solution of the equation.

1. $d + 9 = 25$ $d = 6, 14, 16, 21$

2. $c - 8 = 25$ $c = 17, 28, 33, 35$

3. $2y = 30$ $y = 10, 12, 24, 36$

4. $150 \div h = 50$ $h = 2, 3, 4, 5$

5. $f - 13.2 = 28.9$ $f = 38.7, 42.2, 45.8, 51.4$

LESSON 5-2 **Apply Properties of Equality**

Quick Review

The **properties of equality** allow you to apply the same operation with the same amount to both sides of an equation.

Example

The properties of equality are illustrated in the table.

Properties of Equality	
Addition Property of Equality	$4 + 3 = 7$ So, $4 + 3 + 2 = 7 + 2$
Subtraction Property of Equality	$9 + 8 = 17$ So, $9 + 8 - 5 = 17 - 5$
Multiplication Property of Equality	$3 \times 5 = 15$ So, $3 \times 5 \times 2 = 15 \times 2$
Division Property of Equality	$16 + 2 = 18$ So, $(16 + 2) \div 2 = 18 \div 2$

Practice

1. If $6 + 2 = 8$, does $6 + 2 + 3 = 8 + 3$? Why or why not?

2. If $8 - 1 = 7$, does $8 - 1 - 2 = 7 - 3$? Why or why not?

3. If $4 + 6 = 10$, does $(4 + 6) \times 3 = 10 \times 3$? Why or why not?

4. If $5 + 4 = 9$, does $(5 + 4) \div 3 = 9 \div 4$? Why or why not?

Write and Solve Addition, Subtraction, Multiplication, and Division Equations

Quick Review

Use the inverse relationship of addition and subtraction or multiplication and division to solve equations. To check, substitute your answer back into the original equation.

Example

$$23 + y = 57 \qquad\qquad a - 12 = 16$$

$$23 + y - 23 = 57 - 23 \qquad a - 12 + 12 = 16 + 12$$

$$y = 34 \qquad\qquad a = 28$$

$$9z = 63 \qquad\qquad c \div 4 = 24$$

$$9z \div 9 = 63 \div 9 \qquad c \div 4 \times 4 = 24 \times 4$$

$$z = 7 \qquad\qquad c = 96$$

Practice

Solve for x.

1. $8x = 64$ **2.** $x + 2 = 11$

3. $x \div 20 = 120$ **4.** $x - 17 = 13$

5. $x \div 12 = 2$ **6.** $8 + x = 25$

7. $7x = 77$ **8.** $x - 236 = 450$

9. $26 = 13x$ **10.** $x + 21.9 = 27.1$

11. $2{,}448 \div 48 = x$ **12.** $x + 15 = 31$

Write and Solve Equations with Rational Numbers

Quick Review

You can use inverse relationships and properties of equality to solve each equation.

Example

Solve $w + 4\frac{1}{3} = 7$.

Subtract $4\frac{1}{3}$ from both sides.

$$w + 4\frac{1}{3} - 4\frac{1}{3} = 7 - 4\frac{1}{3}$$

$$w = 2\frac{2}{3}$$

Solve $\frac{3}{5}n = \frac{2}{3}$.

Multiply both sides by the reciprocal of $\frac{3}{5}$.

$$\frac{5}{3} \times \frac{3}{5}n = \frac{5}{3} \times \frac{2}{3}$$

$$n = \frac{10}{9} \text{ or } 1\frac{1}{9}$$

Practice

In 1–8, solve for x.

1. $x + 3\frac{5}{8} = 7\frac{1}{4}$ **2.** $x - \frac{4}{8} = 4\frac{1}{4}$

3. $x \div 15 = 8\frac{1}{3}$ **4.** $\frac{4}{2}x = 6$

5. $\frac{x}{3} = 9$ **6.** $14x = 73.5$

7. $12x = 19.2$ **8.** $17.9 - x = 12.8$

9. Tomas buys a bag of 5 peaches for $3.55. Write and solve an equation to find how much money, m, Tomas paid for each peach.

10. Krys has $1.54 and spends $0.76. Write and solve an equation to find how much money, m, Krys has left.

Quick Review

An **inequality** is a mathematical sentence that contains < (less than), > (greater than), ≤ (less than or equal to), ≥ (greater than or equal to), or ≠ (not equal to).

Example

Situation	Inequality
The age of the house, *a*, is greater than 3 years.	$a > 3$
The cost of the house, *c*, is at least $50,000.	$c \geq 50{,}000$
The number of windows, *w*, is fewer than 10.	$w < 10$
The number of people, *n*, living in the house is at most 5.	$n \leq 5$
The number of trucks, *t*, in the garage is not 2.	$t \neq 2$

Practice

Write an inequality for each situation.

1. Up to 5 people, *p*, visited Mary today.

2. The value, *v*, of the hat is less than $9.

3. The number of guests, *g*, coming for dinner is not 8.

4. The distance of the race, *d*, is at least 6 miles.

5. The time it takes to get to Grandma's house, *t*, is longer than 2 hours.

Quick Review

To graph the solutions of an inequality on a number line, use an open circle for < or > and a closed circle for ≤ or ≥. If the values of the variable are less than the given number, shade to the left on the number line. If the values of the variable are greater than the given number, shade to the right on the number line.

Example

"Molly is less than 15 years old" is represented by the inequality $x < 15$. Write three ages that could represent Molly's age.

To graph the inequality on a number line, draw an open circle at 15 and shade to the left of 15 because *x* is less than 15. Draw an arrow to show all numbers less than 15.

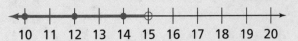

There are many solutions. Molly could be 10, 12, 14, or any age less than 15 years.

Practice

Write the inequality that each graph represents.

1.
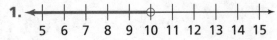

2.
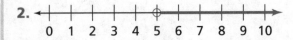

3.
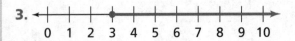

4.
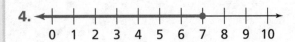

Go Online | PearsonRealize.com

Understand Dependent and Independent Variables

Quick Review

Think about how the values of variables affect each other.

To identify the dependent variable, ask yourself which variable depends on the other.

To identify the independent variable, ask yourself which variable causes the change.

Example

The spirit squad is washing cars. The equation $m = 2c$ represents the money they make, m, for washing c cars. Identify the dependent variable and the independent variable.

The amount of money the spirit squad makes **depends** on the number of cars they wash. The dependent variable is m.

The number of cars washed changes the amount of money made. The independent variable is c.

Practice

Identify the dependent variable and the independent variable in each situation.

1. The distance traveled, d, and the speed, s

2. The calories, c, in a snack and the amount of the snack, a

3. The amount of money you have spent, s, and how much money you have left, m

4. The number of apple slices remaining, r, and the number of apple slices eaten, e

Use Patterns to Write and Solve Equations

Quick Review

Look for patterns between two related variables to find rules and write equations.

Example

Write a rule and an equation that represents the pattern. Then complete the table.

x	3	4	5	6	7
y	12	16	20	24	28

Find the rule and write an equation.

12 is 3 × 4
16 is 4 × 4
20 is 5 × 4

Rule: The value of y is 4 times the value of x.

Equation: $y = 4x$

Evaluate the equation for $x = 6$ and $x = 7$.

$y = 4 \times 6 = 24$

$y = 4 \times 7 = 28$

Practice

1. Find the pattern and then write a rule and an equation that represents the pattern. Then complete the table.

x	0	2	10	16	20
y	0	1	5		

2. Use the equation to complete the table.

$y = 6x + 1$

x	1	2	3	4	5
y					

Quick Review

A table, equation, or graph can be used to analyze the relationship between dependent and independent variables. Ordered pairs that make an equation true can be used to graph the equation.

Example

Complete the table and graph to show the relationship between the variables in the equation $t = s + 1$.

A restaurant has a special that when you buy one sandwich you get a second sandwich for $1.

Let s = price of one sandwich.

Let t = total price of two sandwiches.

Step 1 Make a table. Include at least three values.

$t = s + 1$	
s	t
$1.50	$2.50
$2	$3
$3	$4

Step 2 Graph each ordered pair on a coordinate plane. Then draw a line through the points.

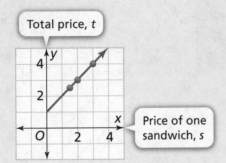

Practice

1. The cross country team practices by jogging on the town's streets. The average jogging rate is 6 miles per hour. One member jogged for 3.5 hours one weekend. How many miles did the team member jog?

   a. Complete the table to relate the number of miles to the number of hours jogged.

x	y
1	
2	
3	

   b. Graph the ordered pairs on the coordinate plane.

   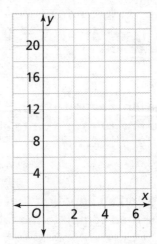

   c. Write an equation that describes the relationship. Then solve the problem.

2. Alex is making puppets for a show. He bought all the string needed for $125. It costs $18 for the remaining materials to make each puppet. What is the total cost to make 50 puppets?

Go Online | PearsonRealize.com

Riddle Rearranging

Find each quotient. Then arrange the answers in order from least to greatest. The letters will spell out the answer to the riddle below.

O $34\overline{)7{,}752}$

T $55\overline{)7{,}645}$

Q $78\overline{)6{,}786}$

N $46\overline{)12{,}834}$

A $11\overline{)682}$

I $81\overline{)15{,}309}$

A $97\overline{)11{,}931}$

E $72\overline{)5{,}256}$

U $83\overline{)8{,}051}$

N $68\overline{)4{,}624}$

What has two sides but can sometimes look like a line?

◯ ◯

◯ ◯ ◯ ◯ ◯ ◯ ◯ ◯

TOPIC 6

UNDERSTAND AND USE RATIO AND RATE

? Topic Essential Question

What are ratios and rates? How can you use ratios and rates to describe quantities and solve problems?

Topic Overview

6-1 Understand Ratios
6.RP.1.1, 6.RP.1.3, MP.1.1, MP.2.1, MP.3.1, MP.4.1

6-2 Generate Equivalent Ratios
6.RP.1.3a, 6.RP.1.3e, MP.2.1, MP.3.1, MP.5.1, MP.7.1, MP.8.1

6-3 Compare Ratios
6.RP.1.3a, MP.2.1, MP.4.1, MP.7.1

6-4 Represent and Graph Ratios
6.RP.1.3a, 6.RP.1.3e, MP.3.1, MP.4.1, MP.7.1

6-5 Understand Rates and Unit Rates
6.RP.1.2, 6.RP.1.3a, 6.RP.1.3b, MP.1.1, MP.2.1, MP.3.1, MP.8.1

6-6 Compare Unit Rates
6.RP.1.3b, 6.RP.1.3a, MP.1.1, MP.2.1, MP.6.1

6-7 Solve Unit Rate Problems
6.RP.1.3b, MP.2.1, MP.4.1, MP.7.1, MP.8.1

3-Act Mathematical Modeling: Get in Line
6.RP.1.3b, 6.RP.1.2, MP.1.1, MP.2.1, MP.3.1, MP.4.1, MP.5.1, MP.7.1, MP.8.1

6-8 Ratio Reasoning: Convert Customary Units
6.RP.1.3d, MP.1.1, MP.2.1, MP.3.1, MP.4.1

6-9 Ratio Reasoning: Convert Metric Units
6.RP.1.3d, MP.2.1, MP.3.1, MP.6.1, MP.7.1, MP.8.1

6-10 Relate Customary and Metric Units
6.RP.1.3d, MP.1.1, MP.2.1, MP.3.1, MP.8.1

Topic Vocabulary

- circumference of a circle
- constant speed
- conversion factor
- diameter
- dimensional analysis
- equivalent ratios
- Pi (π)
- rate
- ratio
- term
- unit price
- unit rate

Lesson Digital Resources

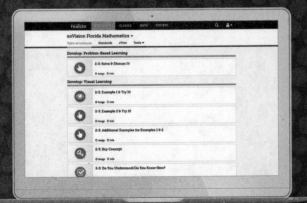

INTERACTIVE STUDENT EDITION
Access online or offline.

VISUAL LEARNING ANIMATION
Interact with visual learning animations.

ACTIVITY Use with *Solve & Discuss It, Explore* and *Explain It* activities, and to explore Example

VIDEOS Watch clips to support *3-Act Mathematical Modeling Lessons* and *STEM Pr*

Go online | **PearsonRealize.com**

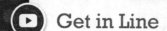

Get in Line

▶ **Get in Line**

It is hard to call it a freeway when you are stuck in the middle of a traffic jam. To keep vehicles moving on the freeway, some on-ramps have traffic signals. Controlling when cars enter the freeway is not only about reducing delays. It can decrease air pollution and collisions.

These ramp meters typically have alternating green and red lights. The time for one cycle depends on the time of day and the amount of traffic on the freeway. Think about this during the 3-Act Mathematical Modeling lesson.

 PRACTICE Practice what you've learned.

 KEY CONCEPT Review important lesson content.

 TUTORIALS Get help from *Virtual Nerd*, right when you need it.

 GLOSSARY Read and listen to English/Spanish definitions.

 MATH TOOLS Explore math with digital tools.

 ASSESSMENT Show what you've learned.

 GAMES Play Math Games to help you learn.

enVision® STEM Project

 VIDEO

Did You Know?

Gears are found in the **mechanisms of many common objects**, such as cars, bicycles, analog watches, and wind turbines.

Gears have been utilized for centuries. Wooden gears, with wooden teeth, can be found in windmills and watermills.

Gears have equally spaced teeth that enable them to interlock with other gears.

The gears of a bicycle are connected and driven by a chain.

Bicycles often have multiple gears that allow riders to make adjustments to power output and speed.

Riders back in the 19th century were not as lucky—no gears meant a lot of pedaling!

Your Task:
Get into Gear ▶

Cyclists strive to achieve efficiency during continuous riding. But, which pairing of gears is the best or most efficient? And does the answer change depending on the terrain? You and your classmates will explore gear ratios and how they can affect pedaling and riding speeds.

Review What You Know!

Vocabulary

Choose the best term from the box to complete each definition.

common factor
common multiple
equivalent fractions
fraction

1. Fractions that name the same amount are called _____.

2. The number 3 is a _____ of 9 and 12.

3. A number that can be used to describe a part of a set or a part of a whole

   is a(n) _____.

Equivalent Fractions

Write two fractions equivalent to the given fraction.

4. $\frac{3}{4}$

5. $\frac{7}{8}$

6. $\frac{12}{5}$

7. $\frac{1}{2}$

8. $\frac{8}{9}$

9. $\frac{2}{3}$

Equations

Write an equation that represents the pattern in each table.

10.

x	2	3	4	5	6
y	16	24	32	40	48

11.

x	2	4	6	8	10
y	5	7	9	11	13

Units of Measure

Choose the best unit of measure by writing *inch, foot, yard, ounce, pound, ton, cup, quart,* or *gallon*.

12. serving of trail mix

13. height of a person

14. weight of a newborn kitten

15. gasoline

Measurement Conversions

16. Michael is 4 feet tall. Explain how Michael could find his height in inches. Then explain how he could find his height in yards.

Prepare for Reading Success

Before you begin the topic, predict whether each statement is true or false. Write *True* or *False* in the first column. After you finish each lesson, write *True* or *False* in the second column based on what you learned. When you finish the topic, see how many of your predictions were correct.

Prediction	Text	Statement
		6-1 When writing a ratio, order does not matter. The ratio of dogs to cats is the same as the ratio of cats to dogs.
		6-2 You can use a table to find equivalent ratios.
		6-3 You can only compare part to whole ratios, not part to part ratios.
		6-4 The ratio 5:2 can be represented as the ordered pair (5, 2).
		6-5 A unit rate is a rate in which the first term is 1.
		6-6 A rate of 5 miles in 2 minutes is faster than a rate of 4 miles in 1 minute.
		6-7 You can use the unit price for oranges in dollars per pound to find the price of 10 pounds of oranges.
		6-8 One method for converting customary units is to use dimensional analysis.
		6-9 The methods for converting metric units are the same as the methods for converting customary units.
		6-10 When converting between customary and metric units, all conversions will be approximate.

Go Online | PearsonRealize.com

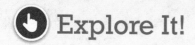 Explore It!

 ACTIVITY

A band just released an album that contains both pop songs and R&B (rhythm and blues) songs.

I can...
use a ratio to describe the relationship between two quantities.

MAFS.6.RP.1.1 Understand the concept of a ratio and use ratio language to describe a ratio relationship between two quantities. Also 6.RP.1.3
MAFS.K12.MP.1.1, MP.2.1, MP.3.1, MP.4.1

A. How can you describe the relationship between the number of pop songs and the number of R&B songs on the album?

B. How does the bar diagram represent the relationship between the number of pop songs and the number of R&B songs?

| Pop Songs | | | |
| R&B Songs | | | |

Focus on math practices

Reasoning Another album has 2 pop songs and 10 R&B songs. Draw a bar diagram that you could use to represent the relationship between the number of pop songs and the number of R&B songs.

 VISUAL LEARNING ASS

EXAMPLE 1 **Write Ratios to Compare Quantities**

Scan for Multimedia

Tom's Pet Service takes care of cats and dogs. Currently, there are more dogs than cats. Compare the number of cats to the number of dogs. Then compare the number of cats to the total number of pets at Tom's Pet Service.

 14 cats

 17 dogs

A **ratio** is a relationship in which for every *x* units of one quantity there are *y* units of another quantity. A ratio can be written three ways. *x* to *y* *x*:*y* $\frac{x}{y}$ The quantities *x* and *y* in a ratio are called **terms**.	Use a ratio to compare the number of cats to the number of dogs. 14 to 17 14:17 $\frac{14}{17}$ Cats 14 17 Dogs This ratio compares one part to another part.	Use a ratio to compare the number of cats to the total number of pets. 14 to 31 14:31 $\frac{14}{31}$ Cats 14 14 17 **Total Number of Pets** This ratio compares one part to the whole.

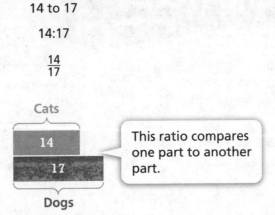

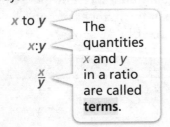

✓ Try It!

What are three ways to write the ratio of the number of dogs to the total number of pets?

Convince Me! Is the ratio of dogs to cats the same as the ratio of cats to dogs? Explain.

Go Online | PearsonRealize.com

EXAMPLE 2 Use a Bar Diagram to Solve a Ratio Problem

 ACTIVITY ASSESS

The ratio of footballs to soccer balls at a sporting goods store is 5 to 3. If the store has 100 footballs in stock, how many soccer balls does it have?

Use a bar diagram to show the ratio 5:3.

Use 5 boxes for footballs.

Footballs

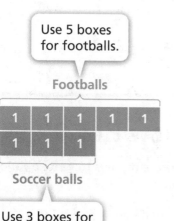

1	1	1	1	1
1	1	1		

Soccer balls

Use 3 boxes for soccer balls.

Use the same diagram to represent 100 footballs.

Because 100 ÷ 5 = 20, write 20 in each red box.

Footballs

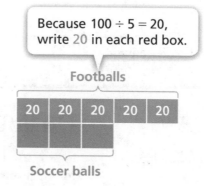

20	20	20	20	20

Soccer balls

Each box represents the same value. Write 20 in each green box.

Footballs

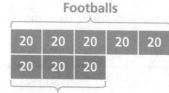

20	20	20	20	20
20	20	20		

Soccer balls

There are 3 green boxes, so the total number of soccer balls is 3 × 20, or 60.

The sporting goods store has 60 soccer balls in stock.

EXAMPLE 3 **Use a Double Number Line Diagram to Solve a Ratio Problem**

Chen can ride his bike 3 miles in 15 minutes. At this rate, how long will it take Chen to ride his bike 18 miles?

Use a double number line diagram. Show 15 minutes for every 3 miles.

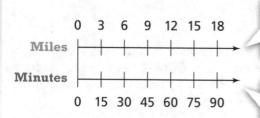

Miles: 0 3 6 9 12 15 18

Minutes: 0 15 30 45 60 75 90

Count by 3s along the top number line until you get to 18 miles.

Count by 15s for the same number of spaces along the bottom number line.

Chen can ride 18 miles in 90 minutes.

3 miles

Model with Math A double number line diagram can represent a constant relationship between two values with different units.

 Try It!

Chen's friend Alisa can ride her bike 2 miles in 7 minutes. Use a bar diagram or a double number line diagram to find how long it would take Alisa to ride 10 miles if she rides at the same rate.

A ratio compares two quantities. A ratio can be written 3 ways: x to y, $x{:}y$, or $\frac{x}{y}$.
Ratios can be represented using bar diagrams and double number line diagrams.

Oranges

Apples

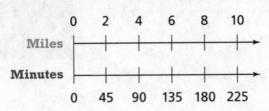

The ratio of oranges to apples is 2:3, 2 to 3, or $\frac{2}{3}$.

The ratio of miles to minutes is 2:45, 2 to 45, or $\frac{2}{45}$.

Do You Understand?

1. **Essential Question** What is a mathematical way to compare quantities?

2. **Reasoning** What are two different types of comparisons that a ratio can be used to make?

3. A science classroom has 5 turtles and 7 frogs. What is the ratio of frogs to total animals?

4. Tye is making trail mix with 3 cups of nuts for every 4 cups of granola. If Tye has 6 cups of nuts, how many cups of granola should he use?

Do You Know How?

In 5–7, use three different ways to write a ratio for each comparison.

A sixth-grade basketball team has 3 centers, 5 forwards, and 6 guards.

5. Forwards to guards

6. Centers to total players

7. Guards to centers

8. The ratio of blue cards to green cards is 2 to 5. There are 8 blue cards. Complete the diagram and explain how you can find the number of green cards.

Blue cards ☐ ☐

Green cards ☐ ☐ ☐ ☐ ☐

Practice & Problem Solving

Scan for
Multimedia

In 9–14, use the data to write a ratio for each comparison in three different ways.

A person's blood type is denoted with the letters A, B, and O, and the symbols + and −. The blood type A+ is read as *A positive*. The blood type B− is read as *B negative*.

9. O+ donors to A+ donors

10. AB− donors to AB+ donors

11. B+ donors to total donors

12. O− donors to A− donors

13. A+ and B+ donors to AB+ donors

14. A− and B− donors to AB− donors

Blood Donors

Type	Donors
A+	45
B+	20
AB+	6
O+	90
A−	21
B−	0
AB−	4
O−	9
Total	195

15. Which comparison does the ratio $\frac{90}{9}$ represent?

16. Which comparison does the ratio 20:21 represent?

17. Sam is packing gift boxes with fruit. For each apple, he packs 3 plums and 5 oranges. If he puts 3 apples in a box, how many plums and oranges will Sam put in the box? Draw a diagram to solve the problem.

18. Write a ratio that compares the number of teal squares to the total number of squares in the quilt.

19. Reasoning Rita's class has 14 girls and 16 boys. How does the ratio 14:30 describe Rita's class?

20. A math class surveyed students about their musical preferences and recorded the results in the table. Use the data to write a ratio for each comparison in three different ways.

a. Students who prefer classical to students who prefer techno

b. Students who prefer hip-hop to total number of students surveyed

Favorite Music

Music Type	Number of Students
Rock	10
Classical	4
Techno	12
Hip-Hop	15
Country	8
Alternative	4

21. Construct Arguments Justin used blocks to model the following situation: A car dealership sells 7 cars for every 4 minivans it sells. How can Justin use his model to find the number of minivans the dealership sells if it sells 35 cars?

22. Make Sense and Persevere The ratio of adult dogs to puppies at a dog beach in Florida on Monday was 3:2. There were 12 puppies there that day. On Tuesday, 15 adult dogs were at the dog beach. What is the difference between the number of adult dogs at the dog beach on Monday and Tuesday?

23. Higher Order Thinking At 9:30 A.M., Sean started filling a swimming pool. At 11:30 A.M., he had filled 1,800 gallons. At what time will the pool be full?

4,500 gallon capacity

24. The diagram below represents the relationship between the number of students taking Spanish and the number of students taking French in a foreign language class. ⬥ 6.RP.1.1

Spanish

French

What is the ratio of the number of students taking Spanish to the number of students taking French?

Ⓐ 8 : 3

Ⓑ 8 : 5

Ⓒ 8 : 8

Ⓓ 8 : 13

Lesson 6-2
Generate Equivalent Ratios

Solve & Discuss It!

Sally used all of the paint shown below to make a certain tint of orange paint. How many pints of red paint should be mixed with 24 pints of yellow paint to make the same tint of orange?

1 Pint   1 Pint   1 Pint   1 Pint   1 Pint   1 Pint

I can...
use multiplication and division to find equivalent ratios.

MAFS.6.RP.1.3a Make tables of equivalent ratios relating quantities with whole-number measurements, find missing values in the tables, ... Also 6.RP.1.3e

MAFS.K12.MP.2.1, MP.3.1, MP.5.1, MP.7.1, MP.8.1

Look for Relationships How can you use the relationship between the number of pints of yellow paint and the number of pints of red paint to answer the question?

Focus on math practices

Reasoning If Sally uses the same ratio of yellow paint to red paint, how many pints of yellow paint should she mix with 16 pints of red paint?

341

VISUAL LEARNING ASS

Scan for
Multimedia

EXAMPLE **1** **Use Multiplication to Find Equivalent Ratios**

For every 16 basketball players in Crystal County schools, there are 48 soccer players. If the ratio remains constant and there are 64 basketball players, how many soccer players are there?

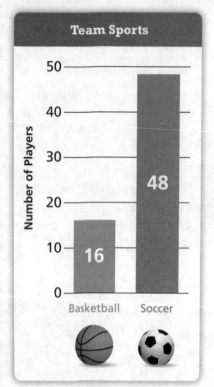

ONE WAY Make a table with equivalent ratios.

Equivalent ratios are ratios that express the same relationship.

> Multiply both terms of the original ratio by the same number to find an equivalent ratio.

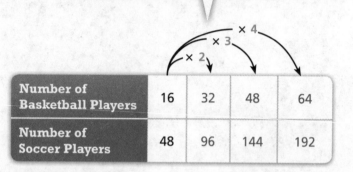

	× 2	× 3	× 4
Number of Basketball Players	16	32	48	64
Number of Soccer Players	48	96	144	192

There are 192 soccer players when there are 64 basketball players.

ANOTHER WAY Use multiplication. Multiply both terms by the same nonzero number.

> Multiply 16 × 4 for the 64 basketball players.

$$\frac{16 \times 4}{48 \times 4} = \frac{64}{192}$$

> Multiply 48 × 4 to find the number of soccer players.

There are 192 soccer players when there are 64 basketball players.

☑ Try It!

If you extend the table above, how would you find the next ratio of basketball players to soccer players?

Convince Me! What is the relationship between the number of basketball players and the number of soccer players in each column in the table?

EXAMPLE **2**

  ACTIVITY ASSESS

Use Division to Find Equivalent Ratios

Sarah made baskets on some of her shots in a basketball game. If she continues to make baskets at the same rate, how many baskets will Sarah make in her next 6 shots?

PLAYER	SHOTS	BASKETS
SARAH	18	12

ONE WAY Make a table with equivalent ratios.

> Divide both terms of the original ratio by the same number to find an equivalent ratio.

÷ 3
÷ 2

Number of Shots Taken	6	9	18
Number of Baskets Made	4	6	12

Sarah will make 4 baskets in her next 6 shots.

ANOTHER WAY Use division.

> **Reasoning** By what number do you need to divide 18 to get 6? Divide 12 by the same number.

$$\frac{18 \div 3}{12 \div 3} = \frac{6}{4}$$

> Divide both terms by the same nonzero number.

Sarah will make 4 baskets in her next 6 shots.

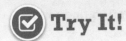 Try It!

Rashida uses 8 cups of tomatoes and 3 cups of onions to make salsa. How many cups of onions should Rashida use if she uses only 4 cups of tomatoes?

EXAMPLE **3** Find Equivalent Ratios

Pi (π) is the ratio of the circumference of a circle to its diameter. This ratio is approximately 66:21. Which of the following ratios are equivalent to 66:21?

22:7, 33:10, 44:14, 88:28

Make tables of equivalent ratios.

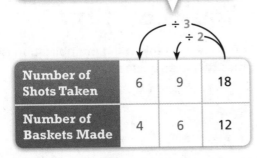

÷ 3

22	66
7	21

× 4
× 3
× 2

22	44	66	88
7	14	21	28

> The **circumference** of a circle C is the distance around the circle.

C

d

> The **diameter** of a circle d is a segment that passes through the center and has both endpoints on the circle.

The ratios 22:7, 44:14, and 88:28 are equivalent to 66:21.

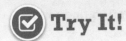 Try It!

Which of the following ratios are equivalent to 16:20?

2:3, 4:5, 18:22, 20:25

You can multiply or divide both terms of a ratio by the same nonzero number to find equivalent ratios.

Multiply both terms by the same nonzero number.

$$\frac{30 \times 2}{40 \times 2} = \frac{60}{80}$$

Divide both terms by the same nonzero number.

$$\frac{30 \div 10}{40 \div 10} = \frac{3}{4}$$

Do You Understand?

1. **? Essential Question** How can you find equivalent ratios?

2. **Critique Reasoning** Deshawn says that the ratios 3:5 and 5:7 are equivalent ratios because by adding 2 to both terms of 3:5 you get 5:7. Is Deshawn correct? Explain.

3. What are two ways you can find an equivalent ratio for $\frac{12}{16}$?

4. How can you show that the ratios 10:4 and 15:6 are equivalent?

Do You Know How?

5. Complete the table using multiplication to find ratios that are equivalent to 4:5.

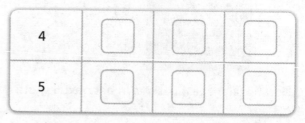

6. Complete the table using division to find ratios that are equivalent to 40:28.

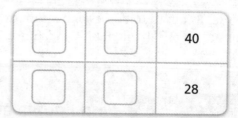

In 7–10, write an equivalent ratio for each given ratio.

7. $\frac{12}{21}$ 8. 1:3   9. 6 to 8

10. Pi (π) can be approximated using decimals as the ratio 3.14:1. Find 3 ratios equivalent to the ratio 3.14:1.

Practice & Problem Solving

Scan for
Multimedia

11. Eva is making French toast. How many ounces of milk should Eva use with 10 eggs?

The recipe calls for 5 ounces of milk for every 2 eggs.

Milk (oz)	5	⬚	⬚	⬚	⬚
Eggs	2	4	6	8	10

In 12–15, write three ratios that are equivalent to the given ratio.

12. $\frac{6}{7}$

13. $\frac{9}{5}$

14. 8:14

15. 7:9

16. A teacher kept track of what students consumed at a school picnic. For three grades, the ratios of the amount of water consumed to the amount of fruit juice consumed were equivalent. Complete the table.

Grade	Water (gallons)	Juice (gallons)
5th	6	7
6th	24	⬚
7th	18	⬚

17. The attendant at a parking lot compared the number of hybrid vehicles to the total number of vehicles in the lot during a weekend. The ratios for the three days were equivalent. Complete the table.

Day	Hybrids	Total
Fri.	4	9
Sat.	⬚	63
Sun.	32	⬚

18. Shiloh is sharing jellybeans. The jar of jellybeans has the ratio shown. If Shiloh keeps the ratio the same and gives his friend 7 pink jellybeans, how many green jellybeans should he also share?

32 green jellybeans
56 pink jellybeans

Green Jellybeans	⬚	⬚	⬚	32
Pink Jellybeans	7	⬚	⬚	56

19. Use Appropriate Tools Equivalent ratios can be found by extending pairs of rows or columns in a multiplication table. Write three ratios equivalent to $\frac{2}{5}$ using the multiplication table.

X	0	1	2	3	4	5	6
0	0	0	0	0	0	0	0
1	0	1	2	3	4	5	6
2	0	2	4	6	8	10	12
3	0	3	6	9	12	15	18
4	0	4	8	12	16	20	24
5	0	5	10	15	20	25	30
6	0	6	12	18	24	30	36

20. If 5 mi ≈ 8 km, about how many miles would be equal to 50 km? Explain.

PEDOMETER

5.00 mi
/8.04 km

21. Vocabulary How is the word *term* defined when used to describe a ratio relationship? How is the word *term* defined in the context of an expression?

22. Higher Order Thinking Three sisters are saving for a special vacation in Orlando, Florida. The ratio of Ada's savings to Ellie's savings is 7:3, and the ratio of Ellie's savings to Jasmine's savings is 3:4. Together all three girls have saved $56. How much has each girl saved? Complete the table. Explain how the table can be used to solve the problem.

Ada's savings	$7		$21	
Ellie's savings		$6		
Jasmine's savings	$4			$16

Assessment Practice

23. Corey is making key lime pies for the school fair. For every 3 egg yolks, he uses 2 tablespoons of key lime zest. 🔵 6.RP.1.3a

PART A

Complete the table to find equivalent ratios.

Egg Yolks	3			
Lime Zest (tbsp)	2	4	6	8

PART B

How can you use the table to find how many egg yolks are needed for 8 tablespoons of lime zest?

24. Which ratios can be represented by Pi (π)? Select all that apply. 🔵 6.RP.1.3e

- ☐ Diameter : Circumference
- ☐ Circumference : Diameter
- ☐ Circumference : Radius
- ☐ Radius : Circumference
- ☐ Circumference : Twice the radius

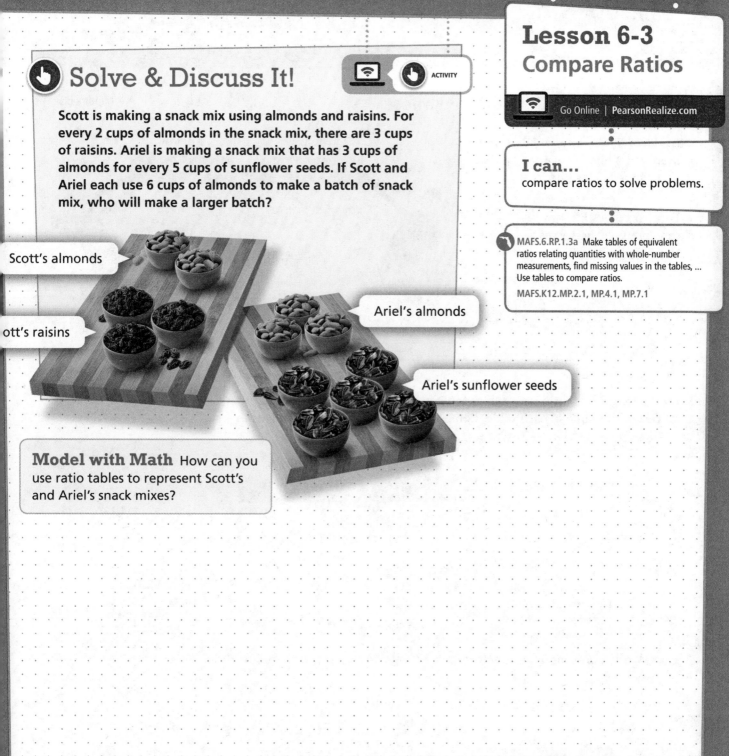

Solve & Discuss It! 📶 ⏱ ACTIVITY

Scott is making a snack mix using almonds and raisins. For every 2 cups of almonds in the snack mix, there are 3 cups of raisins. Ariel is making a snack mix that has 3 cups of almonds for every 5 cups of sunflower seeds. If Scott and Ariel each use 6 cups of almonds to make a batch of snack mix, who will make a larger batch?

Scott's almonds

ott's raisins

Ariel's almonds

Ariel's sunflower seeds

Model with Math How can you use ratio tables to represent Scott's and Ariel's snack mixes?

I can...
compare ratios to solve problems.

MAFS.6.RP.1.3a Make tables of equivalent ratios relating quantities with whole-number measurements, find missing values in the tables, ... Use tables to compare ratios.

MAFS.K12.MP.2.1, MP.4.1, MP.7.1

Focus on math practices

Look for Relationships Scott and Ariel want to make as much snack mix as possible, but no more than 25 cups of mix. If they can use only full cups of ingredients, who can make more mix without going over?

EXAMPLE 1 Compare Ratios

Scan for
Multimedia

Dustin had 3 hits for every 8 at bats.
Adrian had 4 hits for every 10 at bats.
Who has the better hits to at bats ratio?

Use Structure How can you use ratio tables to compare ratios?

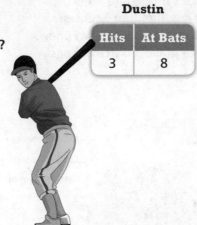

Dustin

Hits	At Bats
3	8

Adrian

Hits	At Bats
4	10

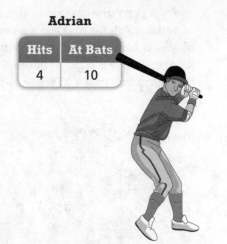

Extend and complete the ratio tables for Dustin and Adrian until the number of at bats is the same in each table. Compare the number of hits that Dustin and Adrian each get with 40 at bats.

Dustin

Hits	At Bats
3	8
6	16
9	24
12	32
15	40

Adrian

Hits	At Bats
4	10
8	20
12	30
16	40

Dustin gets 15 hits for every 40 at bats.

Adrian gets 16 hits for every 40 at bats.

Because Adrian gets more hits in 40 at bats, he has the better hits to at bats ratio.

☑ Try It!

Marlon had 6 hits in 15 at bats. How does Marlon's hits to at bats ratio compare to Adrian's?

Convince Me! Based on their hits to at bats ratios, who would you expect to have more hits in a game, Marlon or Dustin? Explain.

Due to compatibility and size restrictions, only certain types of fish can live together in an aquarium. If there are 15 mollies in each tank with the ratios shown at the right, which tank has more fish?

Tank 1

4 Guppies : 5 Mollies

Tank 2

2 Angelfish : 3 Mollies

STEP 1

Make a table to show the ratio of guppies to mollies in Tank 1.

Guppies	Mollies
4	5
8	10
12	15
16	20
20	25

There are 12 guppies for every 15 mollies.

STEP 2

Make a table to show the ratio of angelfish to mollies in Tank 2.

Angelfish	Mollies
2	3
4	6
6	9
8	12
10	15

There are 10 angelfish for every 15 mollies.

STEP 3

Add to find the total number of fish in each aquarium.

Tank 1: 12 guppies + 15 mollies = 27 fish

Tank 2: 10 angelfish + 15 mollies = 25 fish

27 > 25

Tank 1 has more fish.

Try It!

Tank 3 has a ratio of 3 guppies for every 4 angelfish. Complete the ratio table to find the number of angelfish in Tank 3 with 12 guppies.

Using the information in Example 2 and the table at the right, which tank with guppies has more fish?

Guppies	3			
Angelfish	4			

You can use ratio tables to compare ratios when one of the corresponding terms is the same.

Theresa's Purple Paint Mixture

Cups of Blue Paint	2	4	6
Cups of Red Paint	5	10	15

Hala's Purple Paint Mixture

Cups of Blue Paint	3	6	9
Cups of Red Paint	7	14	21

Theresa used more cups of red paint than Hala.

Do You Understand?

1. **Essential Question** How can you compare ratios to solve a problem?

2. In Example 1, how many hits would Adrian have in 50 at bats? Explain.

3. **Reasoning** During the first week of a summer camp, 2 out of 3 campers were boys. During the second week, 3 out of 5 campers were boys. There were 15 total campers each week. During which week were there more boy campers? Explain.

Do You Know How?

4. To make plaster, Kevin mixes 3 cups of water with 4 pounds of plaster powder. Complete the ratio table. How much water will Kevin mix with 20 pounds of powder?

Cups of Water	3			
Pounds of Powder	4	8	12	

5. Jenny makes plaster using a ratio of 4 cups of water to 5 pounds of plaster powder. Whose plaster recipe uses more water? Use the ratio table here and in Exercise 4 to compare.

Cups of Water	4	8		
Pounds of Powder	5			

6. Kevin and Jenny each use 12 cups of water to make plaster. Who will make more plaster? Explain.

Practice & Problem Solving

Scan for
Multimedia

In 7–10, use the ratio table at the right.

7. Local radio station *WMTH* schedules 2 minutes of news for every 20 minutes of music. Complete the ratios shown in the table at the right.

Minutes of Music	20	?	40	?	60
Minutes of News	2	3	?	5	?

8. What is the ratio of minutes of music to minutes of news?

9. Radio station *WILM* broadcasts 4 minutes of news for every 25 minutes of music. Which radio station broadcasts more news each hour?

10. Which station will have to be on the air longer to broadcast 4 minutes of news? Explain.

11. **Reasoning** The ratio tables at the right show the comparison of books to games for sale at Bert's Store and at Gloria's Store. Complete the ratio tables. Which store has the greater ratio of books to games? Explain.

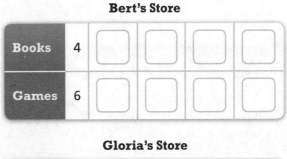

Bert's Store

Books	4			
Games	6			

Gloria's Store

Books	5			
Games	8			

12. The ratio of soy sauce to lime juice in a homemade salad dressing is 7:6. The ratio of soy sauce to lime juice in a store-bought dressing is 11:9. Which dressing has the greater ratio of soy sauce to lime juice?

Homemade Salad Dressing

Soy Sauce	7			
Lime Juice	6			

Store-Bought Salad Dressing

Soy Juice	11			
Lime Sauce	9			

13. One bouquet of flowers has 3 milkweeds for every 5 tickseeds. Another bouquet has 4 tickseeds for every 5 canna lilies. If both bouquets have 20 tickseeds, which bouquet has more flowers?

Milkweeds and Tickseeds

Milkweeds	3			
Tickseeds	5			

Tickseeds and Canna lilies

Tickseeds	4			
Canna lilies	5			

14. Higher Order Thinking Lauren can drive her car 320 miles on 10 gallons of gasoline. Melissa can drive her car 280 miles on 8 gallons of gasoline. Who can drive farther on 40 gallons of gasoline? Complete the ratio tables to justify your solution.

Lauren's Car

Miles Driven					
Gallons					

Melissa's Car

Miles Driven					
Gallons					

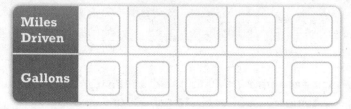

Assessment Practice

15. Fran buys Florida cone seashells in packages that contain 9 purple-dyed Florida cone seashells for every 3 pink-dyed Florida cone seashells. Mia buys Florida cone seashells in packages with a ratio of 2 pink-dyed Florida cone seashells to 4 purple-dyed Florida cone seashells. ⟳ 6.RP.1.3a

PART A

Complete the tables using the ratios given.

Fran's Shell Packages

Purple cone shells	9		27	
Pink cone shells	3	6		12

Mia's Shell Packages

Purple cone shells	4	8		16
Pink cone shells	2		6	

PART B

If the girls each buy packages that contain 6 pink-dyed Florida cone seashells, how many purple-dyed Florida cone seashells would each have? Explain.

Go Online | PearsonRealize.com

Solve & Discuss It!

ACTIVITY

For every 4 adults at the beach one afternoon, there were 3 children. How many children were at the beach if there were 8, 12, 16, or 20 adults at the beach?

Number of Adults					
Number of Children					

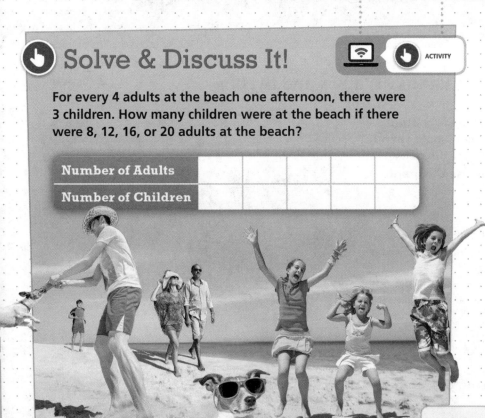

I can...
solve ratio problems by using tables and graphs to show equivalent ratios.

MAFS.6.RP.1.3a Make tables of equivalent ratios relating quantities with whole-number measurements, find missing values in the tables, and plot the pairs of values on the coordinate plane... Also 6.RP.1.3e

MAFS.K12.MP.3.1, MP.4.1, MP.7.1

Model with Math How does the graph show the ratio?

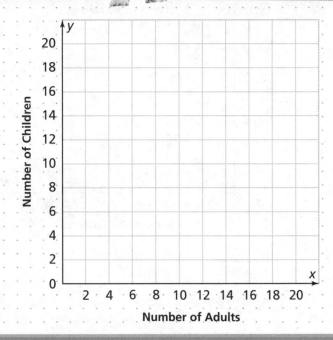

Focus on math practices

Critique Reasoning There were 25 children and 15 adults at the beach. Emery said that there were 5 children for every 3 adults. Is he correct? Explain.

VISUAL LEARNING   ASSES

 EXAMPLE 1   Explore Ratios in Tables and Graphs

Scan for Multimedia

Ellen is shopping for supplies at Jake's Party Store. Make a table to show how much Ellen would spend to buy 3, 6, 9, or 12 balloons. Then plot the pairs of values in a coordinate graph and use the graph to find the cost of 18 balloons.

> **Use Structure** How can you make a table of equivalent ratios or a graph to find the costs for other numbers of balloons?

Jake's Party Store
Balloons 3 for $2
Hats 5 for $3
Streamers 4 for $1

The ratio $\frac{3 \text{ balloons}}{\$2}$ represents the cost of the balloons.

Make a table of equivalent ratios to find the costs of 6, 9, and 12 balloons.

Number of Balloons (x)	3	6	9	12
Cost in Dollars (y)	2	4	6	8

> The values in the table can be used to write the ordered pairs (3, 2), (6, 4), (9, 6), and (12, 8).

Ellen can buy 3 balloons for $2, 6 balloons for $4, 9 balloons for $6, or 12 balloons for $8.

Plot the pairs of values on the coordinate plane for each ratio, x to y.

Connect the points and extend the line.

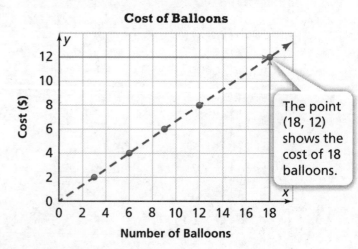

Cost of Balloons

> The point (18, 12) shows the cost of 18 balloons.

The cost of 18 balloons is $12.

☑ **Try It!**

What are the coordinates of the point that represents the number of balloons you can buy for $6?

Convince Me! How can you use the graph to find the cost of 15 balloons?

EXAMPLE **2** Graph Ratios Using Repeated Addition

  ACTIVITY ASSESS

Jack is making juice. He has 25 celery sticks. If Jack uses all 25 celery sticks, how many apples will he need to make the juice?

APPLE CELERY JUICE
5 CELERY STICKS
2 APPLES

Use repeated addition to complete the ratio table.

For each row in the table, add 5 to the number of celery sticks and add 2 to the number of apples.

Celery Sticks	Apples
5	2
10	4
15	6
20	8
25	10

+5 +5 +5 +5

+2 +2 +2 +2

Plot the pairs of values on a coordinate plane.

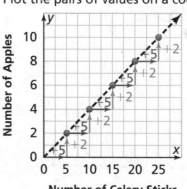

The point (25, 10) shows that 10 apples are needed for 25 celery sticks.

Jack needs 10 apples to make the juice.

EXAMPLE **3** Graph Ratios Related to Pi (π)

The measurements of different circular objects are given in a ratio table. What do you notice about the graph of the pairs of values given in the ratio table?

Plot the pairs of values on a coordinate plane.

Object	Diameter, d	Circumference, C
Fruit Plate	7 in.	22 in.
Clock Face	14 in.	44 in.
Hula Hoop	35 in.	110 in.

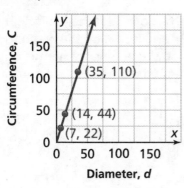

(35, 110)
(14, 44)
(7, 22)

The graph of the values in the ratio table are on the same line.

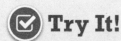 **Try It!**

Can you draw an object with a diameter of 10 inches and a circumference of 50 inches? Explain.

You can use ratio tables and graphs to show equivalent ratios. When ordered pairs representing equivalent ratios are graphed as points in the coordinate plane, they form a line.

Tennis Rackets Sold	Tennis Balls Sold
3	4
6	8
9	12
12	16

For every 3 tennis rackets sold, 4 tennis balls are sold.

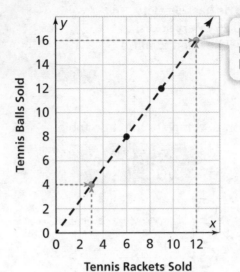

For every 12 tennis rackets sold, 16 tennis balls are sold.

Do You Understand?

1. **? Essential Question** How can you use tables and graphs to show equivalent ratios?

2. **Look for Relationships** In Example 2, how could you use the graph to find the number of apples needed for 30 celery sticks?

3. How could you use repeated addition to show ratios equivalent to 1:3 on a graph?

Do You Know How?

4. Complete the table to show equivalent ratios representing a cost of $8 for every 3 boxes. Then write the pairs of values as points to be plotted on a coordinate plane.

Number of Boxes	Cost of Boxes ($)
3	8
6	16
9	24
⬜	⬜
⬜	⬜

5. **Model with Math** Plot the equivalent ratios (3, 4), (6, 8), and (9, 12) on the graph. Use the graph to find the number of nonfiction books purchased if 10 fiction books are purchased.

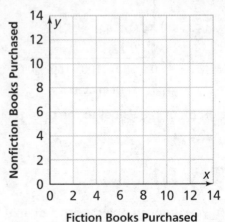

Go Online | PearsonRealize.com

Name: _____

Practice & Problem Solving

Scan for
Multimedia

Leveled Practice In **6** and **7**, complete the table and graph the pairs of values.

6.

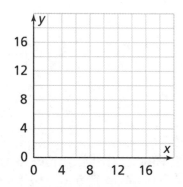

2	3
4	6

7.

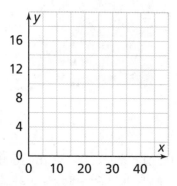

5	2
25	10

---

8. A student runs 2 minutes for every 10 minutes she walks.

a. Complete the table. Graph the pairs of values.

Running (min)	Walking (min)
2	10
4	20

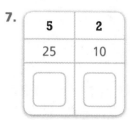

Exercise Times

b. For how long would the student walk if she runs for 7 minutes?

---

9. A car magazine reports the number of miles driven for different amounts of gas for three cars. Which car travels the farthest on 1 gallon of gas? Explain.

Car A

Miles Driven			200	300	
Gallons of Gas	1	4	8		16

Car C Gas Mileage

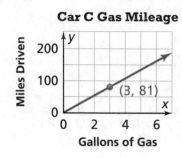

(3, 81)

Car B can travel 140 miles for every 5 gallons of gas.

10. **Model with Math** A bread recipe calls for 4 cups of white flour for every 5 cups of whole-wheat flour. Complete the table to show how many cups of whole-wheat flour are needed to mix with 16 cups of white flour. Then graph the pairs of values.

White Flour (c)	4	8	12	16
Whole-Wheat Flour (c)				

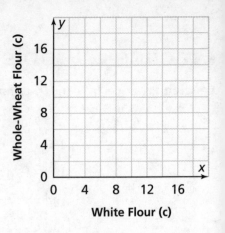

11. The graph shows the relationship between the number of cups of sugar and the number of cups of flour in a key-lime bread recipe. What point on the graph represents the number of cups of sugar that would be used with 8 cups of flour?

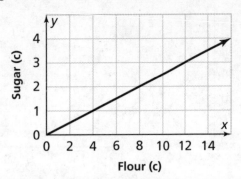

12. **Higher Order Thinking** Ishwar can read 5 pages in 15 minutes. Anne can read 15 pages in 1 hour. Explain how you could use a table or graph to find how much longer it would take Anne to read a 300-page book than Ishwar.

Assessment Practice

13. Some measurements of circular objects are given in the ratio table. 🔵 6.RP.1.3a

PART A

Find the missing dimensions of other circular objects by completing the ratio table.

Diameter, d	42 mm		301 mm
Circumference, C	132 mm	198 mm	

PART B

Graph the pairs of values.

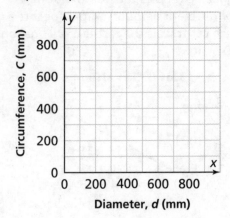

Go Online | PearsonRealize.com

1. **Vocabulary** How can a *ratio* be used to compare quantities? *Lesson 6-1* 🌐 6.RP.1.1

2. The circumference of the outside of a ring is 66 mm, and it has an outer diameter of 21 mm. If the circumference of the inside of the ring is 50 mm, what is the inner diameter of the ring? *Lesson 6-4* 🌐 6.RP.1.3e

3. During the breakfast service, the D-Town Diner sells 12 cups of coffee for every 10 glasses of orange juice. How many cups of coffee would the diner have sold if 40 glasses of orange juice had been sold? Complete the table with equivalent ratios. *Lesson 6-2* 🌐 6.RP.1.3a

Cups of Coffee	12	☐	☐	☐
Glasses of Orange Juice	10	☐	☐	40

4. The ratio of cows to chickens at Old McDonald's Farm is 2:7. Select all the farms that have a greater ratio of cows to chickens than Old McDonald's Farm. *Lesson 6-3* 🌐 6.RP.1.3a

☐ Red's Farm: 3 cows for every 5 chickens

☐ Cluck & Moo Farm: 1 cow for every 5 chickens

☐ T Family Farm: 1 cow for every 3 chickens

☐ Pasture Farm: 2 cows for every 9 chickens

☐ C & C Farm: 3 cows for every 8 chickens

5. A package of 3 notebooks costs $5. Complete the ratio table and graph the pairs of values. How much will 18 notebooks cost? *Lesson 6-4* 🌐 6.RP.1.3a

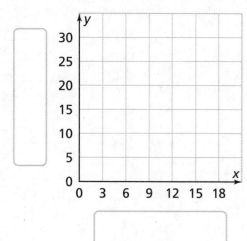

Number of Notebooks	Cost ($)
3	5
☐	10
☐	15
☐	20
☐	25

How well did you do on the mid-topic checkpoint? Fill in the stars. ☆ ☆ ☆

MID-TOPIC PERFORMANCE TASK

Hillsdale Orchard grows Fuji apples and Gala apples. There are 160 Fuji apple trees and 120 Gala apple trees in the orchard.

PART A

Hillsdale Orchard's owners decide to plant 30 new Gala apple trees. Complete the ratio table to find the number of new Fuji apple trees the owners should plant if they want to maintain the same ratio of Fuji apple trees to Gala apple trees. 🔊 6.RP.1.3a

Fuji Apple Trees			160
Gala Apple Trees	30		120

PART B

Use the ratio table to complete a graph that shows the relationship between the number of Fuji apple trees and Gala apple trees at Hillsdale Orchard. 🔊 6.RP.1.3a

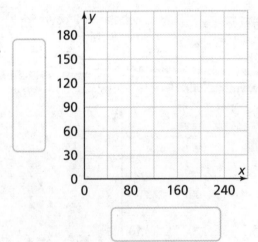

PART C

By the end of the next season, the owners of Hillsdale Orchard plan to have 240 Fuji apple trees. Explain how you could use the graph to find the total number of Fuji and Gala apple trees that Hillsdale Orchard will have if the owners achieve their goal. 🔊 6.RP.1.3a

Solve & Discuss It!

ACTIVITY

What is the cost of 10 bottles of fruit juice?

Fruit Juice
Buy **4** for $**10**

I can...
solve problems involving rates.

MAFS.6.RP.1.2 Understand the concept of a unit rate $\frac{a}{b}$ associated with a ratio a:b with $b \neq 0$, and use rate language in the context of a ratio relationship. **Also 6.RP.1.3a, 6.RP.1.3b**

MAFS.K12.MP.1.1, MP.2.1, MP.3.1, MP.8.1

Make Sense and Persevere
How can you use tables or diagrams to make sense of the quantities in the problem?

Focus on math practices

Critique Reasoning Monica says, "If 4 bottles cost $10, then 2 bottles cost $5, and 8 bottles cost $20. So 10 bottles cost $5 + $20." Is Monica correct? Explain.

VISUAL
LEARNING

ASSESS

EXAMPLE 1 **Find Equivalent Rates**

Scan for
Multimedia

A rate is a special type of ratio that compares quantities with unlike units of measure.

If the race car continues to travel at the same rate, how long will it take it to travel 25 kilometers?

Generalize You can find equivalent rates the same ways that you find equivalent ratios.

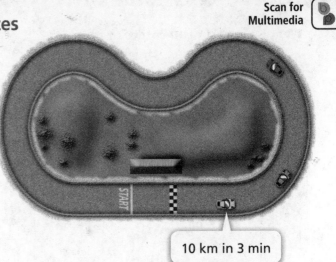

10 km in 3 min

ONE WAY Use a ratio table to find rates that are equivalent to $\frac{10 \text{ km}}{3 \text{ min}}$.

Distance (km)	Time (min)
5	$1\frac{1}{2}$
10	3
15	$4\frac{1}{2}$
20	6
25	$7\frac{1}{2}$

It will take the race car $7\frac{1}{2}$ minutes to travel 25 kilometers.

ANOTHER WAY Write the rate as a fraction. Multiply both terms of the rate by the same number to find an equivalent rate.

Think, $10 \times ? = 25$.

$$\frac{10 \text{ km}}{3 \text{ min}} = \frac{25 \text{ km}}{x \text{ min}}$$

$$\frac{10 \text{ km} \times 2.5}{3 \text{ min} \times 2.5} = \frac{25 \text{ km}}{7.5 \text{ min}}$$

Multiply both terms by 2.5.

It will take the race car 7.5 minutes to travel 25 kilometers.

✓ Try It!

At the same rate, how long would it take the car to travel 60 kilometers?

It will take the car [ ] minutes to travel [ ] kilometers.

$$\frac{10 \text{ km} \times \boxed{}}{3 \text{ min} \times \boxed{}} = \frac{60 \text{ km}}{\boxed{} \text{ min}}$$

Convince Me! Sal draws the double number line diagram at the right. He says it shows that at this rate the race car will travel 35 kilometers in 10.5 minutes. Critique Sal's reasoning. Is he correct? Explain.

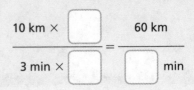

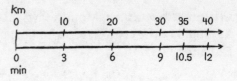 Go Online | PearsonRealize.com

EXAMPLE **2** **Compare Quantities in Two Ways**   ACTIVITY ASSESS

Harvest Market sells a crate of Florida oranges for $12.00. What are two different unit rates that could represent the situation?

Find the unit rate in pounds per dollar.

$$\frac{15 \text{ pounds}}{\$12.00}$$

$$\frac{15 \text{ pounds} \div 12}{\$12.00 \div 12} = \frac{1.25 \text{ pounds}}{\$1.00}$$

The unit rate in pounds per dollar is $\frac{1.25 \text{ pounds}}{\$1.00}$.

Find the unit rate in dollars per pound.

$$\frac{\$12.00}{15 \text{ pounds}}$$

$$\frac{\$12.00 \div 15}{15 \text{ pounds} \div 15} = \frac{\$0.80}{1 \text{ pound}}$$

The unit rate in dollars per pound is $\frac{\$0.80}{1 \text{ pound}}$.

FLORIDA ORANGES
15 lb

 Try It!

A recipe for scrambled eggs uses 2 tablespoons of milk for every 3 eggs. What are two unit rates that could represent the recipe?

EXAMPLE **3** **Use Unit Rates to Solve Problems**

A unit rate is a rate in which the comparison is to 1 unit.

How far could the family travel in 8 hours if they maintain the same rate of speed?

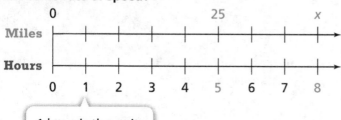

0   25   x

Miles

Hours

0 1 2 3 4 5 6 7 8

1 hour is the unit.

A family bicycles 25 miles in 5 hours.

STEP 1

Find the unit rate in miles per hour.

$$\frac{25 \text{ miles}}{5 \text{ hours}} \text{ or } \frac{25}{5}$$

$$\frac{25 \div 5}{5 \div 5} = \frac{5}{1}$$

Write an equivalent rate with a denominator of 1.

The unit rate is $\frac{5}{1}$, or 5 miles per hour.

Generalize The unit rate is an equivalent rate with a denominator of 1.

STEP 2

Use the unit rate to find how far the family could travel in 8 hours.

$$\frac{5 \times 8}{1 \times 8} = \frac{40}{8} \text{ or } \frac{40 \text{ miles}}{8 \text{ hours}}$$

The family could travel 40 miles in 8 hours.

 Try It!

A canoeing club travels 78 miles in 3 days. How far could they travel in 5 days if they maintain the same speed?

A rate compares quantities with unlike units of measure.

$$\frac{\$3.50}{7 \text{ oranges}}$$

A unit rate compares a quantity to 1 unit of another quantity.

$$\frac{\$3.50}{7 \text{ oranges}} = \frac{\$0.50}{1 \text{ orange}}$$

Do You Understand?

1. **Essential Question** What are rates and unit rates?

2. **Be Precise** Use what you know about ratios to describe a rate.

3. **Reasoning** A bathroom shower streams 5 gallons of water in 2 minutes.

   a. Find the unit rate for gallons per minute and describe it in words.

   b. Find the unit rate for minutes per gallon and describe it in words.

5 gallons in two minutes

Do You Know How?

In 4 and 5, find the value of n.

4.
Miles	45	135
Hours	4	n

5.
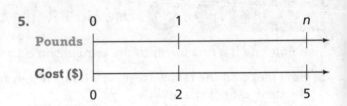

6. Jenny packaged 108 eggs in 9 cartons. Write this statement as a rate.

7. Anna Maria read 40 pages in 60 minutes. What is her unit rate in pages per minute?

In 8 and 9, use the unit rates that you found in Exercise 3.

8. How many gallons of water does the shower stream in 6 minutes?

9. How long can someone shower to use only 10 gallons of water?

Go Online | PearsonRealize.com

Practice & Problem Solving

In 10 and 11, write each statement as a rate.

10. Jan saw 9 full moons in 252 days.

11. It took Hannah 38 minutes to run 8 laps.

In 12 and 13, find the value of x.

12.

Fish	16	48
Bowls	2	x

13.

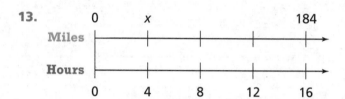

Leveled Practice **In 14 and 15, find the unit rate.**

14. $\dfrac{320 \text{ mi}}{16 \text{ gal}}$

$\dfrac{320 \div 16}{16 \div 16} = \dfrac{\boxed{}}{1}$

$\dfrac{\boxed{} \text{ mi}}{1 \text{ gal}}$

15. $\dfrac{75 \text{ cm}}{5 \text{ h}}$

$\dfrac{75 \div \boxed{}}{5 \div 5} = \dfrac{\boxed{}}{1}$

$\dfrac{\boxed{} \text{ cm}}{1 \text{ h}}$

In 16–19, complete each table.

16.

Pages	9			
Minutes	18	1	10	15

17.

Beans	186			
Bags	3	1	7	11

18.

Ounces		24.6		123
Bags	1	2	5	

19.

Miles	25		125	
Gallons		3	5	12

20. Which runner set the fastest pace? Explain.

Runner	Laps	Time
Martha	20	32 min
Allison	16	25 min
Rachel	17	27.2 min

21. Model with Math Over the summer, Alexis read 15 books in 12 weeks. The diagram below can be used to track her progress. If Alexis read at the same rate each week, how many books had she read in 4 weeks? In 8 weeks? Complete the diagram.

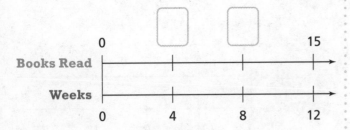

22. An elephant charges an object that is 0.35 kilometer away. How long will it take the elephant to reach the object?

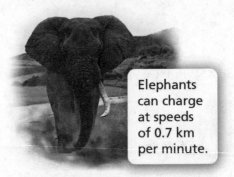

Elephants can charge at speeds of 0.7 km per minute.

23. A machine takes 1 minute to fill 6 cartons of eggs. At this rate, how many minutes will it take to fill 420 cartons?

24. Higher Order Thinking How are the ratios $\frac{24\text{ laps}}{1\text{ hour}}$ and $\frac{192\text{ laps}}{8\text{ hours}}$ alike? How are they different?

Assessment Practice

25. A bakery sells 12 gourmet orange-zest cupcakes for $36.00. Select all the statements that are true. 🔵 6.RP.1.2

☐ $\frac{\$3.00}{1\text{ cupcake}}$ is a unit rate for the cost per cupcake.

☐ $\frac{36}{12}$ represents the ratio of $36.00 for 12 cupcakes.

☐ Using the same rate, the bakery can sell 6 cupcakes for $20.00.

☐ Using the same rate, the bakery can sell 2 dozen cupcakes for $72.00.

☐ Using the same rate, it would cost $24.50 for 8 cupcakes.

Go Online | PearsonRealize.com

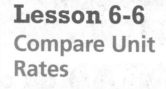
 Solve & Discuss It!  ACTIVITY

Rick and Nikki own remote-control cars. They use a stopwatch to record the speed of each car. Whose car is faster?

Speed of Rick's Car

Distance (feet)	Time (seconds)
150	30

Speed of Nikki's Car

Distance (feet)	Time (seconds)
80	20

I can...
compare unit rates to solve problems.

 MAFS.6.RP.1.3b Solve unit rate problems including those involving unit pricing and constant speed. Also 6.RP.1.3a

MAFS.K12.MP.1.1, MP.2.1, MP.6.1

Rick's Car

Nikki's Car

Be Precise Use precise numbers and units to describe and compare rates.

Focus on math practices

Make Sense and Persevere If each car maintains its rate of speed, how long will it take Rick's car to travel 300 feet? How long will it take Nikki's car to travel the same distance? Explain.

? Essential Question How can you use unit rates to make comparisons?

  VISUAL LEARNING AS

EXAMPLE 1 👁 **Compare to Find the Greater Unit Rate**

Scan for Multimedia

Ethan swam 11 laps in the pool in 8 minutes. Austin swam 7 laps in the same pool in 5 minutes. Which boy swam at a faster rate?

Make Sense and Persevere
Is the faster rate a fewer number of laps per minute or a greater number of laps per minute?

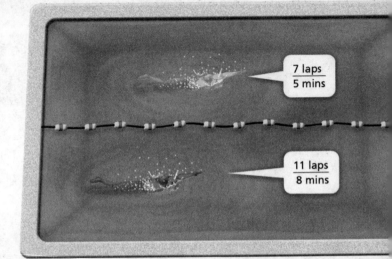

7 laps / 5 mins

11 laps / 8 mins

Ethan swam 11 laps in 8 minutes.

$$\frac{11 \text{ laps}}{8 \text{ minutes}} \text{ or } \frac{11}{8}$$

$$\frac{11}{8} = \frac{11 \div 8}{8 \div 8} = \frac{1.375}{1}$$ — Find the unit rate.

Ethan swam 1.375 laps each minute.

Austin swam 7 laps in 5 minutes.

$$\frac{7 \text{ laps}}{5 \text{ minutes}} \text{ or } \frac{7}{5}$$

$$\frac{7}{5} = \frac{7 \div 5}{5 \div 5} = \frac{1.4}{1}$$ — Find the unit rate.

Austin swam 1.4 laps each minute.

$1.4 > 1.375$, so Austin swam at a faster rate.

✓ Try It!

Ashley is Austin's older sister. She trains in the same pool and can swim 9 laps in 6 minutes. Is Ashley a faster swimmer than Austin?

$$\frac{9 \div \boxed{} \quad \boxed{}}{6 \div \boxed{} \quad \boxed{}} = \boxed{}$$

Ashley swims 1.5 laps per minute. Because $\boxed{}$ $\boxed{}$ 1.4, Ashley is a $\boxed{}$ swimmer than Austin.

Convince Me! How can you use the unit rate in minutes per lap to compare Ashley's speed to Austin's speed?

EXAMPLE **2** Compare to Find the
Lesser Unit Rate

  ACTIVITY ASSESS

Is the lunch special or the weekend special a better value? Find the unit price of each special.

A **unit price** is a unit rate that gives the price of one item.

> **Make Sense and Persevere**
> Is the lesser unit price or the greater unit price a better value?

Find the unit price of the lunch special.

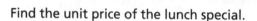
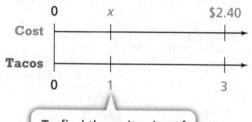

> To find the unit price of the lunch special, find the cost of 1 taco.

$$\frac{\$2.40}{3}$$

$$\frac{\$2.40}{3} \div \frac{3}{3} = \frac{\$0.80}{1}$$ ← Find the unit rate.

The unit price for the lunch special is $0.80 per taco.

Find the unit price of the weekend special.

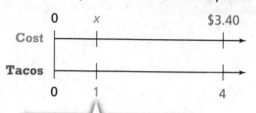

> To find the unit price of the weekend special, find the cost of 1 taco.

$$\frac{\$3.40}{4}$$

$$\frac{\$3.40}{4} \div \frac{4}{4} = \frac{\$0.85}{1}$$ ← Find the unit rate.

The unit price for the weekend special is $0.85 per taco.

$0.80 per taco < $0.85 per taco, so the lunch special is a better value.

✅ **Try It!**

Explain how to decide which is the better value, 4 greeting cards for $10 or 6 greeting cards for $14.

4 greeting cards for $10

6 greeting cards for $14

You can use unit rates to make comparisons.

$8.50 per hour > $8.00 per hour

$$\frac{7 \text{ laps}}{1 \text{ min}} < \frac{9 \text{ laps}}{1 \text{ min}}$$

$$\frac{32 \text{ cm}}{1 \text{ sec}} < \frac{45 \text{ cm}}{1 \text{ sec}}$$

175 words per minute > 95 words per minute

Do You Understand?

1. **? Essential Question** How can you use unit rates to make comparisons?

2. **Critique Reasoning** Paul says that a lower unit rate is a better value only if you can use all the items purchased to get the lower unit rate. Do you agree? Explain.

3. **Reasoning** Car A travels 115 miles on 5 gallons of gas. Car B travels 126 miles on 6 gallons of gas. How can you find which car gets better gas mileage?

Do You Know How?

4. Hakim's car travels 600 feet in 20 seconds. Andre's motorcycle travels 300 feet in 12 seconds. Which is faster, the car or the motorcycle? Explain.

300 ft in 12 seconds

600 ft in 20 seconds

a. Find the unit rates.

b. Compare the unit rates.

In 5 and 6, find each unit price.

5. 7 movie tickets for $56

6. 12 fluid ounces of shampoo for $2.76

7. Which is the better value, 2 books for $15 or 6 books for $45? Explain.

Go Online | PearsonRealize.com

Practice & Problem Solving

Leveled Practice In **8** and **9**, find each unit price.

8. 9 pens for $3.60

$$\frac{\$3.60 \div 9}{9 \div 9} = \frac{\boxed{}}{1}$$

9. 15 ounces of canned beans for $2.25

$$\frac{\$2.25 \div \boxed{}}{15 \div \boxed{}} = \frac{\boxed{}}{\boxed{}}$$

In **10** and **11**, determine which is the better value.

10. 3 kilograms of charcoal for $7.95 or
5 kilograms of charcoal for $12.50

11. 50 envelopes for $2.49 or
90 envelopes for $5.50

In **12–15**, compare the rates to find which is greater.

12. 35 points in 20 minutes or 49 points in
35 minutes

13. 12 laps in 8 minutes or 16 laps in 10 minutes

14. 45 strikeouts in 36 innings or 96 strikeouts in
80 innings

15. 480 stickers on 6 sheets or 120 stickers on
2 sheets

In **16–18**, compare the rates to find which is the better value.

16. $27 for 4 large pizzas or $32 for 5 large pizzas

17. $30 for 100 flyers or $65 for 250 flyers

18. 36 pictures for $8 or 24 pictures for $5

19. **Model with Math** Katrina and Becca exchanged 270 text messages in 45 minutes. An equal number of texts was sent each minute. The girls can send 90 more text messages before they are charged additional fees. Complete the double number line diagram. At this rate, for how many more minutes can the girls exchange texts before they are charged extra?

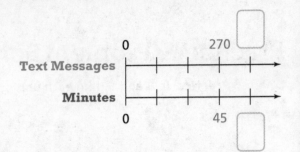

20. **Reasoning** Which container of milk would you buy? Explain.

$\frac{1}{2}$ gallon for $2.29

1 gallon for $3.99

21. **Higher Order Thinking** Amil and Abe rode in a bike-a-thon. Abe rode for 77 minutes at a faster rate per mile than Amil. Find Amil's unit rate. Then explain how you could use it to find a possible unit rate for Abe.

Amil rode 15 miles in 55 minutes.

Assessment Practice

22. A food warehouse sells cans of soup in boxes. Bargain shoppers have four options. 🔵 6.RP.1.3b

PART A

Complete the table to find the unit price for each option.

Boxes of Soup	Unit Price
12 cans for $10.56	
16 cans for $13.60	
20 cans for $17.20	
24 cans for $21.36	

PART B

Compare the unit rates found in Part A and identify the best value.

Go Online | PearsonRealize.com

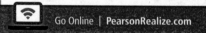
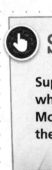 # Solve & Discuss It!  ACTIVITY

Suppose you are traveling by train to visit a friend who lives 275 miles away. How long will the trip take? Moving at a constant speed, how long would it take the train to travel 385 miles?

The train travels at a constant speed of 55 miles per hour.

I can...
use unit rates to solve problems.

MAFS.6.RP.1.3b Solve unit rate problems including those involving unit pricing and constant speed.
MAFS.K12.MP.2.1, MP.4.1, MP.7.1, MP.8.1

Model with Math How can you use what you know about unit rates to model and solve this problem?

Focus on math practices

Reasoning Suppose the train was traveling at a constant speed that is twice as fast as 55 miles per hour. How long would it take the train to go 275 miles? Explain.

EXAMPLE 1 **Solve Constant Speed Problems**

Scan for Multimedia

The jet flies at a constant speed.

Constant speed means that the speed stays the same over time.

If the jet continues to fly at the same rate, how far could it fly in 85 minutes?

The jet flies 175 miles in 7 minutes.

ONE WAY Use a table to record equivalent rates to find how far the jet could fly in 85 minutes.

Time (min)	Distance (mi)
1	25
7	175
25	625
50	1,250
85	2,125

×85 ... ×85

The jet could fly 2,125 miles in 85 minutes.

ANOTHER WAY Use the unit rate to find how far the jet could fly in 85 minutes.

$$\frac{175 \text{ miles} \div 7}{7 \text{ minutes} \div 7} = \frac{25 \text{ miles}}{1 \text{ minute}}$$

$$\frac{25 \text{ miles} \times 85}{1 \text{ minute} \times 85} = \frac{2{,}125 \text{ miles}}{85 \text{ minutes}}$$

Find an equivalent rate.

Look for Relationships The table and the equation represent the same relationship.

The jet could fly 2,125 miles in 85 minutes.

✓ **Try It!**

At the same rate, how far would the jet fly in 75 minutes?

$$\frac{\boxed{} \text{ miles} \times \boxed{}}{1 \text{ minute} \times \boxed{}} = \frac{\boxed{} \text{ miles}}{75 \text{ minutes}}$$

The jet would fly $\boxed{}$ miles.

Convince Me! How could you use the table from Example 1 to find how far the jet would fly in 75 minutes? Explain.

EXAMPLE 2 Solve Unit Price Problems

  ACTIVITY ASSESS

Grocery Giant is having a sale on Swiss cheese. How much would it cost to buy 5 slices of cheese at the same rate?

24 slices for $7.20

Reasoning How can you use the unit price to solve the problem?

ONE WAY Use a ratio table to solve.

Slices	Price
1	$0.30
5	$1.50
24	$7.20

×5 ÷24 ×5 ÷24

ANOTHER WAY Use the unit price to solve.

$$\frac{\$7.20 \div 24}{24 \text{ slices} \div 24} = \frac{\$0.30}{1 \text{ slice}}$$

$$\frac{\$0.30 \times 5}{1 \text{ slice} \times 5} = \frac{\$1.50}{5 \text{ slices}}$$

At this rate, it would cost $1.50 for 5 slices of cheese.

Try It!

Jarod paid $13.80 for 5 tickets to the game. At the same rate, how much would 3 tickets cost?

EXAMPLE 3  Use an Equation to Represent Unit Rate Problems

A ferryboat travels at a constant speed of 57.5 miles in 2.5 hours. How long would it take the ferryboat to travel 92 miles at that rate?

STEP 1 Find the unit rate.

÷2.5

Time (h)	1	2.5
Distance (mi)	23	57.5

÷2.5

The ferryboat travels at a rate of 23 miles per hour.

STEP 2 Find the time.

$d = r \times t$ — The equation shows that distance is the product of rate and time.

$92 = 23t$ — Substitute 92 for distance and 23 for the rate.

$\frac{92}{23} = \frac{23t}{23}$

$t = 4$

Generalize You can use a formula such as $d = r \times t$ to solve constant speed problems.

It would take 4 hours for the ferryboat to travel 92 miles.

Try It!

A submarine travels 19 miles in $\frac{1}{2}$ hour. Write an equation to find out how long it would take the submarine to travel 57 miles at the same rate. Then find the time.

You can use ratio tables or unit rates to solve rate problems, including constant speed problems.

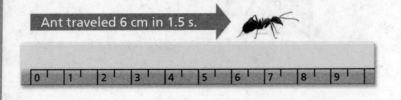

Ant traveled 6 cm in 1.5 s.

Time (s)	Distance (cm)
1	4
1.5	6
3	12
4.5	18
6	24

×6   ×6

Do You Understand?

1. **Essential Question** How can you use unit rates to solve problems?

2. **Construct Arguments** An ostrich runs 6 miles in 12 minutes at a constant speed. Explain how you can use a unit rate to find how far the ostrich could run in 40 minutes.

3. Bananas sell for $0.58 per pound. How could you write an equation to show the relationship between the total cost, c, and the number of pounds of bananas, p?

Do You Know How?

In 4 and 5, use unit rates to solve.

4. A football player runs 80 yards in 25 seconds. If he maintains the same rate of speed, how far could he run in 60 seconds?

5. On a family vacation, Amy's dad drove the car at a constant speed and traveled 585 miles in 13 hours. At this rate, how long would it have taken the family to travel 810 miles? What was the car's rate of speed?

6. Look at Exercise 5. Write an equation to find the total distance, d, that Amy's family traveled after t hours.

Go Online | PearsonRealize.com

Practice & Problem Solving

Scan for
Multimedia

Leveled Practice In 7–9, solve the rate problems.

7. A horse named Northern Dancer won the Kentucky Derby with a time of exactly 2 minutes. At this constant rate, how long would it take Northern Dancer to run the Belmont Stakes?

Use the unit rate. $\dfrac{1.25 \text{ miles} \div \boxed{}}{2 \text{ minutes} \div 2} = \dfrac{\boxed{} \text{ mile}}{1 \text{ minute}}$

Find an equivalent rate. $\dfrac{\boxed{} \text{ mile} \times 2.4}{1 \text{ minute} \times \boxed{}} = \dfrac{1.5 \text{ miles}}{\boxed{} \text{ minutes}}$

It would take Northern Dancer $\boxed{}$ minutes to run the Belmont Stakes.

Kentucky Derby $1\frac{1}{4}$ miles

Belmont Stakes $1\frac{1}{2}$ miles

8. If a cyclist rides at a constant rate of 24 miles per hour, how long would it take the cyclist to ride 156 miles?

9. The price of an 8-minute phone call is $1.20. What is the price of a 17-minute phone call?

In 10 and 11, use the map at the right.

The Garcia family is driving from Sacramento, California, to Key West, Florida. In 5 days, they have traveled 2,045 miles. At this rate, how long will it take them to travel from Sacramento to Key West?

10. How can you use rate reasoning to solve this problem? Explain.

Sacramento, California

3,272 miles

Key West, Florida

11. **Be Precise** Show how to use numbers, units, and symbols precisely to solve the problem.

12. Vik wrote the equation $470 \cdot h = 3,008$, where h is the number of hours it took a plane flying at a constant speed of 470 miles per hour to travel 3,008 miles. Solve for h.

13. A nursery owner buys 7 panes of glass to fix some damage to his greenhouse. The 7 panes cost $15.05. Unfortunately, he breaks 2 more panes while repairing the damage. What is the cost of another 2 panes of glass?

14. Cheyenne drew a circle with diameter 1 meter. She measured the circumference to estimate the value of Pi. Complete the table, and then write an equation to find the circumference, C, for a circle with diameter d.

Diameter, d (meters)	1	2	3	4
Circumference, C (meters)	3.14			

15. Jayden bought 70 feet of speaker wire for $18.20. He needs 30 more feet. If the unit price is the same, how much will Jayden pay for the extra 30 feet of wire? Explain.

16. Higher Order Thinking Sasha runs at a constant speed of 3.8 meters per second for $\frac{1}{2}$ hour. Then she walks at a constant rate of 1.5 meters per second for $\frac{1}{2}$ hour. How far did Sasha run and walk in 60 minutes?

Assessment Practice

17. Suppose that a leatherback turtle swam 7.5 kilometers in 3 hours at a constant speed. At this rate, how long would it take the turtle to swim 10 kilometers? How many kilometers per hour did the turtle swim? Explain. 🔵 6.RP.1.3b

18. The unit rate for Pi (π) can be approximated with the ratio 3.14 : 1. 🔵 6.RP.1.3e

PART A

Find the approximate circumference of a circle (in feet), if the diameter is 4 feet.

PART B

Find the approximate diameter of a circle (in centimeters), if the circumference is 25.12 centimeters.

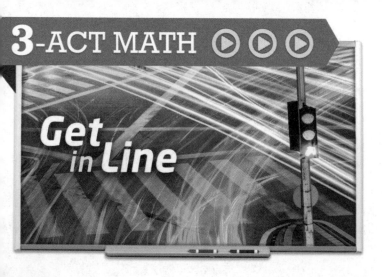

Get in Line

3-Act Mathematical Modeling:
Get in Line

Go Online | PearsonRealize.com

🔍 MAFS.K12.MP.4.1 Model with mathematics
Also MP.1.1, MP.2.1, MP.3.1, MP.5.1, MP.7.1,
MP.8.1
MAFS.6.RP.1.3b Solve unit rate problems
including... constant speed. Also 6.RP.1.2

ACT 1

1. After watching the video, what is the first question that comes to mind?

2. Write the Main Question you will answer.

3. Construct Arguments Predict an answer to this Main Question.
Explain your prediction.

4. On the number line below, write a number that is too small to be
the answer. Write a number that is too large.

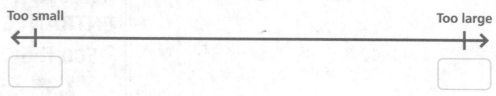

Too small   Too large

5. Plot your prediction on the same number line.

6. What information in this situation would be helpful to know? How would you use that information?

7. **Use Appropriate Tools** What tools can you use to get the information you need? Record the information as you find it.

8. **Model with Math** Represent the situation using the mathematical content, concepts, and skills from this topic. Use your representation to answer the Main Question.

9. What is your answer to the Main Question? Is it higher or lower than your prediction? Explain why.

FREEWAY ENTRANCE 500 feet

Go Online | **PearsonRealize.com**

10. Write the answer you saw in the video.

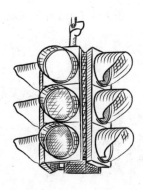

11. Reasoning Does your answer match the answer in the video? If not, what are some reasons that would explain the difference?

12. Make Sense and Persevere Would you change your model now that you know the answer? Explain.

Reflect

13. Model with Math Explain how you used a mathematical model to represent the situation. How did the model help you answer the Main Question?

14. Generalize Will your model work on other lights? Explain your reasoning.

15. Use Structure Later that week, it took between 20 and 21 minutes to get through the same light. How many cars were in line?

Solve & Discuss It!

ACTIVITY

If 6.5 feet of snow were to fall in a 24-hour period, would the 1921 record be broken? There are 12 inches in 1 foot.

THE NEWS

April 15, 1921   Silver Lake, Colorado

RECORD BREAKING SNOWFALL

75.8 INCHES IN 24 HOURS

BREAKING NEWS

Man digging his pickup truck out from snow.

Reasoning Use the relationship between inches and feet to solve the problem.

I can...
use ratio reasoning to convert customary measurements.

MAFS.6.RP.1.3d Use ratio reasoning to convert measurement units, manipulate and transform units appropriately when multiplying or dividing quantities.
MAFS.K12.MP.1.1, MP.2.1, MP.3.1, MP.4.1

Focus on math practices

Make Sense and Persevere How many feet of snow would need to fall in Silver Lake, Colorado, to break the 1921 24-hour snowfall record from 1921?

? Essential Question How can you use ratios to convert customary units of measure?

VISUAL LEARNING · ASSESS

EXAMPLE 1 **Convert Customary Units of Length**

Scan for Multimedia

The sidewalk in front of a store is 4.5 feet wide. The city regulations establish a maximum width for sidewalks of 66 inches. Does the sidewalk meet the city regulations?

4.5 ft

Customary Units

Length
1 ft = 12 in.
1 yd = 36 in.
1 yd = 3 ft
1 mi = 5,280 ft
1 mi = 1,760 yd

Model with Math The conversions in the table can be written as rates that compare equivalent measurements.

ONE WAY

Write the width of the sidewalk in inches.

> Identify the conversion rate that relates feet to inches.

$$12 \text{ in.} = 1 \text{ ft}$$

Find an equivalent rate.

$$\frac{12 \text{ in.} \times 4.5}{1 \text{ ft} \times 4.5} = \frac{54 \text{ in.}}{4.5 \text{ ft}}$$

> Multiply both terms of the rate by 4.5.

The sidewalk is 54 inches wide. It meets the city regulations.

ANOTHER WAY

Use **dimensional analysis** to convert measures by including measurement units when you multiply by a conversion factor. A **conversion factor** is a rate that compares equivalent measures.

$$4.5 \, \cancel{\text{ft}} \times \frac{12 \text{ in.}}{1 \, \cancel{\text{ft}}}$$

$$= 4.5 \times 12 \text{ in.}$$

$$= 54 \text{ in.}$$

> Multiply by the conversion factor that relates the measures and leaves you with the units needed to solve the problem. Divide out the common units.

The sidewalk is 54 inches wide. It meets the city regulations.

✓ Try It!

According to city regulations, how many feet wide is the maximum sidewalk width? Explain.

Convince Me! What conversion factor would you use when converting 66 inches to feet? Explain.

EXAMPLE **2** **Convert Customary Units of Capacity**

Jonah has 15 gallons of water for a camping trip. How many quarts of water does he have?

ONE WAY Use an equivalent rate.

4 qt = 1 gal ◁ Identify the conversion rate.

$\frac{4 \text{ qt} \times 15}{1 \text{ gal} \times 15} = \frac{60 \text{ qt}}{15 \text{ gal}}$ ◁ Multiply both terms of the rate by 15.

Jonah has 60 quarts of water.

- -

ANOTHER WAY Use dimensional analysis.

$15 \text{ gal} \times \frac{4 \text{ qt}}{1 \text{ gal}}$ ◁ Multiply by the conversion factor. Divide out the common units.

$= 15 \times 4 \text{ qt}$

$= 60 \text{ qt}$

Jonah has 60 quarts of water.

Customary Units

Capacity	
1 tbsp = 3 tsp	1 pt = 2 c
1 fl oz = 2 tbsp	1 qt = 2 pt
1 c = 8 fl oz	1 gal = 4 qt

Make Sense and Persevere
How can you use the conversion table to identify an appropriate conversion rate?

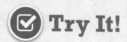 **Try It!**

Brandon is making bread. His recipe says to use $2\frac{1}{2}$ tablespoons of sugar. How many teaspoons of sugar should he use?

EXAMPLE **3** **Convert Customary Units of Weight**

The alpine pika is a small mammal in the rabbit family. How much does the alpine pika weigh in pounds?

The number of ounces in the conversion rate is greater than the number of ounces that the pika weighs. Use division to find the equivalent rate.

Customary Units

Weight
1 lb = 16 oz
1 T = 2,000 lb

ONE WAY Use an equivalent rate.

16 oz = 1 lb ◁ Identify the conversion rate.

$\frac{16 \text{ oz} \div 1.6}{1 \text{ lb} \div 1.6} = \frac{10 \text{ oz}}{0.625 \text{ lb}}$ ◁ Divide both terms of the rate by 1.6.

The alpine pika weighs 0.625 pound.

ANOTHER WAY Use dimensional analysis.

$10 \text{ oz} \times \frac{1 \text{ lb}}{16 \text{ oz}}$ ◁ Multiply by the conversion factor. Divide out the common units.

$= \frac{10}{16} \text{ lb}$

$= 0.625 \text{ lb}$

The alpine pika weighs 0.625 pound.

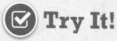 **Try It!**

How many pounds does the elephant weigh?

Stella weighs approximately 3.3 tons.

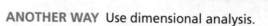

You can convert customary measures by finding an equivalent rate or by using dimensional analysis.

Use an equivalent rate.

1 mi = 5,280 ft

$$\frac{5{,}280 \text{ ft} \times 4.25}{1 \text{ mi} \times 4.25} = \frac{22{,}440 \text{ ft}}{4.25 \text{ mi}}$$

Use dimensional analysis.

$$4.25 \text{ mi} \times \frac{5{,}280 \text{ ft}}{1 \text{ mi}}$$

$$= 4.25 \times 5{,}280 \text{ ft}$$

$$= 22{,}440 \text{ ft}$$

Customary Units

Length
1 ft = 12 in.
1 yd = 36 in.
1 yd = 3 ft
1 mi = 5,280 ft
1 mi = 1,760 yd

Do You Understand?

1. **? Essential Question** How can you use ratios to convert customary units of measure?

2. What is a conversion factor that relates miles to yards?

3. **Construct Arguments** Jenna used the conversion factor $\frac{1 \text{ T}}{2{,}000 \text{ lb}}$ to convert 50 tons to pounds. Did she use the correct conversion factor? Explain.

4. How can you use the conversion rates of fluid ounces to cups, and cups to pints, to find the number of fluid ounces in a pint?

Do You Know How?

5. Convert 27 inches to yards by finding an equivalent rate.

6. Use dimensional analysis to convert 1.8 pounds to ounces.

7. **Critique Reasoning** Sam is tripling a recipe for an organic cleaning solution. The new recipe calls for 15 tsp of orange oil. To find how many tbsp this is, Sam converted this way:

Conversion factor: $\frac{3 \text{ tsp}}{1 \text{ tbsp}}$

$$15 \text{ tsp} \times \frac{3 \text{ tsp}}{1 \text{ tbsp}} = \frac{45}{1} \text{ tbsp} = 45 \text{ tbsp}$$

What error did Sam make?

Go Online | PearsonRealize.com

Practice & Problem Solving

In 8–13, complete each conversion.

8. 5 pt = [ ] c

9. $2\frac{1}{2}$ gal = [ ] qt

10. 2,640 yd = [ ] mi

11. Convert 16 yards to feet.
    Use the conversion rate
    3 feet = 1 yard.

12. Convert 10 pints to quarts.
    Use the conversion rate
    1 quart = 2 pints.

13. Convert 12 ounces to pounds.
    Use the conversion rate
    16 ounces = 1 pound.

14. Two neighbors in a rural area want to know the
    distance between their homes in miles. What
    should the neighbors use as a conversion factor
    to convert this distance to miles?

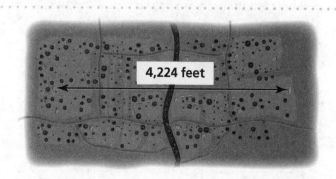

4,224 feet

15. A school custodian discovered a leak in a water
    pipe. The custodian found that 1,920 fluid ounces
    of water had leaked out. How many gallons
    of water is this? Use the conversion
    factor $\frac{1 \text{ gallon}}{128 \text{ fluid ounces}}$.

16. **Critique Reasoning** Two students, Stella and
    Vladimir, complete the conversion statement
    12 feet 8 inches = _____ inches.

    Stella stated that 12 feet 8 inches = 152 inches.
    Vladimir stated that 12 feet 8 inches = 9 inches.

    Which student is incorrect? Explain.

17. The hole for a support post needs to be 6 feet
    deep. It is currently 1 foot 8 inches deep.
    How much deeper must the hole be?
    Use the conversion factor $\frac{12 \text{ inches}}{1 \text{ foot}}$.

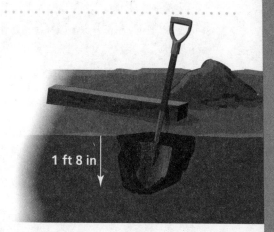

1 ft 8 in

In **18** and **19**, use the recipe card.

18. **Look for Relationships** Cheryl has measured 3 cups of water. Is this enough water for Cheryl to make a double recipe of green slime for a class project? Explain.

Green Slime Recipe

- 1 pint water
- $\frac{1}{2}$ cup cornstarch
- Green food coloring

Add hot water to cornstarch and stir constantly. Then add green food coloring, and stir. Allow the slime to cool to room temperature. This makes a messy slime that goes from liquid to solid. Make sure to play with it on a plastic covered surface. Always have adult supervision when using hot water.

19. There are 16 tablespoons in 1 cup. How many tablespoons of cornstarch would Cheryl need to make the green slime recipe 15 times?

20. **Make Sense and Persevere** Len plans to run at least 3 miles each day to get ready for a cross-country race. One lap of the school track is 440 yards. If Len runs 10 laps each day, will he cover at least 3 miles? Explain.

21. **Higher Order Thinking** Hunter is splitting a quart of ice cream with 7 members of his family. If the quart is split evenly, how many cups will each family member get? Explain.

22. A fully loaded and fueled space shuttle can weigh close to 4.5 million pounds at liftoff. What is this weight expressed in tons?

Weighs almost 4.5 million pounds

 Assessment Practice

23. Select all the conversions that are true.

6.RP.1.3d

☐ 18 ft = 6 yd

☐ 18 yd = 6 ft

☐ 0.5 mi = 10,560 ft

☐ 0.5 mi = 2,640 ft

☐ $\frac{1}{2}$ mi = 880 yd

Customary Units

Length
1 ft = 12 in.
1 yd = 36 in.
1 yd = 3 ft
1 mi = 5,280 ft
1 mi = 1,760 yd

Go Online | PearsonRealize.com

Solve & Discuss It!

 ACTIVITY

Sam needs to fill a 5-liter water jug for his team. If Sam uses the water bottle to fill the jug, how many times does he need to fill the water bottle to fill the jug?

Metric Units of Capacity

1,000 milliliters (mL) = 1 liter (L)
100 centiliters (cL) = 1 liter
10 deciliters (dL) = 1 liter
1 dekaliter (daL) = 10 liters
1 hectoliter (hL) = 100 liters
1 kiloliter (kL) = 1,000 liters

I can...
use unit rates to convert metric measurements.

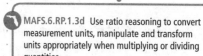

MAFS.6.RP.1.3d Use ratio reasoning to convert measurement units, manipulate and transform units appropriately when multiplying or dividing quantities.
MAFS.K12.MP.2.1, MP.3.1, MP.6.1, MP.7.1, MP.8.1

Reasoning How many milliliters are in 5 liters?

Focus on math practices

Be Precise How many liters of water does Sam's water bottle hold when full?

389

? **Essential Question** How can you use ratios to convert metric units of measure?

 EXAMPLE 1 **Convert Metric Units of Length**

Scan for
Multimedia

Emelia is helping her father build a skate ramp. They cut a board 1.2 meters long to use as the back of the ramp. Is the length of the board as shown in centimeters correct?

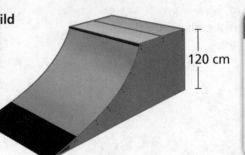

120 cm

Metric Units of Length
1,000 millimeters (mm) = 1 meter (m)
100 centimeters (cm) = 1 meter
10 decimeters (dm) = 1 meter
1 dekameter (dam) = 10 meters
1 hectometer (hm) = 100 meters
1 kilometer (km) = 1,000 meters

Generalize You can use what you know about converting customary units to convert metric units.

ONE WAY Use an equivalent rate to convert meters to centimeters.

100 cm = 1 m ◁— Identify the conversion rate.

$\frac{100 \text{ cm} \times 1.2}{1 \text{ m} \times 1.2} = \frac{120 \text{ cm}}{1.2 \text{ m}}$ ◁— Multiply both terms of the rate by 1.2.

1.2 m = 120 cm

The board is the correct length.

ANOTHER WAY Use dimensional analysis to convert meters to centimeters.

$1.2 \text{ m} \times \frac{100 \text{ cm}}{1 \text{ m}}$ ◁— Multiply by the conversion factor. Divide out the common units.

= 1.2 × 100 cm

= 120 cm

1.2 m = 120 cm

The board is the correct length.

☑ **Try It!**

The middle of the skate ramp is 2.5 meters wide. Emelia and her father want to use a board that is 23.5 decimeters long. Is this board wide enough for them to use? Convert the decimeters to meters to explain.

Convince Me! How can you convert 2.5 meters to decimeters to determine whether the board is wide enough?

EXAMPLE 2 Convert Metric Units of Capacity

  ACTIVITY ASSESS

Raji poured 150 liters of water into an aquarium. How much more water does Raji need to fill the aquarium?

2.2 hectoliters total capacity

Metric Units of Capacity
1,000 milliliters (mL) = 1 liter (L)
100 centiliters (cL) = 1 liter
10 deciliters (dL) = 1 liter
1 dekaliter (daL) = 10 liters
1 hectoliter (hL) = 100 liters
1 kiloliter (kL) = 1,000 liters

ONE WAY Use an equivalent rate.

1 hectoliter = 100 liters

$$\frac{1 \text{ hL} \times 2.2}{100 \text{ L} \times 2.2} = \frac{2.2 \text{ hL}}{220 \text{ L}}$$

220 L − 150 L = 70 L

Subtract 150 L from the capacity of the aquarium.

Raji needs 70 more liters of water.

ANOTHER WAY Use dimensional analysis.

$$2.2 \text{ hL} \times \frac{100 \text{ L}}{1 \text{ hL}}$$

$$= 2.2 \times 100 \text{ L}$$

$$= 220 \text{ L}$$

220 L − 150 L = 70 L

Subtract 150 L from the capacity of the aquarium.

Raji needs 70 more liters of water.

EXAMPLE 3 Convert Metric Units of Mass

Lyle has a bowl that contains 0.8 kilogram of salt. He uses a spoon to remove 850 centigrams of salt. How much salt, in centigrams, remains?

Calculate the conversion rate of kilograms to centigrams.

Metric Units of Mass
1,000 milligrams (mg) = 1 gram (g)
100 centigrams (cg) = 1 gram
10 decigrams (dg) = 1 gram
1 dekagram (dag) = 10 grams
1 hectogram (hg) = 100 grams
1 kilogram (kg) = 1,000 grams

$$1 \text{ kg} = 1,000 \text{ g} \times \frac{100 \text{ cg}}{1 \text{ g}}$$

$$1 \text{ kg} = 1,000 \times 100 \text{ cg}$$

$$1 \text{ kg} = 100,000 \text{ cg}$$

Look for Relationships

You could also convert kilograms to centigrams using dimensional analysis.

Convert 0.8 kilogram to centigrams.

$$\frac{1 \text{ kg} \times 0.8}{100,000 \text{ cg} \times 0.8} = \frac{0.8 \text{ kg}}{80,000 \text{ cg}}$$

80,000 cg − 850 cg = 79,150 cg

Subtract 850 cg from the original mass.

79,150 cg of salt remains in the bowl.

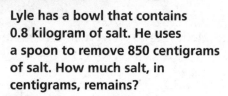 **Try It!**

To make violet paint, Iris mixes 0.25 liter of red paint, 0.25 liter of blue paint, and 4.5 centiliters of white paint. How many centiliters of paint are in the mixture?

You can convert metric measures by finding an equivalent rate or by using dimensional analysis.

Use an equivalent rate.

$1 \text{ kg} = 1,000 \text{ g}$

$$\frac{1 \text{ kg} \times 1.4}{1,000 \text{ g} \times 1.4} = \frac{1.4 \text{ kg}}{1,400 \text{ g}}$$

Use dimensional analysis.

$1.4 \text{ kg} \times \dfrac{1,000 \text{ g}}{1 \text{ kg}}$

$= 1.4 \times 1,000 \text{ g}$

$= 1,400 \text{ g}$

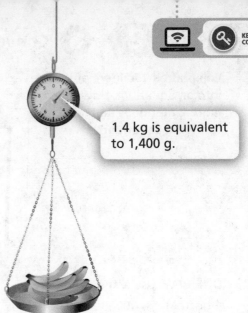

1.4 kg is equivalent to 1,400 g.

Do You Understand?

1. **❓ Essential Question** How can you use ratios to convert metric units of measure?

2. **Be Precise** How are the metric units kilometer and kilogram the same? How are they different?

3. **Reasoning** Which is greater, 250 m or 0.25 km? Justify your reasoning.

4. How can you find the conversion rate for milliliters to kiloliters?

Do You Know How?

5. What is the conversion factor when converting from liters to milliliters?

6. Use an equivalent rate to convert 35 centimeters to meters.

7. **Critique Reasoning** Maddy wants to know how many centigrams are in 0.75 gram. She converted 0.75 gram to its equivalent in centigrams as shown. Is her work correct? Explain.

$$\frac{10 \text{ cg} \times 0.75}{1 \text{ g} \times 0.75} = \frac{7.5 \text{ cg}}{0.75 \text{ g}}$$

8. Look at Exercise 7. Use dimensional analysis to convert 0.75 gram to centigrams.

Practice & Problem Solving

Leveled Practice In **9** and **10**, complete each conversion using an equivalent rate.

9. 4 m = ☐ cm

$$\frac{100 \text{ cm} \times \boxed{}}{1 \text{ m} \times \boxed{}} = \frac{\boxed{} \text{ cm}}{4 \text{ m}}$$

10. 800 mL = ☐ L

$$\frac{1,000 \text{ mL} \div \boxed{}}{1 \text{ L} \div \boxed{}} = \frac{800 \text{ mL}}{\boxed{} \text{ L}}$$

Leveled Practice In **11** and **12**, complete each conversion using dimensional analysis.

11. 200 cL = ☐ L

$$200 \text{ cL} \times \frac{\boxed{} \text{ L}}{\boxed{} \text{ cL}} = \frac{\boxed{}}{\boxed{}} \text{ L} = \boxed{} \text{ L}$$

12. 2.5 kg = ☐ g

$$2.5 \text{ kg} \times \frac{\boxed{} \text{ g}}{\boxed{} \text{ kg}} = \frac{\boxed{}}{\boxed{}} \text{ g} = \boxed{} \text{ g}$$

In **13** and **14**, complete each conversion.

13. 80 cm = ☐ m

14. 2.1 g = ☐ mg

In **15–17**, use the table showing the amount of liquid that Whitney drinks each day.

15. How many liters of water does Whitney drink each day?

Drink	Amount
Juice	250 mL
Milk	400 mL
Water	1,500 mL

16. What is the total amount of liquid, in liters, that Whitney drinks each day?

17. Troy drinks 1.8 L of water each day. How many more milliliters of water does Troy drink each day than Whitney?

18. There are 10 millimeters in 1 centimeter, so about how many millimeters long is this dinosaur bone? Explain.

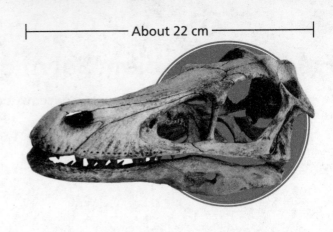
├─── About 22 cm ───┤

19. **Critique Reasoning** Savannah says that 1 kilogram is equivalent to 1,000,000 milligrams. Is Savannah correct? Explain.

20. **Model with Math** Lucas hiked 14,300 meters through the Everglades in the morning. After lunch, he continued hiking. When he finished the hike, he had covered 31.5 kilometers in all. Write an equation that can be used to find how far Lucas hiked after lunch.

21. Tariq has a collection of 35 quarters that he wants to send to his cousin. What is the total weight of the quarters in kilograms?

One quarter weighs 5.67 grams.

5.67 g

22. **Higher Order Thinking** Louis has a bag of 25 pen shells. Each pen shell is 18 centimeters long. What is the combined length of the pen shells in meters?

Assessment Practice

23. Select all the conversions that are equivalent to the capacity of a 5.5-liter pitcher of lemonade. 🐢 6.RP.1.3d

☐ 0.0055 kL

☐ 55 mL

☐ 0.055 kL

☐ 550 mL

☐ 5,500 mL

24. Select all the conversions that are equivalent to the mass of a 425-gram football. 🐢 6.RP.1.3d

☐ 42,000 mg

☐ 42,500 cg

☐ 450 dg

☐ 4.25 hg

☐ 0.425 kg

Explain It!

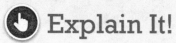

 ACTIVITY

Gianna and her friends are in a relay race. They have a pail that holds 1 liter of water. They need to fill the 1-liter pail, run 50 yards, and dump the water into the large bucket until it overflows. Gianna says that as long as they do not spill any of the water, they will need 7 trips with the 1-liter pail before the large bucket overflows.

I can...
convert between customary and metric units.

2 Gallons

Units of Capacity Conversion Chart	
1 gal ≈ 3.79 L	1 L ≈ 0.26 gal
1 gal = 4 qt	1 L ≈ 1.06 qt
1 qt ≈ 0.95 L	

The ≈ symbol means "about" or "approximately."

1 Liter

MAFS.6.RP.1.3d Use ratio reasoning to convert measurement units, manipulate and transform units appropriately when multiplying or dividing quantities.
MAFS.K12.MP.1.1, MP.2.1, MP.3.1, MP.8.1

A. Which conversion factor could you use to determine whether Gianna is correct? Explain.

B. Critique Reasoning Gianna's friend Linus says that you cannot be certain how many trips it will take because the conversion is approximate. Is Linus's reasoning appropriate? Explain.

C. Construct Arguments Is Gianna correct that 7 trips are needed before the bucket overflows? If not, how many trips will it take? Use the table to justify your answer.

Focus on math practices

Construct Arguments Morgan says that 4 liters is less than 1 gallon. Construct an argument to show that Morgan is incorrect.

EXAMPLE 1 👁 **Convert from Metric Units to Customary Units**

Scan for Multimedia

Tyrel is using a kit to build a robot. The directions use metric units and describe the robot's height as 2 meters tall. About how many inches is 2 meters? Round to the nearest tenth.

> **Make Sense and Persevere** When relating customary and metric units, exact whole-number conversions are rare. The table shows approximate equivalents.

Customary and Metric Unit Equivalents

Length
1 m ≈ 3.28 ft
1 m ≈ 39.37 in.
1 in. = 2.54 cm
1 mi ≈ 1.61 km

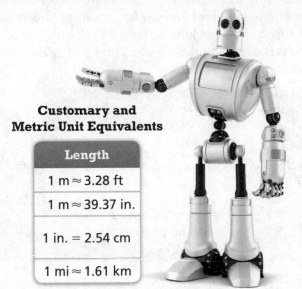

ONE WAY Find an equivalent rate to convert meters to inches.

1 m ≈ 39.37 in.

$$\frac{39.37 \text{ in.} \times 2}{1 \text{ m} \times 2} = \frac{78.74 \text{ in.}}{2 \text{ m}}$$

> Multiply both terms of the rate by 2.

78.74 ≈ 78.7

> Round to the nearest tenth of an inch.

So, 2 m ≈ 78.7 in.

ANOTHER WAY Use dimensional analysis to convert meters to inches.

$$2 \text{ m} \times \frac{39.37 \text{ in.}}{1 \text{ m}}$$

> Multiply by the conversion factor. Divide out the common units.

2 × 39.37 in. = 78.74 in.

78.74 ≈ 78.7

> Round to the nearest tenth of an inch.

So, 2 m ≈ 78.7 in.

☑ **Try It!**

Jacob is building a robot named T3-X that is 75 inches tall. To the nearest tenth, how many centimeters tall is T3-X?

Convince Me! If you want to find the height of T3-X in meters, will you get the same answer if you convert inches to centimeters, and then centimeters to meters, as you would if you convert inches to feet, and then feet to meters? Explain.

1 in. = [ ] cm

$$75 \text{ in.} \times \frac{[\quad] \text{ cm}}{1 \text{ in.}} = 75 \times [\quad] \text{ cm} = [\quad] \text{ cm}$$

T3-X is [ ] cm tall.

EXAMPLE 2 Convert from Customary Units to Metric Units

Jenna's Florida softshell turtle weighs 21 pounds. What is her turtle's approximate weight in kilograms? Round to the nearest tenth.

Generalize When relating customary and metric units, use what you know about converting within one measurement system.

Customary and Metric Unit Equivalents

Weight/Mass
1 oz ≈ 28.35 g
1 kg ≈ 2.20 lb
1 metric ton (t) ≈ 1.102 T

Use dimensional analysis.

$21 \ \cancel{lb} \times \dfrac{1 \text{ kg}}{2.20 \ \cancel{lb}}$

$\dfrac{21 \text{ kg}}{2.20} \approx 9.5 \text{ kg}$ ← Divide to simplify. Round to the nearest tenth.

Jenna's Florida softshell turtle weighs about 9.5 kilograms.

EXAMPLE 3 Convert Using Two Steps

If Deva drank all the water in her bottle, how many cups of water did she drink? Round to the nearest tenth.

Convert liters to quarts, and then quarts to cups.

Customary and Metric Equivalents	Customary Units
Capacity	Capacity
1 gal ≈ 3.79 L	1 tbsp = 3 tsp
1 qt ≈ 0.95 L	1 fl oz = 2 tbsp
1 L ≈ 0.26 gal	1 c = 8 fl oz
1 L ≈ 1.06 qt	1 pt = 2 c
	1 qt = 2 pt
	1 gal = 4 qt

H₂O Ultra 0.75 liter

STEP 1

1 L ≈ 1.06 qt

$0.75 \ \cancel{L} \times \dfrac{1.06 \text{ qt}}{1 \ \cancel{L}}$ ← Multiply by the conversion factor. Divide out the common units.

$0.75 \times 1.06 = 0.795$

$0.75 \text{ L} \approx 0.795 \text{ qt}$

STEP 2

1 qt = 4 c ← Identify the conversion factors: 1 qt = 2 pt and 2 pt = 4 c.

$0.795 \ \cancel{qt} \times \dfrac{4 \text{ c}}{1 \ \cancel{qt}}$ ← Multiply by the conversion factor. Divide out the common units.

$0.795 \times 4 = 3.18 \text{ c}$ ← Multiply the remaining factors.

To the nearest tenth, Deva drank about 3.2 cups of water.

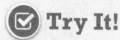 **Try It!**

Find the length of a 100-yard football field in meters. Use 1 yard = 3 feet and 1 meter ≈ 3.28 feet. Round to the nearest tenth.

You can use what you know about converting within one measurement system to relate customary and metric units. You can convert measures with customary and metric units by finding an equivalent rate or using dimensional analysis.

Use an equivalent rate.

$1 \text{ kg} \approx 2.20 \text{ lb}$

$$\frac{1 \text{ kg} \times 5}{2.20 \text{ lb} \times 5} = \frac{5 \text{ kg}}{11 \text{ lb}}$$

$5 \text{ kg} \approx 11 \text{ lb}$

Use dimensional analysis.

$5 \text{ kg} \times \dfrac{2.20 \text{ lb}}{1 \text{ kg}}$

$5 \times 2.20 = 11 \text{ lb}$

$5 \text{ kg} \approx 11 \text{ lb}$

Do You Understand?

1. **? Essential Question** How can you use ratios to convert customary and metric units of measure?

2. **Reasoning** When converting centimeters to inches, do you multiply or divide by 2.54? Explain.

3. **Use Structure** How can you find the approximate number of liters in 1 pint?

   Remember: 1 quart = 2 pints

4. How is the conversion from inches to centimeters different from other conversions between customary and metric units?

Do You Know How?

In 5–8, find the equivalent measure. Round to the nearest tenth.

5. 5 in. = ☐ cm

6. 2 mi ≈ ☐ km

7. 113 g ≈ ☐ oz

8. 14 kg ≈ ☐ lb

9. Convert 30 gallons to liters by finding an equivalent rate.

10. Approximately how many ounces are equivalent to 1 kilogram?

Practice & Problem Solving

In 11–18, find the equivalent measure. Round to the nearest tenth.

11. 9 qt ≈ [   ] L

12. 2 gal ≈ [   ] L

13. 2 in. ≈ [   ] cm

14. 5 km ≈ [   ] mi

15. 10 L ≈ [   ] qt

16. 5.5 t ≈ [   ] T

17. 50 lb ≈ [   ] kg

18. 10 oz ≈ [   ] g

19. A chef at a restaurant uses 12 pounds of butter each day. About how many grams of butter does the chef use each day? Use the conversion factors $\frac{16 \text{ ounces}}{1 \text{ pound}}$ and $\frac{28.35 \text{ grams}}{1 \text{ ounce}}$.

20. Reasoning Simone wants to know whether a new chest of drawers will fit next to her bed. The chest she would like to buy is 73 centimeters wide. She knows that her room is 86 inches wide. The bed is 76 inches wide. Will the chest fit next to her bed? Explain.

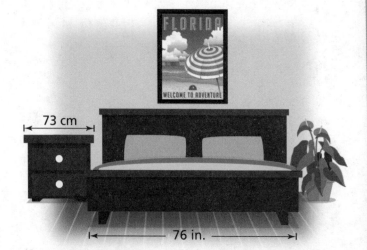

73 cm

76 in.

21. Be Precise Denali is the highest mountain in the United States. What is its height in meters? Round to the nearest whole number.

Denali is approximately 20,320 ft high.

22. Construct Arguments Francesca wants to convert 1 foot to centimeters. Use what you know about customary units to explain how she can do this.

23. Higher Order Thinking At the state fair, a person must be at least 138 centimeters tall to ride the roller coaster. Billy wants to ride the coaster. He is 4 feet 7 inches tall. Is Billy tall enough to ride the coaster? Explain.

24. Paul's car holds a maximum of 19 gallons of gas. About how many liters of gas does Paul need to fill his gas tank?

gallons remaining

Assessment Practice

25. The posted speed limit is 65 miles per hour. Select all the metric measures that are faster than 65 miles per hour. 🕐 6.RP.1.3d

☐ 65 km per hour

☐ 97.5 km per hour

☐ 104 km per hour

☐ 105.7 km per hour

☐ 120.3 km per hour

26. Boys competing in the long jump event must jump at least 15 feet to qualify for the state track and field meet. Select all the metric measures that are less than 15 feet. 🕐 6.RP.1.3d

☐ 6.5 m

☐ 5.0 m

☐ 4.5 m

☐ 3.92 m

☐ 3.5 m

Go Online | PearsonRealize.com

? Topic Essential Question

What are ratios and rates? How can you use ratios and rates to describe quantities and solve problems?

Vocabulary Review

Complete each definition and then provide an example of each vocabulary word.

Vocabulary	constant speed ratio	conversion factor term	rate unit price

Definition	Example
1. A relationship in which there are *y* units of a quantity for every *x* units of a quantity is a _____.	
2. The price of a single item is called a _____.	
3. A ratio that compares quantities with unlike units of measure is a _____.	

Use Vocabulary in Writing

Explain how you can convert 52 ounces to pounds. Use vocabulary words in your explanation.

Concepts and Skills Review

Understand Ratios

Quick Review

A **ratio** is a relationship in which for every *x* units of one quantity there are *y* units of another quantity. A ratio can be written using the word "to," a colon, or a fraction bar to separate the two terms.

Example

The ratio of men to women at a small wedding is 6:4. If there are 16 women at the wedding, how many men are at the wedding?

Draw a diagram to represent the ratio. Because 4 boxes represent 16 women, each box represents 4 women.

Men	4	4	4	4	4	4
Women	4	4	4	4		

There are 24 men at the wedding.

Practice

A florist uses 5 red roses for every 2 white roses in her bouquets.

1. Write the ratio of white roses to red roses in three different ways.

2. Write the ratio of red roses to the total number of flowers in three different ways.

3. If the florist uses 10 red roses in a bouquet, how many white roses does she use?

4. If the florist uses 10 white roses in an arrangement, how many red roses does she use?

Generate Equivalent Ratios

Quick Review

You can multiply or divide both terms of a ratio by the same nonzero number to find equivalent ratios.

Pi (π) is the ratio of the circumference of a circle to its diameter.

Example

Find two ratios that are equivalent to $\frac{21}{126}$.

One Way

Multiply.

$$\frac{21 \times 2}{126 \times 2} = \frac{42}{252}$$

Another Way

Divide.

$$\frac{21 \div 3}{126 \div 3} = \frac{7}{42}$$

Practice

In 1–4, find two ratios equivalent to the given ratio.

1. $\frac{5}{12}$

2. 14:32

3. 3 to 4

4. $\frac{7}{8}$

5. For every 4 bagels sold at a bakery, 7 muffins are sold. How many muffins are sold when the bakery sells 24 bagels? Complete the table.

Bagels	4	8	12	16	20	24
Muffins	7					

Compare Ratios

Quick Review

To compare ratios, make a table to show each ratio and then find a value in which one of the terms is the same in both tables.

Example

Erica

Math Facts	Seconds
25	30
50	60
75	90
100	120
125	150

Klayton

Math Facts	Seconds
38	50
76	100
114	150
152	200
190	250

Erica can complete more facts than Klayton.

Practice

1. The school soccer team buys 3 soccer balls for every 2 players. The school volleyball team buys 7 volleyballs for every 5 players. Which team buys more balls per player?

2. Jenna walks 12 miles in 5 days. Alex walks 7 miles in 3 days. Who walks more miles per day?

Represent and Graph Ratios

Quick Review

You can solve some ratio problems by making a table of equivalent ratios and then graphing the pairs of values on a coordinate plane.

Example

Days of Rain	1	2	3	n
Days of Sun	2	4	6	8

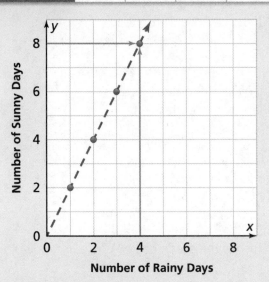

There will be 4 rainy days if there are 8 sunny days.

Practice

1. In gym class, the sixth graders walk 2 laps for every 3 laps they run. If the students run 12 laps, how many laps will they walk? Complete the table. Then plot the pairs of values on the coordinate plane.

Run (laps)	3	6	9	12
Walk (laps)	2			

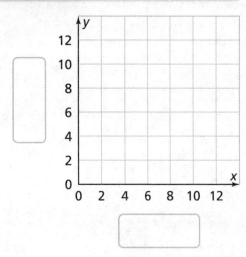

Quick Review

A **rate** is a ratio that relates two quantities with different units. A **unit rate** relates a quantity to 1 unit of another quantity. You can use what you know about dividing fractions to write a ratio of fractions as a unit rate.

Example

Write 20 meters in 4 minutes as a rate and as a unit rate.

Rate:

$$\frac{20 \text{ meters}}{4 \text{ minutes}}$$

Unit Rate:

$$\frac{20 \text{ meters} \div 4}{4 \text{ minutes} \div 4} = \frac{5 \text{ meters}}{1 \text{ minute}}$$

> The unit rate is an equivalent rate with a denominator of 1 unit.

Practice

Write each statement as a unit rate.

1. 78 miles on 3 gallons

2. 18 laps in 6 minutes

3. 48 sandwiches for 16 people

4. 49 houses in 7 blocks

5. 6 desks in 2 rows

Quick Review

A unit rate compares a quantity to 1 unit of another quantity. To compare unit rates, compare the first terms.

Example

On Pet Day, Meg's turtle crawled 30 feet in 6 minutes, and Pat's turtle crawled 25 feet in 5 minutes. Whose turtle crawled at a faster rate?

Write each rate.

Meg's turtle ▷ $\frac{30 \text{ ft}}{6 \text{ min}}$ $\frac{25 \text{ ft}}{5 \text{ min}}$ ◁ Pat's turtle

Find each unit rate.

$\frac{5 \text{ ft}}{1 \text{ min}}$ $\frac{5 \text{ ft}}{1 \text{ min}}$

Both turtles crawled at the same rate.

Practice

1. Which is the better value? Circle it.
   $5.00 for 4 mangoes
   $6.00 for 5 mangoes

2. Who earned more each month? Circle it.
   Atif: $84 over 3 months
   Jafar: $100 over 4 months

3. Which is a faster rate? Circle it.
   3 laps in 5 minutes
   4 laps in 7 minutes

4. Which is the better value? Circle it.
   3 sandwiches for $15.00
   4 sandwiches for $21.00

5. Which is the greater rate? Circle it.
   6 points in 3 attempts
   15 points in 5 attempts

Go Online | PearsonRealize.com

Quick Review

You can use a ratio table or a unit rate to solve problems involving ratios or rates.

Example

A plane travels at a rate of 780 miles in 2 hours. At this rate, how far will it travel in 3.5 hours?

Find the unit rate.

$$\frac{780 \text{ miles} \div 2}{2 \text{ hours} \div 2} = \frac{390 \text{ miles}}{1 \text{ hour}}$$

Find an equivalent rate.

$$\frac{390 \text{ miles} \times 3.5}{1 \text{ hour} \times 3.5} = \frac{1{,}365 \text{ miles}}{3.5 \text{ hours}}$$

The plane will travel 1,365 miles in 3.5 hours.

Practice

1. Doug has 5 hours to make an on-time delivery 273 miles away. Doug drives at a constant speed of 55 miles per hour. Will Doug make the delivery by the deadline? Explain.

2. Marie has 8 hours to write a 45-page chapter for her book. Marie writes at a constant speed of 4 pages per hour. Will Marie complete the chapter in time? Explain.

Quick Review

You can convert customary measures by finding equivalent rates or by using dimensional analysis.

Example

How many pints are equivalent to 4 quarts?

Find an equivalent rate:

2 pints = 1 quart ······· Identify the conversion rate.

$$\frac{2 \text{ pints} \times 4}{1 \text{ quart} \times 4} = \frac{8 \text{ pints}}{4 \text{ quarts}}$$

Use dimensional analysis:

$$4 \text{ quarts} \times \frac{2 \text{ pints}}{1 \text{ quart}} = 8 \text{ pints} \cdots\cdots \text{Multiply by the conversion factor.}$$

So, 8 pints are equivalent to 4 quarts.

Practice

In 1–4, complete each conversion.

1. 2 mi = ☐ ft

2. 144 in. = ☐ yd

3. 4 oz = ☐ lb

4. 3 gal = ☐ qt

5. The hippo at the zoo weighs 1.5 tons. How many pounds does the hippo weigh?

Quick Review

To convert metric units, use the same methods used for converting customary units. Either use the conversion rate to find an equivalent rate or use dimensional analysis.

Example

Tariq rode his bike 15,100 meters. How many kilometers did he ride his bike?

Find an equivalent rate:

$$1,000 \text{ meters} = 1 \text{ kilometer}$$

$$\frac{1,000 \text{ m} \times 15.1}{1 \text{ km} \times 15.1} = \frac{15,100 \text{ m}}{15.1 \text{ km}}$$

Use dimensional analysis:

$$15,100 \text{ m} \times \frac{1 \text{ km}}{1,000 \text{ m}} = \frac{15,100}{1,000} \text{ km} = 15.1 \text{ km}$$

Tariq rode 15.1 kilometers.

Practice

In 1–4, complete each conversion.

1. 3 m = ☐ mm

2. 3,520 mm = ☐ cm

3. 4.2 kg = ☐ g

4. 300 mL = ☐ L

5. Li needs to buy 2 kilograms of apples. If she buys 9 apples that each weigh approximately 150 grams, will she have enough? Explain.

Quick Review

To convert between metric and customary units, use the conversion rate and find an equivalent rate, or use dimensional analysis. Most conversions will be approximate because, except in the case of inches to centimeters, the conversion rates are approximate.

Example

Gwen has a cooler that holds 3 quarts. About how many liters does the cooler hold?

$$1 \text{ qt} \approx 0.95 \text{ L}$$

$$3 \text{ qt} \times \frac{0.95 \text{ L}}{1 \text{ qt}} = (3 \times 0.95) \text{ L} = 2.85 \text{ L}$$

Gwen's cooler holds approximately 2.85 liters.

Practice

In 1–4, find the equivalent measure. Round to the nearest tenth.

1. 100 g ≈ ☐ oz

2. 6 ft ≈ ☐ m

3. 57 gal ≈ ☐ L

4. 27 km ≈ ☐ mi

5. The science class is raising monarch caterpillars. One of the caterpillars weighs 2.3 ounces. About how many grams does the caterpillar weigh? Round to the nearest tenth.

Go Online | PearsonRealize.com

Pathfinder

Shade a path from START to FINISH. Follow the sums and differences in which the digit in the ones place is greater than the digit in the tenths place. You can only move up, down, right, or left.

I can...
add and subtract multidigit decimals. 🌐 6.NS.2.3

START ↓

31.2 − 5.73	1.84 + 19.26	25 − 8.53	2 − 0.95	12.3 − 4.81
14.27 + 4.9	7.29 − 0.8	12.95 + 9.06	1.07 + 0.27	4.22 + 2.8
18 + 4.301	3.007 − 1.71	8.38 − 6.42	10 − 8.94	21 − 3.303
43.397 + 17.81	15.75 − 8.8	4.02 − 3.83	17.54 + 6.82	3.8 + 1.89
2.35 + 1.08	1.035 − 0.641	29.06 + 2.87	28.12 − 5.016	0.62 + 5.38

↓
FINISH

GLOSSARY

A

absolute deviation from the mean Absolute deviation measures the distance that the data value is from the mean. You find the absolute deviation by taking the absolute value of the deviation of a data value. Absolute deviations are always nonnegative.

desviación absoluta de la media La desviación absoluta mide la distancia a la que un valor se encuentra de la media. Para hallar la desviación absoluta, tomas el valor absoluto de la desviación de un valor. Las desviaciones absolutas siempre son no negativas.

Example Data set: 0, 1, 1, 2, 2, 2, 2, 3, 3, 5, 5, 10. The absolute deviations of the values in the data set are:

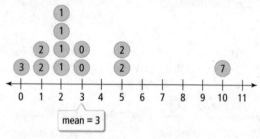

mean = 3

absolute value The absolute value of a number a is the distance between a and zero on a number line. The absolute value of a is written as $|a|$.

valor absoluto El valor absoluto de un número a es la distancia entre a y cero en la recta numérica. El valor absoluto de a se escribe como $|a|$.

Example -7 is 7 units from 0, so $|-7| = 7$.

Addition Property of Equality The two sides of an equation stay equal when the same amount is added to both sides of the equation.

propiedad de suma de la igualdad Se puede sumar el mismo número a ambos lados de una ecuación y los lados siguen siendo iguales.

Example
$$4 + 2 = 6$$
$$(4 + 2) + 3 = 6 + 3$$
$$(4 + 2) + a = 6 + a$$

additive inverses Two numbers that have a sum of 0.

inversos de suma Dos números cuya suma es 0.

Example 7 and -7 are additive inverses.

algebraic expression An algebraic expression is a mathematical phrase that consists of variables, numbers, and operation symbols.

expresión algebraica Una expresión algebraica es una frase matemática que consiste en variables, números y símbolos de operaciones.

Example $x - 7$, $n + 2$, and $5d$ are algebraic expressions.

ENGLISH	SPANISH

Associative Property of Addition For any numbers a, b, and c:
$(a + b) + c = a + (b + c)$

propiedad asociativa de la suma Para los números cualesquiera a, b y c:
$(a + b) + c = a + (b + c)$

> **Example** $(3 + 25) + 4 = 3 + (25 + 4)$
> $(m + 25) + 4 = m + (25 + 4)$

Associative Property of Multiplication For any numbers a, b, and c:
$(a \cdot b) \cdot c = a \cdot (b \cdot c)$

propiedad asociativa de la multiplicación Para los números cualesquiera a, b y c:
$(a \cdot b) \cdot c = a \cdot (b \cdot c)$

> **Example** $(16 \cdot 26) \cdot 55 = 16 \cdot (26 \cdot 55)$
> $(m \cdot 56) \cdot 4 = m \cdot (56 \cdot 4)$

 B

balance The balance in an account is the principal amount plus the interest earned.

saldo El saldo de una cuenta es el capital más el interés ganado.

> **Example** You deposit $100 in an account and earn $5 in interest. The balance is $105.

base The base is the repeated factor of a number written in exponential form.

base La base es el factor repetido de un número escrito en forma exponencial.

> **Example** $3^4 = 3 \times 3 \times 3 \times 3$
> In the expression 3^4, 3 is the base and 4 is the exponent.

base of a parallelogram A base of a parallelogram is any side of the parallelogram.

base de un paralelogramo La base de un paralelogramo es cualquiera de los lados del paralelogramo.

> **Example**

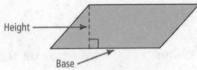

Height ⟶

Base ⟶

ENGLISH	SPANISH
base of a prism A base of a prism is one of a pair of parallel polygonal faces that are the same size and shape. A prism is named for the shape of its bases.	**base de un prisma** La base de un prisma es una de las dos caras poligonales paralelas que tienen el mismo tamaño y la misma forma. El nombre de un prisma depende de la forma de sus bases.

Example

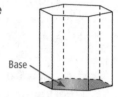

Base

base of a pyramid A base of a pyramid is a polygonal face that does not connect to the vertex.	**base de una pirámide** La base de una pirámide es una cara poligonal que no se conecta con el vértice.

Example

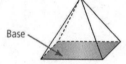

Base

base of a triangle The base of a triangle is any side of the triangle.	**base de un triángulo** La base de un triángulo es cualquiera de los lados del triángulo.

Example

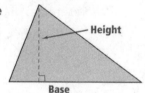

Height

Base

box plot A box plot is a statistical graph that shows the distribution of a data set by marking five boundary points where data occur along a number line. Unlike a dot plot or a histogram, a box plot does not show frequency.	**diagrama de cajas** Un diagrama de cajas es un diagrama de estadísticas que muestra la distribución de un conjunto de datos al marcar cinco puntos de frontera donde se hallan los datos sobre una recta numérica. A diferencia del diagrama de puntos o el histograma, el diagrama de cajas no muestra la frecuencia.

Example Minimum   First quartile   Median   Third quartile   Maximum

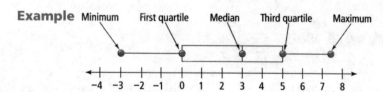

ENGLISH

categorical data Categorical data consist of data that fall into categories.

  Example Data collected about gender is an example of categorical data because the data have values that fall into the categories "male" and "female."

circle graph A circle graph is a graph that represents a whole divided into parts.

  Example Favorite Types of Music

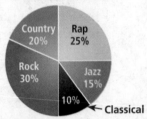

circumference of a circle The circumference of a circle is the distance around the circle. The formula for the circumference of a circle is $C = \pi d$, where C represents the circumference and d represents the diameter of the circle.

  Example

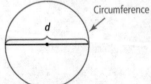

coefficient A coefficient is the number part of a term that contains a variable.

  Example In the expression $3x + 4y + 12$, the coefficients are 3 and 4.

Commutative Property of Addition For any numbers a and b: $a + b = b + a$

  Example $25 + 56 = 56 + 25$
       $x + 72 = 72 + x$

Commutative Property of Multiplication For any numbers a and b: $a \cdot b = b \cdot a$

  Example $17 \cdot 6 = 6 \cdot 17$
       $47x = x \cdot 47$

SPANISH

datos por categorías Los datos por categorías son datos que se pueden clasificar en categorías.

gráfica circular Una gráfica circular es una gráfica que representa un todo dividido en partes.

circunferencia de un círculo La circunferencia de un círculo es la distancia alrededor del círculo. La fórmula de la circunferencia de un círculo es $C = \pi d$, donde C representa la circunferencia y d representa el diámetro del círculo.

coeficiente Un coeficiente es la parte numérica de un término que contiene una variable.

propiedad conmutativa de la suma Para los números cualesquiera a y b: $a + b = b + a$

propiedad conmutativa de la multiplicación Para los números cualesquiera a y b: $a \cdot b = b \cdot a$

complex fraction A complex fraction is a fraction $\frac{A}{B}$ where A and/or B are fractions and B is not zero.

fracción compleja Una fracción compleja es una fracción $\frac{A}{B}$ donde A y/o B son fracciones y B es distinto de cero.

Example $\dfrac{\frac{1}{2}}{\frac{3}{4}}$

composite number A composite number is a whole number greater than 1 with more than two factors.

número compuesto Un número compuesto es un número entero mayor que 1 con más de dos factores.

Example The factors of 15 are 1, 3, 5, and 15. Because 15 has more than two factors, it is a composite number.

constant A constant is a term that only contains a number.

constante Una constante es un término que solamente contiene un número.

Example In the expression $3x + 4y + 12$, 12 is a constant.

constant of proportionality In a proportional relationship, one quantity y is a constant multiple of the other quantity x. The constant multiple is called the constant of proportionality. The constant of proportionality is equal to the ratio $\frac{y}{x}$.

constante de proporcionalidad En una relación proporcional, una cantidad y es un múltiplo constante de la otra cantidad x. El múltiplo constante se llama constante de proporcionalidad. La constante de proporcionalidad es igual a la razón $\frac{y}{x}$.

Example In the equation $y = 4x$, the constant of proportionality is 4.

constant speed The speed stays the same over time.

velocidad constante Tasa de velocidad que se mantiene igual a través del tiempo.

conversion factor A conversion factor is a rate that equals 1.

factor de conversión Un factor de conversión es una tasa que es igual a 1.

Example $\dfrac{60 \text{ minutes}}{1 \text{ hour}}$

coordinate plane A coordinate plane is formed by a horizontal number line called the x-axis and a vertical number line called the y-axis.

plano de coordenadas Un plano de coordenadas está formado por una recta numérica horizontal llamada eje de las x y una recta numérica vertical llamada eje de las y.

Example

ENGLISH

data distribution To describe a data distribution, or how the data values are arranged, you evaluate its measures of center and variability, and its overall shape. See distribution of a data set.

dependent variable A dependent variable is a variable whose value changes in response to another (independent) variable.

deviation from the mean Deviation indicates how far away and in which direction a data value is from the mean. Data values that are less than the mean have a negative deviation. Data values that are greater than the mean have a positive deviation.

Example Data set: 0, 1, 1, 2, 2, 2, 2, 3, 3, 5, 5, 10. The deviations of the values in the data set are:

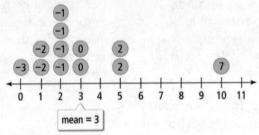

diameter A diameter is a segment that passes through the center of a circle and has both endpoints on the circle. The term diameter can also mean the length of this segment.

Example

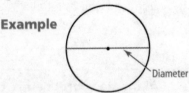

Diameter

dimensional analysis A method to convert measures by including measurement units when multiplying by a conversion factor.

Example $3.5 \, \cancel{ft} \times \dfrac{12 \text{ in.}}{1 \, \cancel{ft}}$
$= 3.5 \times 12 \text{ in.}$
$= 42 \text{ in.}$

SPANISH

distribución de datos Cómo se distribuyen los valores.

variable dependiente Una variable dependiente es una variable cuyo valor cambia en respuesta a otra variable (independiente).

desviación de la media La desviación indica a qué distancia y en qué dirección un valor se aleja de la media. Los valores menores que la media tienen una desviación negativa. Los valores mayores que la media tienen una desviación positiva.

diámetro Un diámetro es un segmento que atraviesa el centro de un círculo y tiene sus dos extremos en el círculo. El término diámetro también puede referirse a la longitud de este segmento.

análisis dimensional Método que usa factores de conversión para convertir una unidad de medida a otra unidad de medida.
Ejemplo: $64 \, \cancel{\text{onzas}} \times \dfrac{1 \text{ taza}}{8 \, \cancel{\text{onzas}}} = \dfrac{64}{8} \text{ tazas}$
$= 8 \text{ tazas}$

ENGLISH

SPANISH

distribution (of a data set) The distribution of a data set describes the way that its data values are spread out over all possible values. This includes describing the frequencies of each data value. The shape of a data display shows the distribution of a data set. *See data distribution.*

distribución (de un conjunto de datos) La distribución de un conjunto de datos describe la manera en que sus valores se esparcen sobre todos los valores posibles. Eso incluye la descripción de las frecuencias de cada valor. La forma de una exhibición de datos muestra la distribución de un conjunto de datos.

Example The distribution of this data set shows that the data are clustered around 2 and 7, and there is one stray data value at 12.

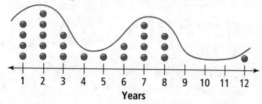

Ages of Cats at a Local Shelter

Years

Distributive Property Multiplying a number by a sum or difference gives the same result as multiplying that number by each term in the sum or difference and then adding or subtracting the corresponding products.
$a \cdot (b + c) = a \cdot b + a \cdot c$ and
$a \cdot (b - c) = a \cdot b - a \cdot c$

propiedad distributiva Multiplicar un número por una suma o una diferencia da el mismo resultado que multiplicar ese mismo número por cada uno de los términos de la suma o la diferencia y después sumar o restar los productos obtenidos.
$a \cdot (b + c) = a \cdot b + a \cdot c$ and
$a \cdot (b - c) = a \cdot b - a \cdot c$

Example $36(14 + 85) = (36)(14) + (36)(85)$

Division Property of Equality The two sides of an equation stay equal when both sides of the equation are divided by the same non-zero amount.

propiedad de división de la igualdad Ambos lados de una ecuación se pueden dividir por el mismo número distinto de cero y los lados siguen siendo iguales.

Example
$$4 + 2 = 6$$
$$(4 + 2) \div 3 = 6 \div 3$$
$$(4 + 2) \div a = 6 \div a$$

E

edge of a three-dimensional figure An edge of a three-dimensional figure is a segment formed by the intersection of two faces.

arista de una figura tridimensional Una arista de una figura tridimensional es un segmento formado por la intersección de dos caras.

Example

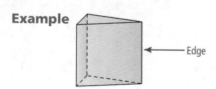

Edge

ENGLISH

SPANISH

equivalent expressions Equivalent expressions are expressions that always have the same value.

expresiones equivalentes Las expresiones equivalentes son expresiones que siempre tienen el mismo valor.

Example 2(12) and 20 + 4 are equivalent expressions.

equivalent ratios Equivalent ratios are ratios that express the same relationship.

razones equivalentes Las razones equivalentes son razones que expresan la misma relación.

Example 2 : 3 and 4 : 6 are equivalent ratios.

evaluate an algebraic expression To evaluate an algebraic expression, replace each variable with a number, and then follow the order of operations.

evaluar una expresión algebraica Para evaluar una expresión algebraica, reemplaza cada variable con un número y luego sigue el orden de las operaciones.

Example To evaluate the expression $x + 2$ for $x = 4$, substitute 4 for x.
$x + 2 = 4 + 2 = 6$

expand an algebraic expression To expand an algebraic expression, use the Distributive Property to rewrite a product as a sum or difference of terms.

desarrollar una expresión algebraica Para desarrollar una expresión algebraica, usa la propiedad distributiva para reescribir el producto como una suma o diferencia de términos.

Example The expression $(5 - x)(y)$ is a product that can be expanded using the Distributive Property.
$$(5 - x)(y) = 5(y) - x(y)$$
$$= 5y - (xy)$$
$$= 5y - xy$$

exponent An exponent is a number that shows how many times a base is used as a factor.

exponente Un exponente es un número que muestra cuántas veces se usa una base como factor.

Example 7^5 ←Exponent
     ↖Base

expression An expression is a mathematical phrase that can involve variables, numbers, and operations. See algebraic expression or numerical expression.

expresión Una expresión es una frase matemática que puede tener variables, números y operaciones. Ver expresión algebraica o expresión numérica.

Example $4 + 9$
     $2x$

ENGLISH

SPANISH

F

face of a three-dimensional figure A face of a three-dimensional figure is a flat surface shaped like a polygon.

cara de una figura tridimensional La cara de una figura tridimensional es una superficie plana con forma de polígono.

Example

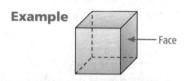

Face

factor tree A factor tree shows the prime factorization of a composite number.

árbol de factores Diagrama que muestra la descomposición en factores primos de un número.

Example

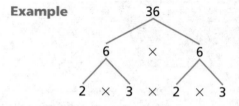

frequency table A frequency table shows the number of times a data value or values occur in the data set.

tabla de frecuencias Tabla que muestra la cantidad de veces que un valor o un rango de valores aparece en un conjunto de datos.

Example

Running Times	Tally	Frequency
14:00–15:59	IIII	4
16:00–17:59	IIIII	6
18:00–19:59	II	2

G

gap A gap is an area of a graph that contains no data points.

Espacio vacío o brecha Un espacio vacío o brecha es un área de una gráfica que no contiene ningún valor.

Example

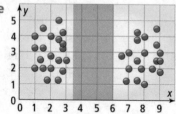

ENGLISH

SPANISH

greatest common factor The greatest common factor (GCF) of two or more whole numbers is the greatest number that is a factor of all of the numbers.

máximo común divisor El máximo común divisor (M.C.D.) de dos o más números enteros no negativos es el número mayor que es un factor de todos los números.

Example The greatest common factor of 12 and 10 is 2.
The greatest common factor of 24 and 6 is 6.

height of a parallelogram The height of a parallelogram is the perpendicular distance between opposite bases.

altura de un paralelogramo La altura de un paralelogramo es la distancia perpendicular que existe entre las bases opuestas.

Example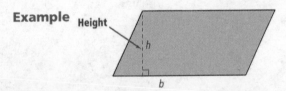

height of a prism The height of a prism is the length of a perpendicular segment that joins the bases.

altura de un prisma La altura de un prisma es la longitud de un segmento perpendicular que une a las bases.

Example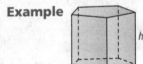

height of a pyramid The height of a pyramid is the length of a segment perpendicular to the base that joins the vertex and the base.

altura de una pirámide La altura de una pirámide es la longitud de un segmento perpendicular a la base que une al vértice con la base.

Example

height of a triangle The height of a triangle is the length of the perpendicular segment from a vertex to the base opposite that vertex.

altura de un triángulo La altura de un triángulo es la longitud del segmento perpendicular desde un vértice hasta la base opuesta a ese vértice.

Example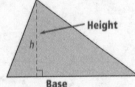

ENGLISH	SPANISH
histogram A histogram is a statistical graph that shows the shape of a data set with vertical bars above intervals of values on a number line. The intervals are equal in size and do not overlap. The height of each bar shows the frequency of data within that interval.	**histograma** Un histograma es una gráfica de estadísticas que muestra la forma de un conjunto de datos con barras verticales encima de intervalos de valores en una recta numérica. Los intervalos tienen el mismo tamaño y no se superponen. La altura de cada barra muestra la frecuencia de los datos dentro de ese intervalo.

Example

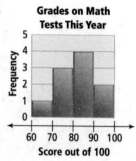

Grades on Math Tests This Year

I

Identity Property of Addition The sum of 0 and any number is that number. For any number n, $n + 0 = n$ and $0 + n = n$.

propiedad de identidad de la suma La suma de 0 y cualquier número es ese número. Para cualquier número n, $n + 0 = n$ and $0 + n = n$.

Example $0 + 41 = 41$
$x + 0 = x$

Identity Property of Multiplication The product of 1 and any number is that number. For any number n, $n \cdot 1 = n$ and $1 \cdot n = n$.

propiedad de identidad de la multiplicación El producto de 1 y cualquier número es ese número. Para cualquier número n, $n \cdot 1 = n$ and $1 \cdot n = n$.

Example $1 \cdot 67 = 67$
$x \cdot 1 = x$

independent variable An independent variable is a variable whose value determines the value of another (dependent) variable.

variable independiente Una variable independiente es una variable cuyo valor determina el valor de otra variable (dependiente).

inequality An inequality is a mathematical sentence that uses $<, \leq, >, \geq$, or $\neq$ to compare two quantities.

desigualdad Una desigualdad es una oración matemática que usa $<, \leq, >, \geq$, o $\neq$ para comparar dos cantidades.

Example $13 > 7$
$17 + c \leq 25$

integers Integers are the set of positive whole numbers, their opposites, and 0.

enteros Los enteros son el conjunto de los números enteros positivos, sus opuestos y 0.

Example $..., -3, -2, -1, 0, 1, 2, 3, ...$

ENGLISH	SPANISH
interest rate Interest is calculated based on a percent of the principal. That percent is called the interest rate (r).	**tasa de interés** El interés se calcula con base en un porcentaje del capital. Ese porcentaje se llama tasa de interés, (r).
interquartile range The interquartile range (IQR) is the distance between the first and third quartiles of the data set. It represents the spread of the middle 50% of the data values.	**rango intercuartil** El rango intercuartil es la distancia entre el primer y el tercer cuartil del conjunto de datos. Representa la ubicación del 50% del medio de los valores.

Example Data set: 1, 3, ⑥, 10, 11, |14, 15, ⑳, 23, 40

First quartile   Third quartile

The interquartile range of the data set is 20 − 6, or 14.

inverse operations Inverse operations are operations that undo each other.	**operaciones inversas** Las operaciones inversas son operaciones que se cancelan entre sí.

Example Addition and subtraction are inverse operations because they undo each other.
$4 + 3 = 7$ and $7 − 4 = 3$

Multiplication and division are inverse operations because they undo each other.
$4 \times 3 = 12$ and $12 \div 4 = 3$

Inverse Property of Addition Every number has an additive inverse. The sum of a number and its additive inverse is zero.	**propiedad inversa de la suma** Todos los números tienen un inverso de suma. La suma de un número y su inverso de suma es cero.

Example 5 and −5 are additive inverses.
$5 + (−5) = 0$ and $(−5) + 5 = 0$

inverse relationship Operations that undo each other have an inverse relationship.	**relaciones inversas** Relaciones entre operaciones que se "cancelan" entre sí, como la suma y la resta o la multiplicación y la división (excepto la multiplicación o división por 0).

Example Adding 5 is the inverse of subtracting 5.

isolate a variable When solving equations, to isolate a variable means to get a variable with a coefficient of 1 alone on one side of an equation. Use the properties of equality and inverse operations to isolate a variable.	**aislar una variable** Cuando resuelves ecuaciones, aislar una variable significa poner una variable con un coeficiente de 1 sola a un lado de la ecuación. Usa las propiedades de igualdad y las operaciones inversas para aislar una variable.

Example To isolate x in $2x = 8$, divide both sides of the equation by 2.

ENGLISH	SPANISH

kite A quadrilateral with two pairs of adjacent sides that are equal in length.

cometa Cuadrilátero con dos pares de lados adyacentes de igual longitud.

Example

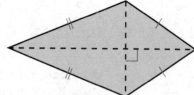

least common multiple The least common multiple (LCM) of two or more numbers is the least multiple, not including zero, shared by all of the numbers.

mínimo común múltiplo El mínimo común múltiplo (m.c.m.) de dos o más números es el múltiplo menor, sin incluir el cero, compartido por todos los números.

Example The LCM of 4 and 6 is 12.
The LCM of 3 and 15 is 15.

like terms Terms that have identical variable parts are like terms.

términos semejantes Los términos que tienen partes variables idénticas son términos semejantes.

Example Like terms
$y + 2.5 - 3y$

markdown Markdown is the amount of decrease from the selling price to the sale price. The markdown as a percent decrease of the original selling price is called the percent markdown.

rebaja La rebaja es la cantidad de disminución de un precio de venta a un precio rebajado. La rebaja como una disminución porcentual del precio de venta original se llama porcentaje de rebaja.

Example A shirt that was originally $28 is on sale for $21. The markdown is $28 - 21 = 7$. The percent markdown is $\frac{7}{28} = \frac{1}{4} = 0.25$, or 25%.

markup Markup is the amount of increase from the cost to the selling price. The markup as a percent increase of the original cost is called the percent markup.

margen de ganancia El margen de ganancia es la cantidad de aumento del costo al precio de venta. El margen de ganancia como un aumento porcentual del costo original se llama porcentaje del margen de ganancia.

Example The original cost of a shirt is $16, and a store is selling it for $28. The markup is $28 - 16 = 12$. The percent markup is $\frac{12}{16} = \frac{3}{4} = 0.75$, or 75%.

ENGLISH

mean The mean represents the center of a numerical data set. To find the mean, sum the data values and then divide by the number of values in the data set.

SPANISH

media La media representa el centro de un conjunto de datos numéricos. Para hallar la media, suma los valores y luego divide por el número de valores del conjunto de datos.

Example Data set: 2, 4, 5, 15, 23, 12, 9

$$\text{mean} = \frac{2 + 4 + 5 + 15 + 23 + 12 + 9}{7} = \frac{70}{7} = 10$$

mean absolute deviation The mean absolute deviation is a measure of variability that describes how much the data values are spread out from the mean of a data set. The mean absolute deviation is the average distance that the data values are spread around the mean.

$$\text{MAD} = \frac{\text{sum of the absolute deviations of the data values}}{\text{total number of data values}}$$

desviación absoluta media La desviación absoluta media es una medida de variabilidad que describe cuánto se alejan los valores de la media de un conjunto de datos. La desviación absoluta media es la distancia promedio que los valores se alejan de la media. desviación absoluta media

$$= \frac{\text{suma de las desviaciones absolutas de los valores}}{\text{número total de valores}}$$

Example Data set: 0, 1, 1, 2, 2, 2, 2, 3, 3, 5, 5, 10.
The mean absolute deviation of the data set is 1.8.

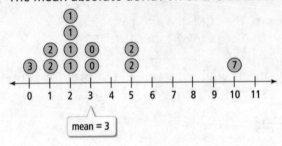

$$\text{mean absolute deviation} = \frac{3 + 2 + 2 + 1 + 1 + 1 + 1 + 0 + 0 + 2 + 2 + 7}{12}$$

$$= \frac{22}{12}$$

$$\approx 1.8$$

measure of variability A measure of variability describes the spread of values in a data set. There may be more than one measure of variability for a data set.

medida de variabilidad Una medida de variabilidad describe la distribución de los valores de un conjunto de datos. Puede haber más de una medida de variabilidad para un conjunto de datos.

Example Data set: 4, 5, 5, 6, 6, 7, 8, 11

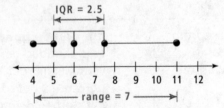

ENGLISH

SPANISH

measures of center A measure of center is a value that represents the middle of a data set. There may be more than one measure of center for a data set.

medida de tendencia central Una medida de tendencia central es un valor que representa el centro de un conjunto de datos. Puede haber más de una medida de tendencia central para un conjunto de datos.

Example Data set: 4, 5, 5, 6, 6, 7, 8, 11

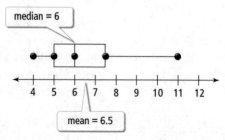

median The median represents the center of a numerical data set. For an odd number of data values, the median is the middle value when the data values are arranged in numerical order. For an even number of data values, the median is the average of the two middle values when the data values are arranged in numerical order.

mediana La mediana representa el centro de un conjunto de datos numéricos. Para un número impar de valores, la mediana es el valor del medio cuando los valores están organizados en orden numérico. Para un número par de valores, la mediana es el promedio de los dos valores del medio cuando los valores están organizados en orden numérico.

Example Data Set A: 3, 5, 6, 10, 11, 13, 18, 21, 25
The median of Data Set A is 11.
Data Set B: 3, 5, 6, 10, 11, 13, 18, 21, 25, 30
The median of Data Set B is $\frac{11 + 13}{2}$, or 12.

mode The item, or items, in a data set that occurs most frequently.

modo El artículo, o los artículos, en un conjunto de datos que ocurre normalmente.

Example In a parking lot there are 18 red cars, 10 blue cars, and 12 silver cars. The mode of the data set is *red*.

Multiplication Property of Equality The two sides of an equation stay equal when both sides of the equation are multiplied by the same amount.

propiedad multiplicativa de la igualdad Ambos lados de una ecuación se pueden multiplicar por el mismo número distinto de cero y los lados siguen siendo iguales.

Example $4 + 2 = 6$
$(4 + 2) \times 3 = 6 \times 3$
$(4 + 2) \times a = 6 \times a$

ENGLISH

SPANISH

negative numbers Negative numbers are numbers less than zero.

números negativos Los números negativos son números menores que cero.

Example The number −5 can represent a temperature of 5 degrees below zero.

---

net A net is a two-dimensional pattern that you can fold to form a three-dimensional figure. A net of a figure shows all of the surfaces of that figure in one view.

modelo plano Un modelo plano es un diseño bidimensional que puedes doblar para formar una figura tridimensional. Un modelo plano de una figura muestra todas las superficies de la figura en una vista.

Example This is the net of a triangular prism.

---

numerical expression A numerical expression is a mathematical phrase that consists of numbers and operation symbols.

expresión numérica Una expresión numérica es una frase matemática que contiene números y símbolos de operaciones.

Example 9 − 17
8 + (28 · 53)

opposites Opposites are two numbers that are the same distance from 0 on a number line, but in opposite directions.

opuestos Los opuestos son dos números que están a la misma distancia de 0 en la recta numérica, pero en direcciones opuestas.

Example 17 and −17 are opposites.

---

ordered pair An ordered pair identifies the location of a point in the coordinate plane. The x-coordinate shows a point's position left or right of the y-axis. The y-coordinate shows a point's position up or down from the x-axis.

par ordenado Un par ordenado identifica la ubicación de un punto en el plano de coordenadas. La coordenada x muestra la posición de un punto a la izquierda o a la derecha del eje de las y. La coordenada y muestra la posición de un punto arriba o abajo del eje de las x.

Example

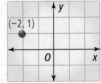

The x-coordinate of the point (−2, 1) is the −2, and the y-coordinate is the 1.

Go Online | PearsonRealize.com

ENGLISH

SPANISH

origin The origin is the point of intersection of the *x*- and *y*-axes on a coordinate plane.

origen El origen es el punto de intersección del eje de las *x* y el eje de las *y* en un plano de coordenadas.

Example The ordered pair that describes the origin is (0, 0).

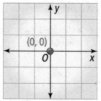

outlier An outlier is a piece of data that does not seem to fit with the rest of a data set.

valor extremo Un valor extremo es un valor que parece no ajustarse al resto de los datos de un conjunto.

Example This data set has two outliers.

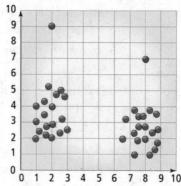

P

percent A percent is a ratio that compares a number to 100.

porcentaje Un porcentaje es una razón que compara un número con 100.

Example $\frac{25}{100} = 25\%$

percent equation The percent equation describes the relationship between a part and a whole. You can use the percent equation (part = percent × whole) to solve percent problems.

ecuación de porcentaje La ecuación de porcentaje describe la relación entre una parte y un todo. Puedes usar la ecuación de porcentaje para resolver problemas de porcentaje. parte = por ciento · todo

ENGLISH	SPANISH

percent error Percent error describes the accuracy of a measured or estimated value compared to an actual or accepted value.

error porcentual El error porcentual describe la exactitud de un valor medido o estimado en comparación con un valor real o aceptado.

Example A person guesses that there are 36 passengers on a bus. The actual number of passengers is 45.

$$\text{percent error} = \frac{|\text{ measured or estimated value} - \text{actual value }|}{\text{actual value}}$$

$$= \frac{|\ 36 - 45\ |}{45}$$

$$= \frac{|-9|}{45}$$

$$= 0.20, \text{ or } 20\%$$

So the guess "36 passengers" is off by 20%.

percent of change Percent of change is the percent something increases or decreases from its original measure or amount. You can find the percent of change by using the equation:

$$\text{percent of change} = \frac{\text{amount of change}}{\text{original quantity}}$$

porcentaje de cambio El porcentaje de cambio es el porcentaje en que algo aumenta o disminuye en relación a la medida o cantidad original. Puedes hallar el porcentaje de cambio con la siguiente ecuación: $\text{porcentaje de cambio} = \frac{\text{cantidad de cambio}}{\text{cantidad original}}$

Example The number of employees changed from 14 to 21.

amount of change $= 21 - 14 = 7$

percent change $= \frac{7}{14} = \frac{1}{2} = 0.5$, or 50%

Pi Pi (π) is the ratio of a circle's circumference, C, to its diameter, d.

Pi Pi (π) es la razón de la circunferencia de un círculo, C, a su diámetro, d.

Example

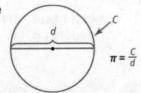

$$\pi = \frac{C}{d}$$

polyhedron A polyhedron is a three-dimensional figure made of flat polygon-shaped surfaces called faces.

poliedro Figura tridimensional compuesta de superficies planas que son polígonos.

Example A rectangular prism is a polyhedron.

positive numbers Positive numbers are numbers greater than zero.

números positivos Los números positivos son números mayores que cero.

Example The number +3 can represent a temperature of 3 degrees above zero. +3 is usually written 3.

Go Online | PearsonRealize.com

ENGLISH	SPANISH
power A power is a number expressed using an exponent.	**potencia** Una potencia es un número expresado con un exponente.

Example 3^4 and 3^5 are powers of 3.

ENGLISH	SPANISH
prime factorization The prime factorization of a composite number is the expression of the number as a product of its prime factors.	**descomposición en factores primos** La descomposición en factores primos de un número compuesto es la expresión del número como un producto de sus factores primos.

Example The prime factorization of 30 is $2 \cdot 3 \cdot 5$.

ENGLISH	SPANISH
prime number A prime number is a whole number greater than 1 with exactly two factors, 1 and the number itself.	**número primo** Un número primo es un número entero mayor que 1 con exactamente dos factores, 1 y el número mismo.

Example The factors of 5 are 1 and 5. So 5 is a prime number.

ENGLISH	SPANISH
principal The original amount of money deposited or borrowed in an account.	**capital** La cantidad original de dinero que se deposita o se pide prestada en una cuenta.

Example You open a savings account with $500. The principal is $500.

ENGLISH	SPANISH
proportion A proportion is an equation stating that two ratios are equal.	**proporción** Una proporción es una ecuación que establece que dos razones son iguales.

Example $\frac{2}{3} = \frac{6}{9}$ and $\frac{9}{12} = \frac{x}{4}$

ENGLISH	SPANISH
proportional relationship Two quantities x and y have a proportional relationship if y is always a constant multiple of x. A relationship is proportional if it can be described by equivalent ratios.	**relación de proporción** Dos cantidades x y y tienen una relación de proporción si y es siempre un múltiplo constante de x. Una relación es de proporción si se puede describir con razones equivalentes.

Example The equation $y = 4x$ shows a proportional relationship between x and y.

Q

ENGLISH	SPANISH
quadrant The x- and y-axes divide the coordinate plane into four regions called quadrants.	**cuadrante** Los ejes de las x y de las y dividen el plano de coordenadas en cuatro regiones llamadas cuadrantes.

Example

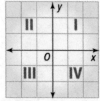

The quadrants are labeled I, II, III, and IV.

ENGLISH

quartile The quartiles of a data set divide the data set into four parts with the same number of data values in each part.

Example Data set: −5, −1, 4, 7, 8, 8, 11
First quartile: −1
Second quartile (median): 7
Third quartile: 8

R

range The range is a measure of variability of a numerical data set. The range of a data set is the difference between the greatest and least values in a data set.

rate A rate is a ratio involving two quantities measured in different units.

ratio A ratio is a relationship in which for every *x* units of one quantity there are *y* units of another quantity.

Example The ratio of the number of squares to the number of circles shown below is 4 to 3, or 4 : 3.

rational numbers A rational number is a number that can be written in the form $\frac{a}{b}$ or $-\frac{a}{b}$, where *a* is a whole number and *b* is a positive whole number. The rational numbers include the integers.

Example $\frac{1}{3}$, −5, 6.4, $0.\overline{6}$ are all rational numbers.

reciprocals Two numbers are reciprocals if their product is 1. If a nonzero number is named as a fraction, $\frac{a}{b}$, then its reciprocal is $\frac{b}{a}$.

Example The reciprocal of $\frac{2}{3}$ is $\frac{3}{2}$.

SPANISH

cuartil Los cuartiles de un conjunto de datos dividen el conjunto de datos en cuatro partes que tienen el mismo número de valores cada una.

rango El rango es una medida de la variabilidad de un conjunto de datos numéricos. El rango de un conjunto de datos es la diferencia que existe entre el mayor y el menor valor del conjunto.

tasa Una tasa es una razón que relaciona dos cantidades medidas con unidades diferentes.

razón Una razón es una relación en la cual por cada *x* unidades de una cantidad hay *y* unidades de otra cantidad.

números racionales Un número racional es un número que se puede escribir como $\frac{a}{b}$ or $-\frac{a}{b}$, donde *a* es un número entero no negativo y *b* es un número entero positivo. Los números racionales incluyen los enteros.

recíprocos Dos números son recíprocos si su producto es 1. Si un número distinto de cero se expresa como una fracción, $\frac{a}{b}$, entonces su recíproco es $\frac{b}{a}$.

ENGLISH	SPANISH

simple interest Simple interest is interest paid only on an original deposit.

interés simple El interés simple es el interés que se paga sobre un depósito original solamente.

simplify an algebraic expression To simplify an algebraic expression, combine the like terms of the expression.

simplificar una expresión algebraica Para simplificar una expresión algebraica, combina los términos semejantes de la expresión.

$$\textbf{Example} \quad 4x + 7y + 6x + 9y = (4x + 6x) + (7y + 9y)$$
$$= 10x + 16y$$

solution of an equation A solution of an equation is a value of the variable that makes the equation true.

solución de una ecuación Una solución de una ecuación es un valor de la variable que hace que la ecuación sea verdadera.

$$\textbf{Example} \quad \text{The solution of } m - 15 = 12 \text{ is } m = 27, \text{ because}$$
$$27 - 15 = 12.$$

solution of an inequality The solutions of an inequality are the values of the variable that make the inequality true.

solución de una desigualdad Las soluciones de una desigualdad son los valores de la variable que hacen que la desigualdad sea verdadera.

$$\textbf{Example} \quad \text{The solutions of } 17 + c > 25 \text{ are } c > 8.$$

statistical question A statistical question is a question that investigates an aspect of the real world and can have variety in the responses.

pregunta estadística Una pregunta estadística es una pregunta que investiga un aspecto de la vida diaria y puede tener varias respuestas.

Example "How old are students in my class?" is a statistical question. "How old am I?" is not a statistical question.

substitution To evaluate an algebraic expression, use substitution to replace the variable with a number.

sustitución Reemplazo de la variable de una expresión por un número.

Example Substitute 4 for n.
$12 + n$
$12 + 4 = 16$

Subtraction Property of Equality The two sides of an equation stay equal when the same amount is subtracted from both sides of the equation.

propiedad de resta de la igualdad Se puede restar el mismo número de ambos lados de una ecuación y los lados siguen siendo iguales.

$$\textbf{Example} \quad 4 + 2 = 6$$
$$(4 + 2) - 3 = 6 - 3$$
$$(4 + 2) - a = 6 - a$$

ENGLISH

surface area of a three-dimensional figure The surface area of a three-dimensional figure is the sum of the areas of its faces. You can find the surface area by finding the area of the net of the three-dimensional figure.

Example

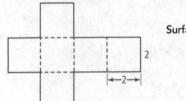

Surface area $= 6s^2$
$= 6(2)^2$
$= 6(4)$
$= 24$

T

term A term is a number, a variable, or the product of a number and one or more variables.

Example In the expression $3x + 4y + 12$, the terms are $3x$, $4y$, and 12.

terminating decimal A terminating decimal has a decimal expansion that terminates in 0.

Example Both 0.6 and 0.7265 are terminating decimals.

terms of a ratio The terms of a ratio are the quantities x and y in the ratio.

Example The terms of the ratio 4 : 3 are 4 and 3.

U

unit price A unit price is a unit rate that gives the price of one item.

Example $\frac{\$2.95}{5}$ fluid ounces $= \frac{\$.59}{1}$ fluid ounce, or $.59 per fluid ounce

unit rate The rate for one unit of a given quantity is called the unit rate.

Example $\frac{130 \text{ miles}}{2 \text{ hours}} = \frac{65 \text{ miles}}{1 \text{ hour}}$, or 65 miles per hour

SPANISH

área total de una figura tridimensional El área total de una figura tridimensional es la suma de las áreas de sus caras. Puedes hallar el área total si hallas el área del modelo plano de la figura tridimensional.

término Un término es un número, una variable o el producto de un número y una o más variables.

decimal finito Un decimal finito tiene una expansión decimal que termina en 0.

términos de una razón Los términos de una razón son la cantidad x y la cantidad y de la razón.

precio por unidad El precio por unidad es una tasa por unidad que muestra el precio de un artículo.

tasa por unidad Se llama tasa por unidad a la tasa que corresponde a 1 unidad de una cantidad dada.

ENGLISH

SPANISH

variability Variability describes how much the items in a data set differ (or vary) from each other. On a data display, variability is shown by how much the data on the horizontal scale are spread out.

variabilidad La variabilidad describe qué diferencia (o variación) existe entre los elementos de un conjunto de datos. Al exhibir datos, la variabilidad queda representada por la distancia que separa los datos en la escala horizontal.

---

variable A variable is a letter that represents an unknown value.

variable Una variable es una letra que representa un valor desconocido.

Example In the expression $3x + 4y + 12$, x and y are variables.

---

vertex of a three-dimensional figure A vertex of a three-dimensional figure is a point where three or more edges meet.

vértice de una figura tridimensional El vértice de una figura tridimensional es un punto donde se unen tres o más aristas.

Example

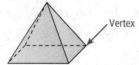

Vertex

---

x-axis The x-axis is the horizontal number line that, together with the y-axis, forms the coordinate plane.

eje de las x El eje de las x es la recta numérica horizontal que, junto con el eje de las y, forma el plano de coordenadas.

Example

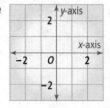

---

x-coordinate The x-coordinate is the first number in an ordered pair. It tells the number of horizontal units a point is from 0.

coordenada x La coordenada x (abscisa) es el primer número de un par ordenado. Indica cuántas unidades horizontales hay entre un punto y 0.

Example The x-coordinate is -2 for the ordered pair $(-2, 1)$. The x-coordinate is 2 units to the left of the y-axis.

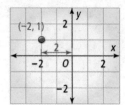

ENGLISH

y-axis The y-axis is the vertical number line that, together with the x-axis, forms the coordinate plane.

Example

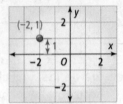

y-coordinate The y-coordinate is the second number in an ordered pair. It tells the number of vertical units a point is from 0.

Example The y-coordinate is 1 for the ordered pair (−2, 1).
The y-coordinate is 1 unit up from the x-axis.

Zero Property of Multiplication The product of 0 and any number is 0. For any number n, n · 0 = 0 and 0 · n = 0.

Example 36 · 0 = 0
x(0) = 0

SPANISH

eje de las y El eje de las y es la recta numérica vertical que, junto con el eje de las x, forma el plano de coordenadas.

coordenada y La coordenada y (ordenada) es el segundo número de un par ordenado. Indica cuántas unidades verticales hay entre un punto y 0.

propiedad del cero en la multiplicación El producto de 0 y cualquier número es 0. Para cualquier número n, n · 0 = 0 and 0 · n = 0.

ACKNOWLEDGEMENTS

Photographs

CVR: fotorince/Shutterstock, grthirteen/Fotolia, Alfgar/Shutterstock, riccamal/Fotolia, Jusakas/Fotolia, Oksana Kuzmina/Fotolia; 4: Nerthuz/Fotolia; 7 (C) Timothy Masters/Fotolia, (CL) Coprid/Fotolia; 12 (BR) Pearson Education, (T) Maxim Pavlov/Fotolia; 13: Pixelrobot/Fotolia; 14: Zelfit/Fotolia; 17: Steve Lovegrove/Fotolia; 18: Snvv/Fotolia; 19: Wckiw/Fotolia; 20 (TCL) Mara Zemgaliete/Fotolia, (TL) olllinka2/Fotolia; 24 (CR) Sergey Nivens/Shutterstock, (TL) Jason Edwards/National Geographic Creative/Corbis; 31: Alexander Zelnitskiy/Fotolia; 32 (C): Jaddingt/Fotolia, (TC) Bombybamby/Fotolia; 33: Maksim Shebeko/Fotolia; 36 (TR) hotshotsworldwide/Fotolia, (TC) Jupiter Images, (TL) Jupiter Images; 37: Amphaiwan/Fotolia; 43: Gabe9000c/Fotolia; 44: Vectorace/Fotolia, TeddyandMia/Shutterstock, DaryaSuperman/Shutterstock; 45 (TCR) D3d/Fotolia, (TR) Kazyavka/Fotolia, Jane Kelly/Shutterstock; 49 (TC) Vipman4/Fotolia, (TL) Iagodina/Fotolia; 52 (BC): Kosmos111/Fotolia, (BCL) Tashatuvango/Fotolia, (BL) Piai/Fotolia; 53: Deniskolt/Fotolia; 62 (BCL) Macrovector/Fotolia, (BCR) KEG/Shutterstock, (Bkgrd) Natbasil/Fotolia, (BR) Igor Stevanovic/Shutterstock, (C) Kudryashka/Fotolia, (CL) Zimmytws/Fotolia, (CR) Kenishirotie/Fotolia, (T) Poltorak/Fotolia, (TC) David Franklin/Fotolia, (TCR) Mizar_21984/Fotolia, (TL) Straghertni/Fotolia; 65 (CL): Africa Studio/Shutterstock, (TL) Sagir/Shutterstock; 71: Alexander Potapov/Fotolia, (BC) Catmando/Fotolia, (C) Andrey Kuzmin/Fotolia, (CL) Dengol/Fotolia, (CR) Andrea Izzotti/Fotolia; 73 (CL) Fenkieandreas/Fotolia, (CR) Fenkieandreas/Fotolia; 77 (TC) Underverse/Fotolia, (TL) Viper/Fotolia; 79: Curiosity/Shutterstock; 95: Catmando/Fotolia; 111: Ryan Burke/DigitalVision Vectors/Getty Images; 113: Mary Rice/Shutterstock; 114 (B) Logra/Shutterstock, (TCL) Garytog/Fotolia, (TL) Javen/Fotolia, (TR) Kenneth Keifer/Fotolia; 117: Picsfive/Fotolia; 121 (BCR) latitude59/Fotolia, (BR) Johan Larson/Fotolia; 123 (C) Css101/Fotolia, (CL) Gvictoria/Fotolia, (CR) Photka/Fotolia; 129 (BCR) Thawats/Fotolia, (BR) Valeriy Kirsanov/Fotolia; 136 (BR) Josefpittner/Fotolia, (CL) Volodymyr Vechirnii/Fotolia; 139 (TC) Anna Bogatirewa/Shutterstock, (TL) Bazzier/Fotolia; 145 (CR): Kletr/Fotolia; 147: Irina Kildiushova/Shutterstock; 155 (Bkgrd) Picsfive/Fotolia, (C) WavebreakMediaMicro/Fotolia, (CL) WavebreakmediaMicro/Fotolia; 160 (BR) Eskymaks/Fotolia, (TR) Marco mayer/Shutterstock; 161: Onairjiw/Fotolia; 171: RapidEye/iStock/Getty Images Plus/Getty Images; 173: mycteria/Shutterstock; 174 (penguin) Kotomiti/Fotolia, destina/Fotolia, leona_44/Fotolia, Mr Twister/Fotolia, Siempreverde22/Fotolia; 177 (BR) Destina/Fotolia, (C) 3dsculptor/Fotolia; 183 (C) Djahan/Fotolia, (CL) Djahan/Fotolia, (T) Rawpixel.com/Fotolia, (TC) Bacalao/Fotolia; 184 (TCR) 103tnn/Fotolia, (TR) Pete Saloutos/Shutterstock; 188: NRT/Shutterstock; 189: Ras slava/Fotolia; 190 (C) Brostock/Fotolia, (T) Violetkaipa/Fotolia; 191 (CR) Nik_Merkulov/Fotolia, (TCR) david_franklin/Fotolia, (TR) Tashka2000/Fotolia; 192 (BCR) Ravenna/Fotolia, (CR) Eric Isselée/Fotolia, (R) Modella/Fotolia; 193 (BCR) dampoint/Fotolia, (BR) Vitaly Krivosheev/Fotolia; 195: castelberry/Fotolia; 209 (C) Natis/Fotolia, (TC) Thomas Barrat/Shutterstock; 211 (TCR) Totophotos/Fotolia, (TR) Igor Mojzes/Fotolia; 215 (C) Nataliia Pyzhova/Fotolia, (TC) Thanakorn Thaneewach/Fotolia; 225 (BCR) Aleksei Lazukov/Shutterstock, (BR) Maximmmmum/Shutterstock; 227: Elvirkin/Fotolia; 235: Georgejmclittle/Fotolia; 233 (TC): Rasulov/Fotolia; 148: Can Yesil/Fotolia; 149: RapidEye/iStock/Getty Images Plus/Getty Images; 251: Marquisphoto/Shutterstock; 252 (Bkgrd) Macrovector/Fotolia, (BR) Zooropa/Fotolia; 255: Voronin76/Shutterstock; 256: Andersphoto/Fotolia; 257 (Bkgrd) 5second/Fotolia, (C) Imfotograf/Fotolia, (CR) Nikolaj Kondratenko/Fotolia, (TC) Gelpi/Fotolia, (TCL) Jon Barlow/ Pearson Education Ltd., (TCR) Kues1/Fotolia; 261: hagehige/Fotolia; 266: letfluis/Fotolia; 274 (CL) Fototaras/Fotolia, (CR) Fototaras/Fotolia, 274 Giadophoto/Fotolia, 274 Weris7554/Fotolia; 285 (BR): Denyshutter/Fotolia; 289: Tom Wang/Fotolia; 295: Racorn/Shutterstock; 296: yossarian6/Fotolia; 311: Rafael Ben Ari/123RF; 313: bloomua/Fotolia; 317: Ron Nickel/Design Pics/Getty Images; 318: Dani Simmonds/Fotolia; 321: Erik Lam/Fotolia; 331: AsiaTravel/Shutterstock; 332 (B) yossarian6/Fotolia, (BCR) AlienCat/Fotolia, (BR) Monika Wisniewska/Fotolia, (CL) olly/Fotolia, (CR) donatas1205/Fotolia, (TC) glyphstock/Fotolia, (TCL) vvoe/Fotolia, (TL) MIGUEL GARCIA SAAVED/Fotolia, (TR) Svenni/Fotolia; 335: Marekkulhavy12/Fotolia; 341 (BC) Exopixel/Fotolia, (BCL) Carlos Santa Maria/Fotolia, (Bkgrd)